DATE DUE			

D1569486

SOUTHERN BIOGRAPHY SERIES

Titles in the SOUTHERN BIOGRAPHY SERIES

Edited by Fred C. Cole and Wendell H. Stephenson

Felix Grundy, by Joseph Howard Parks
Thomas Spalding of Sapelo, by E. Merton Coulter
Edward Livingston, by William B. Hatcher
Fightin' Joe Wheeler, by John P. Dyer
John Sharp Williams, by George Coleman Osborn
George Fitzhugh, by Harvey Wish
Pitchfork Ben Tillman, by Francis Butler Simkins
Seargent S. Prentiss, by Dallas C. Dickey
Zachary Taylor, by Brainerd Dyer

Edited by T. Harry Williams

John Bell of Tennessee, by Joseph Howard Parks
James Harrod of Kentucky, by Kathryn Harrod Mason
Arthur Pue Gorman, by John R. Lambert
General Edmund Kirby Smith, by Joseph Howard Parks
William Blount, by William H. Masterson
P. G. T. Beauregard, by T. Harry Williams
Hoke Smith and the Politics of the New South, by Dewey W. Grantham, Jr.
General Leonidas Polk, by Joseph Howard Parks
Mr. Crump of Memphis, by William D. Miller
General William J. Hardee, by Nathaniel Cheairs Hughes, Jr.
Montague of Virginia, by William E. Larsen
Thomas Mann Randolph, by William H. Gaines, Jr.
James Lusk Alcorn, by Lillian A. Pereyra
Robert Toombs of Georgia, by William Y. Thompson
The White Chief: James Kimble Vardaman, by William F. Holmes
Louis T. Wigfall, by Alvy L. King
L. Q. C. Lamar, by James B. Murphy
Breckinridge: Statesman, Soldier, Symbol, by William C. Davis
Joseph E. Brown of Georgia, by Joseph Howard Parks
David French Boyd: Founder of Louisiana State University, by Germaine Reed
Cracker Messiah: Governor Sidney J. Catts of Florida, by Wayne Flynt
Maverick Republican in the Old North State: A Political Biography of Daniel L. Russell, by Jeffrey J. Crow and Robert F. Durden
Oscar W. Underwood: A Political Biography, by Evans C. Johnson

Oscar W. Underwood

Underwood as a contestant for the presidential nomination in 1912

OSCAR W. UNDERWOOD

A Political Biography

By Evans C. Johnson

LOUISIANA STATE UNIVERSITY PRESS

BATON ROUGE AND LONDON

Designer: Albert Crochet
Typeface: VIP Caledonia
Typesetter: Graphic Composition, Inc.
Printer and binder: Thomson-Shore, Inc.

Portions of the material contained herein have been previously published
in *Historian, Alabama Review*, and *Alabama Historical Quarterly*.

LIBRARY OF CONGRESS CATALOGING IN PUBLICATION DATA
Johnson, Evans C   1922–
    Oscar W. Underwood: A Political Biography
    (Southern biography series)
    Bibliography: p.
    Includes index.
    1. Underwood, Oscar Wilder, 1862–1929. 2. United States—Politics and govern-
ment—1865–1933. 3. Legislators—United States—Biography. 4. United States. Congress—Biography. I. Title. II. Series. E664.U5J63   328.73′092′4 [B]   79–19907
ISBN 0–8071–0582–1

For "Kitty"

Contents

Illustrations

Woodlawn, purchased by the Underwoods in 1925

Underwood after his retirement in 1927

Underwood in 1928

Preface

My interest in Oscar W. Underwood dates from my childhood when, rummaging through the basement of our home, I discovered a sheaf of my father's correspondence with Underwood. Almost twenty years later, at the University of North Carolina, Dr. Fletcher M. Green suggested that I study Underwood's House career for my doctoral dissertation. Finding that Underwood's congressional papers had just become available at the Alabama Department of Archives and History in Montgomery, I agreed.

Although Underwood was considered a titan of his age, few American political figures have suffered such neglect as he. Except for his candidacy for the Democratic nomination in 1924, his political career is largely forgotten even in Alabama. The name once known to most Alabamians faded long ago from the pages of state newspapers and the national press. Since the Wilson and Harding administrations when his constituents regarded with pride his position as majority leader of the House and minority leader of the Senate, Alabama has returned to its natural political insularity, and in recent years its politics has been dominated by Governor George C. Wallace, with whose flamboyant politics Underwood would have had little in common.

Underwood has not been an attractive subject to biographers. Never involved in a scandal, failing to receive the Democratic presidential nominations which he sought in 1912 and 1924, and failing to secure passage of a bill for private operation of Muscle Shoals, he is largely remembered for the Underwood-Simmons

Tariff Act—not an unimportant accomplishment. He was a warm and attractive personality, as scores of his friends have testified. This warmth, however, is seldom reflected in his speeches in the musty *Congressional Record*, and although his personal letters are more interesting, they are cryptic and brief. A number of memoirs and books about the Wilson era were written with hardly more than a passing reference to Underwood. Among those arcane few who remember Underwood, he is generally misunderstood because of his political testament *Drifting Sands of Party Politics* that was widely distributed in Alabama following his death. This book led readers to conclude that Underwood was a doctrinaire advocate of states' rights, immune to interest politics, eschewing participation in the demagoguery engaged in by politicians such as J. Thomas Heflin and, to a lesser extent, Hugo L. Black. All of these impressions are at least somewhat in error.

The one place in which Underwood is well remembered is in the folklore of Congress, where he is widely regarded as a great party leader who had mastered the rules perhaps as thoroughly as any member of Congress. This mastery, together with steady work, personal magnetism, and a willingness to compromise, made him effective as chairman of the Ways and Means Committee in formulating a majority program after the Democrats seized control of the House in 1910. In 1913 and 1914 Underwood piloted through the House the New Freedom, the most ambitious reform program of the Progressive era. His transfer to the Senate in 1915 hardly interrupted his career as a party leader. Beginning in 1919 he served, in effect, as majority leader in the Senate. In April, 1920, he was elected leader of the Senate Democrats—by then a minority. He surrendered the minority leadership in 1923 prior to his presidential race of 1924. Pat Harrison, Underwood's lieutenant as minority leader, referred to Underwood as the "greatest natural parliamentarian, the greatest leader of a law making body that I ever saw."[1]

The use of the word "Bourbon" in this biography will raise ques-

1. Montgomery *Advertiser*, November 12, 1920.

tions among those familiar with the writings of C. Vann Woodward and others with whom the term has lost favor in southern history. Underwood would have disliked the label—he thought he was a "modern man"—but he would have disliked even more Woodward's term "Redeemer" with its theological connotations. Generally, he fits the definition of a Bourbon as given by the late Francis Butler Simkins: a member of the old plantation aristocracy who favored concessions to business and strict economy, and who extolled the glories of the Old South and envisioned a great industrial future for the New South.[2]

My reading of twentieth-century biography reveals, I think, the perils of the life-and-times biographical approach for secondary political figures like Underwood. Sometimes that approach has been necessitated by the lack of personal papers, but the result is almost always the same—the story is taken over by the dominant figure of the era—frequently by Woodrow Wilson. I have chosen, instead, to rely heavily on the huge store of Underwood papers and to focus closely on his career, furnishing background only as it is essential to illuminate my subject.

My debts are so numerous that the footnotes and the bibliography must serve as my note of thanks to most who have helped. In my earlier research, I was aided by a number of people who are now dead. Professor Oscar W. Underwood, Jr., provided a vast quantity of material and devoted much time to me. Judge Robert B. Carr of the Alabama Court of Appeals gave general background for Alabama politics and provided an entree to the Alabama political circle, as did my father, John Will Johnson, Sr. William Hugh McEniry, Jr., then dean of Stetson University, was helpful in securing financial aid through Stetson University and the Southern Fellowships Fund. Above all, I am indebted to my cousin, Lucille McLendon, who provided me with board and lodging on my numerous trips to Montgomery.

It was my pleasure to spend many months working in the Department of Archives and History at Montgomery, and I owe a

2. Francis B. Simkins, *History of the South* (New York: Knopf, 1963), 318–19.

great debt to its staff. I am indebted, too, to the staffs of the libraries of the University of Virginia, the University of North Carolina, and Stetson University. At Stetson, I am especially indebted to Eleanor Anne Hurst, Inter-Library Loans librarian. My wife, Betty D. Johnson, Technical Services librarian, intercepted scores of books containing Underwood material before they went on the shelves of the duPont-Ball Library, and she has read the manuscript with a critical eye. Marc Lovelace, professor of history at Stetson University; Lewis P. Jones, chairman of the Department of History at Wofford College; Allen J. Going, professor of history at the University of Houston; Milo B. Howard, director of the Alabama Department of Archives and History; Charles G. Summersell, professor of history at the University of Alabama; Martin Torodash, professor of history at Fairleigh Dickinson University; Rutland Cunningham of Florence, Alabama; and Lee N. Allen of Samford University served as readers of various chapters. Others who have aided me are: Richard B. Morland, Betty Carr, Mike Reichman, Harold Damsgard, Ann Paden, Sondra Ickes, and Mary Jane di Piero. Jacqueline Wigmore, secretary to the Stetson University Department of History, typed the manuscript with an even hand and an even temper.

Oscar W. Underwood

CHAPTER I

An Aristocrat from the Bluegrass

Preceding the first ballot at the Democratic National Convention at Madison Square Garden in July, 1976, the Alabama delegation was in a fractious mood. Ordered by Governor George C. Wallace, who had withdrawn as a presidential candidate, to vote for Jimmy Carter, the quite conservative delegation rebelled against casting the ballots for a Georgia Democrat with Populist roots. A state representative from Montgomery empathized with his fellow Alabama delegates, saying that naturally they would prefer not to vote for Carter and moved that Alabama's votes be cast for Oscar W. Underwood as they were in 1924—103 times. Great applause and a roar of approval greeted the suggestion prior to Alabama's decision to vote for Carter.[1]

Press attention to the parallels between the Democratic convention of 1924 and that of 1976, both of which were held at Madison Square Garden, and the candidacies of Underwood and Carter, the first serious Deep South contenders for a major party nomination since the Civil War except for Senator Richard B. Russell of Georgia in 1952, renewed speculation about a southern paradox. Oscar Underwood, the personification of tariff reform, represented a Birmingham manufacturing constituency. He was an opponent of the Ku Klux Klan, yet was from one of the nation's most Klan infested cities. He was antilabor and yet he was from an area where labor unions were strong. He was an outspoken "wet" (use of the old

1. Interview with Clay Henderson, August 15, 1976.

Waldorf bar for his presidential headquarters caused raucous laughter), yet he was from a very "dry" state. Unlike most of his southern colleagues, he opposed the use of the filibuster. What kind of man was Oscar Underwood?

Oscar W. Underwood, who served the Birmingham area in the United States House of Representatives from 1895 to 1915 and the state of Alabama in the United States Senate from 1915 to 1927, was born into a prominent Louisville, Kentucky, family. During and immediately after the Civil War, Underwood spent several years of his youth in the frontier town of St. Paul, Minnesota, returning with his family to Louisville in the late 1870s. After graduation from Rugby, a private school in Louisville, he visited with a brother in Texas and then entered the University of Virginia in 1883. Although Underwood attended the Law Department of the University of Virginia, he never graduated. In 1884 after a brief residence in St. Paul, he went to live in Birmingham, where his half-brother William Thompson Underwood had preceded him. He married in 1885, and Birmingham was to remain his home until the eve of his retirement from Congress.

Oscar Underwood's family background was that of Kentucky Bluegrass, Presbyterian and Episcopalian aristocrats who are sometimes referred to as the *vere de vere*. They were people of exceptional family pride, and, after Underwood became a public figure, few reporters concluded a long interview with him without hearing him discuss his forebears. Underwood was a sixth generation American. The first Underwood to arrive in America was Thomas William Underwood, born at Norfolk, England, about 1675. Thomas William came to Virginia as a very young man. First employed in Richmond as a merchant's clerk, he later moved to Hanover County, where he developed Bear Castle, a very profitable plantation. Thomas William married Elizabeth Taylor, and their son, Thomas, like his father, was a Virginia planter. He served as sheriff of Goochland County, as a member of the Virginia House of Delegates, and, just prior to the Revolution, as a member of the Goochland County Committee of Public Safety. Thomas' son, John, a captain in the Revolutionary army, married Frances Rogers, a first cousin of George Rogers Clark. John, too, represented Goochland County in the legislature. Captain John was a handsome man, with a winsome personality but dissolute habits; it was probably his gambling that led to the loss of Licking Hole, the Goochland County estate he had inherited.[2]

The eldest son among Captain John Underwood's eight children was Joseph Rogers Underwood, Oscar W. Underwood's grandfather, born in Goochland County, Virginia, on October 24, 1791. As Joseph's parents were in straitened circumstances, Edmund Rogers, Mrs. Underwood's brother, secured the parents' permission to take Joseph to Kentucky to live with him. Joseph thus experienced the hardships of frontier life in his youth, but he received an elementary education under relatives and Presbyterian ministers in the area. Later, keeping within the orbit of Presbyterianism and moving under the influence of the Reverend David Rice, a prominent Whig and antislavery leader, he entered Transylvania College, where he was a schoolmate of the noted abolitionist, James G. Birney. He began the study of law, but the War of 1812 briefly interrupted his training when he enlisted in General William Henry Harrison's army in March, 1813. He served with distinction as a lieutenant at the Battle of Dudley's Defeat, where he was badly wounded. On his return he married Eliza McCown Trotter, the granddaughter of the Reverend David Rice, on March 26, 1817. He practiced law at Glasgow, Kentucky, and was elected to the legislature. In 1823 he moved to Bowling Green, again practicing law, and served in the legislature as a member of the antirelief or New Court faction. By 1828 Joseph Underwood was a prominent Whig leader in the state. In that year he was defeated for the office of lieutenant governor, but he was appointed to the court of appeals, where he served until his election to Congress in 1835. In 1845 he returned to the Kentucky legislature and served as speaker

2. *Cyclopaedia of American Biographies* (7 vols.; Boston: Cyclopaedia Publishing Company, 1897–1903), VII, 409. See also John H. Gwathmey, *Twelve Virginia Counties Where the Western Migration Began* (Richmond: Dietz Press, 1937), 175, 233; Joseph R. Underwood, "Diary of Joseph R. Underwood, 1834," in Oscar W. Underwood Papers, University of Virginia Library, 21, 228; O. W. Underwood, Jr., "Commentary on the Dissertation of Evans Johnson" (MS in possession of Evans C. Johnson, DeLand, Fla.), 1–2.

of the house until his election to the state senate in 1846. The following year Joseph was elected to the United States Senate. He retired from politics in 1853 but reentered political life in 1860, when he was elected to the Kentucky legislature as a Unionist. At seventy years of age he was a vigorous opponent of Governor Beriah Magoffin's proslavery policies and a powerful factor in holding Kentucky in the Union. When Bowling Green was occupied, Confederate soldiers were detailed to protect from the occupation troops a large tobacco warehouse owned by Joseph Underwood, as he was a known Unionist. The tension was dispelled when Underwood gave the tobacco to the Confederate troops. After the war, he retired to his estate, Ironwood, near Bowling Green, where he lived until his death in 1876. His last important political activity was his attendance as a delegate at the Democratic convention of 1868.[3]

Joseph Underwood kept a diary of personal and political observations in which he recorded his political faith with almost childlike candor but with the perspicacity of a sage. He supported the American Colonization Society and freed several of his slaves, financing their relocation in Africa.[4] His political models were Daniel Webster and John Quincy Adams rather than Henry Clay, whom he regarded as somewhat superficial. He was an extremely strict constructionist. He refused to accept travel pay given him for a "constructive recess" of Congress. He opposed the removal of executive officers without congressional approval. So fundamentalist was he, that he objected to President James Polk's nomination of a minister to Prussia on his last day in office because it fell on a Sunday. He thought the Mexican War was a mistake and, in Whig fashion, accused President Polk of starting it for partisan advan-

3. Lewis Collins, *Historical Sketches of Kentucky: A History of Kentucky* (Rev. ed.; 2 vols.; Louisville: John P. Morton, 1924), II, 740–45; *Biographical Encyclopaedia of Kentucky of the Dead and Living Men of the Nineteenth Century* (Cincinnati: J. M. Armstrong, 1878), 122, 505; interview with O. W. Underwood, Jr., November 24, 1951; undated press release in 1924 Campaign File, Oscar W. Underwood Papers, Alabama Department of Archives and History, Montgomery; Eliza C. Hall, "Bowling Green and the Civil War," *Filson Club Quarterly*, XI (1937), 241–42; Birmingham *Daily Advance*, April 2, 1912.

4. Jean E. Keith, "Joseph Rogers Underwood, Friend of African Colonization," *Filson Club Quarterly*, XXII (1948), 119–29.

tage.[5] He was a conservative in the most pristine meaning of the term. He accepted public office reluctantly, with the Federalist concept of trusteeship of the people, and he despised President Andrew Jackson who used what he considered demagogic devices. Oscar Underwood kept his grandfather's diary in his desk after he went to Congress and, although the Alabama congressman thought that he and Joseph differed widely in political philosophy, often referred to the diary.[6] Oscar Underwood said, many years later, that although he was a "very small boy" (he was fourteen) when his grandfather died in 1876, "I recall him very distinctly and people compliment me by saying that I resemble him in many particulars."[7]

Eugene Underwood, Oscar's father, was born on April 4, 1818, while the Joseph R. Underwoods were living in Glasgow, Kentucky. When he was five his parents moved to Bowling Green, where he was educated prior to entering Miami University at Oxford, Ohio. In 1835 he transferred to Centre College at Danville, Kentucky, where he graduated. He returned to Bowling Green to study law under his father, and he remained his father's partner while the latter was in Congress. In 1848 he moved to Nashville, Tennessee, where, in October, 1846, he married Catherine R. Thompson, the daughter of an outstanding lawyer. Eugene soon established himself in the leading legal circles in Nashville. He became interested in the projected Louisville and Nashville Railroad and was a vigorous advocate of the route that was finally adopted. He became a member of the original board of the L & N, serving from 1852 to 1861.[8]

Eugene Underwood and his wife Catherine had three sons, William Thompson, Joseph R., and Eugene, Jr.; Catherine died in

5. J. R. Underwood, "Diary of Joseph R. Underwood, 1834," 10. "Constructive recess" occurs when the Speaker declares the House to be released in order for Congress to begin the next session on the constitutionally specified date. Controversy usually occurs over the payment of mileage to return home when too brief an interim has occurred for congressmen to go home.

6. Interview with O. W. Underwood, Jr., November 24, 1951.

7. Oscar W. Underwood to M. B. Morton, *ca.* September 10, 1923, in Special Letter File, Underwood Papers, Alabama Archives.

8. *Biographical Encyclopaedia of Kentucky*, 122; Louisville *Times*, December 21, 1893.

1857. On January 31, 1861, Eugene married Frederica Virginia
Wilder, a wealthy, twenty-nine-year-old widow, in her home at 608
Eighth Street in Louisville. The marriage service was performed
by the Reverend Francis M. Whittle, rector of St. Paul's Episcopal
Church where Virginia was a member. Mrs. Wilder had one child,
Marinda Burnett Wilder—a son, Oscar Wilder, had died in in-
fancy. Her late husband, Oscar Wilder, a partner in the large
wholesale drug firm of J. B. Wilder, had been fatally injured in a
fall in the elevator shaft of his warehouse. Mrs. Wilder was descended from a New England family that included one of the original proprietors of Norwich, Connecticut. Her father, Jabez Smith,
was born at Groton, Connecticut, but as a youth he moved to
Petersburg, Virginia, and married Mary Walthall of a prominent
southern family. He established a cotton mill at Petersburg and
was mayor for a number of years preceding the Civil War. A fastid-
ious Yankee, always immaculately dressed, Smith was a Democrat
who sympathized with the South during the Civil War. He died at
Petersburg during the siege of 1865 at the age of seventy-six.[9]

Eugene Underwood was, like so many Kentuckians with Unionist forebears, a southern sympathizer. His pro-Confederate activities allegedly included the smuggling of quinine to General Bragg's
army. Arrested and imprisoned when Louisville was occupied by
the Union army in 1861, he was soon released through the influence of his father. He took no further part in the war and withdrew
from active law practice presumably in the hope of keeping out of
the controversies of the period. He had earlier voted the Whig
ticket of his father, but his Civil War experience converted him to
the Democratic party.[10]

9. "The Underwood Family Book" (in possession of Mrs. Jason Eckford, Charlottesville,
Va.); Josiah Stoddard Johnston (ed.), *Memorial History of Louisville from Its First Settlement to the Year 1896* (2 vols.; Chicago: American Biographical Publishing Company, 1896),
II, 472; Hartford (Conn.) *Times*, April 19, 1924. Virginia Underwood owned in 1861
perhaps $100,000 in real estate, stocks, and bonds. See Deeds Book 110, p. 192, Jefferson
County, Ky.
10. Interview with O. W. Underwood, Jr., November 24, 1951; undated press release
in 1924 Campaign File, in Underwood Papers, Alabama Archives. A Civil War story frequently told in the Underwood family indicates the determination of Frederica Virginia
Underwood. As a train of Union artillery caissons passed in front of her Louisville home,

Oscar Wilder Underwood, the first child of Eugene and Virginia Underwood, was born on May 6, 1862, in a light-colored three story brick house on Eighth Street. The thirteen-pound boy was named for Virginia's first husband or perhaps for the child of her first marriage who died as an infant. On September 14, Oscar was baptized at St. Paul's Episcopal Church by the Reverend Francis M. Whittle.[11] A second child of this marriage, Sidney Smith Underwood, was born in the summer of 1864.

In the fall of 1864 the Underwoods moved to St. Paul, Minnesota. Virginia was ill, and the doctors, fearing tuberculosis, advised Eugene to take his wife to a dry climate. The warlike Sioux Indians had been expelled into the Dakotas leaving the area free for settlement. The Louisville house that Virginia had purchased five years earlier for $10,500 was sold for $19,000, and with $14,000 of the proceeds, Eugene Underwood purchased a house on St. Anthony's Hill in St. Paul in 1865.[12]

The date of the Underwood family's move from Louisville to St. Paul would seem to be of small consequence, but it later proved desirable for Oscar to obscure the fact that his family had moved from Louisville to a northern city during the war. *The Biographical Directory of Kentucky* gives the correct 1864 date, but accounts written after Underwood became politically active, notably Burton J. Hendrick's sketch of Underwood, gave the erroneous 1865 date. In the 1924 campaign, when national political conditions were important, the correct 1864 date was used in the basic Underwood campaign pamphlet.[13]

The numerous Underwoods must have made quite a procession

she was horrified to see that one soldier was being dragged along the street tied to a caisson. She blocked the way, and when the battery commander told her the soldier was being punished for drunkenness she "tongue lashed" the commander, who sheepishly ordered the soldier's release. O. W. Underwood, Jr., "Commentary," 6.

11. Birmingham *Age-Herald*, January 14, 1912; Parish Register of St. Paul's Episcopal Church, II, Louisville, Ky.

12. Deeds Book HH, 344, Ramsey County, Minn.; Deeds Book 106, p. 397, and Book 286, pp. 629–31, Jefferson County, Ky.

13. *Biographical Encyclopaedia of Kentucky*, 122; Burton J. Hendrick, "Oscar W. Underwood, a New Leader from the New South," *McClure's Magazine*, XXXVIII (1912), 404–20; *For President: Oscar W. Underwood* (campaign pamphlet; Washington, 1924); Parish Register of St. Paul's Episcopal Church, II.

to St. Paul. It is not clear how many members moved, but at least
Oscar, Sidney, William T., Eugene, Jr., and Marinda Wilder accompanied Eugene and Virginia to the new Minnesota home. The
family traveled by rail part of the way, but the last leg of the journey was made on sledges up the frozen Mississippi River. St. Paul,
with a population of only thirty thousand, was the kind of frontier
town to fulfill the dreams of the most romantic schoolboy. William
F. "Buffalo Bill" Cody, the famous scout, lived there, and he declared years later that "the Underwood boy was always bothering
my horses." Young Oscar sat on a fence and watched as the buck-
skin-clad, blue-eyed, flaxen-haired General George A. Custer
mustered his Seventh Cavalry Regiment before going to fight the
hostile Sioux Indians in 1876. General Custer lived only a block
from the yellow stone Underwood house on Summit Avenue between St. Anthony and Rice streets, and young Oscar thought him
the greatest man he had ever known. General Winfield Scott Han-
cock, commander of the Department of Dakota, fresh from his lau-
rels in Indian warfare, lived next door to the Underwoods. It was
a fascinating town to young boys, with the pacific Chippewa Indians roaming the streets and plenty of game and wild horses to be
found in the surrounding territory. It was not unusual for the Underwood children to find groups of Chippewa resting in their front
yard, and the boys hunted and fished in the Mille Lacs region,
where many Chippewas lived.[14]

Oscar was not an overly studious boy, but he took advantage of
his recreational opportunities. The stone stable that housed Oscar's
fine, spirited pony was a veritable storm center of youthful activities. He and the other children could hear the creak of primitive
Indian wagons for miles across the prairie, as the Indians drove to
St. Paul to sell their furs, and that was the signal to run home to
get their pennies for the tasty maple candy the Indians brought.
Oscar was deeply impressed by the appearance of the Indians,
their feet encased in great snowshoes, blankets wrapped about

14. Interview with O. W. Underwood, Jr., November 24, 1951; St. Paul (Minn.) *Daily
News*, February 1, 1920; *St. Paul City Directory for 1867* (St. Paul, Minn.: Bailey and
Wolfe, 1867), 219; Hendrick, "Oscar W. Underwood, a New Leader from the New South,"
405–406; Alfred Henry Lewis, "Underwood—House Leader," *Cosmopolitan*, LII (December, 1911), 114.

their bodies, and on their backs bundles of fur and beads which they traded for flour, tobacco, and firewater. On one occasion Oscar heard that a Negro was in town, a specimen he fancied he had never seen before, and he ran breathlessly to see the man and follow him about. In summer he dangled his feet in the Mississippi from scows along the river front. In winter he hunted in western St. Paul on lands owned by his father, coasted down St. Anthony's Hill, and skated on the frozen Mississippi. These activities would seem to have left little time for education, but Oscar went unwillingly to Jefferson School, quarreled a little, got thrashed occasionally, and made trouble for the teacher.[15]

The Underwoods were an attractive family. Eugene was a tall, muscular man with receding hair and a southern colonel's goatee. Virginia, known to neighbors as "Miss Jenny," was an attractive woman, with a sweet gentle face and pale blue eyes, who wore her hair parted in the middle and tied in a bun in the back. Virginia's slight figure and her frequent appeals to her "Heavenly Father" for guidance masked a determined and sometimes stern nature. She was clearly the head of the family.[16] A neighbor remarked many years later of pretty Marinda Wilder, known as "Rin": "I used to think her the most beautiful young lady I had ever seen."[17]

William Thompson Underwood, Eugene's son by his first marriage, married his foster sister, Marinda Wilder, on October 4, 1871, when Will was twenty-three years old. Rin had inherited a sizable estate from her father, and the marriage gave Will considerable financial independence. Will and Rin, however, continued to live at their parents' home. He also was employed by James J. Hill's Northern Pacific Railway as a clerk. He was assigned to an express car, and his first duty was to accompany a corpse to its destination.[18]

Eugene Underwood practiced law and farmed, but his real in-

15. St. Paul (Minn.) Dispatch, January 25, 1929; Lewis, "Underwood—House Leader," 114.
16. O. W. Underwood, Jr., "Commentary," 5.
17. Harry S. Johnson to O. W. Underwood, Jr., December 27, 1917, in Underwood Papers, Alabama Archives.
18. Lois M. Fawcett to author, November 7, 1951, in possession of Evans C. Johnson, DeLand, Fla.; O. W. Underwood, Jr., "Commentary," 6.

terest was in land speculation. In December, 1866, he was a member of a company that proposed to build a street railway in St. Paul, and he gradually acquired large tracts of undeveloped suburban land near what is now Macalester College. He was interested in the development of the Mississippi River, and in 1881, several years after he left St. Paul, he attended the Mississippi River Improvement Congress at St. Louis as a delegate from Minnesota. During his stay in St. Paul he joined the Episcopal church and became a vestryman. He was also a leader in the formation of the Patrons of Husbandry.[19]

St. Paul was growing rapidly. There was a heavy immigration of Catholic Irish into St. Paul, and large numbers of Scandinavians poured into neighboring Minneapolis—a volatile mixture. From the Irish immigrants came the two Underwood servants, Mary Foley and her sister Katie. Mary died, perhaps before the return to Louisville, but "Miss Katie," almost as old as her mistress, remained with the Underwoods for the rest of her long life, dying several years before Virginia.[20]

Even with these interests in St. Paul, the Underwoods retained their Louisville business and social connections and gradually began a return to that city. Eugene and Will periodically returned to Louisville to attend to business matters. In 1875 they shared an office and the father boarded with the son at 490 Third Avenue near Kentucky. By 1876 the move back to Louisville was completed since Eugene and Will are listed in the city directory as sharing the Third Avenue house. This arrangement seems to have been continued until 1881 when Will moved to Birmingham and Eugene went back to the ancestral home, Ironwood, near Bowling Green.[21]

The Underwoods' return to Louisville was probably due to the recovery of Virginia Underwood, who lived to the age of ninety. The ties with St. Paul were not completely broken, however. The

19. William P. Westfall to author, October 10, 1951, in possession of Evans C. Johnson; *Biographical Encyclopaedia of Kentucky*, 122.

20. O. W. Underwood, Jr., "Commentary," 6.

21. *Park City Daily Times* (Bowling Green, Ky.), December 21, 1893.

St. Paul residence was swapped for a parcel of land, which was given to Oscar and his brothers. In Oscar's papers are found references to "Underwood's Acre Lots," which he owned until after 1900, though he realized little from the sale of this land. Oscar and his father, sometimes accompanied by Will, returned to St. Paul every summer until 1884. In Louisville, Eugene Underwood again associated himself with the life of the city and became a vestryman in St. Paul's Episcopal Church. In his latter years he was not an active lawyer, and there is no evidence that he practiced much after the Civil War.[22]

Oscar's activities in Louisville seem not greatly different from those in St. Paul. He played along the wharves of the Ohio River and tagged playmates in the warehouses along Market Street. Like other Louisville boys of the period, he played military games in the Civil War gun emplacements that survived in the city's parks. Doubtless there were battles between the Blues and the Grays, but in that city the Grays outnumbered the Blues. The battlements manned by young Confederate Underwood were the remains of Union forts. Oscar was sent to dancing school if one can trust the account of Mary Anderson, a noted dancer who lived in Louisville in the 1870s and wrote, many years later, of her painful experience with the future congressman. The talented young dancer was assigned as Oscar's partner, and she wept at her inability to dance with him, describing him as lacking all sense of music or rhythm.[23]

In September, 1876, young Oscar visited the Philadelphia Centennial Exposition, and happily, his "nickel notebook" diary has survived. "Brother Will" was along, and although other members of the party are not specifically mentioned, his father and younger brother Sidney probably made the trip. The diary is mainly a catalogue of everything seen, but it demonstrates keen observation and a fondness for statistics. The youngster's spelling was definitely below par, and his expression was sometimes obtuse, occasionally

22. See, for example, Frederick G. Ingersoll to Underwood, March 31, 1905, Underwood to Z. H. Austin, August 11, 1923, both in Underwood Papers, Alabama Archives; *Biographical Encyclopaedia of Kentucky*, 122.
23. Birmingham *Post*, May 6, 1926; St. Louis *Times*, May 20, 1924.

leading to a double entendre as in his description of his party's arrival at La Pierre Hotel in West Philadelphia "where we got two nice rooms and good meals, but will have to give them up tomorrow."[24]

In these years in Louisville, Virginia Underwood "had babies to attend to." In addition to little Frederick Virginius, born in 1877, nieces and nephews were frequently brought in to share the Underwoods' comfortable home. Rin Wilder Underwood, childless at the time, taught Oscar his speeches and lessons. She remembered Oscar as "always well behaved" and "a good student." Virginia Underwood, too, recalled that she "never had any trouble with Oscar." Often Rin would say: "Oscar, you are going to be a senator someday like your grandfather Joseph Rogers."[25]

Oscar and his brother Sidney were sent to Rugby, an English-type preparatory school in Louisville, generally regarded as the best in the city. Oscar played on the football team, and some of his teammates came from prominent Louisville families. He also associated with the high school boys and "punished the ball" on the back lots with them after school. The boy's waggishness, and probably his lack of enthusiasm for Latin, is seen in a verse he wrote in his Latin grammar: "Take not this book, for fear of life, the owner carries a knife." Oscar then amended the verse to end in a lighter vein: "a very dull knife."[26] At Rugby, Oscar was taught a classical curriculum including English, Latin, Greek, French, German, history, mathematics, natural sciences, logic, and intellectual philosophy. He distinguished himself academically, and in the session of 1877–1878 his general average was 96.1, which gave him honors for the year. In 1878–1879, his final year at Rugby, Oscar placed, according to the principal, "third best in the whole school and well earned it is." His general average was 92.4. His best marks were a 90.5 in mathematics (his favorite subject, he

24. Oscar W. Underwood, "Diary of Oscar W. Underwood: Centennial Exposition, Philadelphia, 1876," in Underwood Papers, Alabama Archives, 6.

25. O. W. Underwood, Jr., "Commentary," 8; see also, Virginia Underwood to Underwood, May 15, 1920, in Underwood Papers, Alabama Archives.

26. Inscription in Basil L. Gildersleeve, *A Latin Exercise Book* (New York: University Publishing Company, 1875), in Underwood Papers, Alabama Archives.

later said), and in the final declamation, 100. The "thrill of Oscar's rendition of 'Horatius at the Bridge'" was remembered for many years by one of Oscar's schoolmates, but one hopes that this was not his senior declamation. In later years Underwood attributed his training in classical languages to his father's desires. Oscar's favorite authors were Dickens, Thackeray, and Scott. Little is known of his ideological development in these years, but he knew one-eyed "Marse Henry" Watterson, the Democratic editor of the Louisville *Courier Journal*, and years later, defending his tariff views, Underwood wrote, "many of my views on public questions were drilled into me by the editorials of the Courier Journal." It was at about the time of his graduation from Rugby that Oscar was confirmed in the Episcopal church. For the Underwood family church membership was a feminine concern, and there is no indication that Underwood ever attended services regularly.[27]

Following his graduation from Rugby in 1879, Oscar was not yet ready to pursue a career. He joined his half-brother Will, the operator of a Texas ranch between San Antonio and El Dorado, and, "chapped and spurred," rode the range for a few months. He later recalled "as a boy riding a Texas pony most of the way at a gallop from San Antonio down to one of the old mission churches" and admiring its architecture. In Texas he met Henry F. De-Bardeleben, who later joined Will Underwood in establishing the Mary Pratt Furnace in Birmingham. In the summer of 1882, Oscar first visited Birmingham when the furnace was under construction. While there, clothed in hickory shirt and jumpers, he worked for the furnace company as a locomotive fireman and then as engineer and finally was allowed to take his engine out on the main line.[28] Oscar never intended a career as a cowboy or a locomotive engi-

27. Louisville (Ky.) Rugby School report card, June 6, 1879; E. A. Grant to Underwood, January 5, 1912, Underwood to Harrison Robertson, February 25, 1911, Underwood to R. C. Gordon, February 8, 1924, all in Underwood Papers, Alabama Archives; interview with O. W. Underwood, Jr., November 24, 1951.

28. Underwood to O. W. Underwood, Jr., December 28, 1916, in Miscellaneous Folder, Underwood Papers, Alabama Archives; Birmingham *Times*, December 9, 1910; clipping from *National Democrat*, April 17, 1924, Underwood Scrapbook, III, 244, in Underwood Papers, Alabama Archives.

gineer. His father had often talked to him of becoming a lawyer, and a newspaper reporter said in 1912: "He just grew up with that idea in his head and he never felt any inclination to change it."[29]

Underwood entered the University of Virginia in 1881, at the age of nineteen. The school was no place for young wastrels. The students came from families of modest circumstances; Underwood and one of his classmates were the only students who could afford to maintain a horse. Oscar also had a Negro valet. The town of Charlottesville had an air of genteel poverty and through it ran the muddy or dusty Main Street along which wagons lumbered or parked in front of awninged stores. This atmosphere of respectable dilapidation had a definite charm about it similar to that of Bowling Green, his grandfather's home. During his first year at the university, Underwood took a liberal arts course of history, literature, rhetoric, and natural and moral philosophy. In the fall of 1883 he enrolled in the Department of Law. The university offered a one-year course, but it was recommended that students spread their study over two years. The department was staffed by two able men, the amiable and lovable Stephen O. Southall and the rather stern John B. Minor. Minor, or "Old John B.," as the students called him, was an outstanding teacher of common and statute law, and Underwood studied his *Institutes* as a text. Since Underwood repeatedly stated that he imbibed his Jeffersonian philosophy at the University of Virginia, it seems reasonable that Professor Minor was the source of this Jeffersonianism.[30]

Underwood withdrew from the university on two occasions, on June 1, 1882, and on June 1, 1883. No reason was given for the first withdrawal, and Underwood was not listed as being delinquent academically. He probably withdrew to join his half-brother in Birmingham but decided to reenter college in the fall. He was listed as "proficient" in constitutional and international law on his report of June 27, 1883, but that only meant that he had satisfactorily completed the course. The withdrawal in the summer of

29. Birmingham *Age-Herald*, January 14, 1912.
30. Interview with O. W. Underwood, Jr., November 24, 1951; Philip A. Bruce, *History of the University of Virginia, 1819–1919* (5 vols.; New York: Macmillan, 1920–21), IV, 2–5.

1883 followed a delinquency report of five "counts," probably routine absences, in constitutional and international law. He withdrew on this occasion with the permission of his parents who were deeply distressed at reports from the university administration that Oscar had challenged a Louisville student to a duel. Family memories of the proposed affair of honor cast the Louisville student, Embrey Lee Swearingen, later president of the First National Bank of Louisville, as the aggressor. However, Matthew Fontaine Maury, grandson of the famous oceanographer and a friend of Underwood, wrote his father two years later that the dispute involved a girl, Eugenia Massie, and that Swearingen was a "gentle man." Underwood had written Maury that the duel would have occurred had Swearingen not "failed to put in an appearance at the appointed time and place."[31] The high drama of the youthful dispute must have diminished during the summer months. Or perhaps the appeal of pretty apple-cheeked Eugenia Massie was enough to make Oscar promise good behavior in return for readmission to the college. He returned to school in the fall. His scholarship improved, and in July, 1884, he was cited as a "distinguished" student in constitutional and international law. He did not receive a degree from the University of Virginia; in fact, he was listed as a member of the junior class in 1884, his last year there.[32]

While at the university Underwood was interested in nonacademic pursuits and participated in a broad range of activities. Most important of these was the Jefferson Society, a debating group and the most prestigious organization on the campus. The debates were important events, widely patronized by the citizens of Charlottesville. In January, 1883, Underwood sponsored two resolutions concerning the society's magazine. The first criticized the use of the magazine's funds for suppers; the second urged students to patronize only business firms that advertised in the magazine. On

31. Matthew F. Maury II to Richard L. Maury, October 6, 1885, in R. L. Maury Papers, Duke University.
32. Interview with O. W. Underwood, Jr., November 24, 1951; Faculty Minutes 1879–84 (MS in University of Virginia Library), 243, 315, 318, 335, 410; Catalog of the Officers and Students of the University of Virginia, Fifty-Ninth Session, 1883–84 (Charlottesville: n.p., 1885), 17.

February 10, 1883, Underwood debated with William P. Trent on the subject, "Should an assault on the President of the U.S. be made high treason?" In November, 1883, he took the negative against J. Randolph Anderson on the question, "Should the free school policy of Virginia be abolished?" At the same time Underwood achieved importance as a member of the society. In April, 1883, he was appointed secretary and on October 6, 1883, he was nominated by Trent for the presidency and was elected.[33]

Underwood led a pleasant life at the University of Virginia. A woman acquaintance described him, many years later, as "a handsome young man riding around on horseback, wearing Norfolk jacket suits, and accepting life as if it was a long summer's day." He was a member of the Pi Kappa Alpha social fraternity and the very select Eli Banana Ribbon Society. The Eli Bananas, who wore a patch of blue ribbon on their lapels, were a drinking fraternity, and on moonlit nights they went around beating drums and singing— "bumming," as they called it. They had some wild times, for years later a college friend suggested that the old Eli suppers had sent many members to an early grave. Underwood's carefully completed score card indicates his interest in the field day events of November 10 and 11, 1882, and shows that he was an unsuccessful contender in the one mile walk. Underwood also participated in rowing. There was no football at the university, and the boat races at Rives' Boating Club on the Rivanna River were a major sport. He rode his horse along the banks of the narrow Rivanna and helped judge those races.[34]

At Charlottesville Underwood made a number of friends who remained friends for life. Among them were Edward K. Campbell and Walker Percy who urged him to settle in Birmingham. Other schoolmates were R. Cuyler Gordon, J. Randolph Anderson, J. Hamilton Lewis, William P. Trent, and Joseph W. Bailey. His uni-

    33. "University Jefferson Society, 1875–94" (MS in University of Virginia Library), 193–212 *passim.*
    34. Virginia Harrison to Underwood, April, 1914, William Henry Robertson to Underwood, June 11, 1911, both in Underwood Papers, Alabama Archives; interview with O. W. Underwood, Jr., November 24, 1951.

versity career also gave him a common experience with men like Woodrow Wilson, John Sharp Williams, and Claude Swanson, all of whom attended the University of Virginia and figured in his later public life.[35]

Oscar's boyhood had been substantially southern, but it was somewhat more cosmopolitan than that of the same generation of most southern political leaders. During the Civil War the Underwoods were a divided family, and this led to the necessity for compromise and understanding in the family councils. Perhaps Oscar's experiences on the frontier and spending a few years away from the South were influential in giving him a greater tolerance than was characteristic of southerners of the period. At Rugby the irresponsible child, who had led a Tom Sawyer-like existence on the Minnesota frontier, developed into a disciplined youth whose academic record was well above average. Youthful athletic activities gave Underwood a strong and impressive physique, and there was nothing in his wholesome surroundings to give him less than a sanguine temperament. Yet he was becoming a serious young man who was fond of facts and figures. At the University of Virginia Underwood had not distinguished himself, but he developed a political philosophy and won lifetime friends. The ridiculous and unfortunate challenge to a duel, issued to an unoffending student, showed the fierce temper that he had not yet completely mastered. Leaving college without a degree, he eagerly circumvented this shortcoming by leaving the impression that he had indeed graduated. These youthful experiences, overlaid with a decade of life in Birmingham, a city of the New South, before he entered politics, seem to have acted as a taproot of conservatism for Underwood's eventual development as a national statesman.

35. O. W. Underwood, Jr., "Commentary," 14.

CHAPTER II

Populist-Minded Democrat

Upon leaving the University of Virginia in the summer of 1884, Underwood went to his former hometown, St. Paul, Minnesota, and was admitted to the bar. He practiced in St. Paul for two very idle months. His half-brother, William T. or "Will," then urged him to come to Birmingham, a real estate boomtown where there were good opportunities for lawyers. Most important of all, Will, a director of the First National Bank, the Birmingham Trust and Savings Company, and the North Birmingham Street Railroad Company, manager and part owner of the Mary Pratt Furnace Company, and owner of an interest in coal fields in Etowah County, offered Oscar help in developing a clientele. Oscar accepted the offer, moved to Birmingham, and by September 1, 1884, had been admitted to the Alabama bar. In Alabama, to be admitted to the bar an apprentice lawyer served briefly in the office of a lawyer and then appeared before the circuit judge. According to the folklore of lawyers, the candidate was asked one question: "What is the first rule of a lawyer?" The correct answer: "To collect the fee in advance." Probably Underwood's examination was more rigorous than that, but it was not stringent.[1]

Underwood described Birmingham of the 1880s as a primitive but growing town. When he arrived, the bustling, bragging, dirty little mining town of some five thousand people was in the midst of an iron boom, and its inhabitants called it the "Magic City." Un-

1. Underwood Family Folder, in Oscar W. Underwood Papers, Alabama Department of Archives and History, Montgomery.

like other communities in Alabama, it was a frontier town of the New South, rough and crude with as much of a western as a southern atmosphere. Everyone predicted a great future for Jefferson County because all the raw materials for the manufacture of pig iron—coal, iron ore, and limestone—were located in close proximity. South of the Louisville and Nashville Railroad tracks was a swamp. Underwood recalled going outside Birmingham to clear titles and draw the deeds to the land on which Bessemer was to be built and listening incredulously as Henry F. DeBardeleben, his half-brother's business partner, told of the city that would rise there.[2]

Underwood never mentioned the extraordinary tension between Birmingham's black and white workers. The blacks were employed in the mines, about half of them having learned their mining skills as convicts. After an L & N strike in 1893, they were employed on the railroad as brakemen, switchmen, and firemen. Segregation was strict, and a union organizer reported in 1898 that whites and blacks could not get their mail from the same window.[3]

Soon after his arrival, Underwood joined James J. Garrett, a Confederate veteran, and Major Ellis Phelan, secretary of state of Alabama, in the firm of Garrett, Underwood, and Phelan. Major Phelan soon retired, and the firm became Garrett and Underwood, with offices in the First National Bank building, a three-story "skyscraper" at First Avenue North and Twentieth Street known as "Linn's Folly." The Garrett and Underwood offices were evidently spacious, for on one occasion they accommodated the monthly meeting of the Birmingham Police Commission.[4]

2. Martha C. Mitchell, "Birmingham: A Biography of a City of the New South" (Ph.D. dissertation, University of Chicago, 1946), 21–33, 60–63; Birmingham Age-Herald, April 17, 1920.
3. Paul B. Worthman, "Black Workers and Labor Unions in Birmingham, Alabama, 1897–1904," Labor History, X (1969), 375–407.
4. Birmingham News, November 1, 1903. By 1901 Robert H. Thach, a brother of the president of Alabama Polytechnic Institute, had been added to the firm. In the same year there is reference to Underwood's membership in the United States Supreme Court bar. In April, 1902, a new firm was formed of James Wetherly, Underwood, and Thach. By 1905 the firm was Underwood and Thach, but Oscar Underwood, Jr., thought that his father did not practice after 1910. Birmingham Times, April 4, 1902; O. W. Underwood, Jr., to author, September 26, 1959, in possession of Evans C. Johnson, DeLand, Fla.

Underwood returned to Charlottesville in the fall of 1885 to claim the girl for whom he had threatened to fight a duel while a student at the University of Virginia. His bride, Eugenia Massie, was the daughter of the late Dr. Thomas Eugene Massie, who had left his family a sizable estate. The family lived in Charlottesville on the site of the present-day Dolly Madison Inn. "Genie," as everyone knew her, was a beautiful girl of medium height with chestnut-brown hair and bright-colored cheeks. She had attended Edgehill School at Shadwell, Virginia, and was well known in the university community. Her half-sister married Allen L. Thurman, the grandson of Senator Allen G. Thurman, a Democrat from Ohio. At twenty-four, Genie was more than a year older than her fiance.

The Massie-Underwood wedding on October 8, 1885, was a brilliant occasion. The bride, dressed in white satin with a nun's veiling, advanced to the altar of old Christ Church to the strains of the wedding march, where the party was met by the groom and Dr. James Stuart Hanckel, who read the Episcopal marriage service. Judge John L. Cochran, the bride's stepfather, gave her away. Among the bridesmaids were Daisy Hampton, a daughter of Senator Wade Hampton, Martha Minor, a daughter of Professor Minor, and the bride's sister, Nita Massie, who later became Mrs. Malvern C. Patterson. Oscar's younger brother Sidney served as best man, and William P. Trent was an usher. Will and Rin Underwood attended the wedding. The newlywed couple took an evening train for a honeymoon in the North.[5]

The young Underwoods made their home in Birmingham, and for a time they lived with Will and Rin at their large residence on the crest of a hill bounded by Ridge Park Avenue and Sycamore Street. Their modest scale of living as well as the low state and county tax rates is indicated by their tax bill for 1887, which was $2.99, of which $1.50 was poll tax. On March 13, 1890, Oscar purchased for $5,400 a house on the corner of Lower Highland Avenue and Thirtieth Street. Oscar and Genie were a happy couple and

5. Charlottesville (Va.) *Jeffersonian Republican*, October 14, 1885.

Genie bore two children, John Lewis, born September 3, 1888, and Oscar Wilder, Jr., born July 27, 1890.[6]

Underwood engaged in a variety of business enterprises during his early years in Birmingham. He was an organizer and secretary of the Birmingham Fire Brick Works, capitalized at $50,000. He was listed on August 4, 1887, as one of four incorporators of the Peoples Savings Bank which had $50,000 capitalization, but there is no evidence that this organization materialized. In 1887 Will and Rin gave Oscar and Genie a tract of land at Nineteenth Street and Tenth Avenue, now in downtown Birmingham. Within four years Oscar and his wife had sold this tract in three parcels for $9,150. In 1889 Oscar was an organizer and director of the Garrett Spoke and Handle Company, a corporation largely owned by Garrett, to which Underwood subscribed only $100. A year later he was an incorporator of the Alabama Building and Loan Association, which had a capitalization of $2,000. His participation in the incorporation of the Garrett, Underwood Abstract Company on January 2, 1890, was far more important to him than his other corporate activities. This land abstract company was capitalized at $10,000, of which Underwood subscribed $4,900, Garrett $5,000, and Harry W. Hyde, the secretary and treasurer, $100. The stock was paid for by transfer of the stockholders' interest in Sisson's *American System of Abstracts*. Garrett was a specialist in land titles and presumably did much of the work, but there is evidence of Underwood's handwriting in the property records of the period.[7]

One may infer from Garrett's specialization in title work that Underwood did much of the courtroom practice, although one account refers to him as the "library lawyer" of the combination. The firm handled a variety of civil cases but evidently did little criminal work. However, Underwood liked to tell a story of receiving a gallon of St. Clair County "moonshine" from a client who sent a note

6. Deeds Book 138, pp. 16, 374, Jefferson County, Ala.; tax receipt, March 14, 1887, Jefferson County, Ala., in Underwood Papers, Alabama Archives.
7. Underwood's legal activities in the 1880s and 1890s appear in the deed books and corporate records of the Jefferson County, Ala., Probate Court. See especially Corporation Records A–C. In the same probate court see Deeds Books 87, 90, 111, and 156.

to identify it as a sample of the product that Underwood had gotten him acquitted of making. Although most of their clients were individuals, the firm handled some work for corporations, such as the First National Bank, DeBardeleben Coal and Iron Company, and the North Birmingham Street Railroad Company, perhaps their most important client.[8]

Underwood won his first major courtroom victory in the case of *John A. Hambleton and Company of Baltimore* v. *Decatur Land Improvement and Furnace Company* in January, 1890. Underwood sued the latter in federal district court in Huntsville for forty thousand dollars, plus interest. He based his argument on a decision made in a similar case by the opposition lawyer, Robert Coman Brickell, when he was chief justice of the Alabama Supreme Court. After several days of sustained argument in which Underwood single-handedly argued the case involving an interpretation of new federal laws, the court gave a judgment for all that Underwood asked. The defendant made a bond for appeal, but the judgment was then settled out of court, presumably for somewhat less than face value.[9]

In 1912 a reporter for the Birmingham *Age-Herald* assessed Underwood's early legal ability:

Young lawyer Underwood didn't spring into the limelight, he didn't win any sensational case, and he didn't display any extraordinary traits of genius. He just worked. He soon built up a reputation for honesty, thoroughness, and fairness. When young Underwood argued a case in court the matter was presented in a clear, concise manner. He did not say one man was a criminal and another man was a saint just because they were on opposite sides in a law suit and one happened to be his client. He was square. It was fairly shone out of the man that he was asking for a square deal in a square way and for square reasons. He made friends by the wholesale, and when he made one he never lost him. His mind and reasoning powers were well-balanced and he always based his arguments on cold facts and hard statistics and did not fly off into passionate appeals to sentiment.[10]

8. Birmingham *Post*, May 6, 1926.

9. Federal Records Center, Case No. 1477, Record Box 28572, East Point, Ga.; clipping in Frederica Virginia Underwood's Box, Underwood Papers, Alabama Archives.

10. Birmingham *Age-Herald*, January 14, 1912. O. W. Underwood, Jr., recalled that his

Underwood participated in many civic affairs in Birmingham. He was secretary of the Birmingham Bar Association at the time of its formation in 1885. In May, 1887, he was one of three inspectors appointed by the probate judge to supervise an incorporation election for the town of Highland, now the South Highland section of Birmingham. On May 7, 1889, he joined the Knights of Pythias, and two years later he served as chancellor of Jones Valley Lodge Number 11. He was initiated as a Mason, and he also joined the Elks. In 1893 he served on the Committee on Legislation of the Birmingham Commercial Club.[11]

The struggling young lawyer suffered financial reverses in 1892, and in August of that year he and Genie mortgaged for $3,000 the frame house on Lower Highland Avenue that they had purchased two years earlier for $5,400. In 1893 Eugene Underwood, Oscar's father, died in insolvency in Bowling Green, Kentucky. The Mary Pratt Furnace, of which his half-brother was manager and a partner, remained idle much of the time, and in 1898 it was sold for a fraction of its cost.[12]

Underwood's financial reverses just prior to the panic of 1893 coincided with his emergence into politics. He had served for several years as a member of the District Democratic Congressional Committee, and in 1892 he became a delegate-at-large to the Alabama State Democratic Convention which would select the Democratic nominee for governor. Democratic control of Alabama politics had been restored in 1876, and the Republicans in the state split into warring Lily White and Black and Tan factions which had no nope of winning statewide office against the party that now styled itself the Democratic and Conservative party. In 1890 the

father liked the celebrated trial manual of Joseph Wesley Donovan, *Tact in Court* (Rochester, N.Y.: Williamson Law Book Company, 1898). His father, he said, "had very sound ideas about trial strategy, one of which was that, when a lawyer has presented a point upon which he should win, he should rest his case and await the result. . . . He was certainly a good lawyer, well trained, careful, with a deep sense of responsibility." O. W. Underwood, Jr., to author, September 26, 1959, in possession of Evans C. Johnson.

11. George M. Cruikshank, *History of Birmingham and Its Environs* (2 vols.; Chicago: Lewis Publishing Company, 1920), I, 213; Birmingham *News*, October 27, 29, November 3, 1913; Birmingham *Age-Herald*, May 27, 1893.

12. Deeds Book 138, pp. 229, 374, Jefferson County, Ala.; Mortgage Book 175, p. 87, Jefferson County, Ala.; W. T. Underwood to Oscar W. Underwood, August 23, 1907, in Underwood Papers, Alabama Archives.

charismatic Reuben F. Kolb, a well educated agrarian leader, was clearly the most popular candidate for governor, but opposition candidates coalesced around conservative Thomas Goode Jones. The effects of the panic of 1893 were felt early in Alabama, and the distress of the state's farmers augured well for Kolb's effort to capitalize upon his earlier record as commissioner of agriculture and promoter of the state in an "Alabama on Wheels" program that carried state products over the Midwest through the courtesy of the L & N Railroad. Kolb, the developer of "Kolb's Gem" watermelon seed, had availed himself of railroad passes while commissioner of agriculture; he had enough conservative associations to create doubt that his program was as radical as the conservatives charged. Jones, an L & N attorney, was cut from the spare cloth of Bourbonism, and in the minds of most observers the contest was a clear-cut choice between agrarian radicalism and Bourbon conservatism.[13]

The elections for delegates to the Democratic convention to be held in the early summer of 1892 resulted in utter confusion. Both Jones and Kolb claimed enough delegates to win the nomination. The Democratic Executive Committee, in partisan fashion, gave Jones more than twice as many delegates as were given to Kolb, virtually assuring Jones of the nomination. The Democratic convention, which met in Montgomery, had only to ratify Kolb's defeat.

Underwood was chairman of the Credentials Committee, assigned to confirm the Democratic Executive Committee's work in allotting delegates to Jones. Underwood, however, served as a healing element in making a concession to the Kolb followers. His majority report recommended the seating of Kolb supporters as delegates from Populist-dominated Bibb County. Opponents of the majority report viewed the concession as a bid by Jefferson County delegates for support in the coming congressional race, but the report prevailed. The chairman of the Bibb delegation thanked the

13. Albert B. Moore, *History of Alabama* (University, Ala.: University Supply Store, 1934), 607–14. The Black and Tan Republicans had more Negroes and mulattoes in proportion to their numbers than had the Lily Whites.

convention for seating him, and the convention concluded on a more harmonious note than had seemed possible. Nevertheless, Kolb had already made plans to bolt the Democratic party and run as a "Jeffersonian Democrat."[14]

The seating of the Kolb delegation at the state convention was a prologue to Underwood's attempt to block the nomination of Representative Lewis W. Turpin of Greensboro at the district convention held in Blount Springs. The spectacular growth of Birmingham gave Alabama a new congressman in 1892, and the legislature gerrymandered Jefferson County into the new Ninth District with Bibb and Blount, and two black-belt counties, Hale and Perry. The black-belt counties, with the Negro vote under firm control, were almost solidly Democratic and were expected to offset Republican majorities in Jefferson, Blount, and Bibb. Turpin was from Hale in the old Fourth District, and he sought renomination from the new Ninth District. Birmingham Democrats, especially a young and vigorous group led by Underwood, were reluctant to accept Turpin as their nominee, feeling that Birmingham should furnish the congressman.

Favorite son candidates from Jefferson and Blount counties opposed Turpin. Underwood reasoned that since Jefferson County held twenty-six of the total of sixty-three delegates in the congressional convention, it could control the convention by establishing the two-thirds rule. Jefferson's 26 votes added to Blount's 5 and the 4 from Bibb, whose delegates owed their seats to him, would be sufficient to establish the two-thirds rule. Underwood urged adoption of the rule as the "standard of Democracy" and as a method of reducing discord. William C. Cross, chairman of the Committee on Permanent Organization, countered by referring to the two-thirds rule as an "antique" idea and denying that majority rule had produced discord. The defection of Bibb County and one Blount delegate led to defeat of the two-thirds rule by a vote of 33 to 30. This defeat sealed the doom of Jefferson County's congressional candidate, James E. Hawkins, who received only the 26 votes of

14. Charles G. Summersell, "The Alabama Governor's Race in 1892," *Alabama Review*, VIII (1955), 5–33; Birmingham *Age-Herald*, June 10, 1892.

the Jefferson delegation, and Colonel Bret Randolph of Blount who received Blount's 5 votes. Turpin won the nomination with the 32 votes cast by the delegates from Bibb, Hale, and Perry. Perfidious Bibb County had ruined Underwood's plans. Despite his opposition to Turpin's nomination, Underwood was unanimously elected chairman of the Congressional Executive Committee which managed Turpin's campaign as well as the local fortunes of Grover Cleveland and Adlai E. Stevenson. The Democrats won the district handily with a majority that was greater than that of any other Alabama congressional district. The Birmingham *Age-Herald* saluted Underwood's generalship and observed that he had devoted his undivided time and energy to the campaign.[15]

The feeling that Birmingham should furnish the Ninth District congressman was stronger by 1894, and the state Democratic Executive Committee recognized the growth of the city by reapportioning the delegates to the district convention so that burgeoning Jefferson County would have about half the delegates. Urged on by his closest friend, Edward K. Campbell, and by other energetic young Democrats, Underwood sought the nomination. Another Birmingham man, Frank P. O'Brien, was prominently mentioned as a candidate, but in April he announced that he would not run.[16]

Underwood launched his campaign in the spring of 1894, but he did not call a meeting of the Congressional Executive Committee to resign. At the regularly scheduled meeting on August 9, he stated that he had not done so because there was no other business to discuss. Actually, Underwood hoped that the state convention's reapportionment plan would be accepted as a fait accompli. After accepting Underwood's resignation, however, the congressional committee, which favored Turpin, refused to approve the state committee's reapportionment, and Jefferson County received only one third of the members in the convention. Infuriated by these tactics, Underwood's followers called an indignation meeting at

15. Birmingham *Age-Herald*, September 15, November 10, 1892.
16. Bessemer (Ala.) *Weekly*, April 7, 1894.

Birmingham's Elks Hall and appealed the apportionment plan to the state convention committee. The new congressional committee chairman pleaded that he had inadequate time in which to prepare a defense, but most of the Turpin supporters recognized that their case was lost. The state committee overruled the congressional committee, and Jefferson County received about half the delegates.

The campaign for the congressional nomination focused on the monetary issue, with Underwood supporting free silver and Turpin standing "flat-footed" in support of Cleveland's hard-money policies. The newspapers divided on the nomination according to the position they took on the monetary question. The Birmingham *Age-Herald*, Bessemer *Weekly*, Blocton *Courier*, and Oneonto *News-Dispatch* attacked Turpin's hard-money views. The Blountsville *Sentinel*, Bessemer *Journal*, and Marion *Standard* supported Turpin. Assuming that he had the support of Jefferson County, Underwood campaigned most vigorously in Perry County in the black belt. Edward K. Campbell, a University of Virginia classmate who had located in Birmingham before Underwood, was his campaign manager.[17]

The Democratic primaries and conventions, held throughout the district in August, resulted in a clear victory for Underwood. In Jefferson County the Turpin followers made almost no effort to campaign. Jefferson County's convention instructed its thirty delegates to vote as a unit for Underwood. Perry County's convention voted overwhelmingly in favor of Underwood. Bibb County held primaries and prorated its delegates, giving Underwood two and Turpin three. Blount County's delegates unanimously supported Bret Randolph, a favorite son. Hale County, Turpin's home, was the only county to give him a solid delegation.[18]

17. Birmingham *Age-Herald*, April 8, August 8, 10, 12, 15, 18, 1894; Bessemer (Ala.) *Weekly*, April 7, 14, 28, 1894; Bessemer (Ala.) *Journal*, April 12, 19, 1894; Marion (Ala.) *Standard*, March 1, May 10, June 28, 1894.
18. Birmingham *Age-Herald*, August 19, 22, 26, 1894; Marion (Ala.) *Standard*, August 21, 24, 1894.

Turpin's defeats in the district's multifarious party nomination machinery left the district convention at Blount Springs the task of ratifying Underwood's nomination. The convention, meeting on September 4, turned into a Democratic love feast as Turpin, who was drunk at the meeting, had given up any real hope of being nominated. Ed Campbell sponsored a resolution endorsing Turpin's "ability and patriotism" and placed Underwood's name before the convention.[19]

Underwood was nominated by acclamation. In ornate language he pledged party loyalty and fidelity to the Democratic platform:

> Believing in the great principles of our party, as enunciated by our great leaders and as expressed in the national platform of 1892, I shall be guided by those principles.
>
> For the great principles of the Democratic faith the wisdom of our sages and the blood of our heroes have been freely expended. They are like the bright star in the Northern firmament, fixed and unchanging, and when the storms of misfortune or political strife have driven us from the true course of good government they stand as a tower of truth.[20]

Underwood endorsed a revenue tariff which would give his district a "fair share of any incidental benefits that may arise." He favored an expanded currency and the free and unlimited coinage of silver and gold at a sixteen to one ratio; he thus rejected the gold Democrats who had offered their support in return for Underwood's omission of the free-silver plank from his platform.[21]

As the congressional nominee, Underwood was allowed to choose the members of the Democratic Congressional Committee. He chose Ed Campbell as chairman and young Henry Howze as secretary. Both of these men, especially Campbell, were to act as Underwood's local political representatives, dominating the committee and preparing for Underwood's renomination and reelec-

19. Bessemer (Ala.) *Weekly*, September 8, 1894.
20. Birmingham *Age-Herald*, September 6, 1894.
21. Bessemer (Ala.) *Weekly*, September 8, 1894.

tion every two years until Campbell left Birmingham in 1913 and was replaced as chairman by Howze.[22]

The Republicans nominated Truman H. Aldrich, a respected Tennessee Coal, Iron and Railroad Company official who was handicapped by the fact that he was thought to have been in the process of moving to Cincinnati to join his family when he accepted the nomination. A man of considerable wealth, Aldrich had contributed greatly to the industrial development of Birmingham. In accepting the nomination, he advocated a protective tariff as an aid to the diversification of Birmingham's industries. With evident reference to election frauds, he punned, "There is one plant on which the Democrats have gotten ahead of us, and we don't want to rival them on that. It is a s-t-e-a-l plant." About half of the delegates to the convention were Negroes, and having the support of the Black and Tans, Aldrich had the Republican party united behind him.[23]

The outlook for Underwood's election was not bright. Joseph H. Woodward of the Woodward Coal and Iron Company, later Underwood's father-in-law, expressed the prevailing Republican opinion when he said: "Too bad Oscar's trying to get to Congress, he's a nice boy and I don't like to see him beaten, as he's sure to be."[24] Effective fusion between the Republicans and the Populists would likely bring defeat for Underwood. There was little doubt that Populist leaders would support Aldrich's candidacy, but the *Age-Herald* confidently predicted that the "wool hat boys," the sturdy farmers in the Populist ranks, would not find the wealthy Aldrich appealing. Despite the predictions of the *Age-Herald* that the Populists would endorse Underwood or place their own candidate in the field, the agrarian party met at Blocton, Aldrich's home and a Populist stronghold, and endorsed the Republican nominee.[25]

The Democrats were much better supplied with speakers and

22. Henry R. Howze to Underwood, May 23, 1913, in Henry R. Howze Papers, Alabama Department of Archives and History, Montgomery.

23. Birmingham *Age-Herald*, September 18, 28, 13, 1894.

24. Burton J. Hendrick, "Oscar W. Underwood, a New Leader from the New South," *McClure's Magazine*, XXXVIII (1912), 410.

25. Birmingham *Age-Herald*, September 11, 16, 1894.

much better organized than the Republicans. Several prominent Democrats, including Joseph F. Johnston and Ed Campbell, spoke in Underwood's behalf. Congressman Lewis W. Turpin, the defeated candidate for the Democratic nomination, sportingly made a number of speeches for Underwood. Charles F. Crisp of Georgia, Speaker of the United States House of Representatives, came to Birmingham to speak for Underwood. Underwood clubs were organized throughout the district, and at least one Underwood Irish Democratic club was formed. In Perry County in the black belt, a black Underwood Democratic club was formed. The Democrats' claim that their club had as members sixty-five of the eighty-five registered blacks in Perry County may have been exaggerated, but evidently the Negroes were politically controlled by whites.

Underwood methodically and extensively toured the district by horse and buggy averaging a speech a day but concentrating on meeting the voters personally. He went into areas barely accessible by the rutted and muddy roads of the day where congressional candidates were seldom seen. He stopped at the farmers' houses, ate at their tables, and slept in their beds.[26]

There was little that Underwood's supporters could say of the accomplishments of their thirty-three-year-old candidate. Underwood was a tall, gangling man, and a friendly reporter observed that with his "beardless innocent face" he did not appear to be more than twenty-five years old. Opponents ridiculed Underwood's fondness for bicycling, but cycling was popular in the Birmingham area, and the charge backfired.[27] The Age-Herald recommended Underwood as a "thorough gentleman, an able lawyer, a fine business man, and a Democrat from spur to plume."[28]

Underwood attacked the Republican protective tariff policy. At

26. *Ibid.*, September 29, October 4, 11, 12, November 2, 3, 1894; interview with Hugh Morrow, Sr., August 11, 1951; clipping from the Marion (Ala.) *Standard*, in Underwood Scrapbook, C, 8, Underwood Papers, Alabama Archives.

27. Atlanta *Constitution*, quoted in Bessemer (Ala.) *Weekly*, April 14, 1894; clipping in Frederica Virginia Underwood's Box, *ca.* 1898, in Underwood Papers, Alabama Archives. A well-remembered physical exploit of Underwood's was a bicycle trip of over a hundred miles made in 1890 from Birmingham to Montgomery. He won an arm-band award for the accomplishment. Hill Ferguson to author, July 10, 1953, in possession of Evans C. Johnson.

28. Birmingham *Age-Herald*, November 1, 1894.

Greensboro, on October 17, he spoke of Aldrich as an honorable man and stated that the "gauge of battle hinged on party principles embodied mainly in the McKinley Bill." Southern industries were not infant industries, he said, they were capable of competing with any in the world. European labor might be cheaper, but American employers got better value for the same amount expended for labor. Underwood stated that the tariff should be no higher than necessary to support economical government and called the McKinley tariff an important cause for bankruptcy among American businesses. He charged that the number of business failures during Harrison's administration was some two or three times higher than in the Cleveland administration, following the repeal of the McKinley tariff. The workers had been promised wage raises upon the passage of the McKinley act, but instead, wages were cut 10 to 40 percent. Industrial strife resulted, and "cold lead and bayonets was the strikers' portion." He pointed out cogently that Aldrich had reduced the wages of his own miners after the passage of the McKinley act, and he cited the benefits being derived from the free list in the Wilson-Gorman Act.[29]

Second in importance to the tariff question was the Democrats' time-honored charge that the election of a Republican would mean the return of Reconstruction and Negro rule. The *Age-Herald* alleged that the Aldrich followers presented the colors of "Salt, Pepper, and Mustard." The Republicans were attacked for having Negroes on Aldrich's campaign committee, but the Democrats found to their delight that the Negroes were actually on the executive committee, a powerless organization that handled no funds. Aldrich was also denounced for having Bill Stevens, leader of the Black and Tans, in his ranks. Despite its criticism of Republicans for seeking Negro votes, the *Age-Herald* appealed for Negro votes for Underwood. An allegedly prominent Negro, E. E. Carlisle, in several articles in the *Age-Herald* urged Negroes to vote for Underwood as a means of restoring their political rights by keeping in harmony with the whites. He maintained that by helping to elect Under-

29. *Ibid.*, October 21, 1894.

wood, Negroes would have some claim on their representative; if Aldrich were elected, the Lily White Republicans and the Jeffersonian Democrats would be in control. He pointed out that the Aldrich group had three headquarters, one for the Republicans, one for the Jeffersonian Democrats, and one for the Negroes.[30]

Both candidates endorsed bimetallism, but Aldrich's platform failed to endorse specifically the coinage of silver at the sixteen to one ratio. As Underwood had declined the offer of a trade with the gold Democrats for their support in return for repudiation of free silver, these Democrats in the Birmingham area favored Aldrich.[31]

Underwood attacked Republican policies as favoring the wealthy. With the fervor of a Populist, he charged that the tariff made the rich man richer and the poor man poorer. He stated that two thirds of the money in the United States was controlled by millionaires and that most of the people were left to struggle for the remaining one third. He unequivocally and emphatically endorsed free silver at a ratio of sixteen to one, maintaining that the depression of commodity prices was due to the contraction of the currency. He endorsed radical currency expansion and said that he would vote to repeal the 10 percent tax on state bank notes. He was opposed to direct taxation but favored putting the income tax back in force, despite the Supreme Court's decision declaring it unconstitutional. Referring to the hybrid platform on which Aldrich was running, Underwood said that he would refuse to be the standard-bearer of his party when he could not stand "hip to hip" with his party and its principles. Concluding his campaign at Bessemer, a Populist stronghold, Underwood addressed the followers of Reuben F. Kolb.

> The Republican party is struggling to carry with it the Jeffersonian democrats, who separated from us on local issues. To do that they have secured the services of Captain Kolb and others who were prominent in his cause. I ask you to consider well and long before doing some-

30. *Ibid*., September 15, October 9, 16, 21, 31, November 3, 8, 1894.
31. *Ibid*., November 3, 1894; Samuel Will John to Underwood, May 11, 1908, in Underwood Papers, Alabama Archives.

thing that will be detrimental to your interests. Are you going to let them lead you into the Republican party, the party that has done your country so much harm? Captain Kolb and other leaders have nothing to lose by going into the Republican party; they go for the loaves and fishes. You will get none of the loaves and fishes.[32]

The Democrats had demonstrated quite effectively that as a candidate Aldrich was neither fish nor fowl nor good red herring. If he were elected to Congress, he would have divided allegiance. His protectionist views would be distasteful to the Populists and his free-silver position equally distasteful to the Republicans. The Democrats also maintained that Aldrich would be of little help to Alabama Senator John Tyler Morgan in securing passage of a Nicaraguan canal bill because the House was Democratic. Aldrich's claim that he had been a great benefactor of the region in freely spending his own money to foster a study of the geological structure of the Birmingham district brought a bitter election day reply from the *Age-Herald*. Aldrich was accused of spending forty thousand dollars in the "swell days" of high protection to get up a geological paper that presented the atheistic theory that "neither Moses nor his inspirer knew anything about the creation of the world."[33]

The general election revealed that in the state at large, Alabama was safely Democratic. Only half as many voters cast ballots in the statewide November election as had voted in the August gubernatorial primary. The Ninth Congressional District, however, remained a battleground between Democrats and Republicans, and the vote in Jefferson County was only 30 percent lighter than in the gubernatorial primary. Several Republicans were arrested on election day, November 6, for possessing marked or printed mock ballots in violation of Alabama's Sayre law which was designed to make it difficult for Negroes to vote. Republicans began the cry of fraud before the morning was over, and watchers were placed outside the polls to make rosters of the voters for use in contesting the

32. Birmingham *Age-Herald*, November 3, 1894.
33. *Ibid.*, September 13, October 12, 24, November 6, 1894.

election if Aldrich should lose. Some Republicans asserted that Aldrich would be seated whether or not he was elected. Underwood received 7,463 votes and Aldrich 6,153 votes. Jefferson County voters, casting about half the ballots, voted 3,615 to 2,030 in favor of the Democrat. Underwood carried Birmingham, but Aldrich carried most of the peripheral mining settlements. In Blount County, where the Republicans controlled the voting machinery, canvassers threw out two Democratic beats (precincts), and Aldrich received a vote of 1,451 to 1,033 for Underwood. Bibb County went for Aldrich by a majority of 503. Perry and Hale, the two black-belt counties, gave Underwood majorities of 758 and 988, with many Republicans not voting.[34]

At the outset of his campaign, Underwood had appeared to have little chance of nomination or election. Opposition to his nomination disintegrated in the face of a strong movement in Birmingham for the "Magic City" to furnish the district's congressman. The victory in the general election was a result of good organization and effective campaigning. The Republicans had an able nominee in Aldrich, but the hardy Dutch iron master was a poor speaker. The Negro and small-farmer constituents of the Republican and Populist parties were not interested in him. The Republicans had less capable leadership, less effective organization, less newspaper support, and more factionalism than did the Democrats. Underwood had campaigned on the basis of loyalty to the Democratic party, but while standing on the party platform he had used the language of Populism so often that he clearly differentiated himself from the Bourbon Democrats in philosophy. Underwood, in fact, showed a liturgical devotion to the party platform. The revenue tariff, which he emphasized so strongly, was to be the cardinal issue for which he fought during his entire political career. He had proved himself an acceptable though uninspiring speaker, and he conducted the campaign with perhaps more moderation than was characteristic of the period. He showed a fondness for facts and statistics that became an Underwood hallmark.

34. Moore, *History of Alabama*, 640; Birmingham *Age-Herald*, November 8, 1894.

The Republicans were not expected to accept the results of Underwood's election. Indeed, everyone knew that the Republican Congress would, in partisan fashion, vote to unseat Underwood and declare Aldrich elected. Underwood shook hands with Aldrich at the depot before boarding the train to Washington and asked his opponent when he expected to visit the capital. "In about a week" was Aldrich's reply. "Well," said Underwood, "I'll try to keep the seat warm."[35]

According to one account, Underwood returned to the University of Virginia soon after his election to see John B. Minor, his former law professor. When Minor failed to inquire about Underwood's honor, Underwood finally blurted out that he had been elected to Congress. Minor sighed quietly: "I'm sorry, I had great hopes for you. I think you might have made a good lawyer."[36]

35. Birmingham *Weekly State Herald*, November 27, 1895.
36. Clipping in Underwood Scrapbook, III, 130, Underwood Papers, Alabama Archives.

CHAPTER III

In the Twilight of Populism

The panic of 1893 had a searing effect on Birmingham and upon Oscar Underwood and his bride of eight years. For Underwood, at least, the effects of the panic were greatest in the fall of 1895 when he was preparing to enter Congress. In October, 1895, he wrote his wife, who was in Charlottesville with their two boys, John Lewis and Oscar, Jr., that he was "making a hard struggle to save some of our property." His heartrending and self-deprecating letter apologized for his fretfulness, exactitude, and lack of financial achievement. His financial situation was, he said, worse than it had been at the time of their marriage. He pledged, however, that before the end of ten years he would provide well for "my dear little girl" and their two fine sons.[1]

Pretty Eugenia Massie Underwood devoted most of her attention at this time to her two sons. She was, however, interested in art. She liked to paint china and sketch and was one of the organizers of the Birmingham Art League. Much of her time was spent in Charlottesville, at the home of her widowed mother, Mrs. John L. Cochran. These extended visits resulted from filial responsibility, economic necessity, proximity to her husband's new position in Washington, and allegedly, its superior climate.[2]

The Republicans had won an overwhelming majority in the House of Representatives in the election of 1894, and Thomas B.

1. Oscar W. Underwood to Eugenia Massie Underwood, October 8, 1895, in Oscar W. Underwood Papers, Alabama Department of Archives and History, Montgomery.
2. Birmingham News, February 1, 1900.

"Czar" Reed of Maine was easily elected Speaker. Underwood respected Reed, later describing him as "the greatest intellect I have known in public life."[3] Underwood's was one of thirty-two contested seats. With such a Republican majority there was little possibility that he could retain his seat, as the House had in this period largely abandoned any attempt to determine election contests judicially. In the meantime, Underwood set about making his mark.

The new congressman arrived in Washington in late November, 1895. He was quite familiar with the city, having visited it numerous times while a student at the University of Virginia. In his early years in Congress he attracted attention as a dapper dresser, a handsome man, and a "comer" on the Democratic side. Unlike some of his colleagues, he wore suits that were not cheap hand-me-downs. On one occasion minority leader Joseph W. Bailey addressed himself to a Republican bill and began, "Ah, Mr. Speaker," when the dark mustached Underwood passed down the center aisle attracting attention in a white linen suit and novel white canvas, rubber-soled "sneakers." Bailey lost his train of thought as Underwood disappeared into the cloakroom.[4]

Underwood described the Democrats in the Fifty-fourth Congress as divided between extremes. About an equal number were followers of "the heretic religion whose prophet was Bryan" and the other half were Democrats of the "ante-bellum" sort. Underwood described himself as a moderate.[5] Actually, he was a strong free-silverite at this time and represented the infusion of Populist ideas into Democratic politics. Noting that both he and his opponent had run on a free-silver platform, he said upon arriving in Washington: "The people of Alabama are thinking of one thing—that is money. They want more money in circulation." He deplored the gold views of Cleveland: "Alabama will support any man for the presidency who will come out openly and positively for the free

3. Burton J. Hendrick, "Oscar W. Underwood, a New Leader from the New South," *McClure's Magazine*, XXXVIII (1912), 412.

4. Birmingham *Daily Ledger*, June 14, 1898.

5. Arthur B. Krock, "Underwood, an Intimate View of the Man—His Traits, Tendencies, and Prepossessions," *Harper's Weekly*, LVI (July 1, 1912), 10.

coinage of silver at some ratio which shall preserve the parity of
the metals. . . . Among the gold Democrats of the state [Secretary
of the Treasury John G.] Carlisle is the favorite, but the free silver
people are largely in the majority. If Cleveland were only a free
silver man and would take the reins of our free silver coach I would
be sure of success. We regard him as a very able man in Alabama
and are sorry he is not on our side."[6] Although most Alabama
Democrats favored a sixteen to one ratio and Underwood was
elected on this platform, he now claimed that he was not committed to a specific ratio. Alabamians preferred more metallic money,
he said, but inflation through the issuance of more national bank
notes would be acceptable. Denying that free-silver agitation was
holding down prices, Underwood asserted that the scarcity of investment capital resulted from the belief of "capitalists" that the
nation would remain on the gold standard and that prices would
therefore decline further.[7] Such strong criticism of the president
was audacious for a young congressman, but Cleveland was exceedingly unpopular with Underwood's constituents.

Despite his caustic criticism of Cleveland's gold policy, Underwood agreed with Cleveland in denouncing Britain's refusal to arbitrate its dispute with Venezuela over lands lying between British
Guiana and Venezuela. Both sides had the mistaken impression
that valuable gold lands were at stake. Cleveland's annual message
of December 3 discussed the dispute, and the president reiterated
his demand that Britain agree to arbitration. Underwood applauded Cleveland's imperious attitude toward Great Britain. The
speech, he said, "is thoroughly American, and if maintained must
culminate in recognition by the British Government of the Monroe
Doctrine. When considered in connection with the ultimatum of
Britain to Venezuela last summer it can mean only one thing, that
is the English nation must retract its ultimatum and submit its
boundary dispute to arbitration or the United States will consider
its refusal to do so in the light of an unfriendly act."[8] Underwood

6. Clipping from the Washington (D.C.) *Star*, in Underwood Scrapbook, C, 32, Underwood Papers, Alabama Archives.
7. *Ibid.*
8. Birmingham *Age-Herald*, December 7, 1895.

never recanted his support of Cleveland's vigorous role in the Venezuelan dispute, despite a dislike for Cleveland which he nourished for the remainder of the president's career.

Cleveland's annual message also proposed to preserve the rapidly melting gold reserve by retiring greenbacks and treasury notes through short-term, low interest bonds. Underwood, differing with the president, urged that the government pay its debts in silver. Opposing currency contraction in any form, he maintained that the retirement of greenbacks and treasury notes would contract the currency by $500 million, or by one fourth, and lead to a panic.[9]

The Republicans proposed to meet the monetary crisis by restoring the high tariff rates of the McKinley act. Their "emergency tariff" bill would have boosted tariff rates across the board by about 15 percent and would, they argued, increase federal revenues by about $40 million. The proposed Republican tariff bill was expected to pass the House and to fail in the Senate, but even if it passed the Senate, it would be vetoed by the president.

The spirited debate over the tariff bill gave Underwood the opportunity to make a brief maiden speech. Attacking the Republican claim that the bill's higher tariff rates would produce additional revenue, he illustrated by citing the proposed increased duties on pig iron. Duties under the Wilson-Gorman Act were four dollars a ton as compared with six dollars a ton in the McKinley act. Iron was being produced in Birmingham for less than six dollars a ton, and the current tariff rate was prohibitive. Therefore, he argued, increasing the rate could not increase government revenue. According to Underwood, the repeal of the McKinley Tariff Act had stimulated the economy generally and thus had brought renewed prosperity to Birmingham. Describing the prosperity with evident exaggeration, Underwood said that after repeal, Birmingham's blast furnaces reopened and wages of miners and furnace laborers shot up by 25 percent. "Where manufacturing industries are located at advantageous points a protective tariff is not necessary for their prosperity," he concluded.[10] Nevertheless, the House speed-

9. *Congressional Record*, 54th Cong., 1st Sess., 13–15.
10. *Ibid.*, 325.

ily passed the Republican tariff bill by a vote of 228 to 83. The bill's passage was strictly a political maneuver, and it died in the Senate Finance Committee.

The Republicans then offered the coin redemption fund bill in the House. The vague and hastily drawn bill would have authorized the secretary of the treasury to sell low-interest bonds, redeemable at the end of five years, to retire legal tender notes. In its original form the bill would have repealed a proviso of the Bland-Allison Act of 1878 which prohibited further withdrawal of greenbacks from circulation, but to counter this objection the Republican silverites inserted a clause to stipulate that nothing in the bill would modify the Bland-Allison Act. The bill also provided for the issuance of $50 million in low interest, small denomination bonds. Unlike the first mentioned issue, the money from these bonds was to be used for temporary deficiencies of revenue. Silverites objected to the bill as an attempt to place the country strictly on a gold basis. Despite Republican insistence that the bill provided that Bland-Allison Act purchases of silver would continue, Underwood charged that the bill would contract the currency by eliminating greenbacks and silver certificates. The Treasury, he noted, already had a surplus, the emergency tariff bill would add more (in contrast with his earlier tariff argument), and the coin redemption fund bill would authorize the "temporary" retirement of an additional $50 million in legal tender to meet current expenditures. Once redeemed, Underwood doubted that the silver certificates and greenbacks, which he regarded as essential circulating media, would ever be reissued. Currency contraction was, he asserted, the basic cause of economic distress, and he described a cycle of "contraction of the currency from one cause or another; business paralyzed, want, poverty, and distress the necessary result." The gold reserve, Underwood maintained, had no effect on the "solvency" of the dollar and should be abolished. The alternative to the elimination of the gold reserve was the contraction of currency by a third, taxation to provide "free gold," and discrimination against the "solvency" of the silver dollar.[11]

11. *Ibid.*, 368.

The coin redemption fund bill passed the House, but the Senate Finance Committee substituted a bill for the free coinage of silver at the sixteen to one ratio without provision for the maintenance of that parity through gold redemption. The Ways and Means Committee reported the Senate substitute to the House unfavorably, but the silverite minority on the committee favored concurrence with the Senate bill. Underwood spoke in favor of concurrence, and presented figures from Maurice I. Muhleman's *Monetary Systems of the World* to show that not enough gold was being mined to supply the expanding world and national economy and that the refusal to use silver as coin meant the restriction of coined money by more than one-half.

Underwood disagreed with silverites who opposed the bill because no provision was made for maintaining silver at a parity with gold: "If there is anything of benefit . . . in the coinage of the white metal, it does not lie in the maintenance of the parity of that metal on the same basis that we maintain a paper circulation. It does not lie in the fact that we maintain a silver dollar in circulation by reason of the redemption of that dollar with a gold dollar. . . . It must be in the fact that it is recognized as one of the money metals of the world on equal terms with gold."[12] His argument was that of an inflationist differentiated from that of the western free-silverites who favored the sixteen to one parity at a time when the market ratio was thirty-two to one. The crushing defeat of the Senate free-silver bill by a vote of 215 to 90 dashed the hopes of the free-silverites, who did not again receive serious consideration for their schemes. Underwood's speech for the coin redemption fund bill disturbed embattled free-silverites in Alabama who saw that he no longer favored coinage at the ratio of sixteen to one. However, enthusiasm for free silver had abated in Alabama, and by the spring of 1895 no morning Alabama newspaper advocated it.[13] Underwood was indeed weakening on the issue, and he made his last free-silver speech in 1899.

Truman H. Aldrich's case contesting Underwood's House seat

12. *Ibid.*, 1345–46, 1652–53.
13. Birmingham *Age-Herald*, April 3, 1895.

was the longest case of the session, the testimony and briefs total-
ing over two thousand pages. It was ordinarily a simple matter for
a majority party to unseat a minority congressman with a questioned title to his seat, as election contests have the highest parliamentary privilege. However, Underwood's case was pending until
late May, 1896, when Representative Charles Daniels, chairman of
Elections Committee Number 1, attempted to bring his committee's report to the floor. On June 7 the House refused to consider
the case by a vote of 64 to 55. There was evidently little enthusiasm
in the majority party for unseating Underwood. Daniels was determined, however, and he tried again later the same day. The Democrats attempted to keep the resolution off the floor by dilatory ma-
neuvers, but the speaker *pro tem* ruled that the question was one
of highest privilege, and the House voted to reconsider the case
131 to 68, with 155, including Underwood, not voting. On June 9
consideration was resumed although the House was three days
from adjournment and most of the members had gone home. Representative Benton McMillin of Tennessee, a Democrat, objected
that only four of nine committee members, not a majority, had
signed the report. Chairman Daniels replied that although only
four committeemen had signed, two other Republicans sympathized with their objective. The speaker overruled the point of
order, and the Democratic attempt to delay past adjournment
failed.[14]

Aldrich charged the Democrats with gross fraud and intimidation in Jefferson, Hale, and Perry counties, arguing that in these
three counties the Populist-Republican combination had been discriminated against in the appointment of election inspectors, and
in Birmingham several hundred ballots were fraudulently obtained. Democratic ballot fixers, Aldrich maintained, counted several hundred illiterates for Underwood instead of for Aldrich, as
directed. He claimed that Negro voters in two precincts were prevented from voting by the intimidation of policemen and deputy
sheriffs who arrested several for possessing mock ballots, clearly
identifiable as guide ballots.[15] Republicans charged that the votes

14. *Congressional Record*, 54th Cong., 1st Sess., 6299, 6330–32.
15. *House Reports*, 54th Cong., 1st Sess., No. 2006, pp. 1–21.

of a large number of Hale County Negroes had been improperly cast for the Democrats. The Democrats produced affidavits of 183 Negroes saying that they had indeed voted for Underwood, but the Republicans insisted that the testimonies were perjured, coached, and purchased at seventy-five cents each by Underwood's attorneys. Aldrich maintained that at Greensboro, the county seat of Hale County, more people had voted than were registered, and that in Perry County an election official had altered the returns in Underwood's favor. He further charged that three hundred illegally registered Bessemer voters had cast ballots for Underwood, and armed deputies had prevented some Republicans from voting, whereas many others had stayed away because of the intimidation by police and other Democrats. Aldrich also accused Democratic election officials of knowing that a number of ballots had been stolen and passing out the remaining insufficient supply of ballots to Democratic voters.[16]

Underwood countercharged that he had been defrauded in Blount and Bibb counties, where a Populist-Republican coalition controlled the election machinery. He alleged that Aldrich and J. W. Worthington, both mine operators, had coerced their employees to vote for Aldrich. One Underwood box in Blount County was thrown out on a technicality which, if enforced in other counties, would have voided several Aldrich boxes. Aldrich's friends, Underwood charged, had attempted to bribe election officials and in some cases actually bought votes. In Perry County, for example, the "Democratic" election officer was believed to be in the employ of Worthington. The returns, Underwood agreed, had been altered, but the Republicans had altered them in their favor. The Democrats admitted the Republican claim that Hale County Republicans had refrained from voting and maintained that therefore those Negroes who voted were Democrats. Replying to charges that the testimony of Negroes was purchased, Underwood admitted that Negro witnesses were paid seventy-five cents each as state law provided. This was necessary, he said, in order to get the Negroes to leave their work.[17]

16. Birmingham *Age-Herald*, December 13, 1894, January 22, 1895.
17. *Ibid.*, January 12, 1895.

In each of the contests, the Republicans presented voters' lists and tried to show that the Democrats claimed more votes than were cast or that a number of Negroes who, they maintained, were always Republican, had voted. The Democrats impugned the validity of the lists by attempting to show the irresponsible character of the Republican poll watchers.

The committee report recommended the unseating of Underwood. Chairman Daniels said that the members of the committee spoke highly of Underwood and would have been glad to retain him if they could consistently have done so. The committee's report shifted over 1,000 votes to give the election to Aldrich by fewer than 100 votes. In Birmingham the committee boosted Aldrich's total in two precincts by 69 votes because of the arrests of Negroes for violation of the Sayre election law, which was designed to discriminate against Negro voters and which the committee had termed unfair. The Sayre law, passed following the corrupt gubernatorial election of 1892, provided a modest educational requirement for voting, an Australian ballot, and complex requirements that allowed election officials to successfully challenge black voters. At Bessemer the committee gave Aldrich 365 votes which they said would have been cast for the Republican in a free election. In the black-belt counties of Perry and Hale they reduced Underwood's majorities by 471 votes. Daniels admitted that the Democrats had verified many of their Hale County votes, but he refused to credit Underwood with the votes. The report denied Underwood's charge that Aldrich was not a resident of Alabama.

Republican Representative Romulus Z. Linney of North Carolina refused to sign the Daniels report, explaining that he had been insufficiently informed and would have signed had he had time to consider the case carefully. Linney complimented the handsome young Underwood as one who stood as a "noble piece of God's workmanship" and whose "personal magnetism" had had its effect in the House. However, he condemned the election as fraudulent and supported Aldrich's claim on the assumption that the Jeffersonian Democrats combined with the Populists and Republicans were a "trio omnipotent enough to sweep crippled Democracy [i.e. Democrats] from God's green earth."

Jesse Stallings, a "wool hat" Alabama congressman, presented Underwood's case. He attacked Linney's speech as a "foul and filthy philippic," and he reviewed the depredations of Reconstruction. Yet Stallings also effectively presented the legal aspects of the case, basing his argument on George W. McCrary's *Treatise on the American Law of Elections*. Referring to the disputed votes, he quoted McCrary's statement that it was a rare case in which votes could be counted for a candidate when they were not cast. As to the objection that the Sayre law was unfair, he stated that Congress had no right to rule on the wisdom of Alabama's laws.[18]

Underwood spoke in his own defense, as was customary in election cases. He ended his speech with an ornate farewell, quite unlike his congressional speeches and probably intended for home consumption: "You have put this bitter cup to the lips of the people of Alabama, but I warn you to pause lest some day even-handed justice shall place the poisoned chalice to your own lips, I thank you, gentlemen, for your kind attention."[19] Underwood was unseated June 9, 1896, by a vote of 119 to 98, with 137 not voting. Truman H. Aldrich was immediately sworn in as the representative from the Ninth District of Alabama and drew pay for the entire term of which Underwood had served more than half. However, Underwood was paid for the time that he had served, as was customary.[20]

The unseating of Underwood was based upon widespread recognition by the Republicans that black-belt counties such as Hale and Perry were "rotten boroughs" in which the black vote was controlled by the whites. A black man, familiar with black-belt politics, reflected in 1911 that Underwood had been fraudulently elected, having received the votes of a very small, elitist minority of the population. Commenting on the small number of votes cast in the Underwood-Aldrich contest, the talented but almost unlettered black man said: "you did not get in the whole district one half of the votes that should of been cast in your home City alone not saying anything at all about the whole County much less the other

18. *Congressional Record*, 54th Cong., 1st Sess., 6334–45.
19. *Ibid.*, 6338.
20. *Ibid.*, 6353.

four." He continued that Underwood represented a "gang of Plutocrats" who continued to rob the blacks of their rights.[21] In fact, the total vote cast in the Underwood-Aldrich election (13,616) represented only 7½ percent of the district's total population of 181,085 in the 1890 census. That was elitist politics with a vengeance.

There is, however, little doubt that Underwood was legally elected. Both parties had resorted to fraud, but the Democrats had stayed within the letter of the law better than the Republicans. In order to give the election to Aldrich, it was necessary to assign to him virtually every questionable vote. In later years Underwood described his friendly relations with Aldrich while they waited for the House to decide the contest. His picture of walking "arm and arm" with Aldrich to restaurants for a "quiet dinner" is probably overdrawn, yet in fact, the fight engendered little personal animosity.[22] Underwood's constituents were less philosophical about his removal, and he returned to Birmingham to a noisy reception by a brass band at the L & N station. Aldrich received a less enthusiastic reception on his return three weeks later.

In Alabama Underwood campaigned for Joseph F. Johnston, the redheaded, progressive-minded owner of the Birmingham *Age-Herald*, who was the Democratic gubernatorial nominee opposed by Alfred T. Goodwyn, a candidate of the Populist-Republicans. Underwood spoke at Brookside for Johnston, pointing to the dangers of a return to Republican Reconstruction rule and charging that Goodwyn was trying to lead the white Populists into an "unholy alliance" with the Negro-infested Republican party. In the Bourbon campaign style of the day, he called upon the sacred memory of Stonewall Jackson. Yet Underwood claimed that the Democratic party of Jefferson and Andrew Jackson was the friend of the "toiling masses" of the country—a term associated with the Populists. He urged the people to vote Democratic since the party was battling the trusts which were backed by the tariff barons and

21. Harry L. Burnam to Underwood, February 14, 1911, in Underwood Papers, Alabama Archives. Burnam was once employed by Underwood's brother Sidney.

22. Ralph R. Silver, "Oscar Underwood: The Man of the Hour," Birmingham *Age-Herald*, January 14, 1912.

the "bond gobblers," the Shylocks of Wall and Lombard streets. With Populist verbiage and fervor, Underwood blamed the Republicans for striking down silver, "the people's money," thereby doubling the value of gold, the money of the "plutocrats, the bondholders, and the millionaires."[23]

Johnston was elected, and in September the Democrats renominated Underwood by acclamation. The Birmingham *State Herald* noted that the memory of Underwood's unseating was "still green in the minds of the Democratic voters of the Ninth District" and that there was no doubt of his election. Accepting the nomination, Underwood pledged himself to the Democratic platform, including bimetallism, the income tax, and the denunciation of the courts for governing by injunction and of the Supreme Court for its decision in *Pollock* v. *Farmers' Loan and Trust Company.* He denounced Republican charges that the Democrats advocated anarchy and had made unconstitutional attacks upon the Supreme Court, calling the latter charge an attack upon free speech.[24]

Alabama Populists, who withdrew support from the Republicans after the defeat of their gubernatorial candidate in the August elections, nominated a rural physician, Dr. Grattan B. Crowe, leader of the state party and president of the Alabama branch of the American Protective Association, to oppose Underwood. Crowe favored anti-Catholicism, restriction of pauper immigration, public ownership of railroad and telegraph lines, and support of William Jennings Bryan and Thomas E. Watson for president and vice-president. The Black and Tan wing of the Republican party endorsed Dr. Crowe. The gold Democrats nominated Dr. Archibald Lawson of Hale County. The Marion *Standard* supported Lawson, claiming that since no congressional primaries were held in that county, Democrats were not bound to vote for Underwood. The *Standard* falsely maintained that Underwood's record in Congress consisted only of a speech in his own behalf.[25]

23. Birmingham *State Herald,* June 28, 1896.
24. *Ibid.,* September 2, 1896. Of the Democratic beat meetings in Jefferson County, eight were instructed for Underwood and four had no instructions. *Ibid.,* August 16, 1896.
25. *Ibid.,* August 2, September 16, 17, October 24, 1896; Marion (Ala.) *Standard,* October 8, 13, 16, 20, 1896.

Underwood campaigned methodically and systematically by horse and buggy, accompanied by his campaign manager, Hugh Morrow of Birmingham. To use his own ornate language, he marched to victory "carrying a silver shield." Paying glowing tribute to Bryan, he predicted his election.[26] The result was: Underwood, 13,499; Crowe, 5,168; Lawson, 2,316; an otherwise unidentified candidate, Thomson, received a few hundred votes. Underwood exulted to his brother Sidney that his friends had "made one of the best fights that has ever been made in the district, and our majority is so large that I do not think it possible for even a partisan House to question it." He added that Genie would be home from Charlottesville in about two weeks.[27]

Crowe contested Underwood's election but failed to present an effective case. The Elections Committee told Crowe's manager that he had failed to substantiate his allegations of fraud and that his eulogies of President McKinley and the Republican party were irrelevant. Representative Romulus Linney, who had voted for seating Aldrich, declared that Crowe's case was the flimsiest he had ever seen before the committee. Underwood was declared legally entitled to his seat.[28]

Bryan won an unexpectedly resounding victory in Alabama—in Jefferson County the ticket of Bryan and Arthur Sewall outran Underwood. The election's significance, however, was seen in the four to one margin that the Democratic ticket of Bryan and Sewall (a gold Democrat) held over the Populist ticket of Bryan and Watson (a silverite Populist). Populism and free silver were dying in Alabama. Bryan's defeat in the general election was a shattering blow to the free-silver advocates.

The Birmingham *Age-Herald*, owned by the newly elected Governor Joseph F. Johnston, a free-silverite Democrat, was sold at a receiver's sale in 1896. The Birmingham *News*, an afternoon newspaper owned by Rufus N. Rhodes, was thriving, but with the col-

26. Birmingham *State Herald*, November 3, 1896.
27. Underwood to Sidney S. Underwood, November 7, 1896, in Oscar W. Underwood Papers, University of Virginia Library.
28. Birmingham *Age-Herald*, January 15, 1898; Birmingham *Daily Ledger*, February 17, 1898.

lapse of the *Age-Herald* the city lacked a vigorous morning news-paper. Underwood urged Edward W. Barrett, a native of Augusta, Georgia, whom he knew as a Washington reporter for the Atlanta *Constitution*, to buy the defunct morning Birmingham newspaper. Barrett resurrected the *Age-Herald* name and redirected its edi-torial policies into conservative channels.[29] Barrett was an avid sup-porter of Underwood for the remainder of his career.

Underwood was renominated without opposition in 1898 and in the general election was opposed by candidates from both wings of the Republican party—the Lily Whites and the Black and Tans. The Lily Whites nominated J. T. McEniry of Bessemer, and the Black and Tans nominated Louis T. Schwartz—both white men. Underwood's law partner, Robert Thach, was his campaign man-ager and claimed that the only threat to the Democrats was indif-ference about going to the polls. Underwood made few speeches. The Centreville *Press* noted that although he was not a "ranting 'spread-eagle' orator," he spoke "clearly, forcefully, intelligently, and earnestly." Election day was quiet, and Underwood won a sweeping victory. He received 7,155 votes to 1,302 votes for McEniry, who failed to carry his home town of Bessemer, and 160 for Schwartz.[30]

Underwood's increasing seniority in the House and his friend-ship with the southern Democratic leadership brought him more influence. In the Fifty-fifth Congress (1897–1899) Underwood sup-ported his University of Virginia classmate, Joseph W. Bailey, in his successful race for Democratic majority leader against his Ala-bama colleague, John H. Bankhead. Bankhead, a Confederate vet-eran and old-line politician, was later a close friend of Under-wood's, but Underwood told constituents that he had committed himself to Bailey before Bankhead announced his candidacy. One

29. Birmingham *State Herald*, November 5, 1896; Albert B. Moore, *History of Alabama* (University, Ala.: University Supply Store, 1934), 644; Cassius M. Stanley, "Some Personal Recollections of Oscar W. Underwood Prepared for the Thirteen, October 15, 1959" (MS in Underwood Papers, Alabama Archives); Jennie Kimbrough to author, August 23, 1973, in possession of Evans C. Johnson, DeLand, Fla.
30. Centreville (Ala.) *Press*, September 29, November 3, 1898; Birmingham *News*, No-vember 7, 8, 9, 1898.

grumbling Alabama editor suggested that Underwood should not make promises so far ahead.[31]

Also in the Fifty-fifth Congress, Underwood was appointed to the Judiciary Committee, his first important committee post. A colleague later said that Underwood "got his foot on the bottom of the ladder and began to climb."[32] This important committee post was Underwood's reward for supporting Bailey, but it was only the beginning of Underwood's rise. Even before this appointment, he had interested himself in judicial reform and the elimination of the fee system. He had favored the judicial reforms of the legislative, executive, and judicial appropriation bill of 1896, which proposed to place jury commissioners under the district attorneys. There were many more jury commissioners than necessary, Underwood said, and these officials overzealously sought business. He had seen, he claimed, numbers of good country people dragged into Birmingham and jailed for petty offenses. The fee system was "a relic of the Dark Ages and a travesty on justice," he noted, and 40 percent of the cases presented by the jury commissioners were *nol-prossed*. The system was unduly expensive both to the government and to individuals. Underwood offered an amendment that would have placed the jury commissioners on a salary fixed within limits by the attorney general. There was, he said, no more reason for postmasters to be on salary than for jury commissioners to be. He concluded: "No scourge that can be laid on the back of a suffering people will inflict more torture upon them than a dishonest and corrupt judiciary." Other members of the Judiciary Committee lamely defended the bill on the basis that they could not embody all necessary judicial reforms without considerable preparation. Underwood's amendments were rejected without a roll call.[33]

The lingering results of the panic of 1893 led the Republican-dominated Judiciary Commitee to offer in 1898 the Henderson-Torrey federal bankruptcy bill with a wide spectrum of provisions

31. Centreville (Ala.) *Press*, December 22, 1898.
32. Henry D. Clayton, quoted in Underwood and the Spanish-American War, 1898 File, Underwood Papers, Alabama Archives.
33. *Congressional Record*, 54th Cong., 1st Sess., 2402, 2411, 2506, 2528–29.

for both voluntary and involuntary bankruptcy. Although preferring the use of the more convenient state courts for bankruptcy
action, Underwood acknowledged the necessity for federal bankruptcy legislation as a temporary expedient. Such legislation, he
stated with Populist-scented arguments, should favor risk capitalists who farmed or built factories but should not favor large corporations or the holders of bonds. The involuntary features of the bill
would, he said, aid corporate interests, which could benefit by allowing themselves to be pushed into bankruptcy, thereby clogging
the courts with involuntary bankruptcy suits. The Henderson-Torrey bill returned from conference with many of its involuntary features eliminated, and Underwood supported the measure on its
final passage.[34] Underwood's advocacy of bankruptcy legislation
that favored small businesses and risk capital was in keeping with
the cyclical and independent nature of Birmingham business—including that of his brother Will and Henry F. DeBardeleben.

Underwood served on the Committee on Public Lands in the
Fifty-fourth Congress and on the Committee on Irrigation and Arid
Lands in the Fifty-seventh and Fifty-eighth Congresses. In 1896
the Cleveland administration sponsored a bill designed to force
railroads to disgorge huge quantities of land that they had fraudulently obtained. Although the statute of limitations did not apply
to "fraudulent" titles, the difficulty of proving fraud resulted in retention of lands by railroads that had not fulfilled commitments for
the land patents. A statute passed in 1891 allowed the government
five years to contest titles issued before that date or six years for
patents subsequently issued. The government's opportunity to re-
cover railroad patents with defective titles would soon expire unless the time was extended. The administration proposed to extend
the statute of limitations so that the government would have an
additional ten years in which to contest such titles.

Underwood, who voted against the administration's proposal in
committee, argued that although the extension was an improve-

34. *Ibid.*, 55th Cong., 2nd Sess., 1793–94, 6436; Birmingham *Age-Herald*, February
20, 1898.

ment over existing legislation it allowed inadequate time for suits. Government land officials changed frequently, he said, and there should be no statute of limitations for the recovery of government land. On the other hand, he objected that the administration bill made it necessary for innocent purchasers of lands from railroads to enter suit in order to clear their titles. Nevertheless, the House passed the measure. The Senate reduced the ten-year extension to six years, and Underwood unsuccessfully urged that the House re-fuse to concur in the Senate amendment. Whether Underwood's opposition to the administration bill was motivated by genuine concern for "innocent purchasers" of railroad land or by a desire to see the legislation fail is moot. In view of his friendly attitude to-ward the railroads, it would appear to be the latter.

Underwood opposed President Cleveland's efforts to safeguard the leasing of Arizona school lands. The president vetoed a bipar-tisan bill creating a territorial board to lease the lands because the timber was not reserved and because he wanted the secretary of the interior to supervise the leases. Underwood urged passage of the Arizona school lands bill over Cleveland's veto, pointing out that the bill applied largely to grazing land from which revenue could be derived. The bill was identical, Underwood said, to a bill relating to Oklahoma which had met the approval of the secretary of the interior. The Arizona bill, like the Oklahoma act, relieved the secretary of the interior of the responsibility for reviewing the land leases, a task impractical for the secretary to perform. Under-wood said that without this bill the Arizona cattle barons had been able to graze the lands free. The bill passed the House over Cleve-land's veto, with Underwood voting to override, but it died in a Senate committee.[35]

Underwood reported a bill in January, 1896, from the Commit-tee on Public Lands which lifted some restrictions of the Land Act of 1883 on the sale of public lands in Alabama. The Land Act re-quired that agricultural lands be offered to settlers except for that

35. *Congressional Record*, 54th Cong., 1st Sess., 1904–1905, 2170–71, 2298–99, 2301, 2330.

classified as mineral lands by the Land Office. The committee maintained that many of the lands being withheld from the market as mineral lands were wholly agricultural in character and that the provision was tending to delay settlement. The committee's bill provided that Alabama lands should be subject to purchase with no more proof of their nonmineral character than was required under the homestead laws. Upon being reported from committee by Underwood, the bill passed the House, but it died in the Senate.[36] Underwood had again revealed his eagerness to allow exploitation of lands that might contain the coal or iron Alabama entrepreneurs sought.

Underwood seldom mentioned education on the floor of Congress, for like most public figures of the time, he considered it a function of the state. Yet early in 1896 he reported favorably from the Committee on Public Lands companion bills to make extensive land grants to Tuskegee Institute and to establish Alabama College at Montevallo as a school for "poor white girls." Speaker Thomas B. Reed had attempted to secure passage of a land grant for Tuskegee, but Senator John T. Morgan delayed the bill until proponents of the Tuskegee measure agreed to an identical grant to establish Alabama College. Underwood's report maintained that land grants for a school similar to the proposed Alabama College had been provided in other states but not in Alabama. The bills failed to pass, but in 1899 a bill embracing both schools passed, granting the Negro school and Alabama College each twenty-five thousand acres of select mineral land. Underwood was thus able to use northern interest in black education to obtain a badly needed college for women.

After the passage of the Tuskegee and the Alabama College bills, Underwood replied to criticism of Alabama's failure to provide adequately for education. He noted that only half of Alabama's population was white, yet these people paid 95 percent of the taxes. Alabama, he said, suffered from poverty caused by a heavy Reconstruction debt, declining property values, and Negro suffrage. To

36. *House Reports*, 54th Cong., 1st Sess., No. 73, p. 1.

critics of the provision of the Alabama Constitution of 1875 that
limited the rate of land taxes for education, he pointed out that he
and his friends had tried to secure an amendment to correct this
provision, but their efforts had been blocked by Alabama Republicans.[37]

Underwood blocked in January, 1900, a bill to give the abandoned Ft. Hayes Military Reservation in Kansas to the public colleges in that state, maintaining that valuable lands should not be
given to these schools and not to others. The Kansas lands, he said,
were not a part of the public domain, and the gift would be a precedent for giving away lands that the government was purchasing
from the Indians each year. Two years later Underwood helped
defeat a bill to appropriate $100,000 for training teachers for deaf
and dumb kindergarten children in the famous Garrett School
in Philadelphia.[38] Underwood's interest in education seldom extended beyond Alabama's boundaries.

Underwood's insistence that Alabama mineral lands be rapidly
offered for sale with few safeguards was in contrast to his attitude
toward the sale of western mineral lands—especially Indian
lands—in which he was far more restrained. He helped secure restrictions on a provision in the Indian appropriation bill for the sale
of gilsonite lands on the Uncompahgre Reservation in Utah in
1897. In March, 1902, he criticized a proposal to sell some of the
Colville, Washington, Indian Reservation lands without compensating the Indians. Although the Indians involved were nomads,
Underwood favored compensating them for the lands they once
roamed. Nevertheless, Underwood supported the homestead
policy, and he embraced the "safety valve" concept. In 1900 he

37. *Ibid.*, No. 393, p. 1, No. 1376, p. 1; see also, [Forney Johnston], *Democratic Senatorial Campaign: The Issue and the Facts* (Birmingham: Roberts & Sons, *ca.* 1914), 21–22;
Congressional Record, 56th Cong., 1st Sess., 3403–3405. In 1904, Edward K. Campbell
and Henry B. Gray, two of Underwood's closest political friends, headed a special committee
to secure a special school tax in Jefferson County. Birmingham *News*, May 14, 1904.
38. *Congressional Record*, 56th Cong., 1st Sess., 1221–22, 57th Cong., 1st Sess.,
1035–37. In 1921, Underwood secured for the University of Alabama the only Bureau of
Mines Experiment Station in the South; supporters of Alabama Polytechnic Institute, now
Auburn University, were disappointed that the mine station was not located at Auburn.
George H. Denny to author, July 4, 1951, in possession of Evans C. Johnson.

favored opening former Indian reservations to homesteading. He stated that in hard times homesteading increased wages by providing an outlet for labor. In May, 1902, the House was considering a bill to cede a small amount of land in Puerto Rico to the government of the island, and Underwood asked, with surprising naiveté, if the land had been open to homesteading.[39] Although Underwood was generally favorable to exploitation of western lands by business interests, he retained a romantic view of the Indian, perhaps from his life on the frontier in Minnesota. Likewise, he had an unrealistic view of the importance of homesteading in the settlement of the West.

Underwood consistently opposed legislation sponsored by the dairy interests that attempted to tax out of existence oleomargarine, a relatively new product often made from cottonseed oil. He opposed an oleomargarine tax bill in 1896 which proposed a heavy tax on the manufacture and sale of oleomargarine and required the descriptive labeling of the synthetic product. Underwood said that the bill fostered the dairy industry at the expense of the cotton farmer and noted that the committee was unable to show that the product was damaging to health. If it were not wholesome, he said, states could exercise their police power and prohibit its sale. Congress, he believed, had the power to require the proper labeling of the "oleomargarine cheese," but the purpose of the bill was to prohibit its manufacture. He noted that Secretary of Agriculture J. Sterling Morton favored regulation rather than taxation. Nevertheless, the bill passed with Underwood paired and not voting. In February, 1902, Underwood opposed another oleomargarine levy. The new bill subjected oleomargarine in the original packages to state laws and extended the tax provisions of the federal law. He was especially concerned that the provisions of the act would carry the laws into the homes of consumers. Paraphrasing Jefferson, Underwood stated, "that party which legislates least legislates best," and said that the business interests should be left unhampered by

39. *Congressional Record*, 55th Cong., 1st Sess., 106–107, 816–33, 1005–1007, 1205–1207, 57th Cong., 1st Sess., 2811–12, 5564.

restraints insofar as possible. Underwood's protests were of no avail, and the bill became law.[40] Underwood's opposition to taxes on margarine was consistent with his opposition to consumer taxes. Also, he thus demonstrated his recognition of the potential importance of the margarine industry in the South—something in which his constituents showed surprisingly little interest.

Underwood's rural constituents were vitally interested in rural mail delivery, and postal matters were of concern to city dwellers as well. In March, 1898, he supported an amendment increasing the appropriation for the new free rural delivery system from $150,000 to $300,000. He urged rural free delivery as a practical and self-liquidating system which would give the farmer the equivalent of city delivery service. The amendment passed.[41] By 1901 Underwood had blanketed Jefferson County with a system of rural mail routes no other county in the state could match. No other subject generated as much favorable reaction as Underwood's efforts to secure better mail service.

While Underwood was dealing with prosaic judicial, education, land, tax, and postal questions, the nation—especially the South—interested itself in Cuban independence. In 1897 McKinley was elected on a campaign pledge to "free Cuba." Underwood favored an independent Cuba, but his keenest concern was that the Birmingham area gain economic advantages as the nation prepared for war. He was especially interested in the market for Birmingham's steel and coal. There was a brand of the latter, "Underwood Coal," named for its producer, Underwood's older half-brother Will.

Underwood reflected the widespread southern fear that Spain would attack southern ports. In February, 1898, he attacked the Republicans in the House for "cheeseparing" economy in reducing harbor defense appropriations for Mobile which, he declared, would be the first harbor attacked in a war with Spain. He added, however, that as long as the Republicans were in power, there would be no protection of Americans in Cuba and therefore no

40. *Ibid.*, 54th Cong., 1st Sess., 1179, 3846; Birmingham *Age-Herald*, February 13, 1902.
41. *Congressional Record*, 55th Cong., 2nd Sess., 2947.

war. James A. Hemingway, chairman of the Military Affairs Committee, noted trenchantly that Underwood would be unwilling to
provide the men to man the artillery if the Mobile fortifications
were built. In April, 1898, Underwood attempted to amend the
naval appropriation bill by adding $25,000 for a coaling station and
docks at Ft. Morgan in Mobile Bay, noting that the navy had no
coaling station south of Newport News. Mobile was a mid-point on
the Gulf Coast, cheap coal could be obtained there, no new land
need be purchased, and Mobile harbor was impregnable to an
enemy, Underwood said. The amendment was rejected on a point
of order.

The war crisis with Spain focused attention on the danger of yellow fever epidemics in the South. John Sharp Williams, a doctrinaire advocate of states' rights, argued that appropriations for the
control of yellow fever and other diseases were unconstitutional as
an interference with the states. Underwood defended the appropriation of funds to aid state and local medical boards in the event
of epidemics, urging that the appropriation be increased from
$300,000 to $500,000, but the increase was not made.[42]

Although favoring more appropriations for Alabama, Underwood
opposed administration efforts to finance the war through hard-
money policies. Underwood opposed the issuance of bonds to
maintain the reserve of $161 million that the government held in
gold and silver above legal requirements. He advocated the issuance of $100 million in noninterest bearing treasury notes. The
Republicans had overestimated the cost of the war, he said, and
necessary funds could be raised without withdrawing money from
circulation. Although no longer a free-silverite, he still favored in-
flationary policies.

Underwood outlined his ideas on taxation in speaking against the
administration's war revenue bill, a proposal to raise money for the
Spanish-American War through stamp taxes on consumer goods.
He quoted John Stuart Mill on taxation equality and noted that the
Republicans were placing the tax burden on consumers rather than

42. *Ibid.*, 1373–74, 3138, 3457–58.

on the wealthy. He favored an income tax as an alternative and declared that it was constitutional. It was an idea that he was to repeat with regularity over the years.[43]

Underwood attempted to use the war crisis to advance Birmingham economically, energetically promoting, between 1897 and 1904, a government armor plate plant for the city. The naval bill of 1896 placed a statutory limit of $300 a ton on armor for three new battleships. The Bethlehem and the Carnegie Steel companies, which controlled American output of this product, refused to furnish armor at the government's prices. Not only had these companies pegged their prices to the United States government well above that charged other navies, but, according to Underwood, they failed to make deliveries on schedule and fraudulently furnished the government with defective armor plate. Underwood favored an amendment to the naval bill of 1897 authorizing the erection of a government-owned armor plate plant if armor plate could not be secured within the price limit set by Congress. He maintained that a plant could be built at a cost of only $1,500,000, and armor plate could be produced for about $200 a ton, less than half the amount that the secretary of the navy proposed to allow the companies in payment. Although the amendment passed, it only delayed the armoring of the ships, as the McKinley administration refused to put it into effect.[44]

Congress boosted the armor plate price to $435 a ton in 1898 in order to armor vessels for the Spanish-American War. In 1899 the Committee on Naval Affairs recommended that the government pay $545 a ton for a new Krupp type armor. Underwood charged that the steel companies, supported by the Naval Affairs Committee, had, in their efforts to get more money, continually claimed to have a new, secret process. Explaining to the House the process of making armor plate, Underwood maintained that the Krupp process was only a slight improvement over the old process, and that the effectiveness of the new armor had not been proved. Under-

43. *Ibid.*, Appendix, 406–408.
44. *Ibid.*, 55th Cong., 1st Sess., 21, 2646–47; Birmingham *Age-Herald*, August 8, 1897.

wood proposed to appropriate $4 million for an armor plate plant at a location to be determined by a naval board. He declared that every time the government had gone into the making of implements of war, it had been able to make them cheaper than private industry. The chair ruled that Underwood's amendment was not germane.[45] His sponsorship of the armor plate plant bills shows startlingly how far he was prepared to depart from his laissez-faire philosophy when Birmingham's interests were involved.

Soon after the sinking of the *Maine*, but prior to the report by the naval board, Underwood conjectured that the *Maine* had been destroyed by a hostile agency. He said that the question could be successfully arbitrated, although he considered the recognition of Cuban independence a *sine qua non* of peace. While the nation waited for the naval court of inquiry's report, one of Underwood's sons, presumably nine-year-old John Lewis (Oscar, Jr. was then seven) simulated the sinking of the *Maine* in the bathtub of Underwood's Washington apartment. Young Underwood and a friend secured some cigar boxes and painted them with tar from the street in front of the apartments. The boys placed powder inside the boxes and attached a fuse. After floating their craft for a few minutes, one vessel was exploded, wrecking not only the vessel itself but the bathtub and the room. Underwood returned from the House, and according to the press he assembled a "court of enquiry and witnesses were summoned." Young Underwood was in no hurry to report.[46] Interestingly, he demonstrated the Spanish rather than the United States theory of the sinking.

President McKinley delivered his message on Cuba on April 11, 1898. Although he asked authority to use the army and the navy against Spain in Cuba, he failed to specifically recommend a declaration of war and left Congress with the responsibility for choosing a course of action. Underwood criticized McKinley for having failed to outline a policy, and he somewhat modified his earlier

45. *Congressional Record*, 55th Cong., 2nd Sess., 899; Birmingham *News*, July 8, 1899; *Congressional Record*, 55th Cong., 3rd Sess., 2190–96, 2246.

46. Birmingham *Age-Herald*, March 22, April 12, 1898; Mobile *Daily Register*, March 10, 1898.

warlike views. Like most of his southern colleagues, he was adamant that Spain should give up Cuba and said that "unless the
Spanish government agrees to do so, I do not see how war in the
end can be avoided."[47] Nevertheless, he was eager to avoid war. In
the debate over the president's message, Underwood favored the
Berry resolution, a Democratic proposal that would have recognized the independence of Cuba rather than authorize military intervention as the Republicans proposed. After the failure of this
resolution, Underwood favored unsuccessful efforts to amend the
war resolution to include recognition of Cuban independence. He
eventually voted for intervention and later voted with a unanimous
House for the joint war resolution as it returned from the Senate
with the Teller amendment attached.[48] The Teller resolution committed the United States to foregoing the annexation of Cuba, im-
plying that the island would be independent. Like many other
southerners of the era, Underwood was primarily and genuinely
interested in Cuban independence; there is no evidence that he
had imperialistic aims toward Cuba or other Spanish possessions.

During the Spanish-American War a number of Alabama volunteers contracted typhoid and malaria either in Cuba or in camps in
the South. After the Battle of San Juan Hill, in the summer of
1898, Underwood visited Washington to ask Secretary of War Russell A. Alger to release such soldiers. He recounted the story of an
Alabamian who returned from San Juan Hill with a shattered arm.
The Alabamian, one of Roosevelt's Rough Riders, vividly described
the charge up San Juan Hill and the Spanish army's rain of Mauser
bullets that created havoc in the American lines. At the critical
moment, the Rough Riders were reinforced and rescued by the
black Tenth Cavalry, led by First Lieutenant John J. Pershing. "I
want to tell you, Mr. Underwood," the Alabama boy said, "I was
never as glad in my life to see a nigger."[49] Despite Underwood's use
of the word "nigger," his relating of the incident which was nation-

47. Birmingham *Age-Herald*, April 12, 1898.
48. Underwood and the Spanish-American War, in 1898 File, Underwood Papers, Alabama Archives.
49. Underwood Scrapbook, C, 45, in Underwood Papers, Alabama Archives.

ally reflecting credit upon the Tenth Cavalry indicates that he was less racist than many southerners of the period.

Even after the war began, Underwood continued efforts to check administration spending on the navy and army. He withdrew objections to a small salary increase for naval petty officers only after Republican agreement to limit the increases to the duration of the war. Underwood, in harmony with other Democratic congressmen, opposed Republican efforts to increase the size of the army. The War Department, he said, was creating too many "bombproof" positions in Washington, and he charged the administration with holding volunteers in the army as hostages for enlarging the regular army. Failing to secure added numbers during the war, the Republicans passed, despite Underwood's protest, a House bill increasing the permanent standing army from 26,000 to 100,000. The bill died in the Senate. In 1900, during the Philippine insurrection, the Republicans again attempted to authorize the president to increase the regular army to a maximum of 100,000. Underwood noted that it was the duty of Congress and not the president to determine the army's size, but the bill became law.

Underwood unsuccessfully opposed an army proposal in 1900 to create the rank of lieutenant general for General Nelson A. Miles. Although Miles was a distinguished hero of the Civil War and served in the Spanish-American War, he was anathema to many southerners as he was responsible for Jefferson Davis during Davis' imprisonment at Fort Monroe, Virginia.[50] Underwood was doubtless influenced by charges, unfairly made, that Davis was grossly mistreated during his incarceration.

As the war drew to a close, Birmingham promoters planned a Southern Peace Jubilee. Underwood persuaded Secretary of War Russell A. Alger to muster out the First Alabama Regiment, some twelve hundred reservists, in Birmingham rather than in Mobile as originally planned. It was hoped that President McKinley would visit Birmingham and review a parade of the returning troops to-

50. *Congressional Record*, 55th Cong., 2nd Sess., 5160–61, 6275–76, 55th Cong., 3rd Sess., 73–79, 710, 718, 1262, 2302, 56th Cong., 1st Sess., 4988, 6742–43.

gether with veterans of Union and Confederate armies and members of fraternal orders, but the president failed to come.[51]

Following the signing of the peace treaty, Underwood assured his constituents that the Spanish were anxious for peace and that the withdrawal of Spanish troops from Cuba and Puerto Rico would occur momentarily. The Philippines, he asserted, was a more complex problem, and the establishment of United States control over the islands would take time. In later years Underwood compared the taking of the Philippines with the seizure of territory following the Mexican War and with the purchase of land from the Indians for a few "beads and baubles." These sentiments, however, were expressed long after the acquisition of the Philippines, during the long Democratic fight to free the islands. The partisan nature of Underwood's attitude toward imperialism is seen in his vote on June 15, 1898, when he joined most of his Democratic colleagues in opposing Hawaiian annexation.[52] Indeed, Underwood was generally opposed to imperialism—usually in concert with his party.

The congressional elections of 1898 disappointed the Democrats, as Republicans, flush with victory in the Spanish-American War, retained control of Congress. Populist representation was sharply reduced, however, and the Democrats gained House seats, coming within 13 votes of a majority at the outset of the session.

Underwood's increasing prominence was reflected in the internal politics of the House. Bankhead again ran for minority leader, and this time Underwood served as his campaign manager. Bankhead was defeated by James D. Richardson of Tennessee. Underwood retained his post on the important Judiciary Committee but hoped for appointment to the Committee on Labor. The American Federation of Labor (AFL) Executive Committee endorsed Underwood for the post, and Samuel Gompers asked Speaker David B. Henderson to appoint him. But appointment to the Committee on Labor in addition to the Judiciary Committee, on which Underwood already served, would have violated the Speaker's rule that

51. Birmingham *News*, September 7, 1898.
52. *Ibid.*, September 17, 1898; *Congressional Record*, 57th Cong., 2nd Sess., 4762, 55th Cong., 2nd Sess., 6019.

no congressman could serve on two important committees, and he did not receive the appointment.[53] Minority leader Richardson, however, was favorably impressed with Underwood. Richardson, a Confederate veteran and an able but erratic leader, was more interested in editing papers than in leading the Democrats; he had already published *Messages and Papers of the Presidents* and was then editing *A Compilation of the Messages and Papers of the Confederacy.* The old Confederate veteran had strong ties to the Deep South—his wife was named for her native state, Alabama. He was deeply interested in Masonic affairs, sometimes to the exclusion of those of Congress.

In 1899 Genie Underwood, facing her husband's third term in Congress, reflected on congressional life. The two Underwood boys enjoyed Birmingham, she said, and "groaned whenever Washington was mentioned." She herself much preferred to run a household, but it was really impractical as they rented their house in Birmingham and had only rooms in Washington. She looked forward to returning to Birmingham in October, 1900, since her husband was to be in Washington only three months of the short session beginning in that year. She hoped that Oscar would be reelected for a fourth term since that was what he wanted, but she remarked that "there is nothing so uncertain as politics" and the public is "notoriously fickle and restless." She had never thought that political life was best for her husband and she hoped that after another term he would retire and make a name for himself as a "fine lawyer." She concluded by revealing that she was hardly an ideal housekeeper; her boys were allowed to keep a goat in the kitchen for entertainment, and he had consumed little Oscar's best straw hat and had been led out of the kitchen in disgrace for the crime of eating potatoes and apples in the pantry—seizing his opportunity when the cook was away.[54]

During this early part of his political career, Underwood had adhered generally to progressive Democratic doctrine. Although

53. Birmingham *Age-Herald*, December 20, 1899.
54. Eugenia Underwood to Frederica Virginia Underwood, August 27, 1899, in Underwood Papers, University of Virginia.

elected in 1894 as a free-silverite, he did not relish the more extreme tenets of that faith. By the end of the period, free-silver agitation had largely disappeared among his constituency, and he quietly abandoned the issue. He consistently advocated tariff reform despite his manufacturing constituency, and his support for judicial reforms and taxes directed against the "wealth" of the country rather than the consumers accorded with his general Populist bent. His advocacy of a graduated income tax was in line with standard southern Democratic doctrine since the tax would largely be paid by other sections of the country. The latter part of the period was dominated by the Spanish-American War, and Underwood, like most other Democrats, criticized McKinley's handling of the war crisis. He favored the independence of Cuba and opposed the annexation of Hawaii. But though he generally opposed imperialism, Underwood fundamentally sympathized with the war against Spain.

CHAPTER IV

A Conservative in
the Age of Roosevelt

Underwood's attractive young wife, Eugenia, died in January, 1900, a poignant personal tragedy for the congressman. In September, 1899, his wife and their younger son, nine-year-old Oscar, Jr., were stricken with typhoid fever. Two months later the victims were apparently recovering, and the family headed for Washington. Before they reached Charlottesville, Mrs. Underwood suffered a relapse and was taken to her mother's home there. She then contracted "acute gastritis" or peritonitis and was moved to Dr. Edward M. Magruder's sanitarium. She at first seemed to improve, but in late January her condition worsened and her husband was called to her bedside. She died at eight o'clock the evening of January 31, 1900. Funeral services were held at her mother's home, and she was buried in the University of Virginia cemetery.[1]

The bereaved widower was left with two small sons, John Lewis, eleven years old, and Oscar, Jr., nine. The father faced the difficult choice of entrusting the boys' care to their aged paternal grandmother, aided by their Aunt Rin, a nervous woman in bad health, or sending them to Richmond to be cared for by their maternal Aunt "Nita"—Mrs. Malvern C. Patterson. Both aunts sought the responsibility, and Underwood sadly told Mrs. Patterson that the boys would be entrusted to their grandmother until they were older, at which time he hoped they might be sent to school near Richmond so that Mrs. Patterson could "look after their moral

1. Charlottesville (Va.) *Daily Progress*, February 1, 1900.

training and guidance." Will Underwood went to Charlottesville to pick up the two boys, and their grandmother, Frederica Virginia Underwood, moved from Bowling Green, Kentucky, to Birmingham to live at Will's Ridge Park Avenue house, which was to be the boys' home.[2]

John and Oscar, Jr. stayed only one full year in Birmingham after which they were sent to Richmond to live with the Pattersons and to attend school. In 1904 they were placed in the Bingham School at Asheville, North Carolina. Oscar, Jr., in an uncharacteristic burst of parental criticism, later described the school as "an awful place," and both boys were quite unhappy under the stern regimen there, although they enjoyed their frequent visits with "Aunt Nita" and "Uncle Mal" in Richmond. Malvern Patterson, a man of moderate means, was employed by a tobacco company, and the boys lived off the proceeds of two trust funds left by their recently deceased maternal grandmother and step-grandfather. Over the years the Pattersons were rather firmly established in *loco parentis* for the boys, although the congressman occasionally issued from Washington strict Victorian orders for their training. He was especially eager that they be "dressed neatly and nicely" as his wife had wished. They continued to spend summers in Birmingham, where they played golf and tennis and went to dancing school. In these years the Ridge Park house of Will and Rin was still home in the summers for the boys and their father, the house on Lower Highland Avenue being rented. Grandmother Underwood lived there too, in the extended family arrangement preferred by the Underwoods—or perhaps dictated by economy. Nearly every evening the boys went to her room with a request for "stories of the old farm"—Ironwood at Bowling Green. Grandmother told of many other things: of dancing with soldiers who were leaving Old Point Comfort, Virginia, in the Mexican War, of her marriage to a

2. Oscar W. Underwood to Nita Patterson, March 4, 1900, in Oscar W. Underwood Papers, University of Virginia; O. W. Underwood, Jr., "Commentary on the Dissertation of Evans Johnson" (MS in possession of Evans C. Johnson, DeLand, Fla.), 5.

wealthy Louisville druggist when she was seventeen, of the exciting life in Louisville during the Union occupation of the Civil War.[3]

With his children secure, Underwood concentrated on his career. The year 1900 was a natural watershed for him. Entering national politics in the Populist era, he had adopted the rhetoric and some of the ethos of Populism. By 1900 Populist fervor had receded, and free-silver agitation burned low. Despite his vigorous criticism of the McKinley Tariff Act and McKinley's Cuban policy, Underwood liked the conservative Republican president. It was a time in which even a young congressman had direct contact with the president, and Underwood later recalled having a number of interviews with McKinley while seeking the advancement of Alabama's Spanish-American War hero, Lieutenant Richmond Pearson Hobson. Underwood was even called "the Democratic McKinley" by some admirers who professed to see parallels in the conservative dispositions of the two men.[4] Underwood had campaigned for Bryan in 1896, but in 1900 he was unenthusiastic about Bryan's nomination. Bryan was popular in Alabama, though, and in April, 1900, Underwood predicted his nomination by "acclamation." Underwood did not campaign for the candidate, however, and it appears likely that Underwood's brother-in-law reflected the Alabama congressman's attitude when he wrote from Ohio after Bryan's defeat, "the gentleman got just exactly what he deserved."[5]

Hardly more than six months after his inauguration for a second term, McKinley was assassinated by an anarchist. Underwood served on the joint congressional committee that planned Congress' participation in the president's funeral. Despite Underwood's personal admiration for McKinley, he objected strongly, but

3. Interview with O. W. Underwood, Jr., November 19, 1951; Underwood to Nita Patterson, June 25, 1902, in Oscar W. Underwood Papers, Alabama Department of Archives and History, Montgomery. The trust funds totaled $16,559.03 in 1909. R. H. Wood to Underwood, March 31, 1909, in Underwood Papers, University of Virginia.

4. [Forney Johnston], *Democratic Senatorial Campaign: The Issue and the Facts* (Birmingham: Roberts & Sons, *ca*. 1914), 55; New York *Sun*, January 28, 1912.

5. Birmingham *Age-Herald*, April 19, 1900; Albert L. Thurman to Underwood, December 12, 1900, in Underwood Papers, Alabama Archives.

unsuccessfully, to the passage of a bill making it a crime to attack any government official or to speak in justification of such an attack. Underwood's effort to narrow the bill so that it would not cover "fourth class postmasters" failed.[6] McKinley's assassination brought Roosevelt, whom Underwood hardly knew, to the presidency.

Although Underwood had encountered opposition in his first two reelection contests, by 1900 his House seat was secure. He completely controlled the Congressional Executive Committee of the Ninth District. Edward K. Campbell, Underwood's closest political associate, was chairman of the committee. Both of Underwood's law partners, W. C. Garrett and Robert H. Thach, served on the committee, though Garrett held only a proxy. The Republicans had tired of running against Underwood, for although two independents opposed him in the general election of 1900, they received a total of 14 votes to his 10,591. Only 11 percent of the population of the Ninth Congressional District were registered to vote, and of that number almost 45 percent, or less than 5 percent of the population, cast their votes for Underwood.[7] Even prior to the restriction of the franchise under the constitution of 1901, a very small number of voters participated in congressional elections.

In the first few years of the century, Underwood advanced rapidly in the House and in the Democratic party. He called, just prior to the beginning of the Fifty-sixth Congress (1899–1901) for closer organization of the Democratic minority. "The Democrat," he said, "is the most independent animal that roves the earth," and it is "high time for us to begin to fight fire with fire and perfect our organizations as the Republicans do theirs."[8] Underwood was appointed to the Ways and Means Committee as the Democrats' junior member.

House Democrats had allowed the practice of caucusing to fall

6. *Congressional Record*, 57th Cong., 1st Sess., 93, 6467.
7. Birmingham *Age-Herald*, March 16, October 6, November 7, 1900; Alabama Official Election Returns, November 6, 1900, in Secretary of State files, Alabama Department of Archives and History, Montgomery.
8. Birmingham *Age-Herald*, December 12, 1899.

into disuse, but on January 9, 1900, minority leader James D. "Slim Jim" Richardson called an organization meeting. Underwood proposed the creation of two posts of House whip to aid the minority leader in arranging pairs. The positions were created, and Underwood and Congressman Stanley M. Epes of Virginia were elected to them. Underwood, generally regarded as Richardson's choice, accepted the post with an initial show of reluctance.[9] Epes died two months later leaving Underwood as Richardson's sole assistant.

In the Fifty-seventh Congress, meeting in December, 1901, the Democrats, following losses in the congressional elections accompanying the reelection of President McKinley, were forced to surrender a place on the Ways and Means Committee, and, as the junior member, Underwood was dropped. He continued, however, as minority whip and became the second-ranking minority member of the Rules Committee, where Richardson held the first Democratic place. A Democratic victory in 1902 would have made Richardson Speaker of the House and Underwood chairman of the Rules Committee.[10]

Birmingham looked back on the 1890s as a period of accomplishment. The panic of 1893 had temporarily halted its growth, and a violent strike in 1894 had virtually wiped out the labor movement, but by 1898 prosperity was returning. On Thanksgiving Day, 1899, the area's first steel was tapped from an open-hearth furnace in Ensley. The cheap open-hearth process made the use of low cost, unskilled labor more productive, and black men eagerly poured into the area. Birmingham's population grew from 26,178 to 38,415 between 1890 and 1900, but more indicative of its growth was the increase of Jefferson County's population from 88,501 to 140,420. Mining occupations, always somewhat in the hands of convicts and blacks, became increasingly the province of the black or immigrant worker. The huge number of blacks added to the basic white population of native southerners and immigrants—especially a colony of

9. Birmingham *News*, January 10, 1900; Randall B. Ripley, *Party Leaders in the House of Representatives* (Washington, D.C.: Brookings Institution, 1967), 36–37.
10. Birmingham *Age-Herald*, December 5, 12, 1901.

Italians in Ensley—resulted in an explosive labor force that was difficult to organize. Unionization, which had failed so abysmally in the 1890s, was resumed with the turn of the century, and District 20 of the United Mine Workers of America (UMW) grew steadily. A brief strike in 1900 brought gains to the workers, and a coal strike begun in 1902 was settled by arbitration in 1903. A strike in 1904 affected the major coal and iron producers in the Birmingham area and, becoming more of a lockout than a strike, ended in failure for the union. By 1906 the UMW could claim only three thousand of its once eleven thousand members.[11]

The rising racial tensions in Birmingham were paralleled in the state at large. Racism culminated in the movement to remove the Negro from the polls by rewriting the Alabama state constitution to add literacy, property, and poll tax requirements. In an article in *Forum* Underwood argued that Negroes' participation in politics had proved disastrous, since they were incapable of following the best Negro political leadership, let alone that of the superior white man. Advocates of unlimited Negro suffrage could not, he said, contemplate with equanimity the political control of northern states by Negroes, and he saw no more reason for the Negroes to be handicapped by disfranchisement than for women to be handicapped by their lack of the vote.[12]

Alabamians voted almost two to one in 1900 for a constitutional convention to disfranchise the Negro. Underwood's Ninth Congressional District voted three to one for the convention, and only Blount County in the district voted against the proposal. The convention adopted the Constitution of 1901, an ultraconservative document opposed by the mildly progressive, including Underwood's good friend Governor Joseph F. Johnston, the Republicans, and the Negroes. The state Democratic Executive Committee approved the new constitution, and by a vote of 12 to 7 Underwood was selected to head the Democratic campaign committee for rati-

11. Paul B. Worthman, "Black Workers and Labor Unions in Birmingham, Alabama, 1897–1904," *Labor History*, X (1969), 376–407; Nancy Ruth Elmore, "The Birmingham Coal Strike of 1908" (M.A. thesis, University of Alabama, 1966), 39.
12. Oscar W. Underwood, "Negro Problem in the South," *Forum*, XXX (1900), 215–19.

fication. Underwood's selection was intended to secure votes in north Alabama, for it was expected that the conservative new constitution would be more popular in the black belt than in the northern part of the state.[13] Underwood had not sought the office, but he and the committee of fifteen campaigned vigorously for ratification.

Underwood was not universally known even among his more politically oriented constituents. While campaigning along an almost deserted street at Blocton in Bibb County, the congressman was stopped by a stranger who asked him to sign a petition. Glancing at the petition Underwood noted that it was addressed to "Hon. Oscar W. Underwood" in Washington and was an endorsement of a woman candidate for postmaster. When Underwood demurred that he was not a resident of the area the petition carrier said: "Oh, that don't make no diff'rence. I'm gettin' niggers an' everybody to sign this. That damned Congressman won't know the difference."[14] Underwood loved to tell the story. Although the young woman got the job, his distaste for petitions and scorn for Negro participation in politics was reinforced.

The campaign to "purify" the ballot box and deny the vote to the Negro was successful, and the Constitution of 1901 was ratified by a large majority. Underwood's efforts to disfranchise the Negro were reflected in his congressional policies. On several occasions between 1900 and 1907, he argued that the Fifteenth Amendment was an unsuccessful "experiment" and urged its repeal in order to disfranchise the Negro nationwide. The demagogic and unrealistic proposal attracted favorable editorial comments in the South. In 1901 Underwood helped maneuver the filibuster that defeated the Olmsted resolution to reduce southern representation in Congress. The Republican platform of 1904 demanded that Congress investigate unconstitutional limitations on suffrage in the South

13. Birmingham *Labor Advocate*, May 11, 1901; Albert B. Moore, *History of Alabama* (University, Ala.: University Supply Store, 1934), 658; Birmingham *Age-Herald*, September 3, 5, 1901; Malcolm C. McMillan, *Constitutional Development in Alabama, 1798–1901: A Study in Politics, the Negro and Sectionalism* (Chapel Hill: University of North Carolina Press, 1955), 348, 358.
14. Underwood Scrapbook, I, 18, in Underwood Papers, Alabama Archives.

and that southern congressional representation be reduced propor-
tionately. Underwood suggested that merchants tell northern
wholesalers that Republican interference in southern elections
would result in the loss of southern customers. In August, 1904,
Underwood, in a Bessemer speech, arraigned President Theodore
Roosevelt for his policy of Negro equality. He traced the history of
the Negro for centuries, alleging the inferiority of the race, and he
declared that Roosevelt's policy denied the teachings of history as
well as of God. Underwood's leadership of the movement to ratify
the Alabama Constitution of 1901 marked him as a statewide political leader, and on the committee that aided him were the names
of men who became leaders in his senatorial campaign in 1913 and
1914. The resounding approval of the new constitution had its political rewards and punishments. Underwood urged that the governor not appoint registrars unfriendly to the new constitution,
and that the men appointed be selected from "those who fought for
us in our recent battle."[15]

Underwood had gained strength in the battle over the constitution, and in the gubernatorial election of 1902 he unabashedly favored William Jelks of Eufaula over his fellow townsman and
friend, former governor Joseph F. Johnston. Jelks, a black-belt
conservative, identified himself with the new constitution.

In 1902 Underwood again was unopposed for the Democratic
congressional nomination. The Republican nomination was passed
around and offered to several Birmingham leaders, including J. A.
Van Hoose, Erskine Ramsey, and others, before it was handed, like
a cold biscuit, to J. Clyde Miller. Miller, a native of Pennsylvania,
had lived at Powderly, near Birmingham, for several years and was
a mine prospector. In accepting the nomination, Miller said that it
would not be the first forlorn hope he had led, hardly inspiring
confidence in the ticket. Miller's platform favored a protective tar-

15. *Congressional Record*, 56th Cong., 1st Sess., 1841–43; Birmingham *Age-Herald*,
February 25, 1900; W. S. Cowherd to Underwood, August 4, 1904, based on Underwood's
suggestion, in Underwood Papers, Alabama Archives; Birmingham *News*, August 27, 1904;
Birmingham *Age-Herald*, October 15, 1901; Underwood to W. B. [P.] Browne, November
27, 1901, in William Phineas Browne Papers, Alabama Department of Archives and History,
Montgomery.

iff, sound money, a shipping subsidy, liberal appropriations for internal improvements, and imperialistic expansion. Congressman Underwood received 6,783 votes to 1,792 for Miller and 195 for Fred Lennon, the Socialist nominee.[16] Underwood ran slightly ahead of Jelks, the victorious Democratic gubernatorial nominee. Underwood could take satisfaction in his success in riding the tide of conservative sentiment and strengthening the Democrats against the Republicans.

Birmingham's rampant growth, in addition to fostering racial discord, created a spirit of enterprise among its leaders. In keeping with that spirit, Underwood outlined a program for the New South in a speech before the Merchants and Manufacturers Association at Baltimore in 1902. He attributed the South's new industrial development to the destruction of the romantic Old South and urged a reexamination of the region's abundant industrial resources. In the absence of local capital, he said, it was essential for the South to compete with the new and vigorous West for financial support. Underwood vigorously promoted the Birmingham area's interests. From his early years in Congress he had urged generous appropriations for the Geological Survey so that the mineral survey for Jefferson County might be unhampered. He favored the creation of the Bureau of Mines in 1908, and he worked consistently and successfully for large appropriations to aid the bureau in testing coals and investigating mine accidents. He urged that the Bureau of Mines test relatively unknown and unstandardized Alabama coals for private mine operators. He favored large appropriations for mine rescue work, and he arranged for a mine rescue station to be built on land given by Joseph H. Woodward.[17]

Birmingham's increasing foreign-born element exacerbated the area's xenophobia, and the national labor unions were deeply involved in the movement to restrict immigration. Underwood's ru-

16. Birmingham *News*, February 26, August 25, 29, September 3, 24, 25, October 9, 11, 1902; Alabama Official Election Returns, November 8, 1902, in Secretary of State files, Alabama Archives.

17. Birmingham *Age-Herald*, January 31, 1902; *Congressional Record*, 60th Cong., 1st Sess., 6705, 6707; Birmingham *News*, June 17, 1908.

ral constituents had fixed upon foreigners and Catholics as convenient scapegoats for their troubles, and many rural folk, imbued with white supremacy ideals, generalized the concept into a spectral hierarchy of racial supremacy.[18] Underwood launched a fight for immigration restriction in 1902 when he offered the Watson-Underwood literacy amendment, almost identical with Henry Cabot Lodge's earlier proposal. It passed the House but was rejected in the Senate. In presenting restrictive legislation Underwood argued that American laborers must be protected from the influx of cheap foreign labor, and he estimated that the literacy provisions would reduce "undesirable" immigration by half. He declared that the South was burdened with one inferior race and did not want another. He attributed American civilization to the energetic Celtic and Teutonic stocks and described an elaborate hierarchy of races, labeling southern Europeans as inferior mixed races. Underwood spoke confidently, but when questioned he was unable to fit into his scheme the great civilizations built by non-Teutonic races. The South was attempting, he declared, to reduce its acreage of cotton, and the importation of cheap labor would militate against this. He also saw an evil in the "assisted immigrant," whom he wanted to exclude by a higher head tax. He offered the literacy amendment unsuccessfully several times before 1910 and chafed at Roosevelt's failure to promote restrictive immigration legislation. A Roosevelt partisan stated that the president had done everything constitutionally possible to restrict immigration, but Underwood snapped that he was unaware that Roosevelt habitually kept within his constitutional limitations. Copies of Underwood's major immigration speech were mailed all over the country, and the text was published in the magazine of the Junior Order of United American Mechanics; many chapters of that union endorsed Underwood's stand. Objections to Underwood's position were made by some southern manufacturers, eager for immigrant labor, and by Roman Catholics, who resented the discriminatory feature of the bill. Underwood first won national

18. See, for example, Samuel Gompers form letter, January 19, 1907, and R. H. Fitzgerald to Underwood, January 28, 1908, both in Underwood Papers, Alabama Archives.

attention on the immigration issue, and it gave him added labor support. In Wilson's administration he again favored the literacy amendment, and such a bill was passed over Wilson's veto in 1917 as the Burnett Act, sponsored by one of Underwood's closest friends.[19]

Racial tensions in Alabama were paralleled by a conflict between capital and labor over proposals for regulation of railroads and for the protection of railway labor. On the one side were the nine railroads that served Birmingham, and on the other were the four powerful railway brotherhoods. Underwood was a member of the Judiciary Committee when the Erdman Act of 1898 was written. He voted against the compulsory arbitration feature of that bill and for the revision that made arbitration voluntary, the version that was eventually passed. Underwood supported the Elkins Act of 1903, but he stated that the mild, Republican-sponsored railroad regulation measure was inadequate, failing as it did to provide criminal penalties for violation of the rebate provision. He strongly supported passage of the Safety Appliance Act of 1903. At the behest of a lobbyist for the railroad brotherhoods, he offered an amendment, similar to one that passed, to require that at least half of the railroad cars equipped with air brakes be coupled before the train could be placed in motion. In the fall of 1905, Underwood endorsed Roosevelt's railroad reform legislation. He described railroad regulation as "the paramount issue in American politics" and asserted that Roosevelt's being a Republican would not deter the Democrats from supporting his program of railroad regulation.[20]

In 1905 Underwood supported the unsuccessful Esch-Townsend bill to regulate railroads, and he offered amendments to strengthen the bill—amendments that failed. The Hepburn bill, similar to the Esch-Townsend measure, was reported from the Senate early in 1906. Underwood again expressed interest in effective railroad

19. *Congressional Record*, 59th Cong., 1st Sess., 551–55, 59th Cong., 2nd Sess., 3118, 63rd Cong., 3rd Sess., 3072. See, for example, Charles T. Sharer to Underwood, January 22, 1906, and other papers in the January, 1906 File, Underwood Papers, Alabama Archives.

20. Birmingham *News*, September 25, 1911; *Congressional Record*, 57th Cong., 2nd Sess., 2151, 2518–22; Hugh R. Fuller to Underwood, August 10, 1912, in Underwood Papers, Alabama Archives; Birmingham *Age-Herald*, November 11, 1905.

regulation, noting that among the great powers only the United States and France had failed to adopt an effective system of rate control. He cited *Smyth* v. *Ames* as the constitutional authority for regulation. Regulation would not reduce railway wages, he contended, since the courts would reject as confiscatory rates that provided insufficient operating revenue. Admitting that European railroad regulation had held railway wages down, Underwood explained that the American worker was more productive and that the trade union movement had kept wages high in the United States. He thought, incorrectly, that the bill would not be construed to include express and Pullman cars, and he unsuccessfully offered an amendment to cover them.[21] Railroad employees and newspaper editors in Alabama objected to the antipass provision of the Hepburn bill, as publishers of small newspapers wanted to continue the practice of trading the use of their columns for railroad passes. Underwood, who had requested and secured passes from the Southern Railway on occasion, offered an amendment exempting railway employees and their families from the provisions of the antipass stipulation. His amendment failed, but a similar provision was included in the Hepburn Act of 1906. In 1908 Underwood favored an appropriation of $350,000 to enforce the provisions of the Hepburn Act, although he thought even this amount too small.[22] He opposed the substitution of the Esch Hours of Service Act of 1907 for the more stringent LaFollette sixteen hour bill, which limited workers' hours on railroads and was favored by the unions. Underwood believed the failure of the United States to regulate hours on railroads as was done in other nations was reflected in the higher American accident rate.[23]

Underwood revealed privately, however, that he was a moderate on the railroad rate question in relation to state politics. Under-

21. *Congressional Record*, 59th Cong., 1st Sess., 2092, 2257; New York *Times*, February 8, 1906, p. 4.

22. J. H. Kitchum to Underwood, January 7, 1907, A. B. Andrews to Underwood, May 25, 1904, Underwood to J. F. Melbis, June 6, 1906, all in Underwood Papers, Alabama Archives; *Congressional Record*, 60th Cong., 1st Sess., 5490–91.

23. *Congressional Record*, 59th Cong., 2nd Sess., 4596–97. The Esch bill was not as definite as the LaFollette bill in placing responsibility for safety measures on the railroads.

wood's close friend Ed Campbell, an attorney for the Frisco Railroad, wrote Underwood in 1907 that Governor Braxton Bragg Comer and his radical, antirailroad legislature were passing measures "with a vengeance" and that the railroads would have been spared much trouble had they adopted the suggestions for reform that he and Underwood had made long before. In 1908 Underwood refused Governor Comer's request that he protest the Interstate Commerce Commission (ICC) increases in freight rates in Alabama. Acknowledging the desirability of changing the Hepburn Act so that new rates might be adjudicated before taking effect, Underwood said that the ICC had the authority to examine rates, and he was unqualified to question them. He defended an annual subsidy of $143,000 to the Southern Railway for a special fast mail train to the South. Opponents argued that the subsidy had been authorized before the Southern developed into a trunk line and that the heavy regular mail payments made such a bonus unnecessary. Underwood argued that because of the subsidy the South received better mail service, thus the entire nation benefited. He charged that the South was discriminated against in appropriations since the foreign mail service and city delivery systems primarily benefited the North. John Sharp Williams pointed out that the Southern Railway was owned in New York, but the subsidy was nonetheless retained.[24]

In addition to immigration restrictions and railway labor legislation, Underwood supported a variety of measures endorsed by organized labor and the Roosevelt administration. In 1902 he favored an appropriation for the Anthracite Coal Commission and applauded President Theodore Roosevelt's prolabor arbitration of the coal strike. In 1906 he vigorously opposed the repeal of the eight-hour law for alien workers on the Panama Canal and opposed the repeal of the compulsory pilotage system as being destructive to the efficient river and harbor pilotage system. In 1907 he opposed

24. Edward K. Campbell to Underwood, February 3, 1907, Underwood to Braxton B. Comer, August 7, 1908, both in Underwood Papers, Alabama Archives; *Congressional Record*, 56th Cong., 1st Sess., 4716–30, 57th Cong., 1st Sess., 2740–42; Birmingham *Age-Herald*, March 14, 15, 1902.

a ship subsidy bill which included a naval conscription provision objectionable to labor. He advocated the Roosevelt-backed Pure Food and Drug Act of 1906 and helped defeat an amendment offered by the bill's sponsor exempting medicine packaged by drugstores from the labeling provisions of the act.

Underwood generally supported Roosevelt's antitrust legislation, though he attacked aspects of it. In December, 1902, he favored a large appropriation for enforcement of the antitrust laws but stated that existing laws, if enforced, were sufficient to control the trust evil. Only three months later, however, Underwood complained that two minor Republican antitrust measures that were before the House were halfway measures that did little to strengthen the laws.[25]

Underwood was ambivalent toward reclamation legislation sponsored by the Roosevelt administration. He favored passage of the Newlands Reclamation Act which created a revolving fund to receive money from the sale of western public lands for the reclamation of other lands by irrigation. Underwood declared that Congress must aid in attracting people to the western states. He predicted that the products of the newly developed farms in the reclaimed areas would be marketed largely on the West Coast or in the Orient, and thus would offer little competition with the East. The alternative, Underwood stated, was development of western lands by land barons. He defended the constitutionality of the act by stating that the money received from the sale of the lands would become a part of the "private purse" of the nation over which Congress had greater latitude than over ordinary tax revenues. Agricultural colleges, he said, had already been sufficiently provided for without these lands, but ultimately some of the proceeds might be used for schools. He noted that little of the land involved was open to homesteading, and much of it was being used by trespassers. In the fall of 1903, Underwood accompanied William Randolph Hearst, chairman of the Committee on Irrigation

25. *Congressional Record*, 57th Cong., 2nd Sess., 34, 418, 59th Cong., 1st Sess., 1607, 8996–9000; New York *Times*, June 23, 1906, p. 3; *Congressional Record*, 59th Cong., 2nd Sess., 3944–49.

and Arid Lands, and other committee members to inspect the Salt River Valley near Phoenix, Arizona, the scene of the first Newlands act irrigation project. In February, 1905, Underwood opposed the compensation of Mexican citizens for damages arising from diversion of water to a Rio Grande, New Mexico, dam project. Distinguishing the principle in the bill from that of the Reclamation Act of 1902, he opposed the use of public funds (as opposed to the "private purse" trust funds) for western irrigation projects even though treaty claims were involved. Underwood doubted the validity as well as the constitutionality of these claims. However, the bill passed. In the same month, Underwood supported the Roosevelt administration in opposing a bill to increase the homestead provision from 160 to 640 acres for nonirrigable South Dakota and Colorado lands. Underwood's protests were unavailing, and the bill passed the House but failed in the Senate.

Underwood's most notable work for the farmers of his congressional district was in promoting diversification of crops in preparation for the expected arrival of the boll weevil. As early as 1898 he scored the secretary of agriculture for providing farmers common garden seed rather than experimental seed. However, Underwood was prompt in sending to the Department of Agriculture lists of thousands of Alabama farmers to be given free seeds. He fought off efforts to reduce the print order on the *Report on the Diseases of the Horse*, a book popular with his constituents. By 1905 Underwood had arranged for soil surveys in the three agricultural counties in his district. In Blount County the fruit-producing possibilities of the soil were explored, and the Perry County survey found that first-class filler tobacco and alfalfa could be raised on the Orangeburg soils around Marion. Underwood strongly urged the planting of tobacco and alfalfa, and he emphasized that cotton production should be limited through diversification rather than by restriction resolutions. He worked for liberal appropriations for the Bureau of Soils, and in 1908 he was influential in securing an almost 100 percent increase in its appropriation.[26]

26. *Congressional Record*, 57th Cong., 1st Sess., 6671–72, 6736–37; Birmingham *News*, September 28, 1903; *Congressional Record*, 58th Cong., 3rd Sess., 1902–1905, 3674–86,

Underwood was sectionally minded concerning Civil War pensions and war claims in Congress, vigorously opposing the extravagant claims presented by the Republicans. His opposition to an omnibus claims bill in 1902 illustrated his viewpoint. In the Senate, the House appropriation to cover claims approved by the court of claims was increased to indemnify Union contractors for ironclad vessels ordered by, but never delivered to, the Union. When the bill returned to the House, Underwood vigorously opposed payment of the claims and refused to compromise. Republicans threatened to oppose southern Civil War claims if northern claims were not accepted, and Underwood replied with some exaggeration that he always voted for legitimate northern claims as approved by the court of claims. The additional claims attached by the Senate were rejected, and about $1 million was saved. In 1904 Underwood led the Democratic fight against an appropriation of $1,500,000 to carry out McKinley's and Roosevelt's service pension orders, upon which Union army veterans without disability were to be retired at age sixty-two. Republicans cited a Cleveland executive order for the pensioning of senile veterans without a statutory provision as a precedent, but Underwood denied that Cleveland's order was justified. He saw the service pension orders as a dangerous presidential assumption of authority which would destroy congressional control over appropriations. The conference committee on the bill struck out the service pension appropriation, but it was restored in the succeeding session of Congress.[27]

Underwood's constituents often considered patronage issues even more crucial than sectional matters. To judge from the volume of mail involved, one would conclude that securing patronage was the major function of a congressman. Underwood maintained that he was opposed in principle to allowing congressmen a voice

55th Cong., 2nd Sess., 598–99; B. G. Galloway to Underwood, May 18, 1905, in Underwood Papers, Alabama Archives; *Congressional Record*, 57th Cong., 1st Sess., 2495; Birmingham *Age-Herald*, December 29, 1905; Marion (Ala.) *Standard*, June 22, July 6, 1905; Birmingham *Age-Herald*, April 4, 1908.

27. *Congressional Record*, 57th Cong., 1st Sess., 3677, 4530–41, 5371, 5567–5632, 58th Cong., 2nd Sess., 4882–87, 5036; Birmingham *Age-Herald*, April 13, 16, 1904; *Congressional Record*, 58th Cong., 3rd Sess., 2857–65.

Eugene Underwood (1818–1893), father of Oscar Underwood

Oscar Underwood, seated with a cane, and his law class at the University of Virginia in 1884

Underwood's first wife, Eugenia "Genie" Massie (1861–1900)

Underwood photographed in Birmingham in 1883

Underwood at the time of his remarriage in 1904

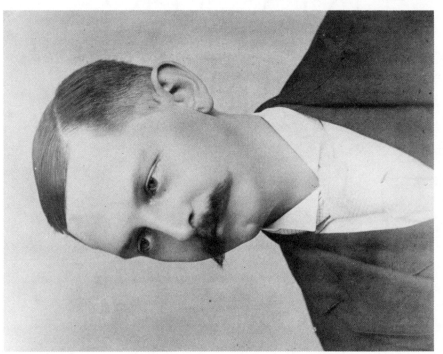

The young congressman in the 1890s attempted to make himself appear older by growing a mustache.

Underwood and his second wife, Bertha (*ca.* 1870–1948), in front of the Capitol around 1915 after his election to the Senate

Underwood's sons, John Lewis (1888–1973) and Oscar, Jr. (1890–1962)

An Underwood family gathering around 1916 includes Oscar's half-brother Will (1848–1916), a coal mine operator; Oscar; his brother Fred, a utilities executive; his brother Sidney, a civil engineer; his second wife, Bertha; his mother, Frederica Virginia Underwood; and his daughter-in-law, Mary Campbell Underwood.

in the distribution of public offices, believing that Republican use of presidential patronage handicapped the Democrats in attempting to block the Republican program. Congressmen, he felt, were generally honest but could not resist the pressure for jobs. Underwood, however, amply used his patronage. During the lean years between 1897 and 1913, when the Republicans were in power, he had a working agreement with them for a division of the patronage in the Ninth District between himself and the Republican "referee" or patronage distributor. The main patronage plums were post office jobs—especially the rural delivery routes which were created soon after the turn of the century. Not only did Underwood secure government jobs for his constituents, but he frequently urged business friends to aid constituents in obtaining employment or promotions.[28]

While making an effort to share in post office patronage, Underwood continued his attempts to get better mail service for the South. In 1909 he tried unsuccessfully to reduce mail rates to Cuba to the level of those to Canada, arguing that southern merchants and newspapers were entitled to the same advantages as those along the Canadian border. In March, 1902, he vigorously opposed placing rural mail routes on a contract rather than a salaried basis on the rather surprising ground that the contract system, which was not adopted, might become enmeshed in favoritism.[29]

Foreign affairs was generally of little concern to Underwood, but in 1902 he assisted Democratic House leader Richardson in obtaining an investigation of the abortive treaty for the purchase of the Virgin Islands from Denmark. Underwood demanded an investigation after the Danish representative, Walter Christmas, informed the Danish government that he had contracted to spend $500,000 on members of the United States Congress. The Republicans, embarrassed but unable to oppose the resolution to inves-

28. Oscar W. Underwood, "Corrupting Power of Public Patronage," *Forum*, XXI (1901), 557–60; Birmingham *News*, June 24, 1899; Russell Smith to Underwood, January 10, 1900, William Vaughn to Underwood, December 6, 1900, H. C. Ansley to Underwood, August 18, 1911, all in Underwood Papers, Alabama Archives.
29. *Congressional Record*, 56th Cong., 2nd Sess., 2099, 57th Cong., 1st Sess., 2409–2410.

tigate, helped pass it unanimously. The investigation failed to confirm Christmas' direct implication of two congressmen, but it confirmed Marcellus' famous observation on the state of Denmark, at least relative to a citizen named Christmas.[30]

Underwood consistently opposed large appropriations for the conduct of foreign affairs. In March, 1901, he successfully opposed a $75,000 appropriation for a junketing commission to study the American consular service. On May 8, 1902, Mt. Pelee, a volcano on the French island of Martinique exploded, destroying the town of St. Pierre, the commercial capital of the island. Thirty thousand islanders were killed by the boiling cauldron, and President Roosevelt asked that Congress provide $500,000 in relief funds. The House appropriations bill provided only $200,000 on the theory that substantial private contributions would be made. Underwood led a handful of congressmen who opposed even this lesser appropriation. He expressed sympathy for the victims of the Mt. Pelee disaster but declared that the United States Treasury was not an eleemosynary institution, and he doubted that Congress had constitutional authority to make the appropriation. Even with that power, he felt that the first duty of the United States was toward its own citizens. Passage of the appropriation was delayed for forty-eight hours, and the national press scolded Underwood for his inhumane attitude. The Kansas City *Star* found his opposition "almost incredible." The Springfield (Massachusetts) *Union* unfavorably compared Underwood's parsimony with his requests for rivers and harbors appropriations for the Chattahoochee River (the editor meant the Black Warrior.) Only the Louisville *Commercial* defended Underwood's position, saying that the appropriation had proved unnecessarily large.[31]

30. *Ibid.*, 57th Cong., 1st Sess., 3335–36; Birmingham *News*, July 2, 1902.
31. *Congressional Record*, 57th Cong., 1st Sess., 5332–33. Underwood was more generous toward the victims of the San Francisco earthquake of 1906. He heartily supported a bill to appropriate $1,000,000 in addition to a previously appropriated $500,000 for the earthquake sufferers, although he asked in vain that Secretary of War William Howard Taft, a man whom he trusted implicitly, be required to account to Congress. *Congressional Record*, 59th Cong., 1st Sess., 5661–62; Kansas City *Star*, May 13, 1902; Springfield (Mass.) *Union*, May 14, 1902; Louisville *Commercial*, May 20, 1902.

Underwood followed Democratic doctrine in attacking the Republican party's imperialistic policy toward new American possessions. In March, 1900, he inveighed against the impending passage of a bill levying a 15 percent duty on imports from Puerto Rico. On the question of whether the Constitution followed the flag, Underwood gave a resounding affirmative, citing Supreme Court decisions and denying categorically that there could be a legal distinction among the territories. He criticized the Republicans for disregarding the constitutional rights of the Puerto Ricans by burdening them with unjust taxes. The Supreme Court confirmed Underwood's opinion on the unconstitutionality of the Puerto Rican Tariff Act, but in *Downes* v. *Bidwell* the Court declared in favor of the incorporated and unincorporated territorial classifications that Underwood had attacked. Underwood even pushed aside his objection to traveling commissions to approve, in March, 1901, a Republican proposal for inspection of United States insular possessions. He strongly supported an act passed in 1902 to give the Puerto Ricans a congressional delegate. In 1909 he favored placing a duty on Puerto Rican rum to offset the United States internal revenue tax on alcohol, though he believed that the internal revenue laws of the United States should themselves apply to Puerto Rico. He declared that Puerto Rico was "a sentry box on our southern coast" which "for all time to come" would be a part of the United States. He approved of the establishment of a civil government for the Philippines in 1902 and praised the Democratic minority members of the Insular Committee for accepting the first opportunity offered by the Republicans for organizing such a government.[32]

As assistant minority leader, Underwood advocated the repeal of the Spanish-American War revenue tax. This tax included business privilege and inheritance taxes, and stamp taxes on alcoholic beverages, tobaccos, and business documents. Underwood felt that the war revenue tax fell heaviest on the "active, energetic, produc-

32. *Congressional Record*, 56th Cong., 1st Sess., 142, 57th Cong., 2nd Sess., 2927, 60th Cong., 1st Sess., 910, 57th Cong., 1st Sess., 6867.

ing wealth" and not on the idle accumulated wealth which had never borne its share of the tax burden. He favored repeal of all the stamp taxes of the war revenue bill, but not the inheritance tax, since the latter had been a good source of revenue in England and Underwood thus thought it an equitable tax for the United States. He sought unsuccessfully to amend the inheritance tax by reducing the exemption from $10,000 to $5,000 per heir. In January, 1902, the Republicans unexpectedly presented an omnibus bill to repeal all war revenue taxes, incorporating a provision introduced by Underwood to repeal the tax on domestic wines. Underwood criticized the Republicans for failing to allow a separate vote on the inheritance tax so that it might be retained, and it, along with all other war revenue taxes, was repealed by a unanimous vote.[33]

The repeal of the war revenue taxes touched off a debate on tariff revision and imperial policy—especially toward the new American dominions. Roosevelt urged that general tariff revision be avoided because of the danger of causing a panic. He advocated instead the ratification of the recently completed Cuban reciprocity measure and of several reciprocity treaties negotiated by McKinley. The Cuban treaty provided for a reduction of at least 20 percent in the tariffs between Cuba and the United States. Acknowledging the obligation of the United States to Cuba, which had just become a protectorate by ratification of the Platt Amendment, Roosevelt said that "reasons of morality and national interest" bound the United States to approve the agreement. To the pleasant surprise of the Republicans, Underwood agreed with Roosevelt's suggestion that general tariff revision be avoided, since such revision might "lead to disorder." Underwood said, however, that any reciprocity agreement should be approved by the House as well as the Senate, and he read an amendment for this purpose that he would have offered had the Republicans allowed amendments.[34] The Senate accepted

33. *Ibid.*, 56th Cong., 1st Sess., 5908–11, 56th Cong., 2nd Sess., 127, 335, 2264, Appendix, 53–54, 57th Cong., 1st Sess., 637, 1830–33; Birmingham *Age-Herald*, January 24, February 18, 1902.

34. James D. Richardson (comp.), *A Compilation of the Messages and Papers of the Presidents, 1782–1892* (20 vols.; New York: Bureau of National Literature, 1897–1914), XV, 6660; *Congressional Record*, 57th Cong., 1st Sess., 1829–31.

a House resolution, similar to Underwood's amendment, that the Cuban reciprocity treaty must be ratified by the House as well.

Both political parties favored approval of the Cuban treaty, but since it was a tariff measure some Democrats wanted to use the occasion to attempt general tariff revision, or at least a lowering of the tariff on refined sugar, in order to build a platform for the fall elections. The Democratic caucus in the spring of 1902 considered the advisability of seeking general tariff revision. Underwood shocked the caucus by charging that Republican leaders had offered a deal whereby they would smother an investigation of the disfranchisement of Negroes in several southern states, including Alabama, in return for southern Democratic cooperation in forgoing tariff reform. The proposed franchise investigation, the Crumpacker resolution, envisioned reducing southern representation in the House, a punishment the Constitution provides for denial of the franchise. Underwood refused to say who had made the overtures, and some Democrats scoffed at the charge, but John Sharp Williams and John H. Bankhead affirmed the report. Underwood urged that those members from the states covered by the Crumpacker resolution be exempted from the caucus rule and be permitted to cooperate with the Republicans. Critics of the proposed deal argued that the Crumpacker resolution was already moribund, but Williams maintained that continued discussion of it caused unrest among the Negroes. The angry and turbulent Democratic caucus ended by overwhelmingly committing the Democrats to an attempt to add general tariff amendments to the Cuban reciprocity bill and more specifically to do away with the differential (higher rate) on refined sugar as compared to that on raw sugar. The next day, Republican Congressman William P. Hepburn of Iowa declared that Underwood was misinformed, and Republican Congressman Charles E. Littlefield of Maine angrily accused Underwood of describing an offer to enter into an "unholy, ungodly, and infamous alliance to sacrifice human rights" for the purpose of maintaining the prestige of the "leader of the House" and the sugar industry. Underwood's colleagues urged him to keep quiet, but under questioning by Littlefield, he categorically denied that he had ever mentioned any such offer. Underwood's in-

sertion of "Laughter and applause" following his statement in the
Congressional Record showed that although he was clearly misrep-
resenting the facts, he did so knowing that no one was deceived.

The Democrats, favoring elimination of the differential or higher
rate on refined sugar, unexpectedly acquired an ally—the "Oxnards," protectionist beet sugar Republicans, named for an important beet sugar center in California. Seeing no hope of defeating
Cuban reciprocity in the House, the Oxnards intended to make it
unpalatable to the protectionist Senate, and their votes, added to
those of the Democrats, resulted in a tally of 199 to 105 to strike
the higher rate on refined sugar coming from anywhere outside the
United States. The Cuban reciprocity bill itself passed by an overwhelming 246 to 54.[35] The Democrats thus won their first victory
of the session, but the Senate did not approve the Cuban reciprocity bill until 1903 after the restoration of the differential on refined
sugar.

Richardson's and Underwood's hedging on the issue of immediate tariff reform created renewed resentment against their leadership—dissatisfaction that manifested itself in opposition to
Underwood. Minority leader Richardson, not one who relished
parliamentary battles, had found that he could safely leave the floor
in the hands of Underwood and usually left for home by two o'clock
in the afternoon. One western Democrat noted that "Richardson is
Underwood" and that the removal of Underwood from the Rules
Committee and as Democratic whip would preclude Richardson
becoming Speaker if the Democrats controlled the next House.
David DeArmond of Missouri, Underwood's competitor for the
post of whip, vigorously opposed cooperation between southern
Democrats and northern Republicans. The Missourian's supporters argued that he would participate more actively in the deliberations of the Rules Committee than had Underwood. Inherent in
the criticism of Underwood was the feeling that he was not genuinely committed to tariff reform. The two Democratic leaders re-

35. Birmingham *Age-Herald*, April 18, 1902; *Congressional Record*, 57th Cong., 1st
Sess., 4382, 4418–19.

tained their positions, but in 1903 Richardson, who had little relish for leading what he termed a "lunatic asylum," announced at a Masonic convention that he would retire from Congress in 1905 and devote his life to Masonry. Richardson resigned at the end of the Fifty-seventh Congress as House minority leader and was succeeded by John Sharp Williams of Mississippi. The mid-term election of 1902 cut the Republican majority in the Fifty-eighth Congress in half, and the new Speaker, Joseph G. Cannon, conceded Williams full control over Democratic appointments. Williams, a doctrinaire "old school" Democrat planning to emphasize tariff reduction and faced with a choice between DeArmond, with whom he had had a bitter personal altercation, and the rapidly rising Underwood, chose DeArmond as his assistant. Underwood's moderate tariff views had received Republican plaudits, and he had not been known as a Williams supporter. Williams punished Underwood by preventing his return to the Ways and Means Committee, which now had a Democratic opening, and removing him from the second Democratic spot on the Rules Committee. He was assigned as the last-ranking Democrat on the Appropriations Committee. It was a bitter pill for Underwood, but he professed to be pleased.[36]

In the preconvention maneuvering for the Democratic presidential nomination of 1904, Underwood, no longer a free-silverite, still harbored bitter memories of the Cleveland administration. In November, 1903, he noted that sentiment had developed for the nomination of an eastern man who would be acceptable to the West. His statement was, of course, directed against William Jennings Bryan, the Democratic nominee in 1896 and 1900, against whom Underwood was to wage a long political battle. Underwood favored the nomination of Richard Olney, a conservative corporation attorney who had served as Cleveland's attorney general and secretary of state. Less than two months later Olney endorsed Cleveland for a fourth nomination and a third term. In an interview with the Washington *Evening Star*, Underwood recoiled at the suggestion

36. New York *Times*, February 26, 1911, Sec. V, p. 2; St. Louis *Globe-Democrat*, April 23, 1902; Birmingham *News*, November 10, 13, 1903; New York *Times*, November 7, 1903, p. 8.

that Cleveland be nominated and stated that although southern
Democrats were ready to accept a gold Democrat who "took his
medicine" by backing Bryan in 1896 and 1900, they were certainly
not ready to accept Cleveland who had refused to support Bryan.
He even hinted that southerners might prefer Roosevelt to Cleveland.[37]

Underwood's statement was not published in Birmingham newspapers, presumably because friendly editors felt it would hurt him.
The Nashville *Banner* and the Montgomery *Advertiser*, however,
commented unfavorably, the *Advertiser* noting Underwood's inconsistency in his enthusiasm for Olney and his opposition to
Cleveland, as both shared the same philosophy. Underwood's opposition to Cleveland, the *Advertiser* commented, was an irra-
tional "old habit," and the statement seemed to address this lingering personal animus rather than any disagreement with Cleveland's
views. Some Cleveland supporters claimed to see a threat that Underwood would bolt the party and support Roosevelt.[38] But more
remarkable than the denunciation of the aging Cleveland was the
open attack upon Bryan who had considerable popularity in Alabama, even though he was anathema to most business interests,
including Birmingham's wealthiest man, Joseph Woodward, who
was about to become Underwood's father-in-law. Although Underwood had at one blow alienated Cleveland and Bryan Democrats,
seemingly a politically unrewarding feat, he had identified himself
as a conservative opponent and rallying point against Bryan.

Underwood's tight control of the Democratic Congressional
Committee for the Ninth District, however, was again evident in
his renomination without opposition in 1904. Underwood received
10,570 votes in the primary, and there were none in opposition.
Ed Campbell reported district committee expenses for renomination to be fifty dollars, including a twenty-five-dollar contribution

37. Birmingham *News*, November 14, 1903; Washington (D.C.) *Evening Star*, January
7, 1904.
38. N. P. T. Finch to Underwood, January 10, 1904, with clipping from the Nashville
Banner quoting the Montgomery *Advertiser*, in Birmingham File, Underwood Papers, Alabama Archives.

to an educational conference sponsored by Dr. J. H. Phillips and "one cocktail and some poor wine" consumed after the dinner. Campbell insisted that Underwood return to Birmingham after the end of the congressional session in March. His failure to return to Alabama, Campbell said, might "be construed as a want of interest especially since you could not come to the primary." Campbell was elected on a slate of delegates to the Democratic National Convention over a slate proposed by Governor Joseph F. Johnston, and he persuaded Underwood to attend the convention which met in St. Louis.[39]

The Republicans fared poorly in the Alabama campaign of 1904 when, after considerable indecision, they nominated John T. Blakemore to oppose Underwood. The Birmingham *News* reported that the nomination was perfunctory and that the Republican party in the state was one of "loaves and fishes" and of "color." A small number of votes were cast, including those of a very few Negroes, and Underwood received 9,615 to 1,775 for Blakemore and 377 for F. X. Waldhorst, the Socialist candidate. Blakemore was rewarded by being appointed assistant postmaster of Birmingham.[40]

After the death of Underwood's wife in 1900, etiquette required a long wait before the congressman could begin a new courtship, but by December, 1902, Ed Campbell knew that Underwood was quietly courting Bertha Woodward. That courtship was interrupted by Underwood's visit to Hot Springs, Arkansas, where he had a brief vacation romance with Mary A. Wherry of Detroit, a young, pretty widow, who was a stenographer. They climbed a mountain above Hot Springs, picking early violets along the way, took snapshots of each other, and visited an ostrich farm. Vacation romances, according to folklore, seldom result in marriages, and when Underwood remarried, it was to Bertha Woodward, a spin-

39. Campbell to Underwood, April 18, 12, 27, 1904, Underwood to John B. Knox, June 29, 1904, all in Underwood Papers, Alabama Archives.

40. Birmingham *News*, September 16, 1904; Alabama Official Election Returns, November 8, 1904, in Secretary of State files, Alabama Archives; Birmingham *Times*, December 23, 1904.

ster whose father he had known since his arrival in Birmingham, and whose home was less than a block from his. According to one account he had known her since late childhood, and according to another he met her on a Birmingham golf course. Underwood joined Miss Woodward in Asheville, North Carolina, in mid-September, 1904, having gone to Asheville from Birmingham to take his sons back to Bingham School.[41] He met her at the Kenilworth Inn, where she had been staying for several days, and on Saturday afternoon, September 10, they were married at two o'clock by the Reverend William Theodotus Capers at Trinity Episcopal Church. Underwood's age was listed as forty-three and his bride's as thirty-four. The proprietor of the inn announced the marriage to the press the following day. Although the couple had been engaged for several months, the wedding surprised friends who expected them to marry in the fall.[42]

Bertha, described by the Birmingham *News* as "a young woman of rare graces," had had the advantages of wealth and culture, and she had aesthetic interests. She was born in Wheeling, West Virginia, studied singing from childhood, and graduated at St. Alban's School in Cincinnati. She was petite and vivacious, but her small triangular face was not pretty. Her father, Joseph H. Woodward, was president of the Woodward Iron Company and a multimillion-aire Birmingham tycoon. "Mr. Woodward," as the congressman unfailingly called him, was not one to suffer his physical ills, which included deafness, in silence; nor did he mind bothering his congressman son-in-law with trifles as small as securing government aid in clearing his Orlando, Florida, lake of water hyacinths. However, Mr. Woodward was generous to his daughter and son-in-law, neither of whom was unaware of his vast wealth—sixteen million dollars at the time of his death in 1917.

There was no time for a honeymoon. The couple spent several

41. Campbell to Underwood, December 23, 1902, Mary A. Wherry to Underwood, May 13, 1903, July 8, 1904, Campbell to Underwood, March 9, 1903, all in Underwood Papers, Alabama Archives.

42. Birmingham *News*, September 12, 1904; Parish Register of Trinity Church, 1890–1913, Trinity Church, Asheville, N.C.

days in Asheville with Underwood's sons prior to heading for New York to join the Democratic presidential candidate, Judge Alton B. Parker at his Esopus, New York, home for a thirty speech campaign tour. A month earlier Underwood had spoken at Bessemer, lauding Judge Parker's character and ability. He felt comfortable supporting the conservative Parker and was relieved that the party was free, for the moment, of the incubus of Bryan. Underwood's campaign speeches passed unnoticed by the northern press, but upon his return to Birmingham, he spoke confidently of Parker's victory—mistakenly of course.[43]

Such a campaign foray was hardly a honeymoon, especially for the daughter of such an ardent Republican. By early November the couple had returned to Birmingham for the marriage of Annie Hill Jemison, daughter of a Birmingham real estate entrepreneur, to Bertha's brother, Allen Harvey "Rick" Woodward. Later the same month Underwood and his bride vacationed at the Tate Springs Hotel at Tate Springs, Tennessee, a fashionable spa of the period where Bertha had vacationed since childhood. This two-week stay cost Underwood $70.90. Tate Springs, in its lovely Great Smoky Mountain setting, was to have a lasting attraction for the Underwoods.[44]

Roosevelt's reelection complicated efforts to solve the thorny problem of Birmingham's congested federal court docket. Alabama had been divided into judicial districts before the rise of Birmingham, and Birmingham's judicial district had no judge of its own but depended on the Montgomery judge and aid from neighboring federal judges. Underwood and other Alabama congressmen had repeatedly attempted, as early as 1899, to redraw the judicial boundaries, but each plan foundered on the conflicting interests of judges and local bar associations. In 1905 Underwood attempted to cut the Gordian knot by means of a law requiring the Birmingham court to operate continuously for six months each year. The act gave Birmingham a more equitable share of the judge's services

43. Birmingham *News*, September 12, October 6, 1904.
44. *Ibid.*, October 6, November 2, 1904; Ledger, November, 1904, in Tate Springs Hotel, Tate Springs, Tennessee.

but was intensely unpopular with the bar outside of Birmingham and with the presiding judge, Thomas Goode Jones. In 1906 Underwood secured the passage of a bill creating a new judgeship, thus risking the chance that Roosevelt, whose chief patronage advisor in Alabama was Booker T. Washington, would appoint a Black and Tan to the new post. Underwood attempted, through his Republican father-in-law, to secure the appointment for Ed Campbell, but Roosevelt appointed Oscar R. Hundley, a Black and Tan. When southern Democrats blocked the Hundley appointment in the Senate, Roosevelt and later President William Howard Taft, gave Hundley recess appointments to keep him in office until 1909.[45]

Underwood regained his place on the Ways and Means Committee when the Fifty-ninth Congress (1905–1907) met following Roosevelt's inauguration for a second term. He was pleased to return to the powerful seventeen-member committee, although he was at the same time dropped from the important Appropriations Committee. He returned to Ways and Means at the suggestion of minority leader John Sharp Williams, whose faith in Underwood's reliability on the tariff issue was restored. The Ways and Means Committee appointment again brought Underwood to a position of leadership on tariff legislation. In 1906 he secured passage of a largely unopposed bill to remove a levy of $2.07 a gallon from denatured grain alcohol. He argued that removal of the duty might foster a new southern industry for the production of rayon through the use of grain alcohol and nitrated cotton. In the same year Underwood favored an ill-fated House bill that would have reduced the Philippine tariff rates to the United States by a fourth. In 1908, although agreeing that the Republicans' bill that became the Philippine Tariff Act was a much-needed reform, similar to the Democrats' House bill of 1906, he criticized the failure to remove export

45. Underwood to Thomas Goode Jones, February 4, 1905, in Thomas Goode Jones Papers, Alabama Department of Archives and History, Montgomery; Birmingham *Age-Herald*, April 6, 1906, February 8, 1907; Birmingham *Times*, December 7, 1906; Campbell to Underwood, March 4, 1907, in Underwood Papers, Alabama Archives; Birmingham *News*, May 8, 1909; interview with Judge Walter B. Jones, June 30, 1951.

taxes on important Philippine products such as sugar, copra, and tobacco.[46]

In the summer of 1906, Underwood received from his father-in-law a substantial gift of one hundred shares of stock in each of the Woodward companies—Woodward Iron Company of Birmingham and LaBelle Iron Works of Wheeling, West Virginia. The shares, worth an estimated $20,000, gave Underwood an added feeling of security. To the dismay of his wife, he then opposed in December, 1906, an increase in salaries for congressmen from $5,000 to $7,500 a year. In objecting to the salary raise that eventually passed, Underwood said that though he was unable to save any money while in Washington, he could do so in the months that he was in Birmingham. His increasing affluence permitted a trip to Europe in the late spring of 1907. He and Bertha sailed after Congress adjourned and returned on June 13. They spent much time at the Louvre in Paris, partially because Bertha was preparing a paper for delivery to a woman's club in Birmingham, and in Italy they were impressed at riding over ancient Roman roads still in use. Underwood purchased an expensive suit in London.

Underwood's conservatism in government spending was matched by his careful management of personal expenditures—doubtless accentuated by the panic of 1907. In August, 1907, he asked the management of the Cochran Hotel at 14th and K streets Northwest, where he had previously stayed, for a room with a bath rather than the suite of rooms (parlor, bedroom, and bath) that he had previously occupied. The Cochran's management refused to rent only a room—they probably had only suites—so Underwood agreed to rent his former quarters over the "corner store" at $270.00 a month, including board, for Mrs. Underwood and himself. He invested in four suits of underwear at $6.50 each, and his dues at the Metropolitan Club in Washington were slightly more than $6.00 a month. Personal expenses in Birmingham in 1907 were modest. Underwood received a requested 50 percent dis-

46. Birmingham *News*, December 23, 1905; *Congressional Record*, 59th Cong., 1st Sess., 5331; Birmingham *Age-Herald*, January 30, 1906; *Congressional Record*, 60th Cong., 1st Sess., 7096–97, 61st Cong., 1st Sess., 2004–2008, 2120–22.

count on his telephone bill, presumably because of his political office, and had the telephone "plugged up" in his absence. In addition to his expenses in Washington and Birmingham, Underwood paid Nita Patterson, in Richmond, Virginia, $70.00 a month for maintenance of his two sons. He also furnished Mrs. Patterson a generous supply of seed, which as a congressman he received free. The boys did not stay with their father and Bertha, as they called their step-mother, because of the frequent moves to Washington, but they all spent summers together.[47]

The panic of 1907, which marred Roosevelt's second administration, was a bankers' panic in that money accumulated in some financial centers but failed to flow properly into the cities where the need was greatest. The Republican solution was the Aldrich-Vreeland Act which authorized the issuance of emergency currency and the creation of the National Monetary Commission.

Underwood sponsored a bill to create a federal insurance deposit fund for national banks that would have anticipated the later Federal Deposit Insurance plan. His extensive, though restrained, comments on the panic of 1907 showed that he had abandoned his earlier Populist-scented ideas and had embraced moderate financial views. He rejected the idea of a central bank as monopolistic and incapable of solving the problem of concentration of reserves. He suggested facilitating the transfer of reserves between reserve centers by requiring country banks to keep most of their reserves in their own vaults or by preventing reserve banks from paying interest on reserves. Hoarding could be checked and confidence restored in banks through the passage of his deposit insurance plan, Underwood said. Underwood's bill never reached a vote, but his speech was an able analysis of the currency problem. He op-

47. Underwood to Joseph H. Woodward, May 25, 1906, in Joseph H. Woodward Papers, in possession of Mrs. Joseph H. Woodward II, Birmingham; Underwood to Katie Hendricks, July, 1907, in Underwood Papers, Alabama Archives; Congressional Record, 68th Cong., 1st Sess., 8181; Birmingham News, November 14, 1913; A. J. Keegan to Underwood, August 18, 24, 1907, in Underwood Papers, Alabama Archives. Underwood's expenses at the Cochran for the month of January, 1907, were $218.49 including extra meal charges of $3.50 and newsstand charges of $1.00. Presumably, Mrs. Underwood was not in Washington that month. See 1907 Accounts File, in Underwood Papers, Alabama Archives.

posed the Aldrich-Vreeland Act of 1908, describing it as a make-shift solution, unsatisfactory even to its advocates. Years later he recalled that three of the nation's leading bankers had come to his office to plead unsuccessfully for his support of the measure. He privately said that Senator Aldrich was serving big business inter-ests by passing a bill that would create a market for the sale of bonds.[48] Despite Underwood's increasing conservatism, his bank-ing views were still within the orbit of Democratic doctrine. His speech, widely distributed, is an early indication of his national aspirations.

Underwood was a carping critic of military spending during most of his service in Congress. In the Spanish-American War, he at-tacked military spending—although he voted for the war itself. In the first Roosevelt administration, while Richardson's assistant, he had perfected his technique of making points of order against mili-tary appropriations for petty items such as extra clerk hire, pen-sions, and a submarine cable in Alaska. Usually his efforts failed, but he occasionally succeeded. In 1906 he successfully blocked an appropriation to fortify the Philippine Islands, saying that the is-lands were in no immediate danger, were impossible to defend, were not a permanent possession, and the money could better be used for the defense of Hawaii.[49]

Underwood harshly criticized the ambitious naval program of the second Roosevelt administration. Between 1906 and 1908 he railed against the navy's failure to broaden the competition for con-structing submarines by considering submarine blueprints other than the Holland-type vessels to which the navy was committed. He succeeded in 1908 in amending the navy bill to broaden the submarine competition. Underwood vigorously opposed the pro-posal to build America's first super battleship or Dreadnaught in 1906. He joined the successful effort to delay authorization for the ship although the ship's proponents were victorious in 1907. In the

48. *Congressional Record*, 60th Cong., 1st Sess., 1037–42, 64th Cong., 1st Sess., 13510; Underwood to J. H. Woodward, April 20, 1908, in Woodward Papers.
49. *Congressional Record*, 58th Cong., 2nd Sess., 1081–87, 59th Cong., 1st Sess., 2571–72.

debates Underwood echoed the sentiments of experts who had told him, he said, "that battleships cannot live in the same water" with the new, fast, "submarine torpedo boats." He suggested that the best defense against the submarine might be cruisers carrying submarines on board. Sounding a Jeffersonian note on defense he said: "The battleship is an instrument of offense, not of defense. I believe that all that is necessary for our nation at the present time to keep up with the nations of the world is defensive weapons, weapons that will protect our great coast line against attacks."[50] Underwood saw a threat to international peace in the building of a large navy, though in 1906 he claimed that he had voted for every "naval programme" offered by the Committee on Naval Affairs. At the outset of his career, however, the United States Navy had been small, he recalled; it was now the third largest in the world. With Canada as a hostage to the United States he saw no danger of attack from Britain, concluding that "the best interests of our peace at home is to cultivate the art of peace and not become embroiled in foreign alliances that may bring us in danger of war." The navy, he said, should be maintained only at the existing level.[51]

Although Underwood opposed Roosevelt's nationalistic "big navy" program, he liberalized his highly sectional views toward Confederate claims and Union pension legislation. In 1906 he offered a bill to appropriate money for the care of Confederate graves although the legislation was opposed by Confederate women's associations who preferred to care for the graves themselves. Presumably, the bill was presented at the urging of his uncle, John C. Underwood, a Confederate veteran and a fanatic on the subject of genealogy. In 1908 Underwood voted for a generous raise in Union veterans' pensions, making the excuse that the general bill avoided the necessity for large numbers of private bills. The significance of Underwood's conversion was not lost on the galleries, who applauded his vote.[52]

50. *Ibid.*, 59th Cong., 1st Sess., 6987–91, 60th Cong., 1st Sess., 4822–23, 4838–39, 59th Cong., 1st Sess., 8822, 59th Cong., 2nd Sess., 3052.
51. *Ibid.*, 59th Cong., 2nd Sess., 3052.
52. *Ibid.*, 59th Cong., 1st Sess., 3240–41, 60th Cong., 1st Sess., 1467–69; unidentified clipping dated February 2, with letter from Rosa L. Malgan to Underwood, May 19, 1908, in Underwood Papers, Alabama Archives.

Underwood had grown steadily in political strength in the Ninth District in Alabama, but in 1906 his popularity was damaged when he supported his close friend J. P. Stiles in a bitter intraparty dispute in the election for sheriff of Jefferson County. Stiles was nominated in the Democratic primaries of 1906 over E. L. Higdon, but Higdon charged the Underwood-dominated Democratic Executive Committee with election irregularities and termed them a "court house ring." Higdon hoisted the flag of revolt and entered the November general election maintaining that he was the regular Democratic nominee. Higdon campaigned aggressively while Underwood campaigned vigorously and vituperatively for Stiles, making speeches that he later labeled the only "hot" speeches of his career. Claiming an unbroken record of party regularity, Underwood called for the support of every Democratic candidate from constable to governor. He angrily and intemperately characterized the Higdonites as "professional bolters" and as "sheep-killing dogs with mouths besmeared with Democratic blood."[53] Higdon won by a vote of 5,191 to 4,139 for Stiles, who trailed well behind the Democratic candidates in Jefferson County. More significantly, in his uncontested race Underwood received only 5,694 votes in Jefferson County, fewer than the Democratic candidates' average of 6,300, and his vote throughout the district fell from 9,615 in 1904 to 7,865 in 1906. Some of this loss was due to the bitterness of the sheriff's race which brought out the opposition vote. Indeed, there was no doubt that Underwood had supported an unpopular cause and lost political strength.[54]

The unpleasant Stiles-Higdon contest appeared to set the background for a hard race for reelection in 1908. Many union members, some of whom had never registered to vote, were paying their back poll taxes and preparing to vote—presumably against Underwood. The *Age-Herald* reminded constituents that Underwood had secured a number of local improvements, listing "a hand-

---

53. Birmingham *News*, October 1, 15, 1906; clipping from the Jones Valley (Ala.) *Times*, in Portfolio File, Underwood Papers, Alabama Archives.

54. Birmingham *Age-Herald*, November 11, 1906; Thomas M. Owen (comp.), *Alabama Official and Statistical Register, 1907* (Montgomery: Department of Archives and History, 1907), 236–37.

some government building at Bessemer," the assurance of an appropriation for a post office building at Ensley, increased appropriations for operation of the Birmingham post office and enlargement of its floor space, a weather station for Birmingham, and a government engineer assigned to study Jefferson County's roads. Also, through his position on the Ways and Means Committee, Underwood had been able to keep Birmingham in the running for a subtreasury. The *Age-Herald* noted, too, that Underwood might soon become Democratic minority leader if Champ Clark and John Sharp Williams were elevated to the Senate. Underwood himself announced that he would campaign for the addition of a good roads amendment to the federal Constitution.[55]

Underwood circularized his constituents, announcing that he would seek renomination. He emphasized his services to agriculture, pointing out that he had secured the first soil survey in the state for his district, had secured the establishment of some of the first rural mail routes, expected to secure soil utilization experts from the Department of Agriculture, had promoted the good roads movement, and had advocated restriction of immigration. Hundreds of Underwood's constituents used the enclosed envelope to thank their congressman. Barely literate farmers wrote joyfully of their mail being delivered to their doors. One Blount County schoolteacher reported that all of the children, and presumably their parents, favored him because he had arranged for them to get their rural delivery mail from Oneonta instead of the more distant Chapultepec. Others thought Underwood was getting the district its share of federal patronage and that the rural mail routes were providing jobs for deserving young men. The deliverymen themselves were appreciative of their jobs. Many farmers expressed thanks for seeds and for the Department of Agriculture "horse book." Underwood had also struck a responsive chord in his immigration restriction fight. The people wrote splenetic letters against the "yellow peril" and jealously spoke of fear that immigrants would take their

55. Jerry Jeraslie to Underwood, April 8, 1908, in Underwood Papers, Alabama Archives; Birmingham *Age-Herald*, March 3, 1908; Birmingham *Ledger*, March 19, 1908.

coveted land. One camp of United Confederate Veterans endorsed Underwood.[56]

Despite Underwood's large reservoir of political strength, several candidates sought to capitalize on the Higdon-Stiles controversy by opposing him for the nomination. Former Birmingham mayor W. M. "Mel" Drennen, a wholesale grocer who had forged strong ties with the Farmers' Union by giving them discounts, was a possible candidate on a prohibition platform. Another reputed candidate was J. A. Van Hoose, a wholesale grocer and the promoter of a plan to connect the Black Warrior River with the Tennessee River by a canal. A third possibility was Judge Samuel L. Weaver, a convivial Odd Fellow who had delivered a popular charge to the jury in a Cullman habeas corpus case and who was expected to receive the support of the Higdonites. Meanwhile, Underwood's friends applied pressure to see that the putative candidates got no newspaper support. The *Age-Herald* claimed credit for removing Van Hoose from the race by launching a campaign against high groceries and reminding the people of their vested interest in Underwood's reelection. Judge Weaver suddenly withdrew after three weeks of campaigning, explaining that Drennen seemed ready to make it a three-cornered race if he should enter, and such a contest might embarrass the party in the fall elections and would be expensive. He did not, he said bitterly, have as friends the owners of banks, furnaces, and rolling mills. Weaver concluded that his candidacy had shown Underwood and his friends that since the purification of the ballot box under the new constitution and the discard of machine rule, the people were no longer to be dictated to. Former mayor Drennen then announced his candidacy for mayor of Birmingham, and Underwood was left without Democratic opposition. The political victory was quite complete, as Underwood's friend, J. P. Stiles, defeated for sheriff in 1906, was elected probate judge.[57]

56. Form letter from Underwood to T. H. Logan, January 22, 1908, J. W. Edwards to Underwood, January 27, 1908, both in Underwood Papers, Alabama Archives.
57. See letters in March, 1908 File, Underwood Papers, Alabama Archives; Birmingham *Age-Herald*, January 27, February 5, 8, March 3, 1908.

Underwood returned to Washington and wrote Ed Campbell of the relaxation of returning to Congress without Democratic opposition; everything was going "smoothly." Campbell replied in a characteristically humorous vein with a jibe at Mrs. Underwood's electric automobile: "I suppose that your reference to evething [sic] going 'smoothly' does not refer to the automobile, which Mrs. Underwood said was in the repair shop. By the way, she rather warmed me for writing [you] about her machine but did confess that she applied the power and the brake at the same time. This was probably done by analogy to your prospective race, inasmuch as you seemed to be putting on the power and the brake in some quarters [at] about the same time."[58]

Underwood was exceedingly fortunate in having no Democratic opposition, especially since the summer of 1908 coincided with a renewed effort by the United Mine Workers to organize the Birmingham district, where their membership had fallen to three thousand. Strengthened by the coming of United States Steel to Birmingham, the coal operators announced a pay cut that would have pushed Birmingham miners' pay, already below that of northern miners, further below the national standard.[59] A violent strike resulted, and Underwood wrote his father-in-law, sympathizing with the operators: "The strike situation seems . . . very bad here as far as lawlessness is concerned. I believe the companies are getting in new men and going on with their work fairly well but there seems to be a number of ruffians in the community that have no regard for life or property and it is going to take some forcible treatment to rid the county of them. I suppose you have seen in the papers that there has been no trouble on the Woodward Iron Company's property, and I think . . . that Rick [Woodward] is handling the situation in first-class shape."[60] A few days later he assured his father-in-law that "Public sentiment in Birmingham is

58. Campbell to Underwood, April 8, 1908, in Underwood Papers, Alabama Archives. The Underwood electric auto was damaged that summer on its trip by rail from Washington. J. C. Turner to Underwood, July 31, 1908, in Underwood Papers, Alabama Archives.

59. Virginia Hamilton, *Hugo Black: The Alabama Years* (Baton Rouge: Louisiana State University Press, 1972), 33–35.

60. Underwood to J. H. Woodward, August 5, 1908, in Woodward Papers.

very strongly against the miners," and that "Rick said recently that he had practically all the men he needed." Underwood was confident that the strike would end when the miners who wanted to work felt secure. He expressed satisfaction when the strike collapsed and noted approvingly a community rumor that the strike leaders had been told that the disorders in the community must cease or they would be held personally responsible. The collapse of the coal strike in August, 1908, left the coal miners with a 20 percent pay cut and bereft of political friends. Governor Comer, a progressive-minded governor whom Underwood and Woodward thoroughly disliked, called out the troops to cut down the strikers' tents. Sheriff Higdon, who had to enforce many of the governor's orders, became anathema to the strikers, who called him a "little Czar."[61] Organized labor's power in the Birmingham district was almost destroyed until the 1920s.

With the decline of unionization and the collapse of Democratic opposition to Underwood, the Republicans could only go through the motions of opposing him in the general election of 1908. They nominated a lawyer, James B. Sloan. Sloan favored a federally aided road program, larger appropriations for rivers and harbors, a protective tariff, and Van Hoose's plan to connect the Black Warrior and Tennessee rivers with a canal. In the election Underwood received 11,288 votes to Sloan's 2,567.[62]

While Roosevelt was perfecting domestic reforms on the national level, the prohibition movement was gaining strength in Alabama—especially during Roosevelt's second term. Underwood first opposed federal regulation of whiskey traffic in 1899 when he opposed a bill to prevent the shipment of whiskey into the District of Columbia on Sunday. He objected strenuously to the bill, which passed, as an attempt to regulate interstate commerce. In 1907 the Alabama legislature passed two general local-option bills, and

61. Underwood to J. H. Woodward, August 13, 15, 26, 1908, in Woodward Papers; Elmore, "The Birmingham Coal Strike," 45.

62. Birmingham *Times*, October 16, 1908; Thomas M. Owen (comp.), *Alabama Official and Statistical Register, 1911* (Montgomery: Department of Archives and History, 1912), 270.

forty-five counties, including Jefferson, prohibited the sale of liquor by the end of the year. On the federal level, prohibitionists concentrated on the passage of federal antishipping laws to prevent liquor from entering dry jurisdictions in violation of state laws.

Although Underwood was generally consistent in opposing prohibition legislation, pressure mounted in Alabama and other southern states to stop the flow of alcoholic beverages into dry states. In 1902 Underwood reversed his earlier position and supported an antishipping bill, and in 1908 he favored the Littlefield antishipping bill, which had widespread support in Alabama. In advocating the Littlefield bill, Underwood reversed arguments he had earlier used in the House and said that though the liquor traffic was a matter within the police power of the states, without antishipping laws state prohibition laws would be ineffective and would merely substitute the "jug trade" for the open saloon. The Littlefield bill failed to pass, but Underwood supported the passage of the similar Webb antishipping bill which became law in 1913. He also approved the efforts of prohibitionists in their attempt to exclude whiskey advertising from the mails in prohibition states.[63] Nevertheless, Underwood was not really converted to the prohibition cause. On the state level, the cause of good bourbon was lost in 1907 with the adoption of statewide, statutory prohibition. In 1909 the Alabama prohibitionists, exultant over their success, proposed to write prohibition into the state constitution. Underwood joined Senator John H. Bankhead, former governor Joseph F. Johnston, and others in fighting the amendment. The dashing young congressman, Richmond Pearson Hobson, always an abstainer, adopted the prohibition political doctrine and campaigned fervently. But the drys suffered a humiliating defeat, perhaps because of Alabama's resistance to changing the constitution. In 1910 Underwood

63. *Congressional Record*, 54th Cong., 3rd Sess., 2239–41; James B. Sellers, *The Prohibition Movement in Alabama, 1702 to 1943* (Chapel Hill: University of North Carolina Press, 1943), 104, 114; *Congressional Record*, 60th Cong., 1st Sess., 2945–46; see, for example, Wallace M. Glass to Underwood, February 12, 1908, S. D. Weakley to Underwood, March 29, 1913, Underwood to Postmaster General, December 12, 1908, all in Underwood Papers, Alabama Archives.

backed for governor Emmet O'Neal, a local-optionist who, upon winning the office, reciprocated Underwood's favor by sharing state patronage with him.[64]

Few congressmen could have exceeded Underwood in advocating economy during the Roosevelt years. In his economy forays he was, at times, merely harassing the administration. At other times he was self-denying, as when he opposed a raise for congressmen and payment for travel during a "constructive recess" of Congress— a recess that Congress never took. In general, however, he advocated economy as an act of faith. He opposed a travel fund for President Roosevelt to replace his lost perquisite of traveling free on public conveyances, discovering, as he usually did on such occasions, a constitutional prohibition against the expenditure—that against increasing the emoluments of office during a term. He consistently criticized the customs service as obsolete and unduly expensive. An interesting exception to Underwood's penury was his proposal in May, 1900, that House employees be given an extra month's pay "as customary." Republicans hooted at Underwood's generosity toward their employees, and he was voted down. In no area did Underwood more consistently demand economy than in the Revenue Cutter Service; in 1901, for example, he declared in discussing pensions for the Revenue Cutter Service that government employees should provide for their own retirements.[65] Underwood's advocacy of economy, except for spending within his own district, was a hallmark of his career. He was a harsh critic in the Roosevelt period of army, navy, and pension appropriations and was appalled by what he said was the doubling of the cost of government from the McKinley to the Roosevelt administration. Like the Bourbon regimes in the South which had preceded his congressional tenure, Underwood favored a particularistic economy that was sometimes stultifying in its effects. Like Jefferson, he felt

64. Emmet O'Neal-Underwood correspondence, February 1911, in Underwood Papers, Alabama Archives; Sellers, *Prohibition Movement in Alabama*, 136, 142–48.
65. *Congressional Record*, 59th Cong., 1st Sess., 8809–11, 58th Cong., 2nd Sess., 1210, 56th Cong., 1st Sess., 5512, 56th Cong., 2nd Sess., 3243–45.

that the purpose of national defense is just that, and he looked upon the navy as an offensive weapon that might complicate relations with the rest of the world.

Underwood had entered the Age of Roosevelt with the vestiges of the progressive ideas with which he had entered Congress in 1895. Alabama and Birmingham had changed, however, and though the state showed some semblance of a progressive movement in the sentiment for railroad regulation, progressivism was dampened by racial discord. This discord was reflected in the conservative Alabama Constitution of 1901, which Underwood played an important role in ratifying. As a representative from a labor district, he supported legislation favored by organized labor, although there is reason to doubt his devotion to labor's cause.

Underwood and Roosevelt differed politically—Underwood was to be especially critical of Roosevelt for appointing Negroes and members of the Black and Tan wing of the Republican party to offices in the South—yet he had no personal animus against "Teddy." Indeed, on one occasion in Roosevelt's second term, he delightedly took his close Birmingham friend, attorney Walker Percy, for a visit with Roosevelt in the spirit of a host furnishing his guest with the best entertainment in town.[66]

Underwood's marriage to a wealthy woman in 1904 strongly influenced him to take more moderate economic views. These views were reflected in his weak support of antitrust legislation, railroad regulation, and conservation legislation. Underwood's interest in moderate tariff reduction was, however, unaffected by his close relationship with the Woodward Iron Company. The tariff was not of vital interest to the Birmingham area, but Underwood knew that without dispelling skepticism about his "regularity" on the tariff issue he could not expect to advance in Democratic councils.

Underwood's remarriage gave him many of the financial resources needed to augment his national aspirations, and his return to the Ways and Means Committee in 1905 restored him to a po-

66. Underwood to Bertha Underwood, December 5, 1906, in Underwood Papers, Alabama Archives.

sition of influence among House leaders. By 1908 his increasing national ambitions were seen in his more generous attitude toward Civil War pensions for Union veterans. While Underwood was generally inclined toward economic conservatism, the nation was still in the vortex of the progressive movement. Though the South lagged behind the rest of the nation in progressivism, it was strongly committed to prohibition, which Underwood strongly opposed. It was too early in 1908 to envision the chances for a conservative to achieve the Democratic nomination in 1912—much depended upon the uncertain internal chemistry of the Democratic and Republican parties.

Underwood had the essential requirements for advancement in Congress. An attractive, young southerner from a one-party state, he had more time to devote to congressional politics than did most of his colleagues. Possessing a safe congressional seat, protected for him by friends at home, notably Ed Campbell, he was free to devote his organizational abilities to advancement in the House. These abilities together with the seniority system helped to buoy him toward congressional leadership.

CHAPTER V

The Magic City Seeks
an Outlet to the Sea

Like many men of any era, Underwood considered himself a "modern man." In a 1902 speech he drew a picture of the Old South that would have done credit to the most ornate of brigadier orators, sentimentally recalling the "stately homes" and "fair women" of that idyllic time. Yet he described the New South of smoke stacks and foundaries "that light up the heavens with the proclamation of a new life and a new era" as the world in which he preferred to live.

River transportation and power were of vital interest in industrializing the South, and Underwood fully comprehended their significance to the landlocked Birmingham area. His family had been entrepreneurs who successfully exploited the resources of the frontier. His father was interested in the building of the Louisville and Nashville Railroad and developing the Mississippi and Ohio rivers. Cheap transportation, the Alabamian asserted, was the key to the industrialization of the South, as transportation costs usually exceed by far profits in manufacturing. He believed that railroads had to be fostered and developed, not stifled, and that because water transportation was vital an interoceanic canal should be built to bring the South closer to new western and foreign markets.[1]

In the 1890s John Tyler Morgan, Alabama's highly popular senior

1. Birmingham *Age-Herald*, January 31, 1902; Underwood Scrapbook, II, 189, in Oscar W. Underwood Papers, Alabama Department of Archives and History, Montgomery.

senator, acquired fame as an advocate of the Nicaraguan route for the proposed canal. In the canal debates of 1898–1902, Underwood argued cogently both for an isthmian canal and for the Nicaraguan route. In May, 1900, he urged that the president be authorized to make treaties with Nicaragua and Costa Rica preparatory to the building of a Nicaraguan canal, shunting aside arguments that the Nicaraguan route had been inadequately explored. The negotiation of the Hay-Pauncefote Treaty (the first of two treaties by that name) whereby Britain released the United States from the obligation to accept Britain as a partner simplified the canal problem. Underwood opposed a proposal that the House attach this treaty to the Nicaraguan canal bill, arguing, in contrast with the position he later took on reciprocity treaties, that the House had nothing to do with the approval of treaties. The bill passed unfettered by the treaty provisions, but it bogged down in the Senate.

Again in 1902 Underwood championed the Nicaraguan route, which was closely identified with Morgan and the Democrats. He saw the canal as a lever to force a reduction in transcontinental railroad rates. There was, he said, nothing new or unusual about the engineering problems in building the Nicaraguan canal. The cost would be heavy, but compared with the benefits and the costs of rivers and harbors legislation and pensions, the expense was small. The canal, he suggested, would pay for itself in ten years, American ships would then be given free passage, and tolls on foreign vessels would pay the maintenance cost. Not only was the Nicaraguan route better from an engineering viewpoint, Underwood asserted, but it would better stimulate trade in the Mississippi Valley and the Gulf of Mexico than would the Panama route and was therefore preferable even at a greater cost. The Nicaraguan route would open a trade lane through the Caribbean, and ships would stop at Gulf ports. The Democratic platform of 1900 expressly favored the Nicaraguan route, which was untainted by the scandals surrounding the French concession and the Panama route. When the Senate adopted the latter in the summer of 1902, Underwood was unconvinced that the United States could secure title to the Panama route and mistakenly predicted ultimate acceptance of the Nicaraguan.[2]

While southern congressmen were fighting a losing battle for the Nicaraguan canal route, speculators were attracted at the turn of the century by the hydroelectric potential in Alabama's powerful tumbling rivers and energetically sought power sites. In 1901 Underwood objected to a bill to allow the Knoxville Power Company to build a dam near Knoxville on the Tennessee River. A proponent of the bill insisted that the river's navigation potential would not be affected, and though Underwood's fears of interruption of navigation delayed the measure, the bill later passed by unanimous consent.[3] Presumably, Underwood's opposition was based on particularistic considerations since a corporation without Alabama connections was involved.

Underwood's eagerness to serve private interests—when they were Alabama interests—was seen in a proposal to add to the rivers and harbors bill of 1905 an item to survey Mobile Bay. Underwood proposed to spend five thousand dollars of rivers and harbors funds for a survey of a channel to Little Dauphin Island. Mobilians criticized the survey of the channel to a nonexistent harbor, and even Underwood's father-in-law told him that speculators held an option on Little Dauphin Island and planned to build a summer resort. Underwood had indeed known of these plans through correspondence with the Birmingham promoters, but Mr. Woodward's warning did not stop him from securing passage of the amendment.[4]

Underwood's enthusiasm for waterways development led him to bury his penurious attitude toward expenditures and to advocate a comprehensive and expensive national internal waterways system. In 1906 the *Manufacturers' Record*, that indefatigable promoter of southern industry, urged that the government build an internal

2. *Congressional Record*, 56th Cong., 1st Sess., Appendix, 272–73, 57th Cong., 1st Sess., 7438–39, 7441–42.
3. *Ibid.*, 56th Cong., 2nd Sess., 935, 2148, 3481.
4. Joseph H. Woodward to Oscar W. Underwood, February 28, 1905, J. H. Parsons to Underwood, March 2, 1905, both in Underwood Papers, Alabama Archives.

waterways system financed by a half billion dollar bond issue instead of depending on what it considered to be uncertain and parsimonious governmental appropriations for rivers and harbors. Ordinarily an opponent of bond issues, Underwood stated that because of the extraordinary benefits of the rapid completion of internal waterways, he heartily favored such a program. In 1907, speaking before the Mobile Basin and Tennessee River Association, Underwood advocated an immediate appropriation of a billion dollars for rivers and harbors. At a dinner at Harvey's Restaurant in Washington in 1910, he recommended the building of a dam at Henderson, Kentucky, recalling that his father had once prepared a statement setting forth plans for the navigational development of the Ohio River.[5]

While supporting a national plan of waterways development, Underwood pushed strongly for the development of a seaway for the Birmingham district, an effort that was to continue for the remainder of his House career. Birmingham desperately needed a cheap water outlet to the sea for the heavy products of its mines and furnaces. Interest focused on canalization of the shallow, rocky Black Warrior River which had its headwaters just north of Birmingham. This trickling stream seemed rather unpromising for transportation, but it was the only available route to the Gulf. The Black Warrior (or the Warrior as it is usually called) is part of a chain including the Tombigbee and Mobile rivers, the last of which empties into Mobile Bay. Warrior River navigation would have provided Birmingham with a cheaper route for the export of coal to South America and the West Indies. Underwood noted that whereas run-of-the-mine coal at the pit's mouth around Birmingham cost only about sixty-five cents a ton, railway transportation from Birmingham to Mobile cost a dollar a ton, making it impossible for Birmingham coal to compete with Welsh and English coals in Latin American markets. The canalization of the Warrior would develop barge traffic that would bring coal to the ship's side at

5. *Manufacturers' Record*, XLIX (February 22, 1906), 142; Birmingham *News*, November 20, 1907; Underwood Scrapbook, I, 3, in Underwood Papers, Alabama Archives.

Mobile for a transportation cost of only twenty-five cents a ton.
With such an outlet Birmingham coal could drive British coals from
the Latin American market and attract new industries to the city.
The Warrior canal, Underwood noted, was largely unopposed as it
would affect no competing interest.[6]

The proposal to canalize the Warrior River included plans for
building a canal and nineteen locks at an estimated cost of
$9,500,000. A slack water channel, six-feet deep, would extend the
river's navigability northward to the railroad lines at Bessemer. The
river was already navigable as far north as Tuscaloosa, but above
that point barge traffic was blocked by shoals.

In 1900 Underwood and Bankhead got the Warrior project, otherwise known as the Birmingham Canal, on a continuing contract
basis, thus avoiding the necessity for annual appropriations. Underwood's Appropriations Committee membership in the Fifty-
eighth Congress of 1903–1905 gave him an important base for
pushing Warrior development. In 1907 Bankhead, temporarily out
of Congress, was appointed to the Inland Waterways Commission
by Roosevelt, further strengthening the Bankhead-Underwood
team. On his trip to Europe in 1907, Underwood traveled up the
Rhine River and compared German river transport with that in
America. He was impressed with the use of barges on the Rhine,
noting that it was not a river to rival the Mississippi in size or
navigability. Yet, he noted, the Germans had developed a channel
to the sea so that barge transportation competed effectively with
railroads along the banks of the river. Underwood helped secure
an appropriation for the completion of three Warrior locks only to
have the appropriation reduced in the final Rivers and Harbors Act
of 1910.[7]

Underwood fretted about Congress' parsimonious attitude toward the completion of the Warrior system, and in 1911 he introduced in the House a simplified Black Warrior canal plan. The new

6. Birmingham *Age-Herald*, November 5, 1899; Bessemer (Ala.) *Weekly*, October 6, 1900.
7. *Congressional Record*, 67th Cong., 4th Sess., 3192, 3195; Birmingham *Age-Herald*, January 19, 1900, February 2, 12, 1910.

bill was energetically promoted by the Birmingham Water Light and Power Company, a "paper" organization of dubious financial stability whose lobbyist, the indefatigable J. W. Worthington, later figured in attempts at private development of Muscle Shoals. The new plan eliminated three proposed dams and locks on the Mulberry and Locust Fork rivers and proposed to replace them by a single higher dam with two tandem locks below the confluence of the two small rivers. The project, about $250,000 cheaper than the old one, would provide the same six-foot slack water canal, and the surplus power would be sold to the Birmingham Water Light and Power Company for a nominal fee. Underwood justified leasing the power by arguing that Birmingham had abundant power sources on the larger Coosa River and through utilization of gases from the coke ovens. The generous terms given to the power lessee were necessary, he said, because there was a limited amount of water power available on the Warrior, the lessee must make a considerable expenditure, and otherwise the power would go to waste. The bill was vociferously opposed from both sides of the aisle as a largess to a private company, with Democratic Representative Ollie James of Kentucky, the acknowledged spokesman for William Jennings Bryan, Underwood's arch enemy, leading the attack. Even Underwood's good friend Walker Percy wired that it should be entitled "A BILL FOR THE SPECIAL BENEFIT OF THE BIRMINGHAM WATER LIGHT AND POWER CO."[8] Opponents heatedly attacked the lack of provisions in the lease for rate regulation, auction of power, early termination, and adequate charges for power. Underwood angrily defended the water power lease and accused Representative James, in words he later retracted, of "playing up to the galleries."[9] Restrictive amendments were added, however, and the power leasing provisions were finally stricken entirely, although the bill itself passed.

After the power provisions of his bill were rejected by Congress,

8. *Congressional Record*, 62nd Cong., 1st Sess., 3782–84; Birmingham *News*, August 16, 22, 1911; telegram from Walker Percy to Underwood, August 17, 1911, in Underwood Papers, Alabama Archives.
9. *Congressional Record*, 62nd Cong., 1st Sess., 3786.

Underwood attempted to negotiate a franchise for the Birmingham Water Light and Power Company with the War Department. Secretary of War Henry L. Stimson cannily fended off Underwood's efforts to secure the power lease. Although Stimson agreed that the Warrior's surplus power should be used, he noted that Congress had rejected the company's proposal, suggesting that Underwood again seek congressional action or that the War Department lease the power with the proper safeguards. Neither course was followed.[10]

While the Birmingham Canal inched northward toward the railroad bridges of the Southern and Frisco railways just west of Birmingham, Birmingham became a subport of entry largely through Underwood's efforts. The subport made it possible to ship foreign goods in bond to Birmingham, paying duties after their arrival instead of upon arrival at New Orleans, Pensacola, or other ports. Passage of the bill was smoothed in the Senate by Bankhead, whose national reputation in transportation matters led to his placement on the Commerce Committee while still a freshman senator. Bankhead's home, Walker County, was a coal producing area with interests similar to those of Jefferson County. The efforts of Underwood and Bankhead were carefully coordinated in seeking transportation legislation, and they were aided by Alabama's senior senator, Joseph F. Johnston, a resident of Birmingham.[11]

The Birmingham Canal was sufficiently complete for the first barge to make the trip from New Orleans to the coal fields below Birmingham by October, 1913. Underwood presided at ceremonies in Tuscaloosa opening the canal and gave Bankhead credit for its development. By the end of the fiscal year in June, 1915, over nine million dollars had been spent on the canal, and the dams and locks were complete. Vessels with a six-foot draft could go as far as Cordova, the southwest corner of Jefferson County on the edge of

10. John C. Forney to Underwood, February, 1912, Henry L. Stimson to Underwood, February 3, 1912, both in Underwood Papers, Alabama Archives.

11. *Congressional Record*, 61st Cong., 3rd Sess., 4336. Bankhead replaced Senator John Tyler Morgan in June, 1907, and became senior senator upon the death of Senator Edmund Pettus the following month.

the Black Creek coal fields. During World War I the government operated the barge line on the Warrior, and after the war Underwood and his colleagues fought for and secured continued government operation under the War Department in the Transportation Act of 1920.[12]

Related to the development of the Warrior River was the Van Hoose plan to dig a canal connecting the Tennessee River with the Warrior, a project Underwood opposed. This plan, sponsored by J. A. Van Hoose of Birmingham, a potential rival for Underwood's seat in Congress, anticipated a canal of several hundred miles beginning at Guntersville on the Tennessee, proceeding southwestward to join the Warrior northwest of Birmingham, and continuing through the river system to the Gulf. In 1905, frightened by a recent drought, the Birmingham Commercial Club endorsed the Van Hoose canal as a guise to obtain government surveys of water sources north of Birmingham. Manufacturing interests feared that unless an additional gravity-flow water source could be found, Birmingham's industrial development was at an end.[13]

Underwood tried to provide for the surveys, but he opposed the canal. He pointed out that the Van Hoose project was an independent canal rather than a river improvement project and that the government had never financed such canals. Representative Theodore E. Burton, chairman of the Rivers and Harbors Committee, had stated that plans for a canal leading into the Warrior were premature until the Birmingham Canal was complete. At a meeting of the Mobile Basin and Tennessee River Association in 1907, Underwood hooted at the impracticability of "making the Tennessee run up hill" to join the Warrior and cited expert opinions adverse to such a canal. Underwood urged the association to reject a resolution asking him to pursue the Van Hoose plan. He suggested that after the completion of the Birmingham Canal it would be possible

12. Birmingham *News*, November 1, 1913; Thomas M. Owen, *History of Alabama and Dictionary of Alabama Biography* (4 vols.; Chicago: S. J. Clarke Publishing Company, 1921), II, 1380; Birmingham *Age-Herald*, March 2, 1920.

13. W. P. G. Harding to Underwood, *et al.*, February 2, 1905, Underwood to Joseph Babb, February 6, 1906, both in Underwood Papers, Alabama Archives.

to determine if the tonnage would justify the expenditure of the necessary thirty million dollars on the Van Hoose plan. The association accepted Underwood's suggestion and refused its endorsement.[14]

The Cahaba River, which flows from the coal fields of Bibb County southward to Centreville and into the Alabama at old Cahaba, also offered possibilities for the cheap transportation of coal to Mobile. Underwood secured an appropriation for examining the possibility of canalizing the Cahaba River in 1908, but the army engineers reported that the river had too many obstructions and was too shallow for navigation. In the same year an Underwood bill granted the Centreville Power Company the right to dam the Cahaba at Centreville, the uppermost point on any proposed Cahaba River canal. Centreville was an excellent power site, but, perhaps because of the limited market, the company never built the dam.[15]

The Warrior and the Cahaba are small rivers compared to the powerful Coosa, the third largest river in the South. Because the Coosa was navigable only on paper, Underwood maintained that the river's hydroelectric potential was far more important than its navigation prospects. In 1903 Underwood favored a bill to grant rights to Robert Chapman and Associates to build a series of six dams on the Coosa near Wetumpka. Chairman Burton of the Rivers and Harbors Committee strongly opposed the franchise. Congress had spent heavily to make the river navigable, Burton said, and the franchise would destroy the possibility of navigation at the dam sites. Underwood defended the bill as a commonplace franchise. Riparian owners would be reimbursed for damages, and, though the river lacked any practical potential for navigation, the dam would be removed if the government decided to make it navigable. Underwood and his colleagues failed to secure the two-thirds vote to suspend the rules and pass the Chapman franchise. In 1905 the army engineers agreed with Underwood's view that

14. Birmingham *News*, November 20, 1907.
15. *House Documents*, 61st Cong., 2nd Sess., No. 697; *Congressional Record*, 60th Cong., 1st Sess., 1954.

the development of the Coosa River for navigation was impractical, except the shallow water navigation already possible between Gadsden, Alabama, and Rome, Georgia, on the upper reaches of the river. Two power franchises were granted on the Coosa in 1904 and 1906 with Underwood's support, but neither franchise was exercised. Underwood introduced a bill to expand the terms of the 1906 franchise below Gadsden in 1909, but it died in committee.

Underwood opposed passage of the Republican-sponsored Southern Appalachian and White Mountain Reserve bill in March, 1909. The Commercial Club of Montgomery favored the bill as necessary to conserve water and to maintain the steady flow of the Coosa River. Underwood had hitherto favored bills to create a Southern Appalachian Mountain Forest Reserve, but he maintained that the Republican bill would be ineffective and would only create a roving commission with unchecked authority to spend nineteen thousand dollars. The bill became law despite his opposition.[16]

In 1912 Underwood supported the Alabama Power Company's application for a Coosa River franchise at lock 18, seven miles above Wetumpka, where the American Cyanamid Company proposed to build a nitrate fertilizer plant using vast amounts of the power that Alabama Power would produce. The bill was vigorously opposed as it exempted the power company from the regulations of the General Dam Acts. Opponents also charged that the Alabama Power Company was part of "the power trust," that rates on power produced at the dam should be regulated, and that the company should pay for use of the power. Underwood and his Alabama colleagues charged that the regulation of electric rates was unconstitutional. The federal government could regulate navigation but had no right to regulate water power, Underwood argued. It could sell power only if it built the dam; otherwise, the power belonged to the people of Alabama. He charged that if the government could levy such a "tax" on water power, it could tax the water that one

16. *Congressional Record*, 57th Cong., 2nd Sess., 2284–88; 60th Cong., 2nd Sess., 3562–67; 61st Cong., 2nd Sess., 138.

drinks. Such a fee would violate the constitutional provision that all taxes be uniform. He expressed doubt that a power trust existed but suggested that Congress could levy an excise tax on corporations that might compose such a trust if it wished to regulate the alleged combine. Financing for the Coosa project had been turned down by General Electric and other New York sources. The proposal was, he said, that of Alabama citizens with Canadian funding. The Coosa River Lock 18 franchise bill passed without amendment by a vote of 94 to 87 but was vetoed by Taft. Underwood's claim that New York interests were not involved was hardly substantiated when J. W. Worthington, the power company lobbyist, stated that he would have to consult his New York associates before deciding what to do next. Underwood and his colleagues vowed to override the president's veto at the next session, but it was an idle threat.[17]

The government's restrictive policy toward dam building on navigable streams stopped the development of hydroelectric dams. The Wilson administration presented the Adamson dam bill to provide a more liberal but uniform power policy. Underwood enthusiastically supported the Adamson bill, noting that power production was a natural monopoly and that federal regulation was provided in the bill when state regulation proved ineffective. His only fear, he said, was that the bill was too restrictive to attract capital. Conservation leaders opposed the bill as originally offered, but after the addition of regulatory safeguards their opposition dissipated and the bill passed.[18]

Underwood's activities in river transportation and power in the period 1898 to 1916 were exceedingly localistic and particularistic. Like most congressmen before and since, he was conditioned by the needs of his district, regardless of national considerations. He energetically promoted the development of the Black Warrior River and was largely responsible for getting Birmingham limited navigation to the Gulf through the Birmingham Canal. He opposed

17. *Ibid.*, 62nd Cong., 2nd Sess., 11567, 11586–89; Birmingham *Age-Herald*, August 27, 1912.
18. *Congressional Record*, 63rd Cong., 2nd Sess., 12334–38; New York *Times*, July 19, 1914, Sec. 2, p. 8.

an impracticable idea to tie the Black Warrior to the Tennessee with a canal. However, as his district was amply endowed with coal as an energy source, Underwood seemed unconcerned with safe-guarding for public control the power sites on Alabama's rivers. He was quite willing for special interests to seize control of dam sites across the Coosa or the Cahaba rivers which offered little prospect for navigation. Yet he was not wedded consistently to private de-velopment as opposed to federal control, as seen in his advocacy of government operation of the Warrior barge line during and after World War I. He waived his principle of rigid economy and urged heavy government spending to give Birmingham the advantages of oceanic transport.

CHAPTER VI

The Path to House Leadership

The panic of 1907 furnished a gloomy backdrop for the last days of Theodore Roosevelt's administration. Birmingham, with its sharply cyclical steel industry, was in a deep depression, and the acquisition by United States Steel of the Tennessee Coal and Iron Company, placing a third of the district's steel capacity in the hands of the huge corporation, stood as a monument to the recent panic. By 1908, however, economic activity resumed at a quickened pace, and Underwood could again see the black smoke belching forth from the smokestacks in view from the rear window of the home he had owned since the 1890s. A few automobiles had begun to appear, and he could watch them from his front window as they traveled toward the fashionable Highland Country Club area to the south and east. Mrs. Underwood's small electric car was billeted in a tiny garage outside the Underwood home.[1] Roosevelt's popularity had been damaged by the panic of 1907, and he had lost control of Congress. Aware of the president's commitment against a third term, the nation waited uneasily to see who his successor might be.

Upon Underwood's return to Birmingham in the summer of 1908, following the first session of the Sixtieth Congress, he complained of Congress' lack of accomplishments. Other than appropriation bills, the only measure Congress passed was the Aldrich-Vreeland Act which provided emergency currency to end the panic

1. New York *Times*, November 26, 1911, Sec. 5, pp. 1–2.

of 1907, and everyone agreed that at best it was no more than a makeshift solution to the monetary crisis. Underwood was not outspokenly anti-Roosevelt, but he complained that the expenses of the government had doubled since the McKinley administration. With no apparent sense of the irony involved, he bragged that Congress had given Birmingham all that it asked and that the state of Alabama had fared well in appropriations—the kind of "bread and butter" politics that made Underwood popular with his constituents. Letter writers who endorsed him for reelection in 1908 largely confined themselves to local issues, but those who commented on national questions talked only of Underwood's campaign for immigration restriction, which was dear to the hearts of the racist populace.[2]

William Jennings Bryan was the front-runner for the Democratic presidential nomination. Despite Bryan's popularity in Alabama where he was well known for his Chautauqua speeches, Ed Campbell, Underwood's chief political lieutenant, abortively attempted to capture the Alabama delegation to the Democratic convention for Governor John Johnson of Minnesota. Underwood cannily kept his opposition to Bryan under cover, and, when it became apparent that Bryan would win, insisted that failure to nominate Bryan would set the party back ten years.[3] Bryan received the nomination with the support of most of the Alabama delegation, but, as in 1900, Underwood did not campaign for him.

Secretary of War William Howard Taft, as Theodore Roosevelt's anointed heir, was expected to be the Republican nominee. Underwood and Taft had distant political ties through Underwood's Republican father-in-law, and both held stock in Mr. Woodward's LaBelle Iron Works of Wheeling, West Virginia. Each admired the other, although as members of different parties they were often political antagonists. In an interview with a Washington reporter at the "New" Willard Hotel, Underwood blamed the Republicans for

2. Birmingham *Age-Herald*, June 17, 1908; 1908 File in Oscar W. Underwood Papers, Alabama Department of Archives and History, Montgomery.
3. Samuel Will John to Oscar W. Underwood, May 11, 1908, citing a letter from Underwood, in Underwood Papers, Alabama Archives.

the panic and commented that Birmingham was enjoying "old fashioned Democratic prosperity." He appraised Taft warmly, however, noting that the candidate was being enthusiastically received on his southern tour and observing that although the South would continue to vote Democratic, the people there "admire Mr. Taft's charming personality and ability." Underwood wrote his father-in-law in March, 1908, that Taft was "very cheerful" about his presidential prospects. He predicted that Taft would be the Republican nominee and "a very difficult man to beat." Underwood expressed strong admiration for Taft as "able, conscientious and conservative" and one who would give "one of the best administrations we ever had, and be absolutely fair to the South."[4]

That Taft would defeat Bryan was hardly in doubt in 1908, although there was, of course, little question that Bryan would win Alabama. Taft was more popular in Alabama than Roosevelt had been, polling 24 percent of the Alabama popular vote, better than the 20 percent polled by Roosevelt in 1904. Taft's vote in Jefferson County was 20 percent of the overall vote compared with only 14 percent for Roosevelt in 1904.[5] Underwood's lack of support for Bryan undoubtedly influenced the Jefferson County result.

Taft had hardly been inaugurated when Underwood began to urge the appointment of Ed Campbell as judge for the Northern District of Alabama, to replace Oscar R. Hundley, the Black and Tan Republican whom Roosevelt and Taft had kept on the bench through recess appointments. Responding to an appeal from Underwood, his Republican father-in-law, who had important business holdings in West Virginia, wired the two West Virginia senators urging Campbell's appointment. Taft refused to appoint a Democrat to the judicial post, but in May, 1909, he appointed his

4. G. D. Etter, Jr., to Underwood, January 13, 1908, with undated clippings from the Washington *Herald* and the Washington *Post*, in Underwood Papers, Alabama Archives; Underwood to Joseph H. Woodward, March 9, 1908, in Joseph H. Woodward Papers, in possession of Mrs. Joseph H. Woodward II, Birmingham.

5. Thomas M. Owen (comp.), *Alabama Official and Statistical Register, 1907* (Montgomery: Department of Archives and History, 1907), 231–33; Thomas M. Owen (comp.), *Alabama Official and Statistical Register, 1911* (Montgomery: Department of Archives and History, 1912), 264–66.

Yale classmate William I. Grubb, a Birmingham attorney. Grubb, although a Republican, was acceptable to the Alabama senators and was confirmed.[6]

In the meantime, Underwood was emerging from a chrysalis stage of development and moving toward leadership of the Democratic minority. In 1903 he had lost his positions as minority whip and as a member of the Rules Committee, but had regained his Ways and Means Committee post in 1905 and resumed his climb to power. The Democrats were greatly outnumbered in the Sixty-first Congress (1909–1911), but Underwood advanced in the Democratic hierarchy. John Sharp Williams had retired from the minority leadership in 1908, and Underwood supported Champ Clark's successful effort to succeed Williams. Clark rewarded Underwood by returning him to the powerful Rules Committee while he retained his position on the Ways and Means Committee, where he was listed as the second ranking Democrat despite the greater committee seniority of John J. Fitzgerald of New York.[7]

Well before Taft's nomination and commitment to tariff reform in the campaign of 1908, the Republicans had authorized the Ways and Means Committee to gather information on the tariff during the congressional recess prior to the meeting of Congress in December, 1908. Underwood objected to the Republican move as mere electioneering, charging that the Republicans had no intention of lowering the tariff. The Dingley Tariff had been undisturbed in the Roosevelt years, and Underwood later remarked that the only tariff reform Roosevelt ever recommended was to remove the levy on coal, which was already on the free list—an exaggeration since there had been a small duty on coal.[8] Taft, however, had committed himself to lower the tariff and thereby equalize the costs of production while allowing the American producer a reasonable profit. Taft's theory of equalizing production costs between domes-

6. J. H. Woodward to Underwood, April 2, 1909, in Underwood Papers, Alabama Archives; Birmingham *News*, May 8, 1909.
7. Champ Clark to Underwood, June 24, 1908, in Underwood Papers, Alabama Archives; Birmingham *News*, March 22, 1909.
8. *Congressional Record*, 60th Cong., 1st Sess., 6430–31; Hartford (Conn.) *Daily Times*, October 15, 1912.

tic and foreign production and Underwood's view of "a tariff for revenue only" differed largely in semantics. Underwood believed that customs should furnish most of the money for government operation, and Taft also emphasized the role of the tariff as a revenue producer. Tariff reduction was implied by both theories as the rates of the Dingley Tariff were prohibitive on many items. Taft's theory of equalizing production costs through the tariff made necessary a study of costs by the Ways and Means Committee. Committee Chairman Sereno E. Payne, florid faced and portly, set vigorously about the task of holding a broad range of tariff hearings that extended through the Christmas holidays prior to Taft's inauguration.

The iron and steel schedule was of particular interest since American mills had adopted the new and vastly more efficient open hearth process that brought a rosy blush of prosperity to the industry. The committee questioned Charles E. Schwab, a former president of United States Steel Corporation, and the corporation's chairman of the board, Judge Elbert Gary. Underwood attempted to demonstrate, with cost data furnished by Mr. Woodward, that pig iron could be produced in Birmingham cheaper than anywhere else in the world. Both Schwab and Gary opposed the rate reductions in the iron and steel schedule, but Schwab admitted under Underwood's probing questioning that a moderate reduction would not damage the industry.[9]

Birmingham industrial leaders recoiled at Underwood's hostile questioning of steel industry executives and his assertion that Birmingham was the world's lowest cost producer of pig iron. W. P. G. Harding, president of Birmingham's First National Bank, and Guy R. Johnson, manager of the Tennessee Coal and Iron Company, the Birmingham branch of United States Steel, strongly objected to Underwood's attitude toward the high tariff on steel. Johnson denied that Birmingham was the cheapest producer of pig iron, claiming that several districts in Germany had lower costs. Half of Birmingham's pig iron was used locally (most was made into cast

9. Birmingham *News*, December 16, 1908.

iron pipe), Johnson admitted, but he noted that the freight charge on Birmingham pig iron shipped to the seaboard equaled the amount of the tariff and thus destroyed any advantage. Thus goaded, the Birmingham Commercial Club resolved to oppose more than a 25 percent reduction in the tariff on pig iron, coal, and lumber.

The Birmingham Commercial Club's action nettled Underwood. He emphasized the necessity for raising revenue through the tariff to counteract the government's large deficit. Incidental protection would result, he admitted, but he asserted that the protective duties on pig iron must be lowered in order to encourage imports and generate revenue. He assured his Birmingham critics that the Ways and Means Committee had no desire to injure the business interests of the country. He again used the cost figures furnished by his father-in-law to demonstrate that Birmingham pig iron could be laid down in New York for less than $15 a ton—a figure comparable to the lowest production cost of foreign pig iron. He added: "Of course in the southern and western markets there would be no chance for foreign competition whatever, as the freight rates entirely exclude the foreign iron from these markets under any circumstances." He said that he had invited representatives of the Birmingham industry to appear before the Ways and Means Committee, but none had done so. Although the hearings had concluded, he offered to try to get the hearings reopened, concluding that he saw no advantage in disguising the fact that Birmingham could make the cheapest pig iron in America (a regression from his earlier statement). Mr. Woodward accepted Underwood's assurances, saying that his son-in-law's views were not dangerous or unreasonable but noted, however, his agreement with United States Steel officials who said that tariff reductions would hurt independent producers (like Woodward) more than United States Steel.[10] Underwood's vigorous defense quieted his Birmingham critics, who were convinced of the futility of efforts to move him toward

10. Birmingham *Age-Herald*, January 9, 13, 1909; J. H. Woodward to Underwood, April 5, 1909, in Woodward Papers.

protectionism. Lumber interests, however, continued to insist upon protection. Underwood agreed that a tariff on lumber was "a correct economic principle" but stated that since his colleagues had made free lumber a party question, he felt bound to support them. The South was, he agreed, discriminated against in the proposed Payne bill, but the solution lay in a reduction to revenue levels of the tariff on goods purchased by the South rather than an increased duty on southern products. [11]

True to his word, President Taft called Congress into special session beginning March 15, 1909, to consider tariff revision. The Payne bill, reported almost immediately from the Ways and Means Committee and accepted by the House with minor amendments, provided an overall moderate tariff reduction, with sharp reductions in the iron and steel schedules. The rate on pig iron was slashed almost in half, from $4.00 to $2.50 a ton. Coal (with certain limitations) and iron ore, raw materials produced in the Birmingham area, were placed on the free list. The tariff on lumber, another Birmingham district product, was cut in half, from $2.00 to $1.00 a thousand board feet—the Republicans having resisted a Democratic move to add lumber to the free list. The duty on lemons was raised by 25 percent as a sop to California lemon growers who wanted to stop the flow of Italian lemons into New York. Underwood attacked this increase, saying that California growers had adequate protection to enable them to market lemons over two thirds of the country under the Dingley act, and that the new higher rate would effectively prohibit the importation of Italian lemons into the Atlantic seaboard.

Underwood advocated the financing of the government by revenue tariffs on those goods used largely by the rich, including lumber, glass, and structural materials in this category. Consumer goods such as coffee and tea, which bore levies in the Payne bill, should be taxed only as a last resort. He had drawn an almost metaphysical distinction between items that should bear a revenue tariff and those that should not.

11. Underwood to T. H. Johnston, *ca.* January, 1909, Underwood to J. H. Eddy, April 27, 1909, both in Underwood Papers, Alabama Archives.

Underwood's speech against the Payne bill emphasized that the tariff must produce revenue adequate to cover the government's estimated deficit of from $100 million to $150 million. Defending himself from charges that he was a free trader or a protectionist, he declared that he favored a "competitive tariff" that would allow enough foreign goods to flow in to create a reasonable amount of competition for domestic manufacturers. He defined a "competitive tariff" as one that would allow about 10 percent imports and would thereby produce the revenue needed by government. Otherwise, he said, "hot house" industries were created that would perish in times of business distress. The Dingley Tariff, he noted, afforded protection for most manufactures in excess of the entire labor cost factor, and he cited Professor Frank W. Taussig's testimony that American industries no longer needed protection because of their natural advantages. In 1905 only 5 percent of United States consumption of goods listed in the Dingley Tariff was admitted from abroad, he said, and the Republican party had presented a tariff designed to protect profits of manufacturers. The iron and steel schedule, he charged, had been scaled down much as a "blind man with an ax would have done it," although he admitted that the reduction of the tariff on pig iron from $4.00 to $2.50 a ton placed the iron duty on a good revenue basis. He believed that the halving of the tariff on galvanized wire and steel rails left those rates too high in relation to the low rates on the raw materials involved. In effect, he said, the new reduced rates on some iron and steel products would be equally as protective as the old Dingley rates.[12]

The Payne bill, satisfactory to many Democrats, was drastically altered by the highly protectionist Senate. A wave of logrolling led Senator Nelson Aldrich, the bill's sponsor, to concede increases averaging 40 percent in *ad valorem* rates above those of the Payne bill. At President Taft's insistence, a corporation tax of 2 percent (later reduced to 1 percent) was added. The corporation tax was the Republican answer to Democratic demands for an income tax,

12. *Congressional Record*, 61st Cong., 1st Sess., 268–80.

and, though a part of its purpose was to replace the revenue lost by the extended free list (now somewhat shortened with the Senate's elimination of iron ore and other items), it was also intended to publicize corporate profits.

The Payne-Aldrich bill was returned to the House and the Republicans immediately moved to send it to conference, allowing no opportunity for amendment. Underwood bitterly complained at this high-handed procedure, but the strength of the Republicans was dramatically shown when the bill was sent to conference by a vote of 195 to 183, with only 19 Republicans opposing.

President Taft was shocked at the high duty level of the Payne-Aldrich bill as it went to conference. He interceded with the conferees, who included Underwood, so that the revised tariff was lower than the Senate version, but the bill's final rates were nevertheless much closer to the high Senate rates than to the Payne bill. In the final debate preceding passage of the Payne-Aldrich Tariff, Underwood angrily set the tone for the coming congressional campaign. The Payne-Aldrich bill represented, he said, an increase in the tariff level of at least 2 percent—80 percent of its rates were the same as those of the Dingley act and many were higher. The reductions on raw materials would benefit the manufacturers, and, he insisted, the corporation tax was the forerunner of federal control of corporations and would burden the small investor rather than the large one. He concluded that the Republicans had demonstrated the inability of their party to revise the tariff downward "in the interest of the people." The Democrats, he warned, were ready to go to the country on the issue.[13]

Taft's victory in the Payne-Aldrich fight was bought at the price of a party split. The president aggravated Insurgent feelings by praising Senator Aldrich and by gauchely saying at Winona, Minnesota, that the Payne-Aldrich Tariff was "the best bill that the Republican party ever passed."[14] Yet the split between Taft and the Insurgents did not appear irreparable until the eruption of the Bal-

---

13. *Ibid.*, 4721–25, 5091; New York *Times*, August 1, 1909, Sec. 2, p. 1.
14. Quoted in Henry F. Pringle, *The Life and Times of William Howard Taft* (2 vols.; New York: Farrar and Rinehart), I, 454.

linger-Pinchot affair in which the attack upon Cannon's rules was renewed. In September, 1909, Chief Forester Gifford Pinchot charged Richard A. Ballinger, secretary of the interior, with a lack of concern for conservation and even corruption in the granting of government mineral lands in Alaska. These charges were widely publicized in the progressive press, and the administration, smarting under criticism, sponsored legislation for the creation of a joint congressional committee to investigate. Under House rules Speaker Cannon, generally considered an enemy of conservation, would appoint the House's representatives on the committee.

The Ballinger investigation furnished Underwood with the vehicle for a renewed attack on Cannonism. Much of the anger of the Insurgent wing of the Republican party had been directed at Cannon's autocratic rules, and in the last days of the Roosevelt administration Cannon reluctantly sponsored a new rule, "Calendar Wednesday," in which each standing committee had one day a week to call up its reported bills without getting a "green light" from the Rules Committee. Rules dissatisfaction was still rife, however, and revolt by a coalition of Democrats and Insurgents appeared imminent as the special session opened. Cannon made a few changes in the rules and strengthened Calendar Wednesday. He bought off some Democrats by promising support of a higher petroleum duty in order to avoid the more drastic revision of the rules planned by Democratic leader Clark. Underwood, together with most House Democrats, opposed Calendar Wednesday since they hoped for more extensive reforms.[15]

Underwood asserted his belief in giving the majority party effective legislative control, but he charged that the Republicans had given the Speaker complete control of the House. Under Cannon's rules even two-thirds of the House were unable to call up a bill, Underwood said, and "no one can say what business we will transact tomorrow morning." He suggested creation of an elective fifteen-man Rules Committee with ten from the majority party. The

15. Richard Lowitt, *George W. Norris: The Making of a Progressive, 1861–1912* (Syracuse, N.Y.: Syracuse University Press, 1963), 147–49; *Congressional Record*, 61st Cong., 2nd Sess., 5751.

Speaker would thus be dissociated from party leadership and become an impartial arbiter. The mantle of House leadership would
then fall upon the chairman of the Rules Committee, thereby di-
vorcing the Speaker from a partisan role. Underwood's plan was
similar to the one Clark had proposed earlier.[16]

Passage of a complete set of new rules was impossible, but Underwood, acting as minority leader in the absence of Champ Clark,
suggested to Insurgent leader George W. Norris that the Ballinger
affair offered an opportunity for a blow against Cannonism. The
two men formulated a plan, and when the resolution to establish
an investigatory committee reached the floor, Underwood explained the importance of the charges against Ballinger without
committing himself to their validity. The House adopted Norris'
amendment to the rules requiring House election of the members
of the Ballinger committee by a vote of 149 to 146. The Democratic-Insurgent triumph against the Speaker was the first important step in the destruction of Cannonism.[17]

The rules fight was renewed on March 16, 1910, a Calendar
Wednesday. Republican Representative Edgar D. Crumpacker
presented a minor amendment to the Census Act as business privileged under the Constitution, and, upon objection from the floor,
Cannon upheld Crumpacker. Underwood appealed the ruling of
the chair saying that if the Speaker could designate privileged business for Calendar Wednesday, Calendar Wednesday would be ineffective; the vote of 163 to 112 against sustaining Cannon demonstrated the strength of the Democratic-Insurgent coalition. The
following day, March 17, Crumpacker again offered his census bill,
which Underwood admitted was now in order, since the precedents for privileged business Cannon had cited on Calendar
Wednesday were quite proper on this regular day. Underwood
maintained, however, that the House was free at any time to refuse
to consider a bill by a majority vote.

16. *Congressional Record*, 60th Cong., 2nd Sess., 816.
17. Birmingham *Ledger*, January 8, 1910; Champ Clark, *My Quarter Century of American Politics* (2 vols.; New York: Harper and Brothers, 1920), II, 273, 281; *Congressional
Record*, 61st Cong., 2nd Sess., 401–405.

The House sustained Cannon's claim of constitutional privilege for Crumpacker's resolution, but the Speaker had fallen into a trap. The Constitution authorizes the House to make its own rules, and though Cannon's supporters maintained the provision was merely permissive in saying that the House "may" make its own rules, the Insurgents argued that the House rules were constitutionally privileged and thus always subject to revision. Norris, sensing a gaping opening in Cannon's position, adroitly and unexpectedly offered a resolution for the election of a Rules Committee of fifteen by the House as a matter of constitutional privilege. Underwood supported Norris, saying that the House could make anything a matter of privilege by a majority vote, as Speaker Cannon had often maintained. Underwood declared that his fight was not against Cannon, but against the system.

Cannon recognized that if he ruled against Norris, the Insurgent-Democratic coalition had the votes to win an appeal from the chair. Caught badly off balance, he declined to rule, dispatched his lieutenants for help, instituted a filibuster, and sent his regulars out of the hall to break the quorum at about two-thirty on the morning of March 18. Underwood secured passage of a resolution directing the sergeant at arms to arrest and bring in the absent members. A quorum did not at first appear, and Underwood charged that the Speaker and the sergeant at arms were not attempting to secure one. A quorum, however, was attained later in the morning. The decisive contest occurred on March 19 following a recess, during the longest continuous session in House history. After Cannon ruled that the Norris resolution was not privileged, the Democrats and Insurgents overruled the decision by a vote of 182 to 164. Norris presented his resolution, amended in accordance with Underwood's and Clark's suggestions, now providing for a Rules Committee of fifteen members elected by the House, nine from the majority and six from the minority, the Speaker not to be a member. The resolution passed. Having broken Cannon's power, the Democrats prevailed on him to retain the speakership. Underwood was actually a close friend of Cannon's; they had once had adjoining apartments, and they often "swapped tobacco across the lines" as Cannon called the practice of fraternizing with the opposition. Cannon wanly retained the speakership to the end of the session.[18]

Norris' new rules made little immediate difference, but they required caucus action to confirm committee assignments. The Democratic caucus of March 25 confirmed Clark with 125 votes as ranking Democrat on the Rules Committee and Underwood as second ranking member with 102 votes. James A. Tawney, previous chairman of the Rules Committee, grumbled that ranking Underwood over John J. Fitzgerald was a violation of the House's seniority principle.[19] There was no serious effort to remove Underwood from the second spot, however, and he now stood ready to assume the majority leader's post in the event of a Democratic victory, which would make Clark Speaker.

Having participated in the revolution against Cannonism, Underwood reversed himself. At the end of the third session of the Sixty-first Congress, the Fuller resolution that motions to suspend the rules should have precedence over the Unanimous Consent Calendar, was offered. The Fuller resolution would have expedited bills before the House on the two suspension days each month. Consistency required Underwood to support the resolution as constitutionally privileged. Looking forward, however, to the Democratic assumption of command, Underwood had no desire to restrict his leadership. He recalled that he had never maintained that the Norris resolution was a matter of constitutional privilege but had considered that a majority of the House favored a "revolution" against the Cannon rules. Another revolution was unnecessary, he said, and Cannon's precedents against consideration of the Norris resolution were perfectly valid objections to the Fuller resolution. The new rules, he said, provided additional suspension days—the real aim of the Fuller resolution—and allowing the House to con-

18. *Congressional Record*, 61st Cong., 2nd Sess., 3242–51, 3284, 3293, 3400–3402, 3426–36; Blair Bolles, *Tyrant from Illinois: Uncle Joe Cannon's Experiment with Personal Power* (New York: Norton, 1951), 222–23.
19. Washington (D.C.) *Times*, March 25, 1910.

sider matters without their having come from committee would lead to the "utmost confusion." The House overwhelmingly upheld Cannon's ruling that the Fuller resolution was not privileged.[20]

The new Democratic-Insurgent inspired rules did not solve the problems of dilatory tactics in the House. Toward the end of the Sixty-first Congress, a filibuster launched by James R. Mann threatened to prevent the passage of the remaining nine appropriation bills, including the naval appropriation bill, and thereby require a special session. Speaker Cannon looked on benignly while Mann filibustered against the war claims bill, which was opposed in two distinctly different quarters. The claims bill provided funds to compensate southerners for losses caused by the Union army, and this provision was objectionable to Mann and many northern congressmen. Many other congressmen, however, objected vigorously to a part of the bill allowing payment of spoliation claims to American citizens whose ships had been seized by the French in the Napoleonic wars. Congress had repeatedly failed to approve these spoliation claims, many of whose claimants were insurance companies which had collected high rates to protect against the very disaster that occurred.

John Dalzell, the majority leader, asked Democratic support of a liberalized suspension rule as a means of ending the filibuster. The existing rules provided that the last six days of the session should be suspension days, and Dalzell urged that the suspension rule be moved forward to take effect immediately and cover the last eleven days of the session. Underwood refused to agree to the new rule to allow suspension by a majority vote. However, when the Republicans made a second proposal, to suspend only by a two-thirds vote, he quickly agreed—recognizing that the Democrats would thereby gain a veto over proposed legislation. The war claims bill and the remaining supply bills then passed. Evidently Speaker Cannon had allowed the filibuster, marked by singing as

20. *Congressional Record*, 61st Cong., 3rd Sess., 680; Underwood to Ernest Abbott, January 12, 1911, in Underwood Papers, Alabama Archives; Birmingham *Times*, January 13, 1911.

well as the usual arid discussion, to force Democratic agreement for even stronger rules.[21]

For practical reasons Underwood had cooperated somewhat with the Insurgents in the rules contest, but he had little interest in the conservation movement to which the Insurgents were so devoted. He had been apathetic toward the conservation movement in the Roosevelt era, and he showed no more enthusiasm in Taft's administration. In January, 1909, he secured insertion of an amendment to the bill creating the Sequoia National Forest to assure that no money would be spent for the project. Since the plan was to swap government lands for those containing the giant sequoias, the bill's sponsor accepted the amendment. In May and June, 1910, faced with the congressional election in the fall, Underwood appeared obstruction-minded in opposing a liberal appropriation for the Department of the Interior. He maintained that Secretary of the Interior Ballinger represented westerners who thought that the public domain belonged to them and who favored the reckless sale of western lands. However, with striking inconsistency, he criticized the Department of the Interior for withholding odd lots of Alabama farm lands from sale; he apparently did not understand that the Alabama lands were under the Department of Agriculture rather than the Department of the Interior.[22] Underwood's criticism of Ballinger, who was still under investigation, ran parallel to the secretary's unpopularity in the press. Ballinger was exonerated by the majority of the joint congressional committee, but his public image was so damaged that he resigned in March, 1911.

By 1910 Underwood's interest in federal railroad regulatory legislation had cooled, and this was reflected in his lack of enthusiasm for the Mann-Elkins Act of 1910. The Taft-supported legislation created a commerce court and allowed the ICC to initiate rate changes. Underwood opposed placing the responsibility for erroneous bills of lading on the railroads, although he favored placing telephone and telegraph companies under the ICC, a feature re-

21. *Congressional Record*, 61st Cong., 3rd Sess., 2881–83, 2972–73.
22. *Ibid.*, 60th Cong., 2nd Sess., 1628, 61st Cong., 2nd Sess., 7084, 8684–98.

tained in the final act. He failed to vote on the overall passage of the measure.[23]

Paralleling Underwood's increasing conservatism on railroad reform legislation was the close liaison growing up between him and representatives of the railroads. Underwood had always had associations with railroad officials through his family, and by the time his House career ended, he, on occasion, frankly represented their interests. The L & N Railroad had, in the 1890s, aided Underwood's brother Will, a coal operator, by financing his operations and by extending spur tracks to his coal fields. Oscar's closest friends were railroad attorneys, and he occasionally met with high railroad officials, including James J. Hill of the Great Northern and B. F. Yoakum of the Frisco system. In 1909 an enterprising, if unscrupulous, reporter rifled the files of the Frisco office in Birmingham and publicized information about strategy conferences between Underwood and Frisco officials in opposing the ill-fated Borah national full crew bill. Underwood had cooperated with the railway officials to defeat the measure, favored by the railway brotherhoods and designed to prevent railway accidents. The Birmingham law firm of Ed Campbell and Forney Johnston, Underwood's close personal and political friends, represented the Frisco Railroad, and in 1912 Underwood brooked powerful opposition to oppose plans of the Rock Island Railway to build a bridge across the Mississippi at Memphis that would render the antiquated Frisco bridge obsolete. The Rock Island proposal had broad support in Memphis, and though Underwood offered amendments ostensibly to prevent a monopoly over that important gateway to Birmingham, he actually intended to delay or prevent passage of the bill. He failed completely, and Congress authorized the new structure.[24]

23. H. W. Coffin to Underwood, August 30, 1910, in Underwood Papers, Alabama Archives; Congressional Record, 61st Cong., 2nd Sess., 5534.

24. Birmingham Age-Herald, November 11, 1907; W. T. Underwood to Underwood, January 19, 1911, in Underwood Papers, Alabama Archives; Birmingham News, November 22, 1911; A. D. Lightner to Underwood, December 4, 1909, in Underwood Papers, Alabama Archives; Memphis Commercial-Appeal, July 26, 30, August 6, 17, 18, 1912; Congressional Record, 62nd Cong., 2nd Sess., 11219–24.

In the nation at large President Taft faced a troubled summer. Forty incumbent regular Republican congressmen had been defeated in primaries, most of them by Insurgents. The Democrats, with Taft's Payne-Aldrich fiasco on their minds, could look sanguinely to the fall campaign.

As the fall elections of 1910 approached, Underwood, facing no opposition in his district, campaigned for Democratic congressional candidates throughout the Midwest, attacking the Payne-Aldrich Tariff and Republican extravagance. If the Democrats would stand squarely for tariff revision, he said, they would elect the president in 1912. The Democratic victory exceeded Underwood's expectations. Democrats won control of the House, and Underwood noted with pleasure the election of Woodrow Wilson as governor of New Jersey. Looking forward, however, he praised the just reelected conservative Governor Judson Harmon of Ohio and endorsed him for the 1912 Democratic presidential nomination, saying, "Mr. Wilson and I are graduates of the same college and I would say aught against him, but the people have been looking towards Mr. Harmon, know him, have the greatest confidence in his ability and have come to the conclusion that he can lead the party to success in 1912."[25] Underwood had no opposition in the general election, receiving 10,114 votes.[26]

The congressional election of 1910 gave the Democrats control of the House of Representatives for the first time in sixteen years, and although the Republicans retained a nominal majority in the Senate, eight or nine Insurgent senators held the balance of power between the almost evenly divided regular Republican and Democratic forces. Following his loss of control of Congress, President Taft's message to the "lame duck" session which assembled in early December, 1910, was conciliatory. The president wanted to go slowly in business legislation but favored passage of Canadian reciprocity, a schedule-by-schedule revision of the tariff, the creation

25. Birmingham *News*, November 9, 1910.
26. Owen, *Alabama Official and Statistical Register, 1911*, p. 272.

of a tariff board, and rigid economy. Although criticizing the president's continuing defense of the Payne-Aldrich Tariff, Underwood generally approved of the speech—especially the advocacy of rigid economy. He seized upon Taft's suggested general tariff revision and talked of Democratic adoption of the schedule-by-schedule approach, not realizing that the president would soon jettison this idea to pave the way for the passage of Canadian reciprocity. Taft's program was soon limited to the Canadian reciprocity bill and several minor measures of "tidying up" progressive legislation. Well before the passage of the Payne-Aldrich Tariff, a tariff war between the United States and Canada had seemed imminent, and the Payne-Aldrich measure exacerbated the problem. Canadian reciprocity was the logical and generally popular solution, but the Insurgents, who objected to the Payne-Aldrich Tariff, feared an influx of Canadian farm goods, and on this issue they were not "progressive."[27]

The new Norris rules proved more valuable to Taft than to the Democrats as the president pushed his reform program. Underwood complained, while opposing the administration's postal savings bank bill, that the Democrats had no opportunity to amend the bill. He told a farm lobbyist that he preferred a plan whereby postal savings would be retained as government guaranteed deposits in local banks. The dangers of removing the deposits from the local area and making them available for speculation would thus be obviated, he argued. Nevertheless, the measure became law. Canadian reciprocity with a tariff board attached passed with strong Democratic support, and Underwood reversed his earlier opposition to the tariff board by supporting the Taft-sponsored measure. The proposal for the creation of a permanent tariff board failed when the House and the Senate were unable to iron out the differences between their bills in conference. President Taft then asked for an appropriation to allow the continuation of the presidential

27. George E. Mowry, *The Era of Theodore Roosevelt, 1900–1912* (New York: Harper, 1958), 282–86; unidentified clipping, *ca.* December 7, 1910, Underwood Scrapbook, I, 12, in Underwood Papers, Alabama Archives.

tariff board to which he had appointed two Democrats. Underwood unsuccessfully opposed the appropriation, saying that Congress should control the writing of revenue bills and the instru-
mentality by which the bills were written.[28]

The Senate failed to approve the Canadian reciprocity agreement, and the president was convinced of the necessity for calling
a special session of the newly elected Sixty-second Congress. Republican leaders could not believe that Taft would commit the folly
of assembling the new Democratic Congress nine months before it
was necessary to meet the body dedicated to his defeat in 1912.
Ignoring advice and facing the adjournment of the "lame duck"
Congress on March 4, 1911, Taft was eager to call the special session as soon as possible after that date. The president intended to
confine the session to Canadian reciprocity and to avoid a Democratic effort at general tariff revision. On the other hand, Underwood and the other Democrats on the Ways and Means Committee
were reviewing the Payne-Aldrich hearings in preparation for general tariff revision. Sixty days between sessions, Underwood said,
would be adequate time for him and his Democratic colleagues on
the Ways and Means Committee to frame a new tariff upon which
the Democratic party could march to victory in 1912.[29]

Underwood publicly pledged that the Democrats would not take
partisan advantage of the special session, though it was not clear to
all that this pledge was limited to cooperation in passage of the
Canadian reciprocity bill. Shoving aside talk of the need for banking reform, Underwood stated that he had not decided what banking reforms were necessary and that the real problem was the failure to reform the tariff. The lack of tariff reform together with the
fight for better government, he felt, were at the bottom of "our
difficulties" and the causes for the growth of insurgency. Indeed,
the fight to reform the mechanics of government was mainly a

28. Underwood to C. S. Barrett, February 26, 1910, in Underwood Papers, Alabama
Archives; *Congressional Record*, 61st Cong., 3rd Sess., 3333–34; Pringle, *Life and Times of
William Howard Taft*, II, 600; Washington (D.C.) *Times*, May 18, 1910.
29. Donald F. Anderson, *William Howard Taft: A Conservative's Conception of the
Presidency* (Ithaca, N.Y.: Cornell University Press, 1973), 139; New York *American*, Feb-
ruary 8, 1911.

"state fight"; the tariff problem was the question over which the Democrats should contest with the Republicans.[30]

Just prior to calling the special session, President Taft consulted Champ Clark, slated to be Speaker of the House, and Underwood, who would be the new chairman of the Ways and Means Committee. Taft knew that he could depend on Democratic support of Canadian reciprocity; he asked Clark and Underwood to confine themselves to passage of this bill. The Democratic leaders declined to give such assurances and asserted that they would attempt comprehensive tariff revision. Although the president refused to delay the session until early May, as Underwood preferred, he agreed to April 4 rather than a mid-March date in deference to Clark's and Underwood's plea that the Democrats needed time to organize.

The selection of Clark as Speaker and Underwood as chairman of the Ways and Means Committee was confirmed by the Democratic caucus of January 19, 1911. Even before the Norris rules increased the powers of the Ways and Means Committee chairman, it was a vastly important post, which Polk, Fillmore, and McKinley had each occupied before being elevated to the presidency. The Ways and Means Committee, under the newly adopted system, served as the committee on committees with its appointments to be approved by the Democratic caucus. Underwood enthusiastically reorganized the House under Democratic control. A regional distribution of committee posts with each member of the Ways and Means Committee limited to one other unimportant committee was agreed upon. The reduction of the Speaker's power in 1910 and the phlegmatic temperament of Clark, who was twelve years Underwood's senior, dictated that although Clark would be Speaker, Underwood would have the real power. A newspaper reporter asked Underwood if his position would not be more important than that of the Speaker. Underwood replied candidly: "It is." Meanwhile Speaker Clark indicated that, unlike previous Speak-

30. New York *World*, February 21, 1911; Carl Hovey, "Underwood of Alabama," *Metropolitan Magazine* (March, 1912), in Underwood Scrapbook, I, 188, Underwood Papers, Alabama Archives.

ers, he intended to play only a subordinate role in committee assignments.[31]

The press generally applauded Underwood's selection as chairman of the Ways and Means Committee and as majority leader of the House Democrats. William S. Couch, in an interview with Underwood in the New York *World*, cited Underwood's patience and diplomacy in dealing with importunate young congressmen seeking committee assignments. Charles Willis Thompson of the New York *Times* emphasized his skill as a parliamentarian and quoted Senator Joseph W. Bailey's characterization of Underwood. Bailey, a classmate of Underwood at the University of Virginia and a Texan, described Underwood as "the only man in either House of Congress who could be locked up in a hermetically sealed room for a week and emerge from it with a perfectly good tariff bill."[32] Underwood fully recognized the hyperbole in Bailey's statement, but the clever characterization followed him throughout his career.

The substantial House Democratic majority of sixty-seven in the Sixty-second Congress presented Underwood with a difficult organization problem. He chose his committees with the aid of a large map on the wall of his office, showing the sectional considerations involved, but in most cases he selected committee chairmen on the basis of seniority. The more important committees were increased from twenty to twenty-one in order to accommodate more claimants. Underwood chose the conservative Tammanyite John J. Fitzgerald, his closest rival as a parliamentary expert, as chairman of the Appropriations Committee in preference to Albert S. Burleson of Texas who had equal seniority. A few congressmen grumbled, but the committee assignments were generally well accepted and the Underwood slate was approved in the Democratic caucus on April 1. At the same meeting House Democrats planned their legislative program: direct election of senators, the Canadian

31. Oscar W. Underwood, *Drifting Sands of Party Politics* (New York: Century Company, 1928), 166–67; Clark, *My Quarter Century of American Politics*, II, 7; Cincinnati *Inquirer*, December 21, 1910; unidentified clipping in Underwood Scrapbook, I, 18, Underwood Papers, Alabama Archives; Birmingham *News*, March 7, 1911.

32. New York *World*, March 26, 1911; New York *Times*, February 26, 1911, Sec. 5, p. 2.

reciprocity agreement, and the admission of Arizona and New Mexico to statehood. Another caucus on April 12 approved the farmers' free list and the reduction of the tariff on wool and cotton.

Underwood offered the rules for the new Congress as a package on April 5, 1911, refusing to allow amendments but noting that the Republicans might offer a new set. Such a course would have been unsuccessful, and Republican leader James R. Mann remarked acidly that the rules were substantially those of the Republican House against which the Democrats had crusaded. Mann complained that Underwood had allowed Republicans only one-third membership on the committees and that this formula had been unfairly applied. Underwood defended the committee allocation as substantially the same proportion as when the Republicans dominated the previous Congress. He effectively noted that never before had the minority been allowed to select every minority member of a committee.[33]

Some of the grumbling came from the Insurgents who resented being excluded from important committee assignments. George Norris, leader of the Insurgents, criticized Underwood's appointment of regular Republican Philip Campbell to the Rules Committee rather than Victor Murdock, an Insurgent. Underwood defended the Campbell appointment, for the Republicans had been allowed to make their own selections. The government was run by parties, he said, and he had repeatedly urged the Insurgents to come over to the Democratic side. Campbell's appointment was confirmed by a vote of 167 to 107, with Murdock receiving support from Insurgents and defecting Democrats. There was little the Republicans could do to stop the Democratic juggernaut. Former Speaker Cannon paid great tribute to Underwood in the debate, acknowledging the increasing talk of Underwood as a presidential candidate, saying that he had "grown more in public sentiment recently than any other man."[34]

33. "Minutes of Democratic Caucus, April 1, 1911" (Typescript in Claude Kitchin Papers, University of North Carolina), 7–15; New York *Times*, April 12, 1911, p. 2; *Congressional Record*, 62nd Cong., 1st Sess., 75–76, 163.

34. *Congressional Record*, 62nd Cong., 2nd Sess., 856, 863–65.

William Jennings Bryan, that bellwether of the Democratic party, strutted across the House floor, taking advantage of having been a member many years before. Years later Underwood recalled his feeling of jealousy as Bryan waved and bowed to the galleries, acknowledging applause that exceeded that for the new Speaker and the new majority leader. Bryan attempted to control the organization of the new House through his Kentucky friend, Congressman Ollie James, who proposed in the Ways and Means Committee that Bryan sit in on their meetings. Underwood successfully opposed James's resolution on the basis that its passage would make it appear that Bryan was in control.[35]

The new Democratic House operated much as the Republican House had under Cannon, but there were a few differences. Under Cannon the Speaker had been supreme; in the Democratic House, Underwood had control as chairman of the Ways and Means Committee and as majority leader. Under Cannon the caucus had rarely been used as an engine of party control; under Underwood the caucus was dominant. Standing committees were formerly appointed by Cannon; in the new order they were appointed by the Ways and Means Committee. The floor leader had been converted from a figurehead to the dominant parliamentary leader. The Rules Committee was still powerful, but although Underwood was no longer a member, it was now dominated by him, since he had appointed the members. On the Republican side the aging John Dalzell was replaced as minority leader by James R. Mann of Illinois, a younger and more aggressive leader. Congressman Mann charged that Cannonism had been replaced by "Underwoodism" and that "the gentleman from Alabama wears his crown and scepter like one to the manner born." Underwood, however, maintained that the difference between his rule and that of Cannon was the same difference as in trial by jury and trial by judge, since he depended upon the party caucus for his power.[36]

35. New York *Tribune*, January 13, 1924; Oscar King Davis, "Where Underwood Stands," *Outlook*, XCIX (September 23, 1911), 198–99.

36. Memphis *Commercial-Appeal*, February 4, 1912; William L. Stoddard, "Underwoodism," *Everybody's*, XXVIII (June, 1913), 802–803. The filibusters of Republican leader

The key to Underwood's aggressive House leadership was rigid
control of legislation by the Ways and Means Committee, based
upon the authority of the Democratic caucus. According to an Un-
derwood-sponsored caucus rule, no committee controlled by the
Democrats could report legislation to the floor without the approval of the caucus. Underwood's control was further enhanced
by another caucus rule which pledged the support of all Democrats
to Ways and Means Committee bills. Within the caucus congressmen were encouraged to talk. "Let 'em have it out here," Underwood would say, and then there will be "no kick afterward." Naturally, there was some criticism of such rigid party regimentation,
and Underwood replied to his critics in the *National Monthly*, the
Democratic party's organ. Praising party organization "as a necessary evolution of free government," he explained that parties could
not exist merely on spoils and that great principles had created
party organizations rather than the reverse. Reflecting on the
Democrats' long history of lack of organization in Congress, Underwood bragged that the Democratic organization in the House
at the time was "as perfect an organization of the Democratic members as was ever witnessed in the history of our Congress." Defending the caucus, Underwood said that it was not undemocratic since
it required a two-thirds vote to make its decisions binding. Although he did not say so, the two-thirds requirement made it possible for the southern Democrats to block caucus action.[37]

Underwood's delicate position as leader of the House depended
not only upon his continuing good relations with Speaker Clark,
with whom he never quarreled, but also upon the good will of
committee chairmen. Especially important was the chairman of the
Rules Committee, Robert L. Henry of Texas. Although Henry was

Mann led Underwood to support measures to restrict the use of the Discharge Calendar,
one of the reforms instituted by the Insurgents against Cannonism. *Congressional Record*,
62nd Cong., 2nd Sess., 1689–90. The Democrats were still concerned over the dangers to
majority party rule in the Discharge Calendar, and, in the special session of 1913, they
suspended it on June 3 for the remainder of the session. Paul D. Hasbrouck, *Party Government in the House of Representatives* (New York: Macmillan, 1927), 147.

37. Davis, "Where Underwood Stands," 199; Oscar W. Underwood, "Party Organization," *National Monthly*, XXXIV (August, 1911), 95.

sometimes styled an agrarian radical, as Underwood was not, he cooperated with Underwood in bringing the desired legislation to the floor.

As floor leader Underwood was supreme. Champ Clark was given the shadow of power, but Underwood had its substance. He could ask and obtain recognition at any time to make motions to restrict debate or preclude amendments or both. A contemporary observer remarked that clothed "with this perpetual privilege of recognition and backed by his caucus," he had it in his power "to make a Punch and Judy show of the House at any time."[38]

Underwood's effective tactics confounded the Republicans. They usually accepted his invitation to criticize the majority's bills and engage in full and free discussion. Ordinarily, however, they were only talking to themselves and their constituents, as they lacked the votes to defeat the Democratic juggernaut. James R. Mann, the new Republican leader, was a bold, shrewd, resourceful parliamentarian, and a master of dilatory tactics. A favorite Mann device was to clog the Discharge Calendar so that Democratic bills would reach the floor before the Democrats were prepared. Underwood countered by simply changing the rules, and in February, 1912, a new Democratic rule relegated the Discharge Calendar to a third order of precedence behind suspension of the rules and the Unanimous Consent Calendar.[39] Underwood's control was as tight as Cannon's had been.

Once organized, the House quickly proceeded to consider the Canadian reciprocity agreement. During the House debate Champ Clark urged Canadian reciprocity as a step toward United States' absorption of Canada, and the Canadian press recoiled with criticism. Underwood said of Clark's blunder: "I suppose Mr. Clark forgot, for a moment, that he had lost the minority leader's freedom of speech, and that, as the coming Speaker, his words have international importance."[40] Underwood concluded the Demo-

38. Lynn Haines, *Law Making in America: The Story of the 1911–12 Session of the Sixty-second Congress* (Bethesda, Md.: L. Haines, 1912), 15–16.
39. James S. Fleming, "Re-establishing Leadership in the House of Representatives: The Case of Oscar W. Underwood," *Mid-America*, LIV (October, 1972), 246.
40. New York *World*, March 26, 1911.

cratic argument for the Canadian reciprocity agreement, arguing
that it would stimulate prosperity as the development of the West
had done in the previous century. Farmers would not be damaged
by the agreement, he said, and he tagged the lumber interests as
the real opponents of the treaty. He criticized the Republican Progressives for opposing the reciprocity agreement and declared that
the Republicans themselves had made the agreement necessary
because of the "gold brick" they had given Taft in the Payne-Aldrich Tariff. Opponents of Canadian reciprocity admitted that Underwood had been "exceedingly generous and fair" in allowing
amendments, but they were unable to alter the bill. Underwood
said that Taft had threatened a veto if the agreement were
amended. The Canadian reciprocity agreement passed the House
on April 21, 1911, by a vote of 265 to 89, with only ten Democrats
voting against it.[41]

Having helped to secure passage of the reciprocity bill, Underwood announced that the House would revise the tariff in "the only
proper manner"—that is, schedule by schedule. Actually, schedule-by-schedule tariff revision was in bad repute, the results having been derisively termed "pop gun" tariffs when attempted with
little success by the Democrats in the 1890s. Such derision,
Champ Clark observed, could not be directed at so serious a tariff
expert as Underwood. Furthermore, the piecemeal approach was
the only method open to the Democrats, since general tariff revision would require more time for preparation than was possible.[42]

First to be considered was the politically ingenious farmers' free
list bill which removed the tariff on agricultural implements, sewing machines, cotton gins, cotton bagging and ties, leather, fencing
wire, lumber, meat, flour, and salt. Wire and cotton gins were important Birmingham products, and the city's industrialists protested that Underwood was sacrificing his district's welfare for that
of his party. United States Steel Corporation ominously suspended
work on a new, largely complete barbed wire plant at Corey (now

41. *Congressional Record*, 62nd Cong., 1st Sess., 533–59; New York *Times*, April 22,
1911, p. 1; Birmingham *Age-Herald*, April 21, 1911.
42. Clark, *My Quarter Century of American Politics*, I, 326.

Fairfield), near Birmingham. Steel company officials attributed the suspension to uncertain conditions within the industry, and indeed, business was slow among the steel fabricators. Underwood, however, denounced the steel company for attempting to intimidate him. He defended the placing of barbed wire on the free list, a popular stand generally regarded as defiance of the steel trust. William Jennings Bryan congratulated Underwood and urged retaliation against the steel trust, concluding, "You are doing a great work."[43]

Underwood assured his constituents that Birmingham's position as a low cost producer would obviate harmful effects of the proposed tariff reduction. Wire and other Birmingham iron products competed effectively in foreign markets. There was no need for protection on these, and the reduction of tariffs on consumer goods would benefit Birmingham consumers. Placing cotton bagging and ties on the free list would benefit Alabama farmers without damaging any Birmingham industry. While Underwood defended his position, his friend Ed Campbell pressured the *Age-Herald*, which had criticized the free list bill at the behest of United States Steel, to reverse its policy. Acceding to the counterpressure, the *Age-Herald* withdrew its criticism and assured its readers that United States Steel had promised to resume construction on the wire plant. Judge Elbert Gary, chairman of the board of United States Steel, disclaimed any intention of influencing the legislation, although he noted that some of the work contemplated by the corporation would not be undertaken at present. He praised Underwood as a man of great ability.[44] The attack upon United States Steel had brought results and demonstrated Underwood's increasing political power.

In Congress, Underwood denied that the free list bill was intended to compensate farmers for Canadian reciprocity. The bill's objectives were, he said, to recognize agriculture as a basic industry, to remove farm implements from the protected list, and to

43. Birmingham *News*, April 21, 25, 1911; telegram from William Jennings Bryan to Ollie James, April 23, 1911, in Odd Lot, Underwood Papers, Alabama Archives.

44. Birmingham *News*, April 25, 1911; Edward K. Campbell to Underwood, April 27, 1911, in Underwood Papers, Alabama Archives; Birmingham *Age-Herald*, April 27, 1911.

reduce the cost of living. The revenue loss from the free list bill and the Canadian reciprocity bills would be small, he said, and some revenue might be recouped by reducing the prohibitive rates on the cotton and wool schedules. The farmers' free list passed without amendment on May 8 by a vote of 236 to 109, with the Democrats and twenty-three Republicans voting for the measure.[45]

Bryan again attempted to influence the House Democrats when the Ways and Means Committee considered the wool bill. The committee split into two factions: Bryan's followers favored free raw wool, and Underwood's followers favored a 20 percent tariff on raw wool as a revenue measure. Bryan charged that a 20 percent tariff on raw wool was protective and that rates on finished woolens in the Underwood bill were hardly lower than those of the Wilson bill of 1894. He further taunted Underwood by asking when the new iron and steel schedule might be expected. Branding Bryan's charges "unjust and unfair," Underwood recalled that Bryan, as a member of the House, had voted for the Wilson bill of 1894 whose rates on manufactured woolens approximated those of the Underwood bill. The duty on raw wool was unanimously endorsed by the Democratic caucus on June 2, although the resolution stated that free wool was the Democratic policy. Underwood stated pointedly that Bryan had his answer from Democrats who, unlike Bryan, had "never bolted a caucus or scratched a party ticket." Bryan was generally criticized in the press, and Underwood was lauded for his effective leadership. Governor Wilson of New Jersey termed the action of the caucus the best that is "possible and practical." The wool bill passed the House without amendment on June 20 by a vote of 221 to 100, with the Democrats and twenty-four Republicans voting for the measure. In addition to reducing the rates on raw wool from 44 percent to 20 percent, the bill cut the Payne-Aldrich rates on manufactured wool in half, from 86 to 43 percent.[46]

The Democratic caucus of July 25 reviewed the Democratic pro-

45. *Congressional Record*, 62nd Cong., 1st Sess., 599–600; New York *Times*, May 9, 1911, pp. 1, 3.

46. New York *Times*, May 3, 1911, p. 2; Birmingham *News*, May 30, 31, June 1, 2, 5, 1911; clipping from *Commoner*, [June, 1911?], in Underwood Scrapbook, I, 75, Underwood Papers, Alabama Archives; *Congressional Record*, 62nd Cong., 1st Sess., 2355–56.

gram of tariff revision. As majority leader, Underwood presented a resolution that the party confine itself to the cotton bill until Taft acted on the free list and wool bills. Speaker Clark, in a rare difference with Underwood, urged that the remaining schedules, including the iron and steel schedule, be presented as soon as possible. Otherwise, Clark argued, Underwood's interest in the iron and steel industry might lead to unjust but effective criticism of the Democratic position. Underwood's position prevailed over that of Clark by a *viva voce* vote although he promised not to move for adjournment without bringing the remaining tariff schedules before the caucus again.[47]

With the iron and steel schedule in abeyance, the cotton bill, embodying the most drastic reductions in the tariff series, was presented on July 28, 1911. The bill would have slashed rates on manufactured textiles from 50 percent to 27 percent. The Payne-Aldrich Act's jungle-like schedule of specific duties had been altered to an *ad valorem* basis. Underwood maintained that the tariff on cotton goods greatly exceeded the labor cost and predicted that the industry would be only moderately affected. The cotton bill passed on August 3 by a vote of 202 to 91, with thirty Republicans joining the Democrats.[48]

Underwood's opposition to revision of the iron and steel schedule was ill-timed. Soon after the caucus's decision not to revise this schedule, the Bureau of Corporations reported the "existence of a price policy described as cooperation" within the steel industry and stated that United States Steel since its organization in 1901 had made an annual profit of 12 percent on capitalization despite the fact that it was heavily overcapitalized. The House's Stanley investigating committee reached substantially the same conclusions and denounced the absorption of the Tennessee Coal and Iron Company.[49] Bryan renewed his attack on Underwood in his newspaper,

47. New York *Times*, July 26, 1911, p. 2.

48. *Congressional Record*, 62nd Cong., 1st Sess., 3305–18; New York *Times*, August 4, 1911, p. 1.

49. *Literary Digest*, XLIII (July 15, 1911), 87, (November 4, 1911), 773; *American Yearbook 1912* (New York: D. Appleton, 1912), 48.

The Commoner, declaring that Underwood's opposition to an immediate reduction of the iron and steel schedule proved earlier charges that he was tainted with protectionism. Citing Underwood's financial interest in the iron industry, Bryan demanded that the Democrats change the caucus rules to require a public record vote on every issue.

Underwood dramatically and angrily denounced the Bryan editorial before the House as "absolutely false." Although he did not contradict the press reports describing his opposition to consideration of the iron and steel schedule in the caucus, he explained that he had initially favored immediate consideration of this schedule before the Ways and Means Committee to relieve himself of personal embarrassment. But other members of the committee had maintained that the wool and cotton schedules were in greater need of revision, and because of differing sectional interests those two had to be considered together. He noted that his father-in-law's Woodward Iron Company could make pig iron as cheaply as any in the world, and cotton gins and barbed wire, important Birmingham products, were on the proposed free list. Underwood recalled that Bryan had congratulated him when he resisted the pressure of United States Steel Corporation at the time the free list was before the committee. He noted that his constituents had no interest in a tariff on raw wool, but he had nevertheless resisted Bryan's demands for placing raw wool on the free list and had placed a revenue tariff on it. Although there were cotton mills in the Birmingham district, the rates of the proposed cotton schedule were far lower than those of the Wilson Tariff which had been favored by Bryan as a member of the Ways and Means Committee. Congressman Claude Kitchin corroborated Underwood's explanation of the committee's action, and no one took the floor to defend Bryan. Underwood received an almost unprecedented ovation, and as he concluded scores of congressmen rushed to congratulate him.[50]

50. *Commoner,* August 4, 1911, quoted in Washington (D.C.) *Herald,* August 3, 1911, clipping in Underwood Scrapbook, I, 83, Underwood Papers, Alabama Archives; *Congressional Record,* 62nd Cong., 1st Sess., 3510–12.

The press almost without exception acclaimed Underwood for his attack on Bryan. A Clifford K. Berryman cartoon showed a battered Bryan leaving the Capitol with a membership card in the Ananias Club, and some reporters noted that Underwood had won an important test of strength, thereby replacing Bryan as the party leader. Bryan declined to retract his statements unless Underwood would deny the accuracy of the newspaper report upon which Bryan had based his charges.[51] The Bryan-Underwood dispute was the culmination of years of conflict, though the two men were to be occasional antagonists for the next decade.

The Bryan-Underwood differences gave Underwood national attention, and he was interviewed for major publications. The New York World, in a flattering and extensive physical description, noted that Underwood was six feet tall, weighed 195 pounds, and had the broad shoulders of an athlete. His brown hair was "divided on an even keel," and his hazel eyes took on darker colors according to the light. He had a boyish, well-groomed look, with his watch on a lapel chain, a neat pearl, set in gold, on his tie, and the broad substantial black shoes of a southern gentleman. On Sundays he was even more dapper in a black coat, flannel trousers, and white shoes. In the House he had as valets or janitors the same two Negroes who had served Sereno E. Payne as chairman. He was noted for generosity by servants at his hotel for whom he regularly "fished out" a dime or a quarter. Underwood had methodical personal habits. He awakened at 6:00 A.M., arose by 6:30, and before 9:00 Mrs. Underwood had deposited him at the House Office Building before the ice in the water coolers had settled. Washingtonians maintained that they could identify the Underwood electric auto by its steady gait for miles away. For recreation Underwood liked to stop by the Metropolitan Club for a game of chess. He had discarded cribbage which "got on his nerves," and he likewise thought whist too fast for his deliberate manner. He loved golf but found no time for it when Congress was in session. He and

51. Washington (D.C.) Herald, August 3, 1911; Washington (D.C.) Evening Star, August 3, 1911; New York Times, August 15, 1911, p. 3.

Mrs. Underwood were devotees of the theater and were well posted on stage events. His reading was largely limited to economics tracts, but he occasionally read a novel. He smoked broad, chunky, rather short cigars and loved to have the fragrance curl up over him as he worked. He confessed to drinking a slug of whiskey when he got his feet wet or had a crick in the back. He drank tea and coffee and ate anything from "predigested cereal to hardtack." As a speaker he was no orator, but he had a voice that carried well, and he used no manuscript. His gestures were few and simple. He usually stood still, a hand resting on his desk, and aimed his voice at the man he was answering. In this 1911 interview Underwood denied all presidential aspirations. The idea of Alabama furnishing a presidential candidate was "absurd," he said. Yet a friendly interviewer noted that thirty-seven of Underwood's House colleagues favored him for president—more than for any other candidate except Wilson.[52]

Underwood's wife Bertha was also interviewed by a Washington reporter in 1911. She feigned an interest in politics, though her avowal of intense concern for the tariff rings hollow. More indicative of her interests were her statements that women did not understand politics, that her hobby was her husband, and that she admired Madame Schumann-Heink because she had both genius and children (Bertha had no children of her own). She had aspired to be an opera singer.[53]

The press identified Underwood closely with the tariff issue, and his strongly racist views, expressed during and following the ratification of the Alabama Constitution of 1901, largely escaped notice after his elevation to chairman of the Ways and Means Committee. Flamboyant demagogues such as Congressman J. Thomas Heflin furnished better copy. As late as 1907, however, Underwood had sponsored the repeal of the Fifteenth Amendment, and his racism did not escape the pungent memory of Harry L. Burnam, a black man who once worked for the Underwood family. Burnam, then

52. New York *World*, August 6, 1911.
53. Washington (D.C.) *Times*, April 5, 1911.

living in Cincinnati, compared Underwood unfavorably with previous Democratic Ways and Means Committee Chairmen Roger
Q. Mills of Texas and William L. Wilson of West Virginia. With
eloquence he wrote bitterly: "Fior [sic] Eaters as you all of today
want to retain representation in Congress and the Electoral College and yet not allow us to have any Voice at all in the selection of
either." Commenting on an Underwood statement that there was
no Republican party in the South, he said that Underwood must
have meant "in those states where you all have disfranchised almost all of the colored Votes for no other reason than that they are
all Rep[ublican]."[54]

Underwood's tariff revision bills were varyingly received in the
Senate. The Canadian reciprocity agreement passed and was
signed by the president. Hopes for Canadian ratification were
dashed by the fall of Sir Wilfred Laurier's government in September, 1911, an incident related to Speaker Clark's rash statement
connecting reciprocity with the annexation of Canada. LaFollette
passed the Underwood wool bill in the Senate, with the finished
woolens rate boosted from the Underwood bill's 20 percent to 35
percent. In conference Underwood and LaFollette compromised
on a 29 percent rate. The cotton bill passed, with Senate amendments reducing tariffs on iron, steel, and chemicals. The farmers'
free list bill was passed, although Underwood failed to obtain Senate approval of the addition of lemons to the list.

Taft vetoed the farmers' free list, wool, and cotton bills, stating
that the Tariff Board was not ready to report and that the Underwood bills had been framed on "uncertain principles with uncertain results." The president later stated that until the Democrats
and the Insurgents joined in framing the three bills, refusing to
wait until the Tariff Board's report in December, he had been convinced that Underwood and LaFollette agreed with him in seeking
scientific tariff revision. He now believed that the Democratic-Insurgent group had refused to wait in order to gain political advan-

54. Harry L. Burnam to Underwood, February 14, 1911, in Underwood Papers, Alabama Archives.

tage. He reaffirmed, however, that he favored orderly tariff reduction based on the recommendations of the board as to the differences in cost of production at home and abroad. Underwood tried in the House to override the wool and free list vetoes but failed by only 31 and 28 votes. Accusing the president of the "arrogance of George the Third," he assailed Taft's vetoes as an attempt to subordinate the legislative branch to the executive. The president, he claimed, had perverted the Payne-Aldrich Act, which authorized the employment of tariff experts for negotiation of minimum rates with foreign countries, when he constituted this group as a Tariff Board to instruct Congress.[55] Congress adjourned without Underwood fulfilling his pledge to reassemble the caucus for consideration of the iron and steel schedule.

With the presidential election of 1912 approaching, the gulf between the Democratic leader and the president widened. Taft's military aide, Major Archie Butt, overheard the president say, "I am going to hammer the life out of Underwood in spite of what Archie may think."[56] Speaking in Hamilton, Massachusetts, Taft ridiculed the Democratic program as "tariff for politics only" and charged that Underwood had erred profoundly in asserting that the wool bill was necessary to avoid a large deficit when a surplus was in prospect. Underwood retorted from Atlantic City that he had based his deficit predictions on the estimates of the secretary of the treasury prior to an unexpected increase in revenues and at a time when approval of the Canadian reciprocity and farmers' free list bills was anticipated. He denied Taft's implication that tariff legislation was unexpected at the extra session, stating that he and Speaker Clark had told the president of their intentions. Taft had not protested this course and had offered data for their use from the so-called Tariff Board. Admitting that he had no proof, Underwood charged that Taft had vetoed the Underwood bills in return

55. Pringle, *Life and Times of William Howard Taft*, II, 595–601; *Congressional Record*, 62nd Cong., 1st Sess., 4103–4104, 4349–53, 4393–95; "Interview Prepared for the Press, August, 1911," in Letterbox M, Underwood Papers, Alabama Archives.

56. Archie Butt to Clara Butt, August 29, 1911, in Lawrence F. Abbott (ed.), *The Letters of Archie Butt, Personal Aide to President Roosevelt* (2 vols.; Garden City, N.Y.: Doubleday, Page, 1924), II, 749.

for regular Republican support of the reciprocity bill. His bills were not perfect, Underwood acknowledged, but he had been forced to compromise with the Republican Senate, and the sections the president said were "loosely drawn" had been taken from the Payne-Aldrich Tariff which he had signed. Popular approval of the Democratic plan was, Underwood maintained, reflected in the passage of the tariff bills by majorities in excess of a hundred when the Democrats held a majority of only sixty-seven seats.[57]

The special session of 1911 also voted to admit Arizona and New Mexico to the union. The Democrats had long favored such legislation since they would thereby gain two states. In 1902 Underwood had favored an omnibus bill for the separate admission of Oklahoma (including the Indian Territory), Arizona, and New Mexico as states, but he was unsuccessful in removing from the bill an option giving the Indian Territory the right to reject admission with Oklahoma. The bill failed. In 1903 Underwood visited Phoenix, Arizona, with other members of the Committee on Irrigation and Arid Lands, headed by Congressman William Randolph Hearst, and absorbed the Arizona viewpoint on statehood. In 1904 he cooperated with Arizona residents in opposing a bill for the admission of Oklahoma (including the Indian Territory) and of Arizona and New Mexico as one state. The 1904 bill did not pass, but in 1906 Roosevelt backed a similar measure, again providing admission of Oklahoma and of Arizona with New Mexico attached. Arizonans, principally Anglo-Saxons or Indians engaged in mining, vigorously opposed the inclusion of agricultural and Spanish-speaking New Mexico into their new state. The two areas had little in common, and Underwood supported the objections of the Arizonans. Although the 1906 bill passed and Oklahoma was admitted, the Arizonans prevented admission of their territory with New Mexico attached by rejecting the measure in a territorial plebiscite. The admission question faced the special session in 1911 after Arizona had adopted a constitution providing for recall of

57. New York *American* clipping, *ca.* August 27, 1911, in Underwood Scrapbook, I, 93, Underwood Papers, Alabama Archives; Birmingham *News*, September 11, 1911.

Although a popular subject for cartoons, Underwood's roundish features did not lend themselves to facile exaggeration. This 1921 cartoon by Henry E. Larimer, following the repeal of the Underwood tariff by the Emergency Tariff of 1921, is a poor likeness of Underwood but is almost unique in being anti-Underwood.

John T. McCutcheon of the Chicago *Tribune* portrayed Underwood as a commanding figure early in the 1924 race for the Democratic nomination.

The Montgomery *Advertiser* cartoonist, Frank "Spang" Spangler revealed
his frustration in attempting to cartoon Underwood.

Clifford K. Berryman of the Washington *Evening Star* regularly cartooned
Underwood—perhaps because Underwood sometimes bought his originals.

Photograph used in Underwood's 1924 campaign for the presidential nomination. The senator's gain in weight seems to obscure his health problems of 1923.

The Underwoods purchased historic Woodlawn mansion near Accotink, Virginia, in 1925.

Underwood at his desk at Woodlawn following his retirement in 1927. He did not type, but the small portable was used by his secretary in typing his *Drifting Sands of Party Politics*.

Old, tired, and uncharacteristically rumpled, Underwood returned in 1928 from a Caribbean cruise that included a trip to Havana for the meeting of the Sixth Inter-American Conference to which he was a delegate.

judges—a provision objectionable to President Taft and to Underwood as well. Underwood swallowed his objections and voted
against requiring the Arizonans to repeal the offending clause, but
quickly reversed himself when the president threatened a veto unless the recall provision was removed. He said that recall of judges
was a "revolutionary idea" and that it was senseless to pass the bill
in a form objectionable to the president. Underwood shoved the
bill forward, but in its final form it provided that Arizona must
remove the offending clause. The clause was restored after Arizona
was admitted.[58]

The special session also submitted to the states for ratification
the Seventeenth Amendment for the direct election of senators. In
May, 1898, Underwood had sponsored an amendment to an unsuccessful House resolution proposing a constitutional amendment to
allow states to elect senators by direct popular vote. Although Alabama was not one of those states with an advisory primary, Underwood proposed to make the popular election of senators manda-
tory, maintaining that the worst boss-ridden states would not
otherwise change; furthermore, Alabama would benefit if senators
from other states were also popularly elected. Some feared that the
Underwood amendment would jeopardize the resolution in the
Senate, but the amendment passed by a vote of 70 to 61. The resolution failed to pass the Senate. A direct election resolution was
offered again in April, 1911, and Underwood favored its passage,
but the House and Senate deadlocked over it. The House's Bartlett
amendment attempted to insure the South against federal control
of elections, and the Senate's Bristow amendment left federal authority over elections unchanged. Unless the House withdrew the
Bartlett amendment in favor of the Bristow amendment, direct
election of senators would not pass. Therefore Underwood voted
with northern Democrats and Republicans for the Bristow amend-

58. *Congressional Record*, 57th Cong., 1st Sess., 5188; *Arizona Republican* (Phoenix),
March 5, 1904; *Congressional Record*, 59th Cong., 1st Sess., 1506, 1562, 1588; Neil M.
Allred to Underwood, August 8, 1911, quoting Underwood interview in a Globe, Arizona,
newspaper, in Underwood Papers, Alabama Archives; *Congressional Record*, 62nd Cong.,
1st Sess., 4242.

ment, a vote for which he was widely criticized in the South.[59]

The special session of 1911 had been little short of a disaster for Taft, and much of the trouble was of Underwood's making. Four important measures were passed: Canadian reciprocity, admission of Arizona and New Mexico, reapportionment of the House from 391 members to 422, and a campaign publicity law. The Senate and the House had failed to agree upon a plan for direct election of senators, and the president had vetoed the farmers' free list, the wool bill, and the cotton bill.

A three-week campaign tour that Underwood made through the Midwest in the fall of 1911 indicated that he was beginning to take his presidential aspirations seriously. He went first to Kentucky where he spoke in Louisville, Stanford, and Corbin. In Louisville he stated that he was not a candidate for the presidency but admitted that he never knew a man "who would not accept the nomination if it were tendered him." In Chicago he addressed the Democratic organization, the Iroquois Club, and in St. Louis he spoke at a banquet meeting of the Young Men's Democratic Club. At St. Louis, although suffering from a severe cold, Underwood excoriated Taft for his tariff policy, saying that he preferred to make the case against the president in the same fashion as he would in the courtroom—that is to select one strong point in his case and win or lose on that basis. The tariff was that issue. He praised Speaker Clark as a "fair and dignified" presiding officer and suggested Henry D. Clayton, chairman of the House Judiciary Committee and an Alabamian, as an appointee to the Supreme Court to replace John Marshall Harlan who had died.[60]

Just as Underwood had predicted, Taft's popularity cascaded to a new low after his tariff vetoes. The president's problems on the eve of the second regular session of the Sixty-second Congress made him look like the central character in a Greek tragedy. Tariff reformers were annoyed by his failure to sign the Democratic tariff schedules into law. His support of Canadian reciprocity, Speaker

59. *Congressional Record*, 55th Cong., 2nd Sess., 4811–25, 62nd Cong., 1st Sess., 204–206; New York *Times*, May 14, 1912, p. 1; Montgomery *Advertiser*, May 21, 1912.
60. Birmingham *News*, October 6, 10, 1911; St. Louis *Post-Dispatch*, October 18, 1911.

Cannon, and Secretary of Interior Ballinger had alienated the Insurgents who were restyling themselves "Progressives." Taft and
Roosevelt broke relations in October, 1911. With the Republicans
so divided, the Democrats could not hide their glee.

In spelling out a Democratic program focused around the tariff,
Underwood stated that the wool, cotton, iron, steel, and perhaps
sugar schedules would be the primary considerations in the session. The program that Underwood suggested for the Democrats
was later expanded to include a chemical schedule and an income
tax under the legal guise of an "excise tax."[61]

Meanwhile, Underwood committed the Democrats to economy.
He asserted that it was the primary duty of the new House to secure an economical administration of the government and a balanced budget. Early in the session Underwood noted that the passage by the House of the expensive Sherwood "dollar a day" Union
pension bill, which he had opposed, made it best to await the fate
of this bill before passing a public buildings or rivers and harbors
bill. Governor Judson Harmon wrote Underwood, endorsing his
economy program and urging Underwood and Clark to halt the
progressives in the party. The Democratic caucus concurred in Underwood's economy program. Some sixteen million dollars was
saved by not presenting a public buildings bill, and another
twenty-four million dollars was saved by eliminating a proposal for
the building of two battleships. It should be noted, however, that
Underwood voted for the Sulloway Age Pension Act of 1912 which
extended the Civil War pension program to virtually all Union veterans and raised the existing pensions, but which was more moderate than the Sherwood "dollar a day" pension bill. The resulting
annual expenditure of some forty-five million dollars a year tended
to offset the other economies that Congress had effected.[62]

The wool tariff was generally regarded as the most unreasonably
high of the schedules, and the Democrats had planned to renew

61. New York *Times*, December 4, 1911, p. 3.
62. New York *Times*, December 16, 1911, p. 2; Judson Harmon to Underwood, December 29, 1911, in Underwood Papers, Alabama Archives; Birmingham *Age-Herald*, January
30, 1912.

the tariff fight by reintroducing the Underwood wool schedule. Underwood was, however, still smarting from Bryan's attack, and the mounting publicity over the huge profits of the steel industry led the Democrats to shift the iron and steel schedule, Schedule C, ahead of the wool bill. Underwood presented Schedule C to the Democratic caucus on January 23, 1912, with proposed additions to the free list of iron ore, machine tools, and several types of machinery, including typewriters and sewing machines. The caucus added baling and fencing wire to the bill. Rates in the metal schedule were reduced about a third. Pig iron and allied products were reduced to 8 percent under the Underwood bill and steel rails to 20 percent *ad valorem*. Iron and steel industry leaders strongly objected to the proposed rate reduction on pig iron, but in presenting the bill to the House, Underwood noted that transportation costs restricted foreign competition in pig iron to the Atlantic and Pacific coasts and argued that the iron industry was no longer in need of protection. He refuted the high wages argument by citing the low wages paid in the iron industry, and he noted the high profits of that industry. Answering Republican criticism, Underwood defended the failure to put agricultural machinery on the free list, arguing that it did not belong in Schedule C. The iron and steel schedule passed on January 30, 1912, by a vote of 212 to 110, with twenty Insurgents favoring the bill and three Democrats opposing.[63]

The chemical schedule, reducing rates on chemicals by 30 percent, was passed on February 21 by a strict party vote of 178 to 127, the Insurgents voting with the regular Republicans against the measure. Underwood explained that though the rates on some luxuries and raw materials had been increased, the rates on consumer necessities had been decreased.[64]

The last of the Democratic tariff bills was the sugar bill, placing

---

63. A contemporary limerick relative to Underwood's candidacy for the Democratic nomination was: "If I cut steel and steel cuts me, can I cut ice as the nominee?" Underwood Scrapbook, I, 78, in Underwood Papers, Alabama Archives. *Congressional Record*, 62nd Cong., 2nd Sess., 1368–74, 1417–1502.

64. *Congressional Record*, 62nd Cong., 2nd Sess., 2251, 2260–62.

sugar on the free list. Free sugar was inconsistent with Under-wood's view that low tariffs on revenue producing imports should be used for the support of the government. In secret Ways and Means Committee sessions designed to avoid difficulty with Louisiana sugar Democrats, Underwood suggested a consumer tax on sugar to make up revenue lost by putting sugar on the list, but he was outvoted and quickly endorsed his party's position. In presenting the sugar bill to the House, Underwood charged the Republican party with obedience to the sugar trust and estimated that the bill would reduce the price of sugar by one and one half cents a pound. The American sugar industry produced less than a fourth of America's consumption, he noted, and he predicted that neither the cane nor beet sugar industry would suffer greatly. The bill passed by a vote of 198 to 103 with the help of twenty-four Republicans, about half of them Insurgents, and the defection of several Louisiana and Colorado Democrats.[65]

Free sugar was expected to reduce revenues by fifty-two million dollars annually, and to offset this revenue loss Underwood introduced an "excise tax," a thinly disguised income tax on the individual's privilege of doing business. The proposed levy of 1 percent on incomes over five thousand dollars attempted to skirt the Supreme Court's Pollock decision of 1895 which declared an income tax unconstitutional. The income tax amendment was then pending in Congress. The excise tax, Underwood said, embodied the modern philosophy of taxation by shifting the burden from the working man to the wealthy. He scored the Supreme Court for abandoning precedents in the Pollock case and charged that the reactionary decision had speeded the growth of socialism in the United States. He presciently noted that the time might come when the nation would need all of its taxing power to sustain a war. The proposed tax, called "Machiavellian cleverness" by one reporter, was well conceived to entice the Insurgents to vote against the regular Republicans. Underwood caustically attacked a Kansas

65. Atlanta *Journal*, March 17, 1912; Raleigh *News and Observer*, February 29, 1912; *Congressional Record*, 62nd Cong., 2nd Sess., 3307–3309; Birmingham *Age-Herald*, March 16, 1912.

Insurgent, who refused to vote for or against the measure, and declared that such a position meant that he stood nowhere. The tax passed easily by a vote of 250 to 40 with eighty Republicans, half of them Insurgents, joining the Democrats for the victory.[66]

The president's Tariff Board rendered its long-awaited report in December, 1911, giving a twelve hundred page report on wool and woolens built around Taft's theory of equalizing production costs at home and abroad through the use of the tariff. The Tariff Board drew no conclusions from its labors, and tariff partisans drew different conclusions from its data although the president himself said that it indicated the necessity for the reduction of wool rates. In late March, 1912, the Tariff Board issued a report on the cotton schedule recommending substantial reductions.

Underwood then reintroduced the woolen bill that Taft had vetoed in August, 1911, berating the Tariff Board's report as "fragmentary and incorrect," based as it was on the erroneous theory that costs of production at home and abroad should be equalized. He described the board as wasteful, inefficient, and ill qualified with a staff composed of "clerks" rather than tax experts. Of four tariff specialists sent abroad in 1911, Underwood noted, only one knew a foreign language and only one knew anything of accounting. He saw nothing in the board's report to justify a change in his earlier bill. The wool bill was passed by a vote of 190 to 92.[67] The Senate substantially altered the Underwood bills. The excise tax and sugar bills died after being loaded with amendments, and the wool bill was replaced by the LaFollette bill with higher rates. However, House and Senate conferees quickly resolved their differences in the LaFollette-Underwood wool bill, identical with the 1911 bill of the same name.

An anonymous poet at the Gridiron Club dinner, an annual Washington press frolic, anticipated a presidential veto of the wool bill in doggerel: "Oh, the tariff talk in Congress halls, Grows sadder by the day, And Underwood unceasingly calls Upon the band to

66. *Congressional Record*, 62nd Cong., 2nd Sess., 3583–88; Montgomery *Advertiser*, March 15, 17, 1912; Washington (D.C.) *Post*, March 20, 1912.
67. Montgomery *Advertiser*, March 28, 30, 1912.

play, A veto fiercely lurks about With musket and with sword, To kill a bill put through without Leave from Taft's tariff board."[68] Indeed, Taft again vetoed the wool bill, this time indicating that its reductions were too severe.

Underwood intended to conclude the Democratic tariff revision program with passage of the wool bill, but he decided to introduce again the cotton bill that the president had vetoed in the summer of 1911. The Tariff Board rendered a special report on the cotton schedule in late March, 1912, and the president sent the message to Congress with the recommendation that duties be reduced. Underwood beamed as the president's message was read, saying that Democrats enjoyed the "spectacle" of a Republican president being applauded for advocating reduction of duties that the Republicans had increased. He expressed concern that unless the cotton schedule were revised, he might be accused of sectional bias in favoring the South.[69] Although the cotton schedule passed the House, the Senate attached an amendment repealing Canadian reciprocity, and the Democrats allowed the bill to die. The chemical schedule met a bipartisan death in the Senate. Passage in the House of the iron and steel and wool schedules over Taft's veto was only a dramatic show of strength, as there was not a chance that the Senate would override the veto.

Although Underwood repeatedly demonstrated a progressivism in his views on the tariff and other forms of taxation, he continued to oppose, usually on narrow constitutional grounds, some of the minor reforms that Taft attempted late in his administration. Among these were the Esch phosphorous bill and the bill for the creation of a parcels post system—both quite popular measures.

No vote in Underwood's career caused more unfavorable comment toward him than did his vote against the Esch phosphorous bill, or the "Phossy Jaw" bill as it was popularly termed. President Taft recommended in December, 1910, that Congress outlaw the manufacture and sale of white phosphorous matches. The manufac-

---

68. Underwood Scrapbook, I, 178, in Underwood Papers, Alabama Archives.
69. Birmingham *Age-Herald*, March 27, 1912.

ture and use of white (or yellow) phosphorous matches had been banned in most nations since the development of the much safer French sesquisulphide process in 1898. Match workers developed a hideous condition known as "phossy jaw" after working with white phosphorous, and matches made with the dangerous poison resulted in numerous suicides and deaths. When Underwood became chairman of the Ways and Means Committee, the committee, unable to reach agreement on Taft's proposal, reported a resolution appropriating a modest five thousand dollars for an investigation. Underwood voted against even this mild measure. Meanwhile, popular magazines took up the cause of the workers. The issue was complicated in that the newer, safer process was owned by the monopolistic Diamond Match Company which did not use it, although it offered to lease the process to other manufacturers.

Underwood not only opposed the House resolution to appropriate funds for investigating the problem, but he joined thirty other constitutional purists in opposing the final measure, the Esch Act, which taxed the white phosphorous process out of existence in April, 1912. Meanwhile, the Diamond Match Company avoided the ire of a thoroughly alarmed public by donating the patent rights to its new and safe sesquisulphide process to the American people. Underwood tenaciously opposed the bill despite an avalanche of letters critical of his position. He later defended his vote saying that there was serious doubt as to the merits of the bill from a humanitarian viewpoint. Although recognizing that "phossy jaw" was a very serious disease, he insisted that the condition could be prevented by proper inspection under state laws and that the use of federal taxing power to "wipe out" industries in order to regulate industrial disease was a "dangerous precedent." He lamely noted that far more people died in textile plants from tuberculosis than in match plants of white phosphorous poisoning.[70] The explanations did him no good, and no other issue better illustrated the extreme to which he would go to avoid federal police legislation.

70. *Congressional Record*, 62nd Cong., 2nd Sess., 2977, 3979; Underwood to Frank A. Hewitt, March 6, 1914, in Underwood Papers, Alabama Archives.

Whereas constitutional objections had been Underwood's rationale in opposing the Esch White Phosphorous Match Act, he opposed the Taft-supported Parcels Post Act on the basis of economy, as well as the danger of centralization. The post office, of course, accepted small parcels, but its rates were high; most of the business was left to the express companies which opposed parcels post just as farmers favored it. Underwood told the Business Men's League of Montgomery in March, 1912, that there would be no parcels post legislation in the second session of the Sixty-second Congress, noting that the relatively small Post Office Department deficit of $7 million would increase to $150 million with parcels post. Complaining of massive government expenses such as those for the Panama Canal, pensions, and the expanding bureaucracy, he said parcels post would add to the dangerous tendency toward centralization and would result in government control of the express companies. Underwood explained to a farm lobbyist that he favored the inauguration of a system of parcels post on rural free delivery routes but opposed plans for a comprehensive system. Parcels post legislation passed, nevertheless, toward the end of the session as a part of the post office appropriation bill. There was no record vote in the House, and the measure involved less reliance upon express companies than Underwood had envisioned.[71] Underwood had thus taken an unpopular stand, and in this case one that could have cost him support among his rural constituents.

Despite this risk, however, Underwood's increasing stature in the House and his capacity to deliver favors to the Birmingham area solidified his position with his constituents. In 1911 an Underwood bill created a subport of entry at Birmingham, giving local merchants the advantage of receiving imports in bond at Birmingham and making payments there rather than in Mobile, New Orleans, or Savannah. In the same year he secured an appropriation for a mine rescue station for Birmingham. For several years he worked energetically for the location of a subtreasury at Birming-

71. Montgomery *Advertiser*, March 20, 1912; Underwood to C. S. Barrett, February 26, 1910, in Underwood Papers, Alabama Archives; *Congressional Record*, 62nd Cong., 2nd Sess., 11819.

ham, though Atlanta, the logical site, won the financial institution.[72]

Underwood could hardly be expected to retain his earlier kindly views of President Taft during the 1912 election year. But if he did, such views were not for public utterance as the Democratic warriors braced for the contest. His opposition to Taft was based on the president's inept domestic policy, but he opposed Taft's foreign policy as well, voicing disapproval of the "dollar diplomacy" employed in Central America and the Orient. American interference in those areas was not stimulating American commerce, he said, and he was harshly critical of Secretary of State Philander C. Knox—especially for seeking expanded appropriations for the Department of State. In 1911 Underwood, urged on by Birmingham's Jewish community, demanded abrogation of the American commercial treaty with Russia as a protest against refusal to honor passports issued to American Jews. The Taft administration yielded to congressional pressure and the treaty was abrogated.[73] Underwood's lowest appraisal of Taft was given in August, 1912, following the president's advocacy of an explanatory resolution that Underwood felt weakened the Panama Tolls Act and following Taft's veto of Underwood's cherished Coosa River franchise bill. Underwood said: "President Taft means well, but he has not the energy to make a profound study of great public issues, and never forms lasting and firm ideas on any public legislation of importance. He wants to do the right thing, but will not probe into questions far enough to find the truth, and find it, stick to it; but relies upon his advisers and they have been his undoing. He will go out of office the most discredited president that ever occupied the White House."[74]

Underwood's continued conservatism was again seen in a dispute with Bryan over the money trust investigation in February, 1912. Agrarian radicals in the Democratic party, insisting that the House of Morgan and other banks controlled access to most of

72. Birmingham *News*, November 16, 1910; Birmingham *Age-Herald*, January 16, 1911; *Congressional Record*, 59th Cong., 2nd Sess., 392.

73. Montgomery *Advertiser*, March 15, 1910; Birmingham *News*, November 21, 1911.

74. Birmingham *Age-Herald*, August 23, 1912.

the nation's capital, demanded a congressional investigation of the money trust. Underwood favored investigation of the alleged trust by standing House committees, especially the Committee on Banking and Currency, rather than by a special committee. Bryan favored creation of a special committee, as he believed that the Committee on Banking and Currency was dominated by the moneyed interests. Underwood noted that members of the banking committee were mostly rural southerners, and he saw no reason to suspect that they were dominated by Wall Street interests. A special committee would have to refer its findings to the banking committee for appropriate legislation anyway with a consequent delay. The Bryan and Underwood plans were offered at the Democratic caucus on February 7, 1912, and Underwood's resolution to refer the matter to the four related standing committees passed by a vote of 115 to 66. A telegram from Bryan to the caucus had failed to stem the tide, and Underwood thus scored another victory over his old opponent.[75]

The allocation of the money trust investigation to four related committees was a face-saving device, since the important action remained in the Committee on Banking and Currency which was divided into two panels. The parent group, headed by Congressman Glass of Virginia, began the framing of the federal reserve bill. A second group, headed by Congressman Arsene Pujo, in the early months of 1913 made a sensational investigation of the money trust. Underwood assured currency reformer J. Lawrence Laughlin that the radical element could easily have been beaten by a margin of two to one and that the investigation was permitted largely because it would "lighten certain political tendencies" by allowing them public expression.[76] Clearly, Underwood had little sympathy with the radicals' views.

Underwood had demonstrated a remarkable capacity for leadership in Congress. He had taken a disorganized party which had forgotten how to function as a majority and had fashioned it into a

75. Washington (D.C.) *Herald*, February 8, 1912.
76. J. Lawrence Laughlin, *The Federal Reserve Act: Its Origins and Problems* (New York: Macmillan, 1933), 80.

well-drilled organization. Republican Nicholas Longworth lamented: "When he pipes they dance, fall down, roll over and play dead."[77] It was difficult to believe that the House Democrats were the fractious group over which Underwood had assumed command in 1911. His techniques of leadership were paradoxically dramatic and prosaic. Lacking the brilliance and wit of John Sharp Williams and the oratorical ability of Champ Clark, Underwood forged ahead slowly with parliamentary skill, patience, dignity, serenity, and courtesy. So engaging and disarming was his genial nature that he sometimes looked like the suave hero of an Anthony Hope novel gallantly destroying his enemies with rapier-like thrusts.

Having participated in the destruction of Cannonism, Underwood realized the necessity for stringent House rules and so helped prevent the dismantling of the House parliamentary structure. He gently shifted himself into the position of party leader, formerly occupied by the Speaker. Speaker Clark, lethargic by nature and charmed by Underwood, tamely submitted. There were complaints against the "Underwoodism," which replaced "Cannonism," but few could attack the genial and soft-spoken gentleman from Alabama as a tyrant. In place of Cannon's boorish dictatorship, Underwood built a genteel machine for party rule. To his harshest critics, "Underwoodism" meant a refined kind of tyranny.

Some historians approve Taft's veto of the Underwood tariff bills of 1911 and 1912. Indubitably, the bills were hastily drawn and were formulated with the 1912 election in mind, and in some cases they were damaged by the Republican Senate, which tacked on irrelevant items. The Underwood bills must be compared, however, not with any chimerical, scientific tariff measure but with the kind of legislation that Congress was capable of passing. Taft had signed the Payne-Aldrich Act, which almost no one claimed to be systematic revision. As Underwood had pointed out, much of the language of the Underwood schedules was identical to that of the Payne-Aldrich Act. He insisted, quite plausibly, that the bills had been drawn with moderate revisions downward in the hope that

77. Underwood Scrapbook, I, 24, in Underwood Papers, Alabama Archives.

the president would sign them into law.[78] The public was apparently convinced that Taft was insincere in requesting tariff reform. With elphantine awkwardness he had lumbered methodically into each trap that Underwood and the Democrats had set. Taft's disapproval of the Underwood bills, other than the Canadian reciprocity bill, indicated that he could almost always find a reason to veto tariff reform.

Underwood had considerable claim to the title "the Pathfinder to the White House" in that he, more than anyone else, was the architect of Democratic victory in 1912. He had focused the nation's attention on the tariff issue, and Champ Clark believed that without the special session of 1911 Taft would have been reelected.[79] The remarkable performance of the Democratic congressional leaders in securing the passage of an extensive legislative reform program and the negative role thereby assigned to the Republicans seemed to acknowledge the Democratic party as the party that could accomplish its aims.

Underwood's presidential ambition was to convert him from his strong southern sectionalism. Certainly, he would not have expected to win the nomination without dissociating himself from the narrow sectionalism that his early career had embodied. He had sponsored Confederate veterans' legislation favored by his pro-Confederate Uncle John and as late as 1907 had sponsored the repeal of the Fifteenth Amendment. He rather consistently opposed Civil War claims from northern sources when they had not been through the court of claims. In 1908, he had relaxed his earlier opposition to Union pension legislation and voted for a general pension bill to increase pensions, saying that the measure would obviate the necessity for numbers of private bills. In 1911 he opposed the Sherwood "dollar a day" pension bill as an expensive giveaway. However, in 1912, Underwood voted "aye" amid gallery applause to the Sulloway Age Pension Act, a measure that raised Union pensions and added even deserters to the pension list.

---

78. Birmingham *News*, September 11, 1911.
79. Clark, *My Quarter Century of American Politics*, II, 7.

In April, 1912, Underwood gave a candid assessment of his predictions for the nomination and election in 1912. The Democrats, he claimed, had demonstrated their capacity to maintain a united front, whereas the Republicans were badly divided: "Our adversaries are torn asunder. They are in two camps: one fighting to maintain the ancient standpat fallacies of the republican party and the other abandoning everything in its effort to overthrow a representative form of government and destroy the federal constitution. We are going to win. The preservation of our republic, the protection of the rights of the people and relief against the present burdens of taxation is dependent upon democratic success."[80] Underwood expected Theodore Roosevelt to be the Republican nominee.

Rather clearly, Underwood had become more progressive and more national as the party conventions of 1912 approached. His support of moderate pension legislation, free sugar, and the admission of Arizona with a recall provision, plus the almost demagogic denunciation of the wealthy with which he supported the income tax were not in keeping with his fundamental conservatism. There were, however, indications that Underwood was unable to break the confines of the parochialism that bound him. His opposition to minor reforms of the Taft administration—postal savings banks, parcels post, and the Esch White Phosphorous Match Act, the first two highly popular with his agricultural constitutents and the last vastly popular with everyone—indicated that there were limits to his political horizons.

Underwood's towering political strength in 1912 resulted from a combination of factors on the national and local scene. The Birmingham congressional district was now safely Democratic, and his key position in the House made him so strong that he could largely disregard local politics and spend his time on national affairs. Ed Campbell and other friends devoted themselves to stamping out local opposition. So safe was his congressional seat that when the Republicans nominated Frederick B. Parker, an Ensley

80. Birmingham *Age-Herald*, April 23, 1912.

draftsman, to oppose him in 1912, Parker praised Underwood as a statesman who had "proved his merits by his works." Underwood received 12,584 votes to Parker's 1,598.[81]

Many of Underwood's activities as House leader in 1911 and 1912 must be viewed as role-playing. In the framing of the Payne tariff bill, he had no feeling that Chairman Payne was being other than fair to the minority members, and his later denunciation of the Payne-Aldrich Tariff Act and the autocratic way in which it was framed must be viewed in relation to the role expected of a Democratic leader. Although Underwood cooperated with Norris in breaking Cannon's lock-hold on legislation, the revolution of 1911 was less important than it seemed at the time. Underwood was unwilling to pursue the revolution against Cannon after the Norris resolution was adopted since he intended, once the Democrats were in full control, to perpetuate the same kind of authority. In terms of his personal relationship with President Taft, there is no indication that the president took personally Underwood's attacks upon him. After all, Underwood was not an "Insurgent" or a "Progressive," anathema to both Taft and Underwood, and the role he played was in keeping with the generally accepted rules of the game.

Late in the Taft administration, while Underwood was being viewed as a contender for the Democratic nomination, he talked reflectively of his philosophy of government. Legislation, he said, "must of necessity be progressive," but "my own inclination has been to proceed along conservative rather than radical lines." Asked if Herbert Spencer were correct in saying that thirty of thirty-one laws passed by the Parliament brought the opposite results than those expected, he judged Spencer's percentage to be entirely too high, adding, however, that the Supreme Court often gives an unexpected meaning to a law Congress has passed. The Sherman Act, he continued, was still in the process of being defined by the courts, and he thought Congress should await further

81. Birmingham *News*, September 29, 1912; Alabama Official Election Returns, November 5, 1912, in Secretary of State files, Alabama Department of Archives and History, Montgomery.

definition of the act before making changes. Asked for a statement
of objectives, Underwood replied that his best qualifications were
in the area of taxation and if he could adjust the burden of taxation
from the masses of the people to the wealthy, he would accomplish
his purpose. He added thoughtfully that he refused to spread his
substance over too great a surface, believing that his talents lay
largely in the financial questions before the Ways and Means Committee.[82]

Underwood explicated his theory of leadership under questioning from a reporter who asked if able leadership succeeds better in
small communities. Not surprisingly, he denied that a man's residence, "whether he lives in New York or Jonesville," was important. "The man who has the personality, magnetism, or by whatever term you may designate that ability for leadership is going to
make himself known, no matter what the size of his environment,"
he said. Ability or talent for leadership "always carries with it an
insistent desire to exercise it to its fullest extent," and great ability
would "drive" a man to a larger scene where he would inevitably
be successful. He gave Napoleon as an example and seemed to
embrace a "mandate of heaven" concept of government in saying
that "mediocrity can never rule, never lead." Underwood denied
that either ignorance or corruption was common in political and
municipal leadership. A political leader, he said, must have the
most valuable kind of knowledge—understanding of human nature—and therefore could not be considered "ignorant." Although
he admitted that there had always been corruption in municipal
affairs, he expressed doubt that it was "a substantial factor in political leadership," concluding "I do not wish to think so ill of my
people."[83] Underwood's analysis of political leadership was rather
Pollyannaish. In any case, the suggestion that a leader could come
from anywhere and rise as far as his talents would carry him offered
the possibility that a leader with a southern background might
reach the presidency of the United States. Seldom had the Demo-

82. Thomas F. Logan, "What I Am Trying to Do: An Authorized Interview with Underwood," *World's Work*, XXIII (March, 1912), 538–43.
83. New York *Times*, August 6, 1911, Sec. 5, p. 1.

crats had such an excellent chance. The Republicans were hope-
lessly divided. The congressional Insurgents, who had begun to
call themselves Progressives, were led by LaFollette, but their real
ideological leader, Roosevelt, waited in the wings to see if La-
Follette might stumble, as indeed he did in February, 1912. With
Roosevelt opposing Taft for the Republican nomination, the Democrats looked on with ill-disguised glee.

Underwood had displayed considerable courage in his fight for
tariff reform. He had resisted the demands of the iron and steel
industry for special consideration, as well as opposing Bryan in a
toe-to-toe confrontation that endeared him to conservatives in both
parties. If Roosevelt were indeed to be the nominee, as Underwood expected, then the Democrats might plausibly offer Underwood as a fresh, new candidate of a conservative bent.

CHAPTER VII

Contesting with Wilson for the Democratic Nomination in 1912

Conservative leaders looked forward to the presidential election of 1912 with considerable apprehension. The bitter internecine warfare between Theodore Roosevelt and Taft made it unlikely that either could win the presidency. Conservatives in both parties feared, almost obsessively, that William Jennings Bryan would be the Democratic nominee. Although Governor Woodrow Wilson of New Jersey attracted a wide popular following among progressives, conservatives pinned their hopes on solid Governor Judson Harmon of Ohio, an outspoken advocate of fiscal conservatism. Their alternate choice for the nomination was Champ Clark, a nominal progressive. Underwood's presidential aspirations may have been as old as Underwood himself. With his remarriage in 1904 he had access to wealth that would be useful in a presidential campaign, and the nationwide distribution of speeches between 1906 and 1908 on good roads, the panic of 1907, and immigration, indicates political aspirations beyond the boundaries of Alabama. National press discussion of his candidacy resulted from his successful leadership of the House in 1911 and 1912 and from his controversy with Bryan in 1911. Initially he was thought of largely as a vice-presidential candidate—probably with Harmon at the top of the ticket. This was based on the assumption that Roosevelt would win the Republican nomination and that a straight-out fight between progressives and conservatives would bring a conservative victory.

As late as the fall of 1911, Governor Wilson and Governor Harmon were the leading contenders for the Democratic nomination. Harmon increasingly identified himself with the conservatives by denouncing initiative, referendum, and recall, those shibboleths of reform. Wilson's progressive principles aroused deep-seated alarm among conservative financial leaders, many of whom were Republicans unabashedly dabbling in Democratic politics. Wilson's enthusiastic reception in the South during the summer and fall of 1911 worsened their fears. He had the political advantage of having lived in four southern states and was welcomed as a southerner returning home.[1]

Speaker of the House Champ Clark, backed by the powerful Hearst press, entered the presidential arena late in the fall of 1911 and created an effective block to Wilson in the West. It was soon apparent, however, that Clark was no more effective in the Southeast than was Harmon. Sectionally minded southerners measured Clark by his vote in favor of the Sherwood pension bill, which proposed a generous "dollar-a-day" pension to Union veterans.[2]

Clark never perfected a political organization in the Southeast, but Governor Harmon set up a rudimentary organization in that area. The Harmon organization was headed in Florida by Pleasant A. Holt, a Jacksonville attorney; in South Georgia by Neyle Colquitt of Savannah; in North Carolina by Henry B. Varner, editor of the Lexington *Dispatch*. In Alabama, Senator John H. Bankhead, Sr., and Underwood were considered to be favorable to Harmon. Despite the efforts of these conservatives, Harmon's campaign faded, especially in the South, as that of Governor Wilson gathered momentum. The aging, pedestrian governor with a "passion for economy" was no match for Wilson as a popular leader in the South. The weakness of Clark's and Harmon's southeastern campaigns presented an opportunity for Underwood to enter the race for the Democratic nomination as a southern conservative.[3] Underwood anticipated no trouble in seeking renomination and election to Congress while at the same time seeking the presidential

1. Charles B. Galbreath, *History of Ohio* (5 vols.; Chicago: American Historical Society, 1925), II, 700–702.
2. Charlotte (N.C.) *Daily Observer*, February 19, 1912.
3. Clark Howell to John H. Bankhead, Sr., February 26, 1912, in Underwood Campaign File, John H. Bankhead, Sr., Papers, Alabama Department of Archives and History, Montgomery; Hugh L. Nichols to Neyle Colquitt, November 27, 1911, in Neyle Colquitt Papers, Duke University; Raleigh *News and Observer*, May 15, 1912; New York *Times*, October 22, 1911, Sec. 5, p. 2.

nomination. He was highly optimistic about Democratic chances for victory, asserting that there had been no better opportunity "since '92. . . . We are united and the Republicans are divided," and "the drift is all our way."[4]

Underwood's appeal to conservatives was based upon his moderation as a tariff reformer, his unalterable opposition to initiative, referendum, and recall, and his pronounced hatred of William Jennings Bryan. His conflict with Bryan dated from 1908 when Ed Campbell tried to prevent Bryan from winning the Democratic presidential nomination. Underwood realized that Bryan would receive the nomination and disassociated himself from this attempt, but the damage to his relationship with Bryan was done.[5] In June, 1911, Bryan's attack on Underwood's motives in failing to take up the iron and steel tariff schedules for revision gave Underwood an unparalleled opportunity to defend himself and attract attention.

Underwood's rise to national fame was aided by his one-time congressional colleague, William Randolph Hearst, who committed himself to stopping the Wilson bandwagon. In September, 1911, Hearst declared that Harmon was too conservative but that Clark or Underwood would make a good president. Hearst assigned one of his top writers, Alfred Henry Lewis, the task of attacking Wilson and building up Clark and Underwood.[6]

The Underwood movement began in New York City, where the Alabama congressman was friendly with tariff lobbyists and businessmen through his chairmanship of the Ways and Means Committee. Italian-American importers were vitally interested in a low tariff on fruits, especially lemons, and they had employed a grandiloquent lobbyist, William C. Beer, to further their interests. Beer, also associated with J. P. Morgan and Thomas Fortune Ryan,

4. Oscar W. Underwood to Thomas M. Owen, August 17, 1911, in Thomas M. Owen Papers, Alabama Department of Archives and History, Montgomery.

5. Samuel Will John to Underwood, May 16, 1908, in Oscar W. Underwood Papers, Alabama Department of Archives and History, Montgomery.

6. New York *American*, September 26, 1911. See Alfred Henry Lewis, "Honorable Champ," *Cosmopolitan*, LI (1911), 760–65; Alfred Henry Lewis, "Underwood—House Leader," *Cosmopolitan*, LII (1911), 109–14; Alfred Henry Lewis, "The Real Woodrow Wilson," *Hearst's Magazine*, XXI (May, 1912), 2265–74.

became an ardent supporter of the Underwood presidential movement. In late August, 1911, Underwood addressed the National Italian Democratic League at the Waldorf-Astoria in New York. His speech was a soft-spoken denunciation of President Taft's position on the tariff. There were titters in the audience when he spoke feelingly of the "Stars and Bars" rather than the "Stars and Stripes," but although he was an uninspiring speaker, his advocacy of the lowering of the tariff by a gradual "jackscrew" method pleased his audience. Joseph S. Auerbach, a prominent New York attorney and tariff lobbyist, shared the platform with Underwood.[7]

After the dinner about twelve of the group, led by Auerbach, followed Underwood to Atlantic City where Mrs. Underwood had rented a house in the Chelsea district. The group urged Underwood to run for the Democratic presidential nomination. Underwood demurred, saying that he bore the stigma of a southerner, but at an early morning breakfast he agreed to let his name be put forward. It was decided that Auerbach would raise campaign funds and that Underwood would not leave his congressional duties in order to campaign. Underwood issued a statement from Atlantic City reassuring business, attacking Bryan, and defending the Democratic attempts at tariff revision.[8]

Underwood returned to Birmingham on September 10, 1911, after an eight-month absence. He denied that he was a candidate for the presidential nomination, saying: "In order to run a man must have a machine or money; I haven't either."[9] Although Underwood was not wealthy, his wife, of course, was, and despite his avowed decision not to be a candidate and not to campaign, Underwood, who had no effective opposition for his congressional

7. New York *Times*, August 24, 1911, p. 3; William C. Beer to Underwood, January 12, 1912, in Underwood Papers, Alabama Archives. Beer, a Republican, was known as the "confidential man" of J. P. Morgan, but Beer's relationship to Underwood appears to have been as representative of the Italian-Americans and of Charles B. Alexander, counsel for Thomas Fortune Ryan's Equitable Life Assurance Society. New York *Times*, April 16, 1911, p. 6.

8. Birmingham *Age-Herald*, April 24, 1912; Joseph S. Auerbach to Underwood, September 6, 1911, in Underwood Papers, Alabama Archives; Birmingham *News*, August 31, 1911.

9. Birmingham *News*, September 11, 1911.

seat, spoke in Chicago, St. Louis, and Louisville. In mid-December he returned to New York for speeches before the Pennsylvania Society, the Southern Society, and the Catholic Club. In his Pennsylvania Society speech he emphasized the need to go slowly on reform measures and to protect the property rights of large corporations as well as individuals. His words were so soothing that a rise in the stock market was attributed to him.[10]

Auerbach entertained Underwood on his New York visit at a dinner to which he invited about twenty prominent New Yorkers. In addition to public figures like Nicholas Murray Butler, the dinner was attended by some of the wealthiest men in the city. Auerbach's statement that "one or two of them have Harmon leanings but not enough to hurt" belied the fact that at least one of the dinner guests, Edward R. Bacon of the Baltimore and Ohio Railroad, was an organizer of the Harmon campaign.[11] By now Underwood had begun to drink strongly of the heady wine of presidential ambition. He wrote his father-in-law of his favorable prospects: "I met a number of leading politicians in New York City as well as up the State. From what they tell me I judge that there is at present a more favorable sentiment for my nomination in New York than for any other candidate. Of course, this may change. I realize fully that I have a very difficult session of Congress ahead of me and there is always the danger of making a mistake, but if conditions remain as good as they are today it looks like I could be nominated."[12]

The Jackson Day dinner at Baltimore on January 8, 1912, was considered a preliminary test of the candidates. Underwood, suffering from an intestinal ailment, at first declined to go. However, when his refusal was taken to indicate fear that Bryan, who followed him on the speakers' program, would again attack him, he changed his mind. Wilson's remarks at the dinner eclipsed those of Underwood and the other candidates, and Frank P. Glass, editor

10. Birmingham *News*, October 28, 1911; New York *Times*, December 10, 1911, Sec. 3, p. 20; Washington (D.C.) *Times*, December 11, 1911.

11. Auerbach to Underwood, undated [December, 1911?], January 8, 1912, both in Underwood Papers, Alabama Archives.

12. Underwood to Joseph H. Woodward, December 22, 1911, in Joseph H. Woodward Papers, in possession of Mrs. Joseph H. Woodward II, Birmingham.

of the Birmingham *News*, was seen conferring amiably with Wilson leaders. It was becoming Wilson against the field. Less noted was the appearance of William Randolph Hearst and his aide John Temple Graves in the friendly company of Hearst's erstwhile enemy, the Tammany tiger, Charles F. Murphy.[13]

In February, 1912, Underwood formally announced for the Democratic nomination. His manager, Senator John H. Bankhead, Sr., wrote to hundreds of newspapers throughout the Southeast, offering them a fee to include a four-page Underwood advertisement with one edition of their papers, thereby revealing that the Underwood forces had money. Ralph Smith, political writer for the Atlanta *Journal*, charged that Senator Bankhead had recently returned from a meeting with Thomas Fortune Ryan, the New York and Virginia utilities and tobacco tycoon who was suspected of financing the Underwood campaign.[14] Bankhead denied these charges, although he and Ryan later admitted that Ryan had contributed thirty-five thousand dollars to the Underwood campaign. Ryan had also previously contributed some fifty thousand dollars to the Harmon campaign.

Ryan, a canny and secretive New York financier, later stated that although he contributed to both Harmon and Underwood, he had no particular interest in who was nominated. He thought, however, that Bryan could not win. Actually, Ryan had long been interested in seeing a southern conservative as the Democratic nominee, and much of Underwood's New York support revolved around him. Another Underwood supporter was S. Davies Warfield, the president of the Continental Trust Company of Baltimore, who had recently purchased most of Ryan's interest in the Seaboard Air Line Railway and was going to the Democratic convention as a delegate pledged to Clark. Ryan had considerable influence with Tammany Hall and with the Martin-Swanson machine in Virginia; he also had been an associate of William C. Whitney, President

13. Montgomery *Advertiser*, January 6, 1912; Henry Morgenthau, *All in a Life-Time* (Garden City, N.Y.: Doubleday, 1922), 140; W. A. Swanberg, *Citizen Hearst* (New York: Scribner, 1961), 275–76.

14. Birmingham *Age-Herald*, January 9, 1912; Atlanta *Journal*, February 8, 1912.

Cleveland's secretary of the navy, and the Underwood supporters in the East were largely the old anti-Bryan and Cleveland Democrats.[15]

In late March, 1912, Underwood assessed his chances of winning the nomination as depending on a deadlock among Wilson, Harmon, and Clark, and on New York's voting for him at the "critical" time:

> The Wilson management seems to be attacking every other candidate. . . . [They] started out with the idea that they were going to have a run away race. . . . [They] now find that Clark is beating their candidate in the West, that the probabilities are that I am getting some of the Southern states away from him and that Harmon is strongest in the East. They are losing their temper and abusing everybody. . . . Wilson will probably go to the Convention with about one-third in the race and I will probably have about one hundred votes on the first ballot. From the information I get Mississippi is as sure to go for me as Alabama. Every indication points to my carrying Georgia. My people think that I have a fine chance in Florida and North Carolina. Virginia and Kentucky will probably both go uninstructed, but I feel sure that they will be for me when the time comes. I also expect to get a few scattering votes on the first ballot from the North. The New York delegation will probably go for [Mayor William J.] Gaynor on the first ballot, but I have every reason to believe that if the nomination ties up that it will ultimately come to me. If it does, there will be a very strong chance of my securing the nomination. If New York does not vote for me at the critical time, why, of course, there will be no chance of my winning. I believe a reaction has set in in the country in both parties, and I do not believe that the radical will win out in either convention.[16]

Underwood was overly optimistic. He had underassessed the strength of both Wilson and Clark.

The first objective of the Underwood campaign, victory in Ala-

15. Birmingham *News*, October 21, 1912. George F. Parker, who edited Cleveland's speeches, worked with the Underwood and Harmon forces to forge an anti-Bryan coalition. Harmon agreed to participate in Parker's plan, but there is no record of Underwood's reply to Parker's proposal. George F. Parker to Judson Harmon, June 7, 1912, in Judson Harmon Papers, Historical and Philosophical Society of Ohio, Cincinnati.

16. Underwood to J. H. Woodward, March 25, 1912, in Woodward Papers.

bama, proved difficult. The Wilson and Harmon campaigns in the state were well underway by the time of Underwood's entry. Underwood and Senator Bankhead had previously been identified with Harmon's candidacy, and Birmingham *News* editor Frank P. Glass, a schoolmate of Wilson and leader of the Wilson campaign in Alabama, harassed the Underwood supporters with charges that Underwood was a foil for Harmon. Even Ed Campbell suspected that Underwood might be serving as a "stalking horse" for Harmon.[17]

On February 28 Glass demanded editorially that Underwood comment on the statement of Harmon's manager, Ohio's Lieutenant Governor Hugh L. Nichols, that Underwood's votes would ultimately go to Harmon. At Underwood's request Campbell, whose daughter had recently married Underwood's older son, denied that Underwood had any interest in who might receive Alabama's votes if he should be eliminated. Senator Bankhead made a similar statement and expressed doubt that Nichols had made the statement attributed to him.[18] Glass and the other Wilson followers in Alabama soon found it impolitic to oppose Underwood's candidacy. They redirected their efforts toward the selection of Underwood delegates who would favor Wilson for second choice. John H. Bankhead, Jr., said that this really meant delegates "who at heart prefer Wilson and will go to his support at the first reasonable excuse."[19]

When the state Democratic convention met at Montgomery on April 17, Senator Bankhead persuaded the turbulent assembly, torn by factionalism on prohibition and other state issues, to endorse Underwood and to avoid endorsement of Wilson as a second choice. However, when Bankhead presented the slate of delegates for the national convention, it was apparent that the Underwood forces had compromised by selecting many delegates who were

17. Birmingham *Ledger*, August 31, 1911; Edward K. Campbell to Underwood, December 21, 1911, in Underwood Papers, Alabama Archives.

18. Birmingham *News*, February 28, 1912; Birmingham *Age-Herald*, February 29, March 2, 1912.

19. John H. Bankhead, Jr., to Underwood, April 9, 1912, in Underwood Papers, Alabama Archives.

known to favor Wilson as a second choice. Some actually favored Wilson as first choice, but Senator Bankhead found it impossible otherwise to avoid a battle with the Wilson forces. The anti-Underwood Montgomery *Journal* stated that Wilson would receive the Alabama votes as soon as Underwood was out of the race.[20]

In Georgia the Underwood movement encountered a well-developed campaign for Wilson, whose Georgia associations were numerous. Underwood's position there was strengthened by the withdrawal of Harmon from the Georgia contest, and the Harmon organization was turned over to Underwood. Harmon's name was not removed from the Georgia ballot as Bankhead requested, but no efforts were made for the Ohio governor after the beginning of 1912.[21]

William Randolph Hearst had purchased the Atlanta *Georgian* with the idea of supporting Champ Clark in Georgia, and John Temple Graves, editor of the New York *American*, was sent to Atlanta to organize the Clark campaign. Graves decided, however, that Underwood was stronger than Clark there, and two of Underwood's friends, Clark Howell, editor of the Atlanta *Constitution*, formerly for Harmon but now for Underwood, and Edward W. Barrett, editor of the Birmingham *Age-Herald*, reached an agreement with Graves whereby the *Georgian* would support Underwood. In return the Underwood spokesmen agreed to keep Underwood out of the Tennessee contest. The full force of the Hearst newspaper was turned against Wilson, a service for which Underwood thanked Hearst.[22]

The Underwood campaign in Georgia, as in other states in the Southeast, was based on a sectional appeal. The Wilson forces replied with arguments that Underwood, reared in Kentucky and

20. Montgomery *Journal*, April 24, 1912. The *Journal* said that of the forty-eight man delegation, forty-five were for Wilson as opposed to either Clark or Harmon.
21. John H. Bankhead, Sr., to Nichols, April 9, 1912, in Harmon Papers. See also letters in the Neyle Colquitt Papers for details of the transfer of the Harmon organization in Georgia to Underwood.
22. John Temple Graves to Underwood, May 9, 1912, Edward W. Barrett to Underwood, May 9, 1912, William Randolph Hearst to Underwood, May 5, 1912, all in Letterbox M, Underwood Papers, Alabama Archives.

Minnesota, was less a southerner than Wilson. The endorsement of Underwood by Thomas E. Watson, the aging agrarian liberal, proved an effective boon in rural areas, but it was a mixed blessing, as Watson attacked Underwood's Georgia managers and attempted unsuccessfully to take over the state delegation. Alabama Underwood supporters launched a letter-writing "friends and neighbors" appeal in Georgia, and they, along with Congressman J. Thomas Heflin, moved into Georgia for the campaign. In some measure the contest was a personal feud between Clark Howell, the pro-Underwood editor of the Atlanta *Constitution*, and Congressman Hoke Smith, a pro-Wilson progressive.[23]

The Georgia primary was a stunning defeat for the Wilson forces. Underwood easily won the state by amassing majorities in the rural areas that Wilson's city majorities could not match. The official tally showed Underwood 71,556, Wilson 58,341, Clark 20,867, and Harmon 8,257. William Gibbs McAdoo, who had regarded Georgia as "essential" to Wilson's success, charged that the only explanation for Underwood's victory was "the prodigal use of money."[24]

Following the Georgia primary victory, Senator Bankhead intensified the efforts of the Underwood organization in Tennessee, and John Temple Graves showered the Underwood leaders with telegrams charging them with bad faith in failing to live up to the Atlanta agreement. Graves recalled that the Clark supporters had agreed not to "antagonize" Underwood in Georgia in return for which Underwood would "not antagonize Clark in Tennessee." Both Underwood and Bankhead denied knowledge of the agreement. Underwood stated that his Tennessee campaign had been in progress during the Georgia contest and he could not abandon the

23. Charlotte (N.C.) *Daily Observer*, May 28, 29, 30, 1912; Dewey W. Grantham, Jr., *Hoke Smith and the Politics of the New South* (Baton Rouge: Louisiana State University Press, 1958), 230–34. Watson was not so much pro-Underwood as anti-Wilson. His attacks on the Underwood managers and outbursts against Catholics in the Democratic party so frightened Underwood that measures were taken to see that he did not get the floor at Baltimore. See J. Randolph Anderson to Underwood, June 7, 1912, in Underwood Papers, Alabama Archives.

24. Charlotte (N.C.) *Daily Observer*, May 3, 1912; William Gibbs McAdoo to Woodrow Wilson, April 3, May 4, 1912, in William Gibbs McAdoo Papers, Library of Congress.

Tennessee race and thereby make himself party to an agreement of which he did not approve and "repudiate the friends in Tennessee who had joined their personal fortunes with mine."[25]

The altercation between Graves and Bankhead had little effect on the result in Tennessee. A deal among the representatives of all the candidates arranged a division of the state in which Underwood was to get only 2½ of the state's 24 votes in the national convention. Hilary E. Howse, the mayor of Nashville and one of the managers of the Underwood campaign, said that Harmon and Underwood men in Tennessee would favor the stronger of the two men in the convention. Howse later wrote Bankhead: "We should not get our wires crossed and thereby defeat the prospects of both Underwood and Harmon and take the chance of delivering the state to the Wilson forces."[26]

In Mississippi, another state with a presidential primary, Underwood and Wilson were the only candidates. Underwood was supported by Governor Earl Brewer and Senator-elect James K. Vardaman. Underwood's long-time colleague, John Sharp Williams, favored Wilson. It was an apathetic election, but Underwood defeated Wilson 14,978 to 7,625.[27]

The close relationship between the Harmon and Underwood campaigns was again seen in Senator Bankhead's angry reaction to the announcement that Champ Clark would campaign in Texas against Harmon and Wilson. Bankhead threatened to disregard Underwood's wishes and enter Underwood's name in Kentucky, where Clark was the sole opponent of Wilson, if Clark remained in the Texas contest. Underwood replied soothingly: "Should we now go into Kentucky it would produce bad feelings, and I do not think

25. John Temple Graves to Underwood, May 9, 1912, Underwood to Graves, May 10, 1912, both in Underwood Papers, Alabama Archives. E. W. Barrett confirmed Graves's understanding of the agreement and stated that he thought Bankhead had suggested the arrangement. E. W. Barrett to Underwood, May 10, 1912, in Underwood Papers, Alabama Archives.

26. Memphis *Commercial-Appeal*, May 17, 1912; Hilary E. Howse to John H. Bankhead, Sr., January 25, February 27, 1912, both in Underwood Campaign File, Bankhead Papers.

27. Memphis *Commercial-Appeal*, May 8, 1912; Birmingham *Age-Herald*, May 15, 1912.

that is good politics. The man who is nominated must receive a two-thirds vote in the convention and Mr. Clark's friends will control a large vote. My friends in Kentucky understand my position . . . and should acquiesce in it."[28] Clark, however, withdrew from the Texas campaign, and Wilson defeated Harmon in that state's primary. One Harmon campaigner in Texas, Senator Joseph W. Bailey, an old schoolmate of Underwood's, not only admitted but defended the combination of Clark, Harmon, and Underwood against Wilson.[29]

In North Carolina, as in Georgia, Alabama, and Tennessee, the Underwood movement was championed by former advocates of Governor Harmon. Underwood's North Carolina manager, Henry B. Varner, editor of the Lexington *Dispatch*, was a former Harmon supporter. Neither Clark nor Harmon made any sustained effort in North Carolina, and the Harmon headquarters declined newspaper offers of publicity in the state. Josephus Daniels' Raleigh *News and Observer* led the attack on Underwood, charging that he had entered a combine with Clark and Harmon against Wilson. Daniels also publicized the charge that Underwood had opposed a proposed provision in the Seventeenth Amendment that would have assured Negro disfranchisement in the South.[30] Varner charged that Wilson had spoken "slurringly of the South" in his *History of the American People*, but Wilson won, and the North Carolina Democratic convention elected a delegation largely composed of Wilson men. Underwood's followers, however, were able to stave off instructions for Wilson.[31]

In South Carolina the Underwood movement ran into heavy Wilson sentiment, but although the state Democratic convention endorsed Wilson, the Underwood followers defeated an effort to

28. Telegram from John H. Bankhead, Sr., to Underwood, April 14, 1912, Underwood to John H. Bankhead, Sr., April 15, 1912, both in Underwood Papers, Alabama Archives.
29. New York *Times*, May 4, 1912, p. 2.
30. Charlotte (N.C.) *Daily Observer*, May 23, 1912; Raleigh *News and Observer*, April 18, May 15, 17, 1912. The *News and Observer* noted with amusement that one of the Underwood leaders, P. D. Gold, Jr., urged the formation of Underwood clubs that would "vote for Harmon." The error was quickly corrected.
31. Henry B. Varner form letter, April 23, 1912, in Owen Folio, Underwood Papers, Alabama Archives.

instruct the delegation for Wilson.[32] In Virginia the Underwood movement had the powerful support of the Martin-Swanson machine which threw its weight against a delegation "instructed" for Wilson. Senator Thomas S. Martin and Congressman Henry D. Flood, pro-Underwood members of the Martin-Swanson machine, considered the defeat of instructions for Wilson to be in accord with their position of "anybody but Wilson."[33]

In Florida, as in Georgia, Alabama, and North Carolina, the Harmon forces transferred their support to Underwood. Pleasant A. Holt had been Harmon's campaign manager in Florida, and he was introduced to Senator Bankhead by Harmon's national manager, Ohio Lieutenant Governor Hugh L. Nichols. Holt then became the manager of Underwood's Florida campaign. In like manner, Nichols sent Florida state representative Eugene S. Matthews to Senator Bankhead, who accepted the former Harmon organizer as one of his own. The Pensacola *Evening News*, also shifting from Harmon to Underwood, even advertised the candidates for delegates as those who preferred "Harmon or Underwood." The Underwood campaign in Florida encountered public apathy and the opposition of William Jennings Bryan who spoke in favor of Wilson. Floridians instructed their delegates to vote for Underwood by a vote of 28,343 for Underwood to 20,482 for Wilson, but the twelve-man delegation consisted largely of men who had first declared for Harmon and included two men whose sympathies were known to be for Wilson.[34]

During these state campaigns Underwood maintained friendly relations with Clark and Harmon. After Underwood's victory in Georgia, Clark called on him to assume the Speaker's rostrum temporarily and looked on approvingly as Underwood received an ovation. Underwood and Harmon exchanged friendly letters on the

32. Charlotte (N.C.) *Daily Observer*, May 6, 16, 1912.

33. Henry D. Flood to Sands Gayle, April 11, 1912, in Henry D. Flood Papers, Library of Congress; Birmingham *News*, June 25, 1912.

34. Nichols to Howell, February 26, 1912, Nichols to John H. Bankhead, Sr., April 14, 1912, both in Underwood Campaign File, Bankhead Papers; Pensacola (Fla.) *Evening News*, March 29, 1912; Charlotte (N.C.) *Daily Observer*, April 27, 1912; Jacksonville (Fla.) *Metropolis*, May 11, 1912.

need for governmental economy, and at a dinner in Harmon's honor the Ohio governor "launched out in unstinted praise of Underwood."[35]

The Underwood campaign to stop Wilson in the Southeast had been fairly successful, but received a sharp setback when the Republicans nominated Taft. Underwood had anticipated that Roosevelt would receive the nomination, and it was generally agreed that such a progressive on the Republican ticket would have strengthened Underwood's chances.[36]

The Alabama delegation reflected the dissensions that had been revealed in the state convention in Montgomery. Delegates seemed marked with a wish for self-destruction, and one Alabama editor suggested that "so many sticks" might as well be sent to Baltimore.[37] Trouble began before the delegation left for Baltimore when Underwood, under pressure from his northern backers, rejected his first choice for nomination speaker. He replaced Congressman J. Thomas Heflin, a superb orator but notorious demagogue, with the young, untried, William B. Bankhead, son of Senator Bankhead. The Eutaw House, where the Alabama delegates had reservations, burned, and their reservations were transferred to the St. James, a second-class hotel. Trouble mounted with the selection of Governor Emmet O'Neal as chairman of the Alabama delegation. O'Neal's choice was a slap at Senator Bankhead and was an early omen of Bankhead's inability to control the brawling delegation. Another blow fell on Bankhead when the Alabama delegates rejected Henry Gray, Bankhead's candidate for Democratic national committeeman, and selected former governor William D. Jelks instead.[38]

The Baltimore convention met on June 25, and controversy flared when Bryan opposed the election of Judge Alton B. Parker

35. Montgomery *Advertiser*, May 3, 1912; Auerbach to Underwood, January 8, 1912, in Underwood Papers, Alabama Archives.

36. Birmingham *Age-Herald*, April 26, 1912.

37. Greensboro (Ala.) *Record*, June 25, 1912.

38. Auerbach to Underwood, June 12, 1912, in Underwood Papers, Alabama Archives; Birmingham *Age-Herald*, June 24, 1912; Owen to J. K. Vardaman, June 10, 1912, in Owen Folio, Underwood Papers, Alabama Archives; Birmingham *News*, June 25, 1912.

of New York as temporary chairman. Senator Bankhead tried to explain to the Alabama delegates that a vote against the conservative Judge Parker would be interpreted as a vote for Bryan, and as discussion waxed hot, he declared: "I tell you with all the strength that I can command . . . that unless the Alabama delegation ardently supports [Parker] our candidate will be eliminated." Bankhead's hand was strengthened when Underwood sent a telegram and a message borne by a personal emissary, saying that the election of Parker was essential to demonstrate that the convention was anti-Bryan. Even after Bryan himself became a candidate for temporary chairman, some of the Alabama delegates professed to see no connection between Underwood's nomination and Parker's election. Six of the forty-eight Alabama delegates voted for Bryan; Parker won. The lack of harmony in the Alabama delegation was apparent in the split vote on almost every organizational issue. However, when Bryan denounced Wall Street influences in the convention and demanded that representatives of J. Pierpont Morgan, Thomas Fortune Ryan, and August Belmont withdraw from the convention, the Alabamians stood together. The resolution was highly adverse to Underwood, as Ryan was a Virginia delegate for Underwood and Belmont of the New York delegation was favorable to him. The Alabama delegation voted against Bryan's resolution, but later voted for it in modified form after learning that Bryan had struck the names from the proposed resolution and that the anti-Bryan bloc had no objection to it.[39]

Underwood, the first candidate to be placed in nomination, was presented by "Bill" Bankhead as "Democracy's real leader and best asset." Bankhead, emphasizing the death of sectionalism and Underwood's mastery of the tariff issue, gave an adequate performance that quieted his critics, but there was limited enthusiasm

---

39. Birmingham *Age-Herald*, June 26, 1912; Urey Woodson (comp.), *Official Report of the Proceedings of the Democratic National Convention Held in Baltimore, Maryland, June 25, 26, 27* (Chicago: Peterson Linotyping Company, 1912), 15, 76–77, 129–36, hereinafter cited as *Official Proceedings*; Perry Belmont, *An American Democrat: The Recollections of Perry Belmont* (New York: Columbia University Press, 1941), 505.

among the convention audience. The mild reception given the Bankhead speech did not dampen the ardor of the Underwood demonstration which lasted a half hour. During the cheering a white dove, symbolizing party peace, was released and flew around the hall, eventually perching on a Georgia delegate. Mississippi Governor Earl Brewer's little daughter, Minnie, dressed in red, was paraded around on the shoulders of Underwood supporters.[40]

On Wednesday night, June 26, the Alabama delegates learned that Frank P. Glass, who accompanied the Alabama delegation, had told a New York *Sun* reporter that Underwood could not win the nomination and that Alabama's votes would go eventually to Wilson. Glass denied that he had consciously spoken for publication, but his explanations did the Underwood cause no good. The Birmingham editor acknowledged that his "heart" was with his old college friend, Woodrow Wilson, and that he had been working for him for second choice. Glass concluded that if the Underwood campaign had been mismanaged, as had been implied, the responsibility was "higher up."[41]

Balloting began on the third day of the convention, June 27. The first ballot showed Underwood, as expected, in fourth place with 117 ½ votes. Clark led with 440 ½ votes, and Wilson was in second place with 324 votes. Harmon, whose candidacy was coldly received by the convention, had 148 votes. A major break came the next afternoon when Murphy shifted his 90-vote New York delegation from Harmon to Clark. Clark surged forward to a peak of 556 votes, still well below the 728 votes needed for nomination. Clark's managers, seeing that the shift of Underwood's delegates would bring Clark within 55 votes of the nomination, urged Underwood to accept second place on the ticket. Underwood made it clear to a steady stream of callers at his home in the Dresden Apartments in Washington that he had absolutely no interest in the vice-presidency. Wilson's managers pleaded with the Underwood

40. New York *Times*, June 28, 1912, pp. 1–2.
41. Montgomery *Advertiser*, June 28, 1912.

delegations to stand firm, but there is no evidence that a shift to Clark was about to occur.[42]

On Saturday, the fifth day of the convention, on the fourteenth ballot Bryan announced that he would support no candidate who won the nomination through New York's support. The Bryan attack frightened J. Randolph Anderson, vice-chairman of the Georgia delegation, who telegraphed Underwood that the convention would expect the anti-Bryan people to line up together behind Clark and implied that they should do so. Underwood wired Bankhead: "We control the situation. I hope my friends will stand firm." The weakness in the Georgia delegation was only momentary, and an hour after his first telegram Anderson wired Underwood, "our lines are perfectly safe."[43] For the moment the interests of the Underwood and Wilson delegations were the same, with both waiting for the Clark boom to expire. Bryan's attack made Senator Bankhead's task more difficult. Underwood's hopes hinged on New York support, and Bryan's charge made it exceedingly awkward for Murphy to make another switch. It was rumored that Murphy insisted on Bankhead's getting added support before the New York delegation would help him. "Show me something first," Murphy reputedly told Bankhead. On the nineteenth ballot Underwood reached a peak of 130 votes, including 15 votes from Tennessee and 8 votes from Connecticut. No major breakthrough came, however, and by the weekend adjournment Underwood's strength had receded to 112 ½.[44]

The weekend recess found the convention deadlocked and Underwood's delegates under tremendous pressure to shift to Wilson. Most observers thought that Clark's boom was dead, that the psychological moment for a shift from Underwood to Clark had passed, and that Underwood's withdrawal would merely precipi-

42. *Official Proceedings*, 196–97, 221; New York *Times*, June 29, 1912, p. 3; New York *Herald*, July 1, 1912.

43. Telegram from Anderson to Underwood, June 29, 1912, in Underwood Papers, Alabama Archives; telegram from Underwood to John H. Bankhead, Sr., quoted in Charlotte (N.C.) *Daily Observer*, June 30, 1912; telegram from Anderson to Underwood, June 29, 1912, in Underwood Papers, Alabama Archives.

44. New York *Times*, June 30, 1912, p. 5; *Official Proceedings*, 253–54, 277.

tate the nomination of Wilson. Within the Underwood delegations there was little talk of going to Clark, although James K. Vardaman temporarily lost faith in Underwood's chances. Some Clark delegates, believing that it was too late for help from Underwood, were becoming bitter. Murphy's hold over New York was weakening. The Fourth of July was approaching, and some of the "shouters" in the delegation had already left. New elements in the party, led by William Gibbs McAdoo and young Franklin D. Roosevelt, were demanding that New York shift to Wilson.[45]

The recess gave Underwood's managers a chance to reassess the deadlock. The New York *Herald* declared that Wilson and Clark were destroying each other and that Underwood should be the nominee. At a conference called by Democratic National Chairman Norman E. Mack, Senator Bankhead spoke bitterly against the Wilson forces. Advancing to within two feet of Wilson's manager, William F. McCombs, he declared that McCombs knew that Wilson could not be nominated and should withdraw him. Bankhead told reporters, however, that Wilson would get his tryout on Monday, and if he could not muster the votes, Underwood would then have his opportunity.[46]

Underwood, in his Washington apartment, emphasized that he was in the fight to the end. Again he attempted to stop persistent rumors that he would accept the vice-presidency by stating that he preferred to be representative in Congress from the Ninth District of Alabama. He said that although Clark's managers had asked him to retire from the race, his friend the Speaker had not approached him. Underwood's supporters talked boldly of "reserve" strength that would show itself once Wilson was exhausted. In addition to New York, it was alleged that Underwood had strength in the New England delegations and that Roger Sullivan had promised to bring Illinois to him at the proper time.[47]

On Monday, July 1, Underwood developed little additional

45. New York *Times*, July 1, 1912, pp. 1–3; Birmingham *News*, June 29, 1912.
46. New York *Herald*, June 30, 1912; William F. McCombs, *Making Woodrow Wilson President* (New York: Fairview Publishing Company, 1921), 164–65.
47. New York *Herald*, July 1, 1912; Birmingham *Age-Herald*, July 4, 1912.

strength. Ohio's Harmon delegation, after a bitter fight, threw 10 of its 19 votes to Underwood on the thirtieth ballot to keep him in the race and with the hope of a return favor. The Harmon addition, which was temporary, was counterbalanced by the loss of most of Underwood's Virginia votes to Clark. Senator Claude Swanson explained that Underwood did not have a "ghost of a chance" and that Virginia would vote for Clark, although it would return to Underwood if he developed additional strength. Further trouble for the Underwood contingent developed on the thirty-ninth ballot when Underwood lost two Florida votes to Wilson. Wilson passed the 500 mark. When the convention adjourned there were rumors that Mississippi, Iowa, and Illinois were about to break to Wilson. Underwood denied reports that he was going to Baltimore to withdraw and stated that he would not go "unless they send for me to approve the platform."[48]

On the last day of the convention some of Underwood's New York friends still hoped to block Wilson and to nominate their candidate, despite the alleged shakiness of the Underwood delegations. New York Supreme Court Justice Daniel F. Cohalan, an Irish Catholic friend of Underwood's, arrived at the convention with the idea of persuading his close friends Murphy and Sullivan to make good their promises to come to Underwood's aid. Cohalan had been instrumental in keeping Sullivan's delegation from being thrown out of the Democratic convention in 1908, and Sullivan had sworn undying loyalty to him. Cohalan, it was alleged, developed a plan whereby Underwood's strength would be held until the late afternoon when a tired convention would see Illinois and New York start an avalanche for Underwood.[49]

Tuesday's first ballot, however, was a shock to Underwood's supporters. Sullivan threw Illinois' 58 votes to Wilson, and Senator Claude Swanson climbed on a chair and announced that Virginia's entire delegation, including Thomas Fortune Ryan, was voting for Wilson. The pressure on Senator Bankhead was indescribable. The

48. John W. Devanney to Harmon, July 1, 1912, in Harmon Papers; Baltimore *Sun*, July 2, 1912; Atlanta *Constitution*, July 2, 1912.

49. Baltimore *American*, September 8, 1912.

Alabama delegation, unruly and turbulent throughout the convention, heard that Mississippi had caucused and would stay with Underwood for only one more ballot. John Sharp Williams was leading Mississippi into the Wilson camp. The Wilson men in the Alabama delegation, and indeed, even Underwood's closest friends, now demanded that Senator Bankhead get additional support or withdraw Underwood's name. Bankhead, pleading from ballot to ballot and afraid to leave the delegation for fear they would break to Wilson, asked Sullivan to make good his promise to support Underwood. Sullivan replied that he would go back to Clark on the next ballot, indicating that he was trying to prolong the deadlock. When the Wilson men in the Alabama delegation became impossible to hold, Bankhead was forced to withdraw Underwood's name.[50]

When Alabama was called on the forty-sixth ballot, a hushed convention watched carefully as Senator Bankhead made his way forward. The old Confederate veteran was master of the occasion. Belying his personal sentiments against Wilson, he told the convention that although Underwood had wanted the nomination, he wanted above all to see the eradication "for all time" of the vestiges of sectionalism. The liberal support in the East, Bankhead said, had satisfied the congressman's friends that a southerner could be nominated, but since Underwood had not entered the contest to block any man, his name was now being withdrawn. Bankhead was interrupted by a delegate who urged Underwood for vice-president, but Bankhead replied that anyone could be vice-president and Underwood had repeatedly said no to such suggestions.

Bankhead concluded that Underwood had directed him to release his delegates to vote for "whom they please." There was no question after this statement that Wilson had won the nomination, but Bankhead voted for Clark as the Alabama delegation began its last poll. However, angry threats of exposure by Wilson men in the Alabama delegation compelled Bankhead and the handful of other anti-Wilson delegates to shift their votes to Wilson.[51]

50. *Official Proceedings*, 337–38; Birmingham *Age-Herald*, July 3, 1912; John H. Bankhead, Jr., to Underwood, undated, in Underwood Papers, Alabama Archives.
51. *Official Proceedings*, 346–47; Montgomery *Advertiser*, July 3, 1912.

Underwood was following the results on a ticker at his office in the Capitol when it was announced that Senator Bankhead had withdrawn his name. He turned to reporters and expressed surprise, stating at the request of friends that his name had been withdrawn without his "knowledge or approval," but adding that Senator Bankhead had complete authority to act for him.[52]

Underwood felt that Bankhead had conceded too early and that he had never had a chance to show his strength in the convention. He wrote his father-in-law:

> I never really got a chance to play my hand. Of course, it was necessary to demonstrate that Clark could not win and that Wilson could not win before there would be any chance for me to get a two-thirds vote. After Bryan's attack on Clark, my friends in the New York delegation felt that it was unwise to come to me unless it could be demonstrat[ed] that I could get a large number of votes from other sources. The Convention had become so tied up by that time and was so tired out that the Clark delegations began breaking to Wilson and there was no chance to turn the tide my way. I do not regret though that I entered the race as I think I came out in good shape. It gave me a standing in the country that I could not otherwise have had.[53]

To another friend he wrote: "We came nearer winning out in Baltimore than the face of the situation shows. I agree with you that the greatest difficulty we had was to wake our own people up to the realization that we had a chance to win." A year later one of Underwood's political opponents quoted Charles F. Murphy as having said: "If Roger Sullivan had played fair, we'd have nominated Oscar Underwood as sure as fate."[54]

Underwood's campaign had been launched in close cooperation with that of Governor Judson Harmon. The campaigns were coordinated by the campaign managers, and strong circumstantial evidence suggests that such coordination had been the condition upon

52. Washington (D.C.) *Post*, July 3, 1912.
53. Underwood to J. H. Woodward, July 30, 1912, in Woodward Papers.
54. Underwood to Jesse F. Stallings, August 8, 1912, in Jesse F. Stallings Papers, University of North Carolina, Chapel Hill; L. Breckinridge Musgrove, *Facts About the Senatorial Campaign: The Vital Issues* (Birmingham: Musgrove Volunteer Committee, 1913), 15.

which Thomas Fortune Ryan contributed to both candidates. The financing of the Underwood campaign, which totaled $106,778.85, substantially in excess of the $52,000 reported by Senator Bankhead in the Clapp committee investigation, is obscure—only the $35,000 contributed by Ryan can be definitely accounted for. Underwood's campaign was also related to that of Speaker Clark through the candidates' personal friendship and through William Randolph Hearst, represented by John Temple Graves.[55]

Underwood's strength in the convention was never thrown to Clark for two reasons. The only time it would have helped Clark was immediately following the tenth ballot when Underwood's followers did not think that they had yet had a chance to develop their strength. Also the Underwood delegations, except for Georgia, were predominantly for Wilson as a second choice. As J. Randolph Anderson, vice-chairman of the Georgia delegation, stated soon after the convention, had Georgia shifted to Clark, it would have precipitated the nomination of Wilson.[56]

The Wilson leaders had repeatedly charged that a "dreibund" existed among Clark, Harmon, and Underwood, and the care taken to see that the three anti-Wilson candidates did not oppose each other is strong evidence of such an arrangement. In the Southeast the Harmon campaign was taken over bodily by Underwood's friends. Whatever arrangements existed before the convention, however, were largely meaningless on the floor at Baltimore. Harmon, once a major candidate, was not a serious contender at the convention. Underwood's votes could not have been delivered

55. Thomas M. Owen checkbook, in Underwood Papers, Alabama Archives.

56. Macon (Ga.) *Telegraph*, July 10, 1912. Arthur Link attaches great importance to a letter from Texas delegate Thomas W. Gregory to Edward M. House, July 9, 1912, in the Edward M. House Papers at Yale University. Gregory, claiming much credit for Wilson's nomination, says that he made agreements with the Underwood leaders not to give any votes to Clark after the tenth ballot. The interests of Underwood and Wilson were at that time largely the same. It is to be noted, however, that both of the Underwood leaders to whom Gregory specifically refers, Senator-elect James K. Vardaman and J. Randolph Anderson, were anxious at one time to shift to Clark. The key Wilson leader in the Mississippi delegation was John Sharp Williams, not Vardaman. There was never any real danger that Underwood's votes would go to Clark. See Arthur S. Link, *Wilson: The Road to the White House* (Princeton, N.J.: Princeton Unversity Press, 1947), 450, Vol. I of Arthur S. Link, *Wilson* (6 vols. projected; Princeton, N.J.: Princeton Unversity Press, 1947–).

to any candidate other than Wilson. There is little evidence of strong support for Underwood in the Clark delegations.

Senator Bankhead's often-cited statement that Underwood's campaign demonstrated the elimination of sectional prejudice and Clark Howell's sentimental assessment that the South is "back in the house of our fathers . . . thank God" are gross exaggerations.[57] Indeed, the Underwood campaign was launched in a spirit of sectionalism. John H. Bankhead, Jr., a keen observer at Baltimore, told Underwood that his vote against the Sherwood Pension Act was a major reason for the Underwood delegates' inability to get northern help.[58]

There are other reasons for Underwood's defeat, including the towering influence of William Jennings Bryan in the convention, but the Underwood campaign was handicapped, above all, by its lack of grass-roots support. In the South, Wilson support had been well developed before Underwood's campaign was launched. The Underwood victories in the Southeast were largely superficial, and the Underwood delegations were laced with pro-Wilson sentiment. Wilson's victory at Baltimore was the result of successful campaigning on the hustings and not of deals in the smoke-filled rooms of Baltimore.

57. Birmingham *Age-Herald*, July 5, 1912.
58. John H. Bankhead, Jr., to Underwood, undated, in Underwood Papers, Alabama Archives.

CHAPTER VIII

House Leader
for Wilson

Underwood adapted easily to the loss of the nomination, and he and his wife consoled themselves by purchasing a home in Washington after years of living in rooming houses and apartments. The house at 2000 G Street was bought from the estate of their friend and President Roosevelt's military aide, Major Archie Butt, who perished on the *Titanic*. Built in the late nineteenth century at a cost of about twenty-five thousand dollars, the house cost the Underwoods twelve thousand dollars. Underwood remarked that many of the "swell people" had moved away years ago, thinking that a swamp behind the nearby White House made the area malarious. The swamp, however, had been converted into Potomac Park, and the area improved as prominent officials moved into the neighborhood. The Underwoods planned to spend two thousand dollars to put in electric lights and hardwood floors, though since Mrs. Underwood was a free spender it is doubtful that the renovation was held to that. They also added a room to the first of the three stories. The congressman thought the house would rent for one hundred dollars a month and be a sound investment or could be resold for the purchase price at any time, but they lived there until 1925.[1]

Prior to Woodrow Wilson's nomination, Underwood knew the New Jersey governor very slightly. Wilson was impressed, how-

---

1. Oscar W. Underwood to Joseph H. Woodward, July 30, 1912, in Joseph H. Woodward Papers, in possession of Mrs. Joseph H. Woodward II, Birmingham.

ever, with Underwood's ability and at one stage in the preconvention campaign said that if he were sure of Underwood's devotion to the fundamentals of democracy, he would withdraw in his favor. The Democratic nominee, however, met Underwood for an hour's conference on June 4, 1911, and was unimpressed with the Alabamian's viewpoint. Even so, Wilson urged Democratic leaders to get him to agree to accept the vice-presidential nomination. Underwood preferred, however, to remain in the House, and he refused the offer.[2]

Following Wilson's nomination, the two Democratic leaders met at the Trenton Country Club where Underwood optimistically appraised the political situation as reported by members of the House. The two men discussed briefly the legislative program and reminisced about their experiences (in different classes) at the University of Virginia. After the conference they gave mutually flattering press statements, with Wilson noting Underwood's "singular frankness and openness and charm," and Underwood expressing appreciation of Wilson as "a very great leader of men."[3]

Wilson and Underwood had apparently similar backgrounds. Both were aristocrats, both were educated at the University of Virginia, and both were southerners. Their differences, however, are more striking. Whereas Underwood was fundamentally conservative, Wilson was progressive. Wilson's governmental experience was entirely executive, Underwood's entirely legislative. Underwood later felt that Wilson's chief weakness was his lack of legislative experience.[4]

With Roosevelt Progressives split from the Republicans, there was little doubt that Governor Wilson would be elected. Underwood predicted a "walk-over" and said that if after its defeat the Progressive party continued to exist, it would mean the end of the Republican party. He agreed to campaign especially in Italo-American areas where he was popular because of his advocacy of

---

2. Frank P. Stockbridge, "How Woodrow Wilson Won His Nomination," *Current History*, XX (1924), 568; interview with Oscar W. Underwood, Jr., November 21, 1951.
3. Mobile *Register*, July 18, 1912.
4. Interview with O. W. Underwood, Jr., November 24, 1951.

the removal of the tariff on lemons. He campaigned enthusiastically, ritualistically, and ebulliently, predicting overwhelming
Democratic success. After a few speaking engagements in Alabama, he campaigned in Connecticut, New Jersey, Delaware, and
Pennsylvania. His speeches, largely devoted to the tariff, were
characteristically surfeited with facts and figures. Although he was
handicapped by throat trouble, he was warmly received.[5]

The Democratic party, Underwood maintained, was the party of
progress, and he denounced Theodore Roosevelt and the Progressives. Underwood charged Roosevelt with hypocrisy on the tariff
and noted that while the real progressives had been fighting Cannonism, Roosevelt was hunting lions in Africa. He termed the Progressive platform a "kimona," which covered everything and
touched nothing. Flaying Roosevelt as a friend of the trusts, he
assailed the sanction of the purchase of the Tennessee Coal, Iron,
and Railway Company by the United States Steel Corporation. He
took a gentler attitude toward Taft who, he said, was not "preaching
in one direction and sailing in another." Calling for a "brick by
brick" lowering of the customs, he charged that the protective tariff
had encouraged the growth of trusts which were charging higher
prices domestically than abroad. Protective rates had increased the
cost of living especially for those in the lower income classes. He
advocated an income tax as a method of making the wealthy pay
their share of the taxes but emphasized his belief in the protection
of property rights. Underwood contended that industry had nothing to fear from Democratic tariff policy. He assured the silk workers of Paterson, New Jersey, that raw silk would remain on the free
list, since only expediency and not principle was involved in taxing
a raw material, and since finished silk was an excellent revenue
producer. Silk cloth, however, was a luxury, a good revenue producer, and a competitive commodity, and he favored maintaining
the existing high tariff rate.

In Pittsburgh Underwood explained that a low tariff was to the

5. William C. Beer to Underwood, August 24, 1912, in Oscar W. Underwood Papers,
Alabama Department of Archives and History, Montgomery; Birmingham *News*, September
11, 1912.

advantage of both Pittsburgh and Birmingham. The destiny of these cities, he said, was "beyond the seas," because there was not enough domestic demand to insure the continued success of the steel industry. Underwood stated that in the past forty years the tariff on iron and steel products had been drastically reduced, that the existing rates were scarcely protective, and that the steel industry needed no protection.

Underwood attacked the Republican controlled Senate for rejecting the free sugar bill which the Democratic House had passed in 1911. Although refiners had denied that the price of sugar was affected by the duty, the price had fallen two cents a pound when the House passed the free sugar bill. The sugar tariff was designed to protect the Louisiana cane sugar interests which provided only 7 percent of the nation's sugar consumption, and yet, he said, this industry was no larger in 1912 than it had been in 1894 when sugar was placed on the free list by the Democrats. A revenue tariff was necessary to meet the rising costs of government, he felt, for even though it was an expensive way of raising revenue, the public seemed to prefer this indirect method.[6]

Election day was cool and crisp in Birmingham, and Underwood was given an ovation when he voted at the Harris Transfer Warehouse on Avenue F. With the announcement of Democratic victory, Underwood engaged in hyperbole in saying that Wilson's victory over Taft and Roosevelt "is unprecedented in the annals of our political history." With convoluted language, he wrote that he was "utterly amazed at the wonderful revulsion of sentiment in favor of the Democratic party." He called for a special session of Congress for tariff revision and assured currency reformer J. Lawrence Laughlin that banking reform was second only to the tariff in importance.[7]

Once elected, Wilson gave Underwood a generous share of the

6. Hartford (Conn.) *Daily Times*, October 15, 1912; Paterson (N.J.) *Guardian*, October 19, 1912; Pittsburgh *Sun*, October 26, 1912. Roosevelt, a severe critic of Underwood's tariff policies, spoke in Montgomery during the campaign, but he ignored Birmingham and Underwood. Birmingham *News*, September 30, 1912.

7. Underwood to J. Lawrence Laughlin, November 9, 1912, in J. Lawrence Laughlin, *The Federal Reserve Act: Its Origin and Problems* (New York: Macmillan, 1933), 180–81.

patronage. There were rumors that the Alabamian might be chosen for secretary of the treasury, but it seems unlikely that the president or Underwood ever seriously considered Underwood's joining the cabinet. Underwood had no influence in the appointment of his political enemy, William Jennings Bryan, as secretary of state, but he exercised considerable influence in the appointment of Albert S. Burleson as postmaster general. In Alabama, Wilson declined patronage requests from those who had fought Underwood in the preconvention campaign and appointed Ed Campbell chief justice of the court of claims. In May, 1914, Wilson appointed another Underwood friend, William P. G. Harding, the able president of the First National Bank of Birmingham, to the board of governors of the Federal Reserve System. In Georgia those who had supported Underwood in the presidential primary shared generously in patronage to the dismay of the pro-Wilson Hoke Smith faction.[8]

Wilson returned from a holiday in Bermuda "impatient" to confer with Underwood about the legislative program, but since Underwood was already busy drafting a tariff bill in the Ways and Means Committee, the conference was delayed. At the same time Underwood was meeting with Senator Thomas S. Martin of Virginia, the Senate majority leader, and other congressional leaders to form legislative plans.[9]

Neither Underwood nor President-elect Wilson considered placing women's suffrage on the agenda of the special session that the Democrats were planning. However, women's suffrage advocates marched from New York to Washington the day before Wilson's inauguration to promote their cause. Jane Addams and Senator John F. Shafroth of Colorado, a women's suffrage state, came to Underwood's office and asked that he allow a joint congressional

8. Daniel C. Roper, *Fifty Years of Public Life* (Durham, N.C.: Duke University Press, 1941), 128; Birmingham *News*, November 27, 1912, March 20, 1913; Birmingham *Age-Herald*, May 5, 1914; Birmingham *Labor Advocate*, December 20, 1912; Dewey W. Grantham, Jr., *Hoke Smith and the Politics of the New South* (Baton Rouge: Louisiana State University Press, 1958), 243–45.

9. Woodrow Wilson to Underwood, December 17, 1912, in Underwood Papers, Alabama Archives.

resolution for a women's suffrage amendment to be reported in the special session. Underwood bridled at the suggestion, stating that under no circumstances would he agree and that whenever a women's suffrage resolution was proposed, he would vigorously oppose it.[10]

At Underwood's suggestion Wilson set April 7, 1913, as the opening date for the special session of Congress. Meanwhile, Underwood conducted open hearings on each tariff schedule, the committee meetings extending from eleven in the morning until well into the night. Underwood said that he saw no necessity for reducing the tariff on competitive items or on luxury goods, but he warned that protective rates must go. He later wrote that the committee had drafted the bill in "almost all its details" before the inauguration.[11]

Underwood presented the Ways and Means Committee draft of the tariff bill to Wilson in late March of 1913. He was mildly displeased because his committee had greatly reduced some revenue-producing schedules and had greatly expanded the free list. But Wilson favored an even more thorough reduction of the tariff. Although Underwood had opposed sharp reductions in committee, he emerged smiling from a two-hour session with the chief executive at ten o'clock in the evening of April 1 saying that he and the president were in harmony. He predicted that the Ways and Means Committee would give in to the president's request that raw wool and sugar be added to the free list—the latter after a three-year delay. Wilson and Underwood agreed that the tariff should be presented in one bill in order to expedite passage and prevent logrolling, but Underwood stated that the president was not adamant; the bill might be split up later.[12]

10. [Forney Johnston], *Democratic Senatorial Campaign: The Issue and the Facts* (Birmingham: Roberts & Sons, *ca.* 1914), 52–53.

11. Underwood to Woodrow Wilson, February 20, 1913, in Underwood Papers, Alabama Archives; New York *Times*, January 25, 1913, p. 18; Oscar W. Underwood, *Drifting Sands of Party Politics* (New York: Century Company, 1928), 171.

12. New York *Times*, April 2, 1913, p. 7; Washington (D.C.) *Post*, April 8, 1913. Although the president and Underwood differed in their tariff conference of April 1, this writer had found no corroboration of Arthur S. Link's statement, based upon newspaper

Underwood dropped the new tariff bill into the hopper as soon as the chaplain finished the prayer on April 7. He accompanied the bill with a statement urging revision of the tariff to stimulate "legitimate" industries. The committee had differentiated between necessities and luxuries, and the rates on the former had been reduced to the lowest point commensurate with revenue requirements. Many manufactured items, produced by monopolies, had been placed on the free list, he noted.

The Democratic majority in the Sixty-third Congress had increased from 67 in the previous congress to 164—a potentially unwieldy majority. Underwood resorted to strong tactics to preserve party discipline. With the consent of the party caucus, he announced that no committee assignments would be made until after the passage of the tariff act. In the Democratic caucus of April 12, dissatisfaction with the Underwood bill focused on the three-year delay before sugar would be placed on the free list. Underwood said that the president preferred the compromise and that the delay would give the sugar industry time to adjust. Without that the entire bill might be defeated. Immediate free sugar was defeated by a vote of 155 to 39.

Physically exhausted, Underwood was ordered to bed by his physician. His absence from the Democratic caucus caused considerable concern, but on April 16 he returned to the caucus to defend the placing of wool on the free list. Again calling for loyalty to the president, he stated that of four thousand items in the bill, the president had made only two suggestions for changes, those concerning sugar and wool. The caucus supported him by rejecting a 15 percent duty on raw wool by a vote of 190 to 42. Some favored a more drastic reduction in the rates on ready-made clothing, but

---

accounts and the "Diary" of Josephus Daniels, that Wilson threatened to veto the Underwood bill if passed without further reductions. In his published diaries Daniels gives no indication of the threat of a veto, and in his *The Wilson Era* he pays tribute to Underwood as the one most responsible for the framing of the tariff. Arthur S. Link, *Wilson: The New Freedom* (Princeton, N.J.: Princeton University Press, 1956), 180, Vol. II of Arthur S. Link, *Wilson* (6 vols. projected; Princeton, N.J.: Princeton University Press, 1947–); Josephus Daniels, *The Cabinet Diaries of Josephus Daniels, 1913–1921* (Lincoln: University of Nebraska Press, 1963); Josephus Daniels, *The Wilson Era: Years of Peace, 1910–1917* (Chapel Hill: University of North Carolina Press, 1946), 222.

Underwood checked the move by pointing out that clothing manufacturers paid an offsetting duty on dress goods that would place them at a disadvantage if the rates were further reduced. Another controversy in the ten-day Democratic caucus resulted from a proposed amendment to give a 5 percent discount on the tariff to goods arriving in American bottoms. Underwood vigorously defended this provision as a method of fostering the merchant marine, and an attempt to strike it failed by a vote of 128 to 60.[13]

Underwood brought the tariff bill from the caucus with only minor changes and reported it from the Ways and Means Committee on April 23. Some felt that Underwood's bill would be emasculated in the Senate, but markedly little bitterness had developed in the caucus; Underwood had pledges of support from all but 13 of the 290 Democratic representatives. Underwood's tariff report and his accompanying speech on April 23 opened a five-day general debate on the tariff. The New York *World* praised the report as a classic on American economy comparable to Hamilton's report on manufactures.[14]

Underwood claimed that the Democratic party was revising the tariff with "an edict from the American people." The Underwood bill, he said, was not new, but it had received the approval of the voters in the elections of 1910 and 1912. Underwood defined the tariff doctrines of the Democratic party:

> The Democratic party stands for a tariff for revenue only, with the emphasis on the word "only." We do not propose to tax one man for the benefit of another except for the necessary revenue that we must raise to administer this government economically.
>
> We adopt the competitive theory. We say that no revenue can be produced at the custom house unless there is some competition between the products of foreign countries and domestic products; that if you put the tariff wall so high that you close the door to importation no revenue can be raised.[15]

13. Washington (D.C.) *Post*, April 8, 13, 17, 1913; New York *Times*, April 20, 1913, Sec. 2, p. 3.

14. Washington (D.C.) *Post*, April 21, 1913; New York *World*, undated clipping in Underwood Family Folder, Underwood Papers, Alabama Archives.

15. *Congressional Record*, 63rd Cong., 1st Sess., 330.

Attacking the Republican theory that the tariff should equal the difference between production costs at home and abroad with an allowance for a reasonable profit, Underwood denied that high American wages resulted from the protective tariff. He said that better industrial organization, greater productivity, and low transportation costs had helped keep American wages high. He concluded in a spirit of moderation: "We have endeavored to lower the tariff wall with a jackscrew, since it was not our commission to lower it with an ax." The new tariff would produce, Underwood said, only slightly less than the Payne-Aldrich Tariff. Sharply rising government costs, however, created an anticipated deficit of some seventy million dollars, which could be erased by a proposed income tax. Underwood admitted that he was figuring rather closely, basing his estimate of a balanced budget on the assumption that pension costs would decline and that the Democrats could reduce defense expenditures.[16]

The debate was *pro forma* since the approval of the Underwood bill by the House was a foregone conclusion. Underwood allowed no other business, and though he reminded the Republicans that they had an opportunity to amend the bill, unlike the procedure used by the Republicans in passing the Payne bill, the Republicans and the sugar and wool Democrats lacked the strength to alter it. The bill's opponents lacked unity; some argued that the rates were too high, while others were equally convinced that they were too low. Underwood defended the free sugar provision, saying that the Louisiana cane sugar industry was doomed even if sugar were not free-listed. A move to strike the free sugar provision failed decisively by a vote of 186 to 88. Efforts to raise the rates on cotton goods above the 5 to 25 percent of the Underwood bill also failed. An attempt to strike raw wool from the free list failed by a vote of 193 to 74.[17]

Underwood opposed Republican suggestions that a maximum and minimum clause be inserted into the bill, whereby the president could increase tariff rates by 25 percent as had been done in

16. *Ibid.*; New York *Times*, April 23, 1913, p. 2.
17. New York *Times*, May 2, 1913, p. 2, May 3, 1913, p. 4; Underwood, *Drifting Sands of Party Politics*, 172.

the Payne-Aldrich Tariff. He noted that European nations had discarded the retaliatory maximum and minimum principle and used instead a maximum rate with the inducement of reciprocal tariff reductions. He preferred the bill's provision authorizing the president to negotiate reciprocal trade agreements subject to congressional ratification as the most practical adjustment. The Underwood bill passed the House on May 8 by a vote of 281 to 139. Only five Democrats voted against the bill, a loss more than offset by a gain of 7 Republican, Progressive, and independent votes.[18]

Underwood had pushed the tariff bill through the House with almost unprecedented speed. His major problem had been to keep the Democrats from logrolling and consuming too much time in speeches designed for the folks at home. Many young congressmen emerged from the office of the Alabamian only to realize that they had relinquished their usual coveted tariff speeches. Republicans found that on the floor of Congress a few words off the subject brought a soft-spoken but firm statement from Underwood that if such dilatory tactics persisted, he would cut off debate by the use of the previous question.

Underwood's Chesterfieldian tactics were praised on both sides of the House. On the Democratic leader's fifty-first birthday, Republican leader James R. Mann paid tribute to Underwood as "one of the ablest men in public life" and praised his "broadness and bigness." One observer noted that Underwood not only looked "hale and hearty," but he did not appear to be within ten years of his age. Underwood's courtly manners had seemed contagious, and the decorous debate over the tariff of 1913 was in marked contrast to the bitter wrangle over the Payne-Aldrich Act of 1909.[19]

Underwood's even disposition on the House floor was not always matched by restraint off the floor. While the tariff bill was under consideration, a Senate Lobby Committee investigated President Wilson's charge that "an insidious lobby" was attempting to defeat the bill. The investigation produced surprising testimony from a

18. *Congressional Record*, 63rd Cong., 1st Sess., 1327.
19. *Congressional Record*, 63rd Cong., 1st Sess., 1210; New York *Times*, May 6, 1913, p. 12.

National Association of Manufacturers (NAM) lobbyist who said that he had protested the appointment of Congressman William B. Wilson as chairman of the Committee on Labor in the Sixty-second Congress (1911–1913), but Underwood had candidly replied that Wilson was appointed not because he was desired, but because there was no other available candidate. The implied criticism of Wilson was certain to cause trouble with Underwood's labor union constituents. The lobbyist further revealed that the Ways and Means Committee had in its employ one clerk who was at the same time on the payroll of the NAM. Underwood reacted angrily to these relatively mild allegations, charging into the committee room, disrupting the hearing, denying that he had ever met the witness, and branding the lobbyist a "liar" and a "blackmailer." Underwood, attempting to make amends to his labor constituents, maintained that Wilson had been selected because of his obvious qualifications, but he did not specifically deny that the Ways and Means Committee had employed an NAM lobbyist. The lobbyist had testified to no more than a brief, casual conversation with Underwood, whose hair-trigger temper was displayed.[20]

The Underwood bill remained in the Senate for four months before it was approved on September 9, 1913. The bill, as returned to the House, contained over six hundred amendments, mainly slight reductions in the rates, but the general pattern of the bill was unchanged. Underwood said: "I am not disposed to fight the Senate for the purpose of maintaining all the House provisions. There are no differences of principle involved. I am convinced the Senate has cut too much revenue from the bill, and if I can convince the conferees that my estimates are correct, I think the Senate will be willing to put some of the revenue back in place."[21]

Underwood and Senator Furnifold M. Simmons of North Carolina conferred with members of the Ways and Means and Finance committees to resolve the differences between the Underwood bill and the Senate amendments. The House conferees agreed to the

20. New York *Times*, July 30, 1913, p. 6.
21. Birmingham *News*, September 3, 1913.

addition of several commodities, including pig iron, to the free list, but cast iron pipe, which the Senate had placed on the free list, was compromised at 10 percent. The Senate had placed a heavy duty on brandies used in fortifying sweet wines, but the conferees added wines to the free list. The Senate conferees accepted the lower House duties on citrus fruits; bananas were left on the free list as in the Underwood bill. The senators reluctantly acceded to Underwood's insistence on a 5 percent tariff discount for goods arriving in American ships, but Underwood lost a fight to reinsert his bill's stringent antidumping clause.[22]

The average rate of the completed Underwood-Simmons bill was 27 percent, slightly lower than either the House or the Senate bill and some 10 percent lower than the rates of the Payne-Aldrich Act. The expanded free list included wool, sugar (after three years), meats, lumber, foodstuffs, farm produce, and many types of farm and office machinery. No tariff board was provided, but a group of experts were to operate under the president in a study of the tariff.[23]

The elimination of the tariff on modern art was quite clearly Underwood's personal achievement. In 1908 he had considered art a "luxury of the rich," but in writing the new bill he cooperated with his good friend John Quinn, who represented the Association of American Painters and Sculptors, in adding modern art to the free list and leaving the secretary of the treasury with the thorny and often ridiculous problem of what was art.[24]

The iron and steel schedules are worthy of special study because of their relationship to Birmingham and Underwood's father-in-law's Woodward Iron Company, and because Senator Simmons, chairman of the Senate Finance Committee, stated that Under-

22. New York *Times*, September 11, 1913, p. 5. Underwood was a close friend of William C. Beer, an agent for Italian fruit importers, who claimed credit for influencing Underwood in favor of a low tariff on fruits. Beer reputedly received $140,000 for his services relative to the fruit schedule, and he was honored with the king of Italy's Cross of the Chevalier. New York *Times*, July 27, 1915, p. 5.

23. Frank W. Taussig, "Tariff Act of 1913," *Quarterly Journal of Economics*, XXVIII (1913), 1–30.

24. Robert Underwood Johnson to Underwood, December 2, 1908, in Underwood Papers, Alabama Archives; New York *Times*, September 26, 1913, p. 10.

wood was "not entirely immune" to those interests. The Underwood bill contained an 8 percent duty on pig iron and a similar duty on ferromanganese, an alloy used in making pig iron. Critics of the Underwood bill charged that the duty on ferromanganese would benefit United States Steel which owned most of the domestic ore deposits. Ferromanganese, however, was a raw material imported to Birmingham. The duties on ferromanganese and on pig iron were eliminated in the Senate. Placing pig iron and coal on the free list was of little importance to land-locked Birmingham. Steel rails and wire for fencing, Birmingham's most important products, were both on the free list as in the original Underwood bill.[25] The Senate slightly reduced the rates on other important Birmingham iron products, and the final bill included 10 percent on cast iron pipe, 5 percent on bar iron, and 10 percent on structural steel.

There was much dissatisfaction in Birmingham with the iron and steel schedule. Underwood repeated the arguments he had made during the Payne-Aldrich debates, saying that Birmingham was protected from foreign competition by freight costs to the inland market. He regretted the loss of a stringent clause that would have assured the steel industry against "dumping" in times of stress. He explained that removal of the tariff on iron ore and coal would lead to some imports into the eastern market, but that the Birmingham district, which had never shipped these heavy raw materials to the East, would be unaffected. Steel rail production, Underwood stated pointedly, was controlled by an international cartel, and the Democratic party could not safeguard such an agreement. He suggested that the Birmingham iron industry might benefit from the new tariff because of its superior natural facilities. Confidence on the part of United States Steel Corporation that the new tariff would be satisfactory was shown by the sudden resumption of work

25. Furnifold M. Simmons, *F. M. Simmons, Statesman of the New South: Memoirs and Addresses*, ed. J. Fred Rippy (Durham, N.C.: Duke Unversity Press, 1936), 58; *Congressional Record*, 63rd Cong., 1st Sess., 855. Simmons said that Underwood was never again "entirely cordial" with him. He thought that this disagreement explained Underwood's denial of Simmons' claim to the position of minority leader and his selection of Joseph T. Robinson of Arkansas as his successor in 1923.

on the large Corey wire plant, which had been suspended during the debates on the steel schedules of 1912.[26] As on past occasions Underwood had answered Birmingham critics of his low tariff position forthrightly and courageously.

Underwood's direct influence was seen in the establishment of virtually free trade between the Philippine Islands and the United States. He had earlier supported tariff advantages for the Philippines, but his current bill embodied the recommendations of the Bureau of Insular Affairs, which dealt generously with the islands. Underwood opposed attempts of cigar manufacturers to limit Philippine cigar production but supported demands of Secretary of War Lindley M. Garrison that the income tax apply to the Philippines, maintaining that the local government needed the income tax revenue that would be remitted by the United States.[27]

In presenting the conference report for the approval of the House, Underwood maintained that the completed bill reduced rates to about 26 percent, lower than any tariff in the last three quarters of a century. The final bill, he said, was lower than the House or the Senate bill and was almost as low as the Walker Tariff of 1845, which he noted had low duties on liquor and tobacco (contrary to the Underwood-Simmons bill). The conference committee had accepted all but three or four of the Senate reductions, and the Senate had receded from over half of its increases. The Democratic party, he asserted, had kept its promise to the American people without injuring the manufacturing interests of the country,

26. Birmingham *News*, May 11, 22, 1913. Representative August O. Stanley of the Steel Investigating Committee charged that Tennessee Coal and Iron Company's low costs resulted from the use of convict labor, including trivial lawbreakers recruited from the streets. Underwood replied that foreigners, except for Scotch and Irish miners formerly employed in the Pittsburgh area, were not employed in the mines. The Birmingham district's Italian community was not employed in the steel industry. The furnaces had never used convict labor, he said, and although TCI once used some convict labor in the coal mines, the practice had been discontinued. Petty criminals from the municipal jail had never been used, Underwood explained, and the only convict labor that remained in the Birmingham steel industry was in the independent coal mines of the area. Stanley's colleagues on the committee declined to support his charges. *Congressional Record*, 63rd Cong., 1st Sess., 817–18.

27. *Congressional Record*, 63rd Cong., 1st Sess., 1245–46, 1329; Lindley M. Garrison to Underwood with memorandum, March 24, 1913, in Underwood Papers, Alabama Archives. See also, Pedro E. Abelarde, *American Tariff Policy Towards the Philippines, 1898–1946* (New York: King's Crown Press, 1947), 94, 103–18.

and the new tariff would result in a surplus of over eighteen million dollars in 1915. The effect of Underwood's oration was somewhat marred when Congressman Victor Murdock, a Republican, humorously related the way in which the majority members of the conference committee had locked him out of the meeting room in order to draw the bill in secret. The bill passed the House on September 30, 1913, by a vote of 255 to 104, with party lines generally adhered to on both sides.[28]

Underwood maintained that the new bill provided a competitive tariff that would ultimately benefit the consumer by lowering the prices on such products as woolen clothing, sugar, and eggs. He warned manufacturers not to cut wages or shut down their plants on account of the new tariff and threatened a congressional investigation if any such move occurred. The New York *Times* considered Underwood's threat to be an intimidation of industry and an invitation to organized labor to make unreasonable demands.[29]

Professor Frank W. Taussig concluded that neither the Underwood-Simmons Act nor its premises were as radical as both friends and enemies of the measure maintained. There was no theoretical difference, Taussig said, between a tariff intended to equalize production costs at home and abroad and a competitive tariff that assumed a partition of the market between the domestic and foreign producer. Nor was Underwood's distinction between "legitimate" and "illegitimate" industries more than a metaphysical subtlety, and if such a difference existed it was disregarded in the framing of the schedules. Taussig thought few economists would agree with Underwood's contention that high tariff rates directly burdened the taxpayer, and he maintained that many of the changes in the Underwood-Simmons Act were inconsistent and "unscientific." The new tariff, he said, abolished rates that were only nominal in a number of cases, and in other instances drastically reduced phenomenally high rates which nevertheless remained effectively prohibitive.

In spite of these criticisms, Taussig called the Underwood-Sim-

28. Birmingham *News*, September 30, 1913.
29. New York *Times*, July 25, 1913, p. 3.

mons Act a good piece of legislation, being especially pleased with the administrative features of the bill. After all, the professor's skepticism about the effect of the act on the lowering of prices was only another way of saying that the tariff did not have the pervasive economic importance that had been attributed to it. Taussig later noted that this tariff remained in force nine years; only one tariff act, the Dingley Tariff, had a longer life. Another financial expert, Secretary of the Treasury William Gibbs McAdoo, later praised the Underwood-Simmons Tariff Act that he helped frame as "an unusually sound and reasonable tariff measure." McAdoo described Underwood as "a well-grounded tariff expert" and said that except for the intercession of World War I the act would have had "a permanent influence for good upon all future tariff legislation."[30]

President Wilson signed the Underwood-Simmons Tariff Act at an elaborate ceremony. Using two gold pens, the president signed "Woodrow" and handed a pen to Underwood, who stood before him in striped trousers and cutaway, and when he completed the signature Wilson handed the second pen to Senator Furnifold M. Simmons.[31] The ceremony symbolized for Underwood the completion of nineteen years of tariff reform effort, and doubtless this was his finest hour.

The income tax provision of the tariff bill was largely the work of Cordell Hull, but Underwood headed a subcommittee to review Hull's draft. Underwood was a strong advocate of the income tax, and he had repeatedly distinguished between an income tax as a tax on wealth, and a protective tariff as a "tax on consumption." Underwood did not, however, perceive the far-reaching significance of the income tax. Asked by a reporter if he thought this tax might become an important basis of government revenue and be-

30. Taussig, "Tariff Act of 1913." This brilliant article is a reply to Underwood's speech of April 23, 1913. See *Congressional Record*, 63rd Cong., 1st Sess., 328–33. Frank W. Taussig, *The Tariff History of the United States* (New York: G. P. Putnam's Sons, 1931), 447; William Gibbs McAdoo, *Crowded Years: The Reminiscences of William Gibbs McAdoo* (Boston: Houghton Mifflin, 1931), 202, 267.

31. New York *Times*, October 1, 1913, p. 2.

come universally applicable, Underwood laughed and refused to speculate.[32]

Southern agrarians used the tariff bill as a vehicle to correct long-standing abuses in the cotton futures market. The Underwood tariff bill returned from conference with the Clarke amendment, added by southern agrarian radicals and designed to prevent speculation in cotton futures. The Clarke antigambling amendment, hardly less drastic than the 1910 Scott proposal that would have destroyed cotton exchanges by forbidding them to use interstate communications media, would have taxed cotton futures sales with the intent of destroying the futures market. Cotton exchanges were little more than gambling institutions since those buyers who demanded delivery of cotton were forced to accept "punk" or unspinnable cotton at an arbitrary price differential from middling cotton. Cotton farmers were convinced that the exchanges were defrauding them, and their unhappiness was reflected in demands that the exchanges be regulated or outlawed. President Wilson objected to the Clarke amendment and asked Underwood to sponsor the less stringent Smith-Lever amendment, which would require brokers to deliver the proper grade of cotton (or one grade different at a realistic price differential) or pay a heavy tax on the transaction. In offering the amendment, Underwood said that it provided the only chance for enactment at that session and that the amendment could be perfected in conference. Underwood argued that the Smith-Lever proposal was regulatory, whereas the Clarke amendment would have destroyed the cotton exchanges.

Underwood piloted the Smith-Lever proposal through the House with considerable difficulty. Richmond Pearson Hobson and other southern agrarians demanded the pound of flesh from the cotton exchanges and were unmoved by arguments that the Clarke amendment would leave the cotton business in the hands of cotton mills and large spot cotton dealers. However, the Smith-Lever

32. Cordell Hull, *The Memoirs of Cordell Hull* (2 vols.; New York: Macmillan, 1948), I, 70; Philadelphia *Record*, October 19, 1913.

substitute passed by a vote of 171 to 161, with party lines almost disappearing in the conflict. The Senate refused to concur with the Smith-Lever substitute, and all hope of cotton futures legislation ended for the session.[33] Similar but more detailed regulation of cotton exchanges was enacted in the Smith-Lever Cotton Futures Act in the summer of 1914 with Underwood's support.

Despite his seeming mastery of House Democrats, Underwood did not always dominate the Democratic caucus. On June 25, 1913, he offered in the caucus a plan for the creation of a budget system. A House Budget Committee of twenty-five members would report to the House the amount of anticipated revenue available for collection during the next fiscal year and apportion the amount among those committees that traditionally made appropriations. The Underwood budget proposal would have concentrated power in the hands of a few members of the House, and it was vigorously opposed. It failed by a vote of 95 to 80, with more than 115 Democrats failing to attend the caucus.[34] Without question budgetary reform was greatly needed, but the House was not ready to surrender its budgetary control to a central committee.

Drafting the tariff bill had been a task of Herculean proportions, and Underwood referred to the early part of 1913 as a "bush winter." In early October Underwood announced his candidacy for the United States Senate and, suffering from a severe cold, vacationed in Atlantic City for ten days before returning to his duties. He spent his time walking on the beach and attempting with limited success to avoid reporters. He said he felt he never wanted to hear the word "tariff" again and had decided to retire from the House.[35]

Underwood had little part in drafting the Glass-Owen federal reserve bill but played an ambiguous role relative to efforts of agrarian radicals to inject agricultural credits legislation into the bill. Democratic sponsors of the Glass-Owen bill religiously maintained that it did not provide "asset currency," or the issuance of

33. New York *Times*, September 28, 1913, p. 3, October 1, 1913, p. 1, October 3, 1913, p. 1.
34. *Ibid.*, June 26, 1913, p. 5.
35. Philadelphia *Record*, October 19, 1913.

currency against a bank's assets. The bill clearly did provide asset currency since commercial paper could be used as security against which currency was issued. To admit that the bill was an asset currency measure would confess departure from the Democratic platform and invite demands from southern agrarians for the inclusion of agricultural credits as security for currency issues.

More candid than other administration leaders, Underwood admitted that the Glass-Owen bill was indeed an asset currency measure. He appeared for a time sympathetic with the aim of the agrarian radicals, and he secured elimination of a provision whereby the currency reserves of rural banks could be removed from their federal reserve districts to correspondent banks in other areas. He further fueled agrarian radical hopes by securing an amendment to the rediscount section of the bill, allowing the use of warehouse receipts against staple crops for credit and currency purposes. The advocates of agricultural credit legislation appeared victorious, but Underwood acceded to President Wilson's request that the rural credits provisions be withdrawn from the federal reserve bill in order that the subject might be dealt with in a separate bill.[36] Whether Underwood had deliberately encouraged the agrarian radicals, intending thereby to make the agricultural credits provisions unpalatable to conservatives, is unclear. In his senatorial campaign, he argued that he had merely acceded to the president's wishes.

The passage of the far-reaching Underwood-Simmons Tariff, with its important income tax, and the Federal Reserve Act did not quell the demand for reform. Attorney General James C. McReynolds' prosecutions of trusts together with continuing revelations of corporate malfeasance contributed to public demands for antitrust legislation. President Wilson responded by calling on the second session of the Sixty-third Congress to pass antitrust legislation and the Harrison narcotics bill, and to repeal the Panama Tolls Act.

Underwood supported the passage of the Harrison Anti-Narcot-

36. New York *Times*, August 18, 1913, p. 6.

ics Act, which placed a tax on opium in order to regulate its sale. The tax was necessary, he said, because the government lacked the power to prohibit the entry of opium. The bill, introduced as a result of international efforts to control the opium traffic, had little opposition, but it furnished an interesting example of Underwood's assent to legislation tending toward development of a federal police power. In later years when he devoted himself almost obsessively to opposing prohibition, Underwood regretted having favored the Harrison Anti-Narcotics law. A dope peddler could conceal a hundred thousand dollars worth of dope in his coat lining, he said, and the law had put the dealers on the street, selling dope even to children.[37]

The second session droned on, seemingly without end. Congress had been in session almost continuously for two years, and almost everyone wanted to go home—especially Underwood, who had been nominated for the Senate in April. Nevertheless, he reluctantly accepted the president's request for the passage of antitrust legislation, and the Democratic caucus agreed to limit the Democratic program to the antitrust bills. In doing so, the caucus shunted aside demands for women's suffrage, prohibition, and rural credits legislation. Agrarian Democrats were keenly disappointed at the failure of the caucus to approve rural credits legislation and, during the debate over antitrust legislation, interrupted Underwood's efforts to secure passage of these bills by a filibuster—demanding that farm credits legislation be passed first. Underwood maintained that although he favored such legislation, the regular Democratic program must first be enacted.[38] Before the session ended, however, the outbreak of war in Europe necessitated the passage of neutrality, revenue, and shipping legislation.

Underwood had been unenthusiastic about antitrust legislation, having assured a business leader in 1913 that he saw "no danger to the country in fair and sane combination." Well after the president endorsed the proposed "definitions bill," a measure designed to

37. *Congressional Record*, 63rd Cong., 2nd Sess., 1543; Velma Chambers to author, February 24, 1969, in possession of Evans C. Johnson, DeLand, Fla.
38. New York *Times*, May 13, 1914, p. 1, May 15, 1914, p. 16, May 16, 1914, p. 6.

strengthen the Sherman Act, Underwood said it was best to leave the act in its present form since the courts had defined its meaning rather well. The passage of new legislation might, he suggested, increase rather than decrease the debatable area around the act. Underwood's reservations about antitrust legislation were reflected in his restive suggestions that Congress had gone on too long. The people, he said, were clamoring not so much for legislation as for a respite in which they might conduct their business. In mid-June, 1914, he suggested an adjournment to Senate leaders with the view of persuading the president that antitrust legislation could be considered at an extra session in November. But the Senate Democratic caucus insisted that there be no adjournment until the antitrust bills were disposed of.[39]

Whatever reservations he had about antitrust legislation, Underwood's doubts seem to have been resolved—perhaps by presidential pressure or by the fact that much of the "definitions bill" became the Clayton bill, bearing the name of Alabama's Congressman Henry D. Clayton, whom Underwood respected greatly. The Clayton bill in its final form contained a provision exempting labor unions from the antitrust laws, an exemption Underwood had voted for in earlier bills. In an effort to get members back from the hustings to pass this legislation, he secured passage of a resolution cutting off salaries of House absentees, and Wilson consented to a thirty-five day recess in November, 1914. The House returned to approve the Clayton bill in October by a vote of 277 to 52, and a bill setting up the Federal Trade Commission passed by an overwhelming majority—325 to 12. A railroad financing regulation bill passed by a *viva voce* vote, and a bill regulating stock exchanges also passed. Thus the House passed four antitrust bills, but the bills providing for government regulation of railroad financing and of stock exchanges met death in the Senate. Wilson signed the Clayton bill on October 15 and wrote Underwood appreciatively of Congress' work in putting through his program to "destroy private

39. John A. Topping to Underwood, September 22, 1914, quoting Underwood, in Underwood Papers, Alabama Archives; New York *Times*, March 1, 1914, p. 12, June 15, 1914, p. 1, July 2, 1914, p. 8.

control and set business free." In reply Underwood attributed progress in Congress to the president's magnificent leadership and looked forward to an era of peace as the "crowning success of the Wilson administration."[40] Wilson's letter was important in Underwood's senatorial campaign.

Three territorial bills in which the president expressed interest were passed during—and after—Underwood's last period of House service. Two of these bills attempted to give home rule to the Philippine Islands and Puerto Rico although neither promised independence. Underwood agreed to the president's request that the Jones bill for broader based civil government in the Philippines be brought up in the House, and it reached the floor and passed in October, 1913. The Senate failed to act, but a similar measure became law in 1916. Another Jones bill, providing self-government for Puerto Rico, failed to reach the floor in the special session but was passed in slightly altered form in 1916. A third territorial bill, the Alaskan railway bill for government ownership and operation of a one thousand mile railroad, was passed in the regular session in February, 1914. Underwood defended the Alaskan railway bill against charges of socialism and compared the project with the Reclamation Act of 1902, saying that the government could finance such a venture out of the "private purse" of the nation. Private enterprise could not, he said, build the Alaskan railroad unaided, and Congress must either build the railroad itself or subsidize a private corporation for the same purpose. He noted that the nation was obligated to develop the potentially wealthy Alaskan territory and to build its defenses.[41]

Before Wilson's New Freedom legislation was completed, national attention shifted to the foreign sphere—first to Mexico, engaged in revolution, and then to Europe, where war broke out in July, 1914. Underwood was essentially interested in domestic eco-

40. Link, *Wilson: The New Freedom*, 425–27; Wilson to Underwood, October 17, 1914, Underwood to Wilson [October 17, 1914?], both in Underwood Scrapbook, II, 135, in Underwood Papers, Alabama Archives.

41. Underwood to Woodrow Wilson, July 22, 1912, in Letterbox M, Arthur Yager to Underwood, January 15, 1915, both in Underwood Papers, Alabama Archives; *Congressional Record*, 63rd Cong., 2nd Sess., 3338–39.

nomic affairs and generally had little awareness of, or interest in, foreign affairs. In some measure, however, he, like President Wilson, was pulled into the international arena. His awareness of European conditions was heightened by his younger son's gloomy reports from Paris where he was practicing law. Oscar, Jr., prophesied, "Europe is on the verge of the greatest war in its history."[42]

The first foreign problem to confront the Wilson administration, however, was not European but was recognition of the Huerta regime in Mexico. Underwood supported the administration's nonrecognition stance, and after Wilson's August 27, 1913, speech elaborating on his policy of "watchful waiting," he described this restrained statement as the "message of a statesman." In September, 1913, responding to an urgent request from Secretary of State William Jennings Bryan, Underwood sponsored passage in the House of an appropriation of $100,000 for Mexican repatriation work. Wilson requested authority to seize Vera Cruz after the Tampico incident in April, 1914, and Underwood, with some flag-waving, offered a resolution authorizing military action against the Huerta government. Expressing hope that peace would result, Underwood declared that "peace never comes to the door of the coward." The resolution passed.[43]

The outbreak of the European war in July, 1914, eclipsed the Mexican situation, and Underwood was soon involved in problems created by the war. With the withdrawal of the British merchant marine, the ports of Mobile and New Orleans lost their capacity to get cotton to market. A rail stoppage between the mid-South and the Atlantic seaboard exacerbated the lack of transportation. The disruption of American shipping sent the price of cotton spiraling downward to six cents a pound, half its former value, and the closing of the cotton exchanges aggravated this situation; cotton farmers in Alabama panicked. Among the measures Underwood supported to relieve the cotton crisis was the Cotton Warehouse Act

42. O. W. Underwood, Jr., to Underwood, July 29, 1914, in Oscar W. Underwood Papers, University of Virginia Library.
43. New York *Times*, August 28, 1913, p. 2, September 13, 1913, p. 1; *Congressional Record*, 63rd Cong., 2nd Sess., 6934–38.

of 1914, which facilitated the inspecting and licensing of cotton warehouses and enabled farmers to readily borrow on cotton warehouse certificates. Urging cotton farmers to be patient, assuring them that the shipping crisis was only temporary, Underwood suggested that they withhold cotton from the market and await higher prices. He predicted that the credit provisions of the Federal Reserve Act and the new warehouse licensing system would help as soon as they became effective. The cotton surplus would be dissipated when exchanges began to find ways of shipping cotton abroad; Britain would quickly clear the seas, and the loss of continental markets would be more than balanced by increased demands in other world markets, he observed, as he resisted frenetic demands of cotton farmers for production taxes, valorization, or destruction of cotton. In opposing such legislation he noted that only a third of the members of Congress were from cotton-growing constituencies and that the remaining representatives would oppose efforts to raise the price of cotton. He maintained that such price-fixing was unconstitutional, producers of other commodities would also demand relief, the cost would be unbearable, and the results would be of dubious value. Limiting production by taxation was, he said, "a rather violent use of the taxing power" and might well boomerang.[44] These were courageous views for one recently nominated for the Senate from a cotton state.

The economic difficulties of 1914 were reflected in disappointing federal revenues reported at the end of the fiscal year on June 30, 1914. Although Secretary of the Treasury McAdoo wired Underwood his congratulations that the Underwood-Simmons Tariff had produced the expected amount of revenue, the income tax fell short of estimates. Underwood charged a widespread hiding of income, and urged an increased appropriation for the use of the commissioner of internal revenue in collecting the tax. Although Underwood explained that the government had ended the year with a surplus, he had excluded expenditures on the Panama Canal, and

44. *Congressional Record*, 63rd Cong., 3rd Sess., 462; Underwood to Henderson-Black Company, August 31, 1914, in Underwood Papers, Alabama Archives.

thus by the usual methods of government accounting the government had a small deficit for the year.[45] Underwood and the Democrats had miscalculated somewhat.

By August the financial recession of the summer amounted to a panic, and with the European and New York stock exchanges closed, borrowers found no available money. The Germans were hammering through Belgium, and the new Federal Reserve System was still in abeyance. The Federal Reserve Act had repealed a provision of the Aldrich-Vreeland Act providing for emergency currency, and the administration proposed to revitalize this plan by issuing one billion dollars in emergency currency to alleviate the European drain on the United States gold supply. Underwood pushed the currency expansion bill through the House quickly, with only the Progressives—still smarting from the lack of a rural credits bill—dissenting. Secretary of the Treasury McAdoo was poised in New York waiting to pump the additional currency into circulation.[46]

War conditions precipitated a further decline in customs receipts, and in the autumn the president determined that additional revenue was essential. In September, 1914, Underwood sponsored an administration war revenue bill that levied license taxes on bankers, brokers, and tobacco manufacturers and stamp taxes, similar to those levied during the Spanish-American War, on a wide variety of luxuries. The original bill included a 3 percent tax on freight to be shared by the shipper and the carrier. Railroad officials opposed the freight tax, and several railroad presidents quietly called on Underwood at his home to emphasize their opposition. The freight levy was removed from the bill (a small stamp tax remained) since the Democrats were almost unanimously opposed. Almost all of the members of the Ways and Means Committee preferred to substitute an increase in the income tax to the stamp and license taxes proposed in the war revenue bill, but Un-

45. Telegram from William Gibbs McAdoo to Underwood, July 1, 1914, in Underwood Scrapbook, II, 117, Underwood Papers, Alabama Archives; *Congressional Record*, 63rd Cong., 2nd Sess., 11240–42; Birmingham *News*, June 28, 1914.
46. *Congressional Record*, 63rd Cong., 2nd Sess., 13167–70.

derwood, with powerful backing from the White House, defeated the income tax advocates. Why did Underwood reverse his usual position and favor consumer taxes rather than an increase in the income tax? The consumer taxes levied by the administration on beer, domestic wines, and licenses were almost identical to the stamp taxes of the Spanish-American War against which Underwood had crusaded. Evidently, presidential pressure led him to change his position.[47] Consumer taxes also had the practical advantage of producing revenue much more quickly than would an increase in income taxes.

The gathering storm in Europe did not alter Underwood's opposition to heavy naval expenditures. In 1913 Underwood had favored the building of one battleship when large-navy advocates were sponsoring a four battleship program, and "little navy" men opposed the building of any battleships at all. With a brief flurry of oratory, Underwood had maintained that there was no danger of invasion, that the country would not be attacked so long as it was "just and right" in its treatment of other nations, and that American integrity and moral courage were the best assurance against attack. The one battleship program was in keeping with President-elect Wilson's wishes, and some observers thought that without Underwood's compromise the House would have voted no battleship at all.[48]

Even the European war did not convince Underwood of the necessity for a large navy, and in 1915, calling for economy, he decried the "hysterical demands" for a heavy naval program. Congressman Richmond Pearson Hobson, defeated by Underwood in the 1913–1914 Senate race, advocated an ambitious naval program. Underwood countered that the nation was in no more danger of war than it had been a year earlier and that an armament race would mean "war at the end of the story." The House refused to follow Underwood's lead in sticking to a one battleship program,

47. New York *Times*, September 11, 1914, p. 18, September 22, 1914, p. 1; John Quinn to Underwood, August 29, September 1, 1914, both in Underwood Papers, Alabama Archives; Birmingham *Age-Herald*, September 24, 1914.
48. *Congressional Record*, 62nd Cong., 3rd Sess., 3980–81, 4080, 4810.

but at his suggestion it eliminated five coastal defense submarines from the bill; however, the naval bill in its final form carried the originally proposed sixteen submarines.[49]

Underwood's bias against the navy was again revealed in his opposition to the Navy Plucking Board, a commission for the removal of unfit officers. Underwood confessed his ignorance of naval affairs but asserted that the board had removed officers unjustly. He voted with the majority of the House and the Senate to abolish the board and allow the president to reinstate the discharged officers.[50]

Underwood was more interested in promoting a strong merchant marine than a large navy, and World War I afforded an opportunity for pressing merchant fleet legislation he had long favored. In 1910 Underwood had joined Champ Clark in proposing a merchant marine bill to give indirect merchant marine subsidies through a 5 percent tariff advantage to goods arriving in American ships. Such a subsidy would have been in excess of ten million dollars a year, but the bill was defeated.[51] He did, however, secure the insertion of a 5 percent discriminatory clause in the Underwood-Simmons Tariff Act of 1913. The discrimination in favor of American-owned ships was in addition to the 10 percent discrimination given to most-favored-nations. The State Department and the Senate conferees had objected to the 5 percent clause, believing the most-favored-nations could claim the advantage of the additional rebate, and since such trade comprised the bulk of United States foreign trade, the effect would have been an across-the-board reduction of tariff rates by 5 percent.

After the passage of the Underwood-Simmons Tariff, the president, sensing a conflict between the 5 percent discriminatory clause and United States treaty obligations, asked Underwood to secure repeal of the discriminatory rebate clause. Noisily supported by the Hearst press, Underwood refused. The rebate was less drastic than the maximum and minimum provision of the Payne-Aldrich Tariff and was advantageous to shippers and ship

49. *Ibid.*, 63rd Cong., 3rd Sess., 3116–17, 3134, 3141–44.
50. *Ibid.*, 2912.
51. Birmingham *Ledger*, March 2, 1910.

owners, Underwood said. The president had been told of the 5 percent rebate before the passage of the bill and could, if he desired, abrogate any trade agreements that were in conflict with the discriminatory clause. Underwood tenaciously favored the 5 percent clause although its advantages to American shipping would have been slight. In the Senate, Democratic leader Furnifold M. Simmons favored repeal of the 5 percent clause, but maintained that such a revenue bill could not originate in the Senate. The House followed Underwood's leadership and did not act. Interpretation of the 5 percent clause was left to the Supreme Court which weakened the clause by ruling that the advantage did not apply to goods coming from most-favored-nations.[52]

Underwood again was supported by the Hearst press when he opposed President Wilson's request for repeal of the Panama Tolls Act, which was especially objectionable to Great Britain. The tolls act, the president thought, violated a treaty commitment requiring United States ships to pay tolls equal with those of foreign ships, and preferring not to deal with the sensitive foreign relations question publicly, Wilson quietly asked congressional leaders to see that the statute was repealed. Underwood objected that the United States merchant marine needed the benefits of the tolls act in order to recapture foreign trade and promote the American merchant fleet. Repeal, he said, would endanger American sovereignty over the canal, and he warned that it could result in the inability of the United States to prevent the passage of foreign warships through the canal. Announcing that he would lead the opposition, Underwood forced the president to make public his fight for tolls repeal. President Wilson appeared personally before a joint session of Congress, dramatically saying that without repeal of the tolls act he would be unable to deal effectively with foreign problems of greater moment. Neither pressure from the president nor from acquaintances such as Andrew Carnegie, Robert Underwood John-

---

52. Birmingham *News*, October 15, 1913; New York *American* editorial, undated clipping [October 9, 1913?] in Underwood Scrapbook, II, 46, Underwood Papers, Alabama Archives; New York *American*, March 1, 1914.

son, and Henry White changed the obdurate Underwood. But tolls act repeal passed the House by a vote of 247 to 162 with Underwood, Clark, and a number of representatives from Irish Catholic areas of the East in opposition. The Senate, unenthusiastic about repeal, attached an amendment that reiterated United States sovereignty over the canal. Although approving of the Senate amendment, Underwood was not mollified, and he called the repeal "one of the most unfortunate legislative acts in history." Members on both sides of the aisle applauded as Underwood restated his views. Having made clear his opposition to the repeal bill, however, he voted with the heavy majority for the Senate amendment and for repeal, which was completed without the necessity for a conference committee.[53]

In August, 1914, Underwood sponsored the creation of a Bureau of War Risk in the Treasury Department to insure American merchant ships against war losses. The United States, he explained, must either pay its European debts in gold or insure the transit of American goods to get the ships out of port. Other nations were insuring their cargoes, the cost would be small, and even with the best conditions the United States was faced with a critical shipping problem. He fought off an amendment to define contraband according to the London Agreement of 1909, arguing that contraband was subject to international treaty, and the London Agreement had never been ratified by the United States. During the debate, Underwood touched off an angry exchange with Republican leader Mann by referring to the opposition as "un-American."

Underwood had long been a critic of restrictive American registry laws, and he sponsored the administration's bill to liberalize registry for American owned vessels as a war measure. The bill, drawn by Eugene T. Chamberlain, commissioner of the Bureau of Navigation, suspended the law excluding foreign-built ships of more than five years of age from American registry. Underwood

53. Andrew Carnegie to Robert Underwood Johnson, undated [ca. February 10, 1913], Robert Underwood Johnson to Underwood, February 12, 1913, both in Underwood Papers, Alabama Archives; Congressional Record, 63rd Cong., 2nd Sess., 10329–30; Link, Wilson: The New Freedom, 307–12.

denied that the bill would bring the nation closer to war, and the bill passed.[54]

Underwood unenthusiastically supported the Alexander ship purchase bill, which proposed to create a United States shipping board to finance the building or purchase of government-owned merchant ships. Although denounced as "socialistic," the bill passed the House only to die in a Senate filibuster. President Wilson thought, with cause, that Underwood had not adequately pushed the measure. After Underwood entered the Senate a similar measure, in which the government was committed to withdraw from ship operation after a period of five years, was passed with Underwood's vigorous support.[55]

Underwood supported the administration in March, 1915, by presenting a neutrality resolution to the House. Counselor Robert Lansing of the Department of State had given him the resolution, stating that its purpose was to fulfill the obligations of the United States under international law. The resolution was hastily drawn, and under close questioning Underwood admitted that he was ill prepared to discuss it. Underwood declined to interpret the resolution, which he had received only a few minutes before, and stated that the basic responsibility for it must rest with the president. Congressmen were thus left to interpret the resolution for themselves. Although the neutrality resolution passed the House, Senate objections led the White House to substitute another, clarifying that an embargo against the belligerents was not authorized.

Congress adjourned following the passage of the neutrality resolution and a resolution defining the president's authority to protect United States maritime rights against abuse by belligerents. Among the bills not acted on were the Alexander ship purchase bill, independence for the Philippines, and a rural credits bill. President Wilson had requested passage for each of these bills, but

54. *Congressional Record*, 63rd Cong., 2nd Sess., 14395–14437; New York *Times*, August 2, 1914, Sec. 2, p. 3, August 4, 1914, p. 6.
55. *Congressional Record*, 63rd Cong., 3rd Sess., 2758, 2804–2806; New York *Times*, August 19, 1916, p. 1.

Underwood had either been unable or unwilling to get them through.[56]

Underwood's sponsorship of the neutrality resolution was his last service for the administration as House leader. In November, 1914, he had overcome nominal Republican opposition and was elected to the Senate. He sadly concluded his career in the House of Representatives on March 4, 1915, as the Sixty-third Congress adjourned. Congressman A. Mitchell Palmer, who was also retiring, paid tribute to Underwood: "Although he is not a genius, he does possess in a greater degree than I have ever known the qualities which are necessary for successful leadership of men. He has infinite patience, consummate tact, and unfailing good humor toward friend and foe alike, and above all absolute and entire command of himself. No matter how fiercely the storm may have been raging about him, his followers have always known that their leader was in absolute control of himself."[57] Palmer announced that members of the House of Representatives had arranged through voluntary subscription to have Underwood's portrait painted and hung in the Ways and Means Committee room alongside those of former chairmen.

The entire House membership rose and cheered Underwood as he began his last House speech. He paid tribute to Republican minority leader Mann and then to Speaker of the House Champ Clark. Referring to the crossing of his and Speaker Clark's political ambitions in the contest for the Democratic presidential nomination in 1912, he said that there had not been "a moment when a spirit of friendship and brotherly love has not existed between us." He concluded extravagantly by calling Clark "the greatest Speaker of the American Congress."[58]

Clark was moved to tears by the tribute. The following day he wrote Underwood: "You have some sense of the bereavement I feel

56. *Congressional Record*, 63rd Cong., 3rd Sess., 5453–55; New York *Times*, March 4, 1915, p. 1.
57. Hartford (Conn.) *Times*, March 5, 1915.
58. Washington (D.C.) *Post*, March 5, 1915.

at your quitting the House. You and I know better than any other how much I will miss you in the next Congress. If you are not promoted [to the presidency] you will probably beat [William B.] Allison's length of service in the Senate."[59] Thus ended a highly successful collaboration between Speaker Clark and his chief lieutenant. Underwood wrote his mother with rather startling egotism and exaggeration that only during his closing speech when he saw "scores of strong men about me with the tears running down their cheeks" did he realize how sad he felt at leaving the House.[60]

Underwood declared that the Sixty-third Congress had completed more work and passed more constructive legislation than any other Congress, but because of the war and subsequent depression the path had been hard. The Democratic administration, he said, had been confronted with almost every possible accident, including the European war and the disruption of world trade. President Wilson summarized the work of the Congress as the Underwood-Simmons Tariff, the Federal Reserve System, the Clayton Act, the Federal Trade Commission Act, repeal of the Panama Tolls Act, the regulation of cotton exchanges, the Alaskan Railway Act, and the act to admit foreign-owned or built ships to American registry.[61]

Perhaps President Wilson never realized fully his indebtedness to Underwood for the passage of his reform program. Several years later Andrew J. Peters of Massachusetts, one of Underwood's colleagues on the Ways and Means Committee, wrote: "Champ Clark did very little and the whole work of leadership came on you. President Wilson didn't seem to realize what the legislative work meant. You certainly received little cooperation from the president and small recognition of your share in carrying out the Legislative program which made the period [in] which you were house leader

59. Champ Clark to Underwood, March 5, 1915, in Underwood Papers, Alabama Archives.
60. Underwood to Frederica Virginia Underwood, March 6, 1915, in Underwood Papers, University of Virginia.
61. New York *Evening Post*, March 10, 1915; New York *Times*, March 5, 1915, p. 4.

so memorable."[62] It is an anomaly that Underwood, a conservative, was largely instrumental in securing the passage of Wilson's New Freedom program, the most comprehensive domestic reform program to that date. Underwood favored moderate but significant tariff reform, and he worked consistently for that purpose. He attempted to secure somewhat protective rates for Birmingham iron products, but this effort was less intense than might have been expected from the representative of an iron and steel manufacturing center. Underwood's fundamental conservatism has been noted, but there is little to indicate that he had in the Wilsonian period evolved any doctrinaire political philosophy. He supported the Harrison Anti-Narcotics Act and the Alaskan Railway Act, although the former involved expansion of the federal police power and the latter provided a subsidy. There is no unified philosophy in Underwood's theory of tariff reform. He rejected free trade just as he rejected the protective tariff idea. His "competitive" tariff scheme lacked the jewel of consistency, but it contained the grit of pragmatism. Unhampered by pedagogical devotion to a systematic philosophy, he was able to secure passage of a moderate tariff reform bill.

Underwood went along with most of the Wilsonian program with varying degrees of enthusiasm; in general, he acted as a moderating influence. Party loyalty, patronage, and Wilson's shrewd management explain Underwood's adherence to much of the New Freedom. Toward the end of his House career, Underwood appeared increasingly independent of presidential control and assertive of his independence as he looked forward to a senatorial career, yet foreign affairs were becoming more important, and in that area he tended increasingly to side with the Democratic president.

---

62. Andrew J. Peters to Underwood, undated, in Undated File, Underwood Papers, Alabama Archives.

CHAPTER IX

The Hobson
Campaign[1]

Underwood's last year and a half in the House overlapped with his campaign for the Senate. He had coveted a Senate seat for many years, but the seats were occupied by two ancient and revered Confederate veterans, John Tyler Morgan and Edmund Pettus. Despite their obvious infirmity Morgan and Pettus were reelected in 1906, but the legislature cannily provided for the election of "Alternate Senators"—"pallbearers" the senators called them. John H. Bankhead and Joseph F. Johnston, both friends of Underwood, were elected as alternates. Both senators died in the summer of 1907, and though Underwood might have opposed Johnston's reelection in 1909 or Bankhead's in 1912, it would have been politically hazardous. Underwood had faced strong potential opposition for his congressional seat in 1908, and it became politically unwise for him to venture forth in statewide politics. In 1912 he was a candidate for the Democratic presidential nomination, and his campaign was managed by Bankhead. The death of Johnston, a fellow Birminghamian, created the desired vacancy. Congressmen Richmond Pearson Hobson and Henry D. Clayton had announced for the seat prior to Johnston's death. Frank S. White, a prohibitionist and candidate for Johnston's unexpired term in a race to be

1. The best sources for this campaign are two intensely partisan campaign pamphlets: [Forney Johnston], *Democratic Senatorial Campaign: The Issue and the Facts* (Birmingham: Roberts & Sons, *ca.* 1914) and L. Breckinridge Musgrove, *Facts About the Senatorial Campaign: The Vital Issues* (Birmingham: Musgrove Volunteer Committee, 1913). See also, J. H. Patten, *Truth About Underwood, Hobson, Clarke, McElderry and Others* (Birmingham: Roberts & Sons, *ca.* 1914).

conducted simultaneously with the race for the full term, was not a candidate for the regular term. Underwood had found the physical demands of his position as House majority leader quite burdensome, and in mid-1913 he had momentarily considered retiring from politics. However, his wife felt that he might find sanctuary in the Senate, and his mother had a sentimental desire to see him in the body once occupied by his grandfather, Joseph Rogers Underwood. Nevertheless, it was with mixed feelings that Underwood decided to leave the House of Representatives. Senator John H. Bankhead, the senior senator, and other friends counseled him against surrendering his tenacious hold on the Ninth District Congressional seat for the uncertainties of a senatorial campaign. Underwood was familiar with Thomas B. Reed's description of the Senate as a place where good politicians go when they die, and his friends pointed out that the Senate was a poor stepping-stone to the presidency. Underwood did not think, however, that his election to the Senate would affect his availability for the presidency.[2] In a lead editorial, September 7, 1913, Victor H. Hanson, publisher of the Birmingham *News*, urged Underwood to announce for the Senate. Underwood replied that he was "disposed to enter the race" but that he could not become a candidate until and unless his new tariff bill became law.[3]

Political pundits speculated that a three-cornered race between Underwood and Clayton, local optionists, and Hobson, a strict prohibitionist, would result in a Hobson victory. Twenty-four hours after the tariff bill was signed into law, Underwood authorized the *News* to announce his candidacy, stating, "With the enactment of the tariff bill I have completed the work in the House that [it] has been my ambition to accomplish." Before retiring from public life, he said, he would like to represent Alabama in the Senate.[4] He

2. Bertha Underwood to Mrs. A. H. Woodward, September 21, 1913, in Joseph H. Woodward Papers, in possession of Mrs. Joseph H. Woodward II, Birmingham; Birmingham *News*, September 19, 1913; Oscar W. Underwood to O. W. Underwood, Jr., October 14, 1913, in Oscar W. Underwood Papers, Alabama Department of Archives and History, Montgomery.
3. Birmingham *News*, September 7, 8, 1913.
4. *Ibid.*, October 3, 1913.

later explained that before deciding to run for the Senate, he had
already decided to retire from the House. In the Senate, he said,
he would not have the "worriment and responsibility" that he had
had in the House.[5]

Frank P. Glass, the local optionist editor of the Birmingham
News, persuaded President Wilson to secure Clayton's withdrawal.
According to the public announcement, Wilson requested Clayton
to withdraw because of the important antitrust legislation pending
before the Judiciary Committee of which Clayton was to be chairman.[6] Wilson's appointment of Clayton to the federal bench following the passage of the Clayton Anti-Trust Act and immediately after
Underwood's victory in the Democratic primaries, suggests that
Clayton was promised a judgeship if he would step aside. Although
the tariff law was already on the books, the president could hardly
risk the displeasure of Underwood, who might well determine the
fate of the federal reserve bill as well as other administration measures in the House.

Clayton's withdrawal left Underwood opposed by Hobson, an
enfant terrible of Alabama politics. Reared in Greensboro, Alabama, the heart of the black belt, and educated at Southern University and Annapolis, Hobson had achieved distinction as a naval
officer in the Spanish-American War. He sank the navy collier
Merrimac in Santiago Bay in an unsuccessful effort to block the exit
of the Spanish navy, but he nevertheless became a popular hero.
After the Spanish-American War he retired from the United States
Navy, entered politics, and, in the election of 1906, unseated veteran Congressman John H. Bankhead. Hobson demonstrated his
independence from his southern colleagues in speaking for and in
voting for a court of inquiry in 1909, established to review the discharge of three companies of Negro soldiers precipitously dis-
missed "without honor" following the Brownsville riot of 1906. An
introspective, grave-faced man with "a smoldering fierceness in his
eyes," Hobson possessed many of the elements of a popular political leader. He was forty-two years old, eight years Underwood's

5. Philadelphia *Record*, October 19, 1913.
6. Birmingham *News*, October 12, 1913.

junior, and was gifted with an eloquence for which Underwood's stilted oratory was no equal. Handsome though balding, abstemious in personal habits, Hobson added to his national fame by Chautauqua speeches in which he inveighed with boundless zeal against drug addiction, alcohol, and the yellow peril and crusaded for a large navy, women's suffrage, federal aid to education, direct popular election of the president, and world government.

However, Underwood had by far the stronger political following of the two candidates. Outside of Alabama many expressed surprise that Hobson, nationally known as an irrepressible alarmist against the threat of Japanese aggression, could defeat Underwood, but the rising prohibition movement made him a powerful candidate. The prohibitionists were strengthened by the unpopularity of the graft-riddled administration of Alabama Governor Emmet O'Neal, whose influence had led to the repeal of statewide prohibition.[7]

Underwood's campaign was aggressively managed by Forney Johnston, son of the late Senator Johnston. A small pugnacious man who wore suits that seemed to swallow him, Johnston was an unrestrained campaigner and wielded a vitriolic pen. He prepared a sixty-four page campaign book which reviewed Underwood's and Hobson's records and attacked Hobson venomously. He organized the state thoroughly, creating Underwood committees in every county and giving special attention to preachers because of their influence with prohibitionists. Johnston's well-laid plans were plagued by those of rival Underwood organizations whose tactics he disliked. Underwood preferred to avoid allowing the contest to become a referendum on the prohibition issue and to stress Hobson's congressional absenteeism and his "unsoundness" on the Negro question. In a positive way the Underwood organization emphasized its candidate's national stature, his favors to agriculture, his prolabor record, and his identification with the popular Wilson administration.[8]

---

7. Montgomery *Advertiser*, October 23, 1949; Birmingham *News*, September 26, 1913.
8. Forney Johnston to Underwood, December 13, 1913, in Underwood Papers, Alabama Archives.

While Hobson campaigned in Alabama, he was scored by Underwood's friends on the floor of the House of Representatives. Congressman Jeremiah Donovan of Connecticut, from the Danbury hatters' district, often a critic of congressional absentees, attacked "the great naval constructor," as he called Hobson, for absenteeism. Stung by these charges, Hobson left his Alabama campaign and attacked Underwood from the floor of Congress. Hobson admitted that the Underwood-Simmons Tariff was the "greatest piece of legislation" that he had seen in the House and "perhaps since the foundation of government," but he noted that the Ways and Means Committee had framed only one tariff in a decade (he overlooked Underwood's bills of 1911 and 1912) whereas his Naval Affairs Committee framed a bill every year.

Hobson maintained that he could not get access to the press, which was influenced by liquor advertising, and had to resort to the lecture platform. Replying to Underwood's charges that he had favored the Brownsville raiders, he said that he had favored reopening the case since there had been no trial. He explained that his endorsement of Underwood in the recent race for the Democratic presidential nomination had been obtained under "false pretenses," as he would not have supported him had he known of Thomas Fortune Ryan's contribution to Underwood's campaign. Underwood was, he said, a "dummy" being used as a tool of Wall Street.

Underwood, replying before friendly House colleagues, pointed out that he had been in almost constant attendance in Congress, having been absent only five times in eighteen years for illness or deaths—never for a political campaign. Underwood denied that he had knowledge of Thomas Fortune Ryan's gift to his 1912 presidential campaign and asserted that he had visited his campaign headquarters no more than three times. He said, but later retracted, that Wilson had received a contribution of ten thousand dollars from Ryan for his New Jersey gubernatorial campaign. Although not charging his opponent with dishonesty, he said that Hobson had voted with the shipbuilding and lumber interests (in voting for a tariff on lumber) while placing products of his district on the free list. Underwood maintained that he had always favored prohibitionist-sponsored antishipping bills and that, except for contributions from his family, he had financed his own campaigns. Turning dramatically to his colleagues, Underwood asked if any other man considered him a "tool of Wall Street" as Hobson had charged. There were cries of "No, no" from both sides of the aisle, and when Hobson tried to interrupt, his fellow congressmen shouted, "Sit down."[9]

Exhausted by his work on the tariff bill and suffering with a hacking cough, Underwood was reluctant to return to Alabama to campaign, but he made three brief visits at the insistence of friends. In late October, 1913, he returned to Birmingham with Mrs. Underwood after an almost continuous absence of two years and was received as a conquering hero. Thousands of people lined the streets to greet the most famous Alabamian of the day. The roll of drums and the blare of trombones announced his arrival, a tired, clean-shaven man in a soft hat, accompanied by his modish wife almost hidden by a bouquet of roses. The senator met for the first time his nine-month-old granddaughter, Eugenia "Ge Ge" Underwood, the daughter of his older son, John Lewis. That evening he delivered a long and tedious address at a Birmingham Board of Trade banquet in his honor at the Hillman Hotel. He described the tariff of 1913 as a method of regulating monopoly through "fair and honest competition." The pending federal reserve bill would correct, he asserted, "the worst banking laws and currency laws in the civilized world." The bill would create a more flexible currency, avoid the peril of tying the nation's credit to New York banks, and prevent currency shortages such as Birmingham had experienced in the panic of 1907 when warehouse certificates illegally circulated as money. Underwood concluded rather dismally that the Balkan Wars had resulted in the withdrawal of money from western Europe to the Balkans and that the nation faced rather "stringent times." His listeners were baffled, as well as bored, as there were no signs of depression in Birmingham.[10]

9. *Congressional Record*, 63rd Cong., 1st Sess., 5549, 5639–49.
10. Birmingham *News*, October 24, 25, 26, 1913.

In a speech at Selma, Underwood defended himself against Hobson's charges with uncharacteristic rancor. Denying that he had prior knowledge of Clayton's retirement from the senatorial race, he said that he had announced to his friends before the death of Senator Johnston that he would be a candidate for the Senate after the tariff bill became law. He refuted Hobson's charges that he was a tool of the liquor interest and had opposed good roads legislation—indeed he noted that he had sponsored good roads legislation soon after entering Congress. Underwood's strongest attack, however, was reserved for the race question. He reminded his black-belt audience that he had been chairman of the committee that secured ratification of the conservative Alabama constitution which was "a great reform in the interest of the integrity of your boys and the safety of your wives and daughters." Developing the same racist theme, he drew a lurid picture of the Brownsville raid, charging, erroneously, that Hobson was the only southerner to vote for the resolution providing for the reinstatement of the Negro soldiers (actually the resolution provided a court of inquiry which resulted in the return of 167 of the black soldiers to service). Concluding his Alabama campaign with eighteen speeches in two days, Underwood returned to his duties in Washington.[11]

Hobson's campaign was managed by L. Breckinridge Musgrove, a wealthy but folksy Jasper industrialist, who published a campaign book that replied in kind to Johnston's brochure. Evidently hoping that the severity of his attacks would so anger Underwood that he would return to Alabama to accept Hobson's challenges for a debate, Hobson conducted a strenuous crossroads campaign, speaking several times a day and drawing large crowds. He excused his absence from Congress by charging that the press was "kept" and by asserting that he could reach the people only by going directly to them. Undoubtedly, the Alabama press was predominantly for Underwood. The Birmingham *News* counted sixty-seven newspapers that had announced for Underwood and forty-five for Hob-

11. *Ibid.*, November 12, 26, 1913. Hobson was not the "solitary" southerner to vote for the board of inquiry. Several congressmen from the border states voted for it. *Congressional Record*, 60th Cong., 2nd Sess., 3399–3400.

son. Among the dailies only the Birmingham *Ledger* and the Montgomery *Journal* favored Hobson. Hobson received fervent editorial
support from two "hand organs," the Alabama *Citizen*, published
by the Alabama Anti-Saloon League, and the Birmingham *Advance*, which he financed and published.

Hobson caustically attacked Underwood as a tool of the liquor
interests—a friend of "liquor, red liquor and straight liquor"—and
he produced affidavits to prove that Underwood had proclaimed
before a group of school children that he took a drink whenever he
liked. He pointed out that Underwood had in 1899 opposed a bill
to prohibit the Sunday sale of whiskey in Washington and had
voted "wet" in a Birmingham local option election in 1907, basing
the latter charge on the statement of a minister who "happened" to
be looking over Underwood's shoulder when he cast his ballot. Underwood had opposed statewide constitutional prohibition in 1909
and had opposed the Webb antishipping bill, Hobson said. He was
backed by the "wet" and graft-ridden administration of Governor
Emmet O'Neal and was the candidate of a "wet," anti-Hobson conspiracy. Hobson's supporters continually arraigned Underwood's
cousin Charles ("Cousin Chawles") Lewis, lobbyist for the Alabama
Wholesale Liquor Dealers Association. Hobson asserted that Underwood had rejected an amendment to the Underwood tariff that
would have provided for a tariff on brandies used in fortifying
wines, and on one occasion he claimed that the liquor interests had
appropriated a half million dollars for Underwood's campaign.[12]

Captain Hobson, who had strong support among Protestant
churchmen, injected religion into the campaign by emphasizing
the fact that Underwood had made a speech before the Catholic
Club of New York. One Hobson committee urged the people to
line up with the Protestants and Masons against Underwood who,
with the Catholic church, was opposed to Hobson's plan of public
education. Underwood felt compelled to deny that he was a Roman
Catholic, but on the other hand the use of the term "Jesuitical

12. Birmingham *Advance*, March 14, 1914; Birmingham *News*, November 12, 18, 27,
1913, January 16, 20, February 17, 1914.

assertion" as an epithet in the campaign book forced Forney Johnston to do some explaining to the Catholics.[13]

Hobson and leaders of the Alabama Farmers Union persistently charged that Underwood was no friend of the farmer, centering their attack on the Underwood-Simmons Tariff Act. Hobson argued that the bill had not been written by Underwood and pointed out that the Senate had revised it downward over six hundred times. Inconsistently, Hobson held Underwood responsible for putting cotton bagging and ties on the dutied list and striking the Clarke amendment which would have prohibited gambling in cotton futures. Underwood produced a telegram from the secretary of the treasury proving that cotton bagging and ties were being admitted free. Referring to the Clarke amendment, Underwood said that he had secured passage in the House of a substitute favored by President Wilson that would have regulated the exchanges, but the amendment was stricken in the Senate. Hobson recalled Underwood's opposition to the "phossy jaw" bill which outlawed the manufacture of matches by the dangerous phosphorous process, but the issue aroused little attention.

Refuting a Hobson charge that he had opposed rural credits provisions in the Federal Reserve Act, a letter was secured from Senator Carter Glass giving Underwood the credit for resolving the only controversy over that phase of the act. When Hobson supporters declared that they meant cooperative credits on improved farm lands rather than short-term, conventional bank loans, Underwood replied that Wilson was opposed to tying this subject to the federal reserve bill. Hobson's charges that Underwood had neglected the farmer were convincingly answered by Underwood's recital of his favors to the farmers.[14]

Hobson described himself as a friend of Underwood's, but early in the campaign he was angered by the publication, unauthorized by the official Underwood committee, of scurrilous cartoons show-

13. Patrick Turner to Forney Johnston, March 29, 1914, and Forney Johnston to Turner, March 30, 1914, both in Underwood Papers, Alabama Archives.

14. Birmingham *News*, January 16, 1914; Greensboro (Ala.) *Watchman*, March 5, 1914; Carter Glass to Forney Johnston, February 9, 1914, in Carter Glass Papers, University of Virginia Library.

ing Hobson receiving money from John D. Rockefeller. If Hobson was mollified by Underwood's repudiation of the cartoons, he was again enraged by Johnston's campaign book—"the blood book," he called it. At times he called Underwood names, but his greatest rage was reserved for Johnston, whom he described as "nothing but a contemptible political thug."[15] In addition to attacking Underwood, Hobson offered a broad, progressive platform of reforms. He proposed federal financing of good roads, federal aid to education, government-sponsored correspondence and vocational schools, and the publication of a free government digest. Hobson said little about his former advocacy of a "big navy" and the direct election of the president.[16]

Underwood maintained that he was a true friend of temperance and favored local option, as did Woodrow Wilson and William Jennings Bryan. But he believed that commitment to national prohibition would destroy the party. He denied charges that he had stated before school children that he took a drink occasionally and denied that he was a "drinking man." Pointing out that he had supported a series of antishipping bills, he produced a letter from Congressman Edwin Y. Webb thanking him for supporting the Webb bill. Johnston condemned the interference of the National Anti-Saloon League in Alabama, emphasizing that only eight Alabama counties were wet and hinting darkly that the prohibitionists would discredit themselves if they used that issue to defeat Underwood. Underwood admitted that he had opposed constitutional prohibition but pointed out that Hobson had, on several occasions, supported local optionist candidates over prohibitionists.[17]

Further emphasizing the race question, Underwood charged that Hobson had sponsored an act to prevent discrimination against the uniform of the United States Army, which, Underwood said, would have had the effect of abolishing segregation. Hobson

15. Birmingham *News*, January 19, 20, 1914.
16. Richmond P. Hobson campaign letter, January 30, 1914, in Richmond Pearson Hobson Papers, Library of Congress.
17. Birmingham *News*, March 3, 1914; [Forney Johnston], *Democratic Senatorial Campaign*, 40–44; Forney Johnston to A. W. Briscoe, February 26, 1914, and Johnston's form letters to ministers, January 29, 1914, both in Underwood Papers, Alabama Archives.

had also sponsored a bill for the admission of ten Filipinos to West Point and Annapolis, and Johnston concluded that this would mean the admission of "Moros, Igarottes, bushmen, stranglers, fast-blacks, and Chinese mixtures" to those hallowed institutions. Adding to these racist accusations, the Birmingham *Age-Herald* stated that Hobson had referred to a Negro minstrel group as "ladies and gentlemen."[18]

Hobson had no politically satisfactory answer to the charges that he was liberal on the Negro question. He pointed out that he was the son of a Confederate soldier and a native of Alabama, but he had voted to reopen the Brownsville case because of "that divine spark in man." His uniform act only applied to the District of Columbia, was intended to prevent discrimination against enlisted men, did not prohibit discrimination for reasons other than enlisted status, and indeed Underwood, though present, had not voted against the bill. Hobson countercharged that Underwood had given patronage on the Ways and Means Committee to three northern Negroes when southern whites would have been glad to have the highly paid jobs. The employees he referred to were janitors. Hobson demonstrated that although he might be slightly less racist than Underwood toward Negroes, he was not free from racial prejudice. He charged that Underwood's homecoming demonstration's size had been greatly exaggerated by the press and that most of the crowd were Greeks and Italians. Furthermore, he suggested that he favored a law whereby California could segregate its white and yellow children.[19]

Underwood charged that Hobson proposals for women's suffrage and direct popular election of the president would destroy the South's control over suffrage and reduce its influence in presidential elections. Hobson had participated, Underwood noted, in a women's suffrage parade in which Negro women marched. Underwood maintained that although he had opposed in Congress a na-

18. Forney Johnston, *Democratic Senatorial Campaign*, 30; Birmingham *Advance*, March 14, 1914.
19. Birmingham *News*, January 16, 20, 1914; Underwood to W. H. Logan, in Blocton (Ala.) *Enterprise*, January 29, 1914; Birmingham *News*, November 24, 1913.

tional women's suffrage resolution, he favored women's suffrage by state action when the majority of the "white women" of the state wanted it. Hobson backed away from the equal suffrage issue, stating that he too favored state action.[20]

The Italian vote was cultivated for Underwood by William C. Beer, a New York attorney and lobbyist for fruit importers. Underwood's stand for a low tariff on lemons had pleased Italian exporters and Italo-American importers. Italian groups in Birmingham and Ensley were contacted in Underwood's interest by the Italian consul at Mobile, and several thousand copies of *L'Italia-Americano*, an Italian language newspaper, were sent to Alabama to spread the Underwood gospel.[21]

Underwood presented an almost impeccable prolabor record. He had, for example, been in the forefront of labor's fight for immigration restriction. He secured the active support of leaders of the American Federation of Labor, including Samuel Gompers, and the Birmingham *Labor Advocate* as well as the Atlanta *Journal of Labor* endorsed him.[22]

On the issue of conservation Underwood was on the defensive. Hobson accused him of being in collusion with the power trust in having proposed a bill that would have granted a "steal" to the Alabama Power Company, allowing them to build a dam across the Coosa River near Wetumpka. He criticized Underwood's opposition to a bill that created a forest reserve in the Appalachian Mountains. Hobson also denounced Underwood's opposition to the proposed grandiose Van Hoose canal which would have connected the Tennessee River with the Coosa and provided Birmingham with a better outlet to the Gulf of Mexico. Underwood replied that Hobson had presented a power franchise bill identical with the Coosa

20. Forney Johnston, *Democratic Senatorial Campaign*, 52–53; Greensboro (Ala.) *Watchman*, November 6, 1913.

21. Gullino to Emilio Yaselli, April, 1914, Vinti, editor of *L'Italia-Americano*, to Underwood, April 8, 1914, both in Underwood Papers, Alabama Archives. Beer later claimed to have elected Underwood to the Senate. New York *Times*, January 20, 1915, p. 5.

22. Birmingham *News*, January 1, 14, 1914; *The Unparalleled Record of Oscar W. Underwood on Legislation of Interest to Labor* (Birmingham: Underwood Campaign Committee, 1920), *passim*.

River dam bill, and although present when the Underwood dam bill was presented, Hobson had not spoken against it. The Van Hoose canal, he said, was an impractical scheme to "make the Tennessee run up hill" and would dry up the river. Underwood maintained that he had favored several Appalachian reserve bills, but he opposed the Republican plan of setting up a commission without making it financially accountable.[23]

Throughout most of the campaign Underwood maintained a gentlemanly attitude toward his opponent, but Underwood's followers treated Hobson with personal vilification and ridicule. It was charged that Hobson, who had a medical discharge, had quit the navy, that some of his family were Republicans, and that he was an egomaniac. Several pages of his oratory were printed in the Underwood campaign book with comments to indicate that he had paranoidal tendencies. It was noted that Hobson, who had married a New Yorker, spent much of his time out of the state. He was labeled "Sobson," and his interest in Dr. Charles W. Stiles's privy-building campaign was derided. He was criticized for refusing to accept Underwood's offer of the chairmanship of the House Education Committee, although acceptance of that minor committee chairmanship would have meant the loss of his important position on the Naval Appropriations Committee.[24]

The Hobson followers replied with similar abuse, branding Underwood's ancestors "Yankees." Hobson maintained that Underwood no longer knew the people of the state and demonstrated this by asking his audiences how many of them had shaken hands with Underwood. Hobson's manager, Musgrove, charged that Underwood was a member of a "kid glove bunch" who could not get up an appetite for dinner unless there was enough tableware to "serve an entire settlement in Walker County."[25]

Hobson was greatly handicapped by the fact that although he was a progressive he was opposed by Alabama Wilson supporters. Birmingham *News* editor Frank P. Glass, one of Wilson's closest

23. Forney Johnston, *Democratic Senatorial Campaign*, 20–21, 51–52, 55.
24. *Ibid.*, 23–24, 35–36, 51.
25. Birmingham *News*, January 21, April 3, 1914.

Alabama friends, vociferously supported Underwood. Wilson's interference with Clayton's candidacy indicated that he preferred Underwood to Hobson, although Hobson's campaign leaders declared that the president had been tricked. When Underwood strongly denounced Wilson's position on the Panama Canal tolls issue, the Hobson men made much of Underwood's difference with the president, but this event was balanced by Wilson's announcement that he would give a state banquet for his House leader.[26]

The Hobson-Underwood controversy flared again on the floor of the House in early December, 1913, when Hobson presented a petition for a prohibition amendment to the Constitution. Congressman Donovan, to the delight of the House, again goaded Hobson about his absences. Hobson's major speech on prohibition was sympathetically received in the galleries where hundreds of Women's Christian Temperance Union (WCTU) members had collected. Replying to Underwood's statement that the Democratic party "would be ground to dust and die" if it adopted prohibition, Hobson waved his hands and pointed his finger at Underwood, who sat almost beside him. "If the fate of the Democratic party depends on the liquor interest," then "let it die," Hobson said. The argument was so intense that some feared a fist fight between the two candidates, and Speaker Champ Clark dispatched the corpulent clerk of the House to sit between them. Underwood calmly replied that it was improper for him as Democratic leader to engage in a personal controversy on the floor. Congressman Richard "Dutch" Bartholdt of St. Louis attempted to denounce Hobson's prohibition proposal but became so entangled in his German syntax that both Hobson and Underwood were convulsed with laughter.[27]

Underwood returned to Alabama just after Christmas for a two-week campaign tour. Traveling by automobile, train, and buggy

26. Greensboro (Ala.) Watchman, October 16, 1913; Birmingham News, March 10, April 5, 1914. Hobson had originally voted with Underwood on the tolls issue.

27. New York Times, December 12, 1913, p. 12; Congressional Record, 63rd Cong., 2nd Sess., 737–45; Champ Clark, My Quarter Century of American Politics (2 vols.; New York: Harper and Brothers, 1920), II, 252; Birmingham News, December 12, 1913.

through sleet and rain, he visited county seat hamlets where Hobson was allegedly popular. He found the courthouses packed with eager followers as early as nine o'clock in the morning. Stung by the bitterness of Hobson's charges, he soon abandoned his Chesterfieldian reserve, and the Captain Hobson who at the beginning of the campaign was termed an "honorable opponent" became a "Prince of Peradventure," "a performing seal" who dove for the sheer pleasure of coming to the surface again. Referring to Hobson's advocacy of expanded federal powers, Underwood called him a believer in the principles of the old Federalist party, not a Democrat. Furthermore, Underwood charged that Hobson was dominated by out-of-state forces in the Anti-Saloon League. Traveling in prohibitionist east Alabama, he attacked political prohibitionists as "pretenders to sanctification," who know nothing of the real cause of temperance. Hobson had embarrassed the Democratic party, he said, and was making the fight for national prohibition for his own personal and political advancement. Underwood privately described the contest as "a very disagreeable, mud-sling campaign," but his crowds were pleased. The Birmingham *News* thought his more pugnacious stance a proper reply to Hobson's "ju jitsu" tactics.[28]

Early in the campaign, Hobson had been confident of victory and had thrown a bad scare into Underwood's organization. As the campaign progressed, however, it was apparent that Hobson lacked the support of many prohibition leaders and that he would lose. Late in the campaign he made a series of errors that sealed his doom—seemingly resulting from a frenetic attempt to regain his momentum. In Montgomery he closed a campaign speech with the tearful statement that he might not see his followers again soon, that his life was a "strenuous one," and that he had had only one meal that day with hardly time to eat that. Musgrove, with uncanny bad judgment, chose April 1 to say that if President Wilson's proposal for a national presidential preference primary be-

28. Birmingham *News*, December 31, 1913, January 2, 4, 6, 1914; Underwood to O. W. Underwood, Jr., January 29, 1914, in Underwood Papers, Alabama Archives.

came law, Hobson would be a candidate of "progressive Democracy" for the presidency. Forney Johnston commented raucously on the "All Fools Day" announcement as well as the news that the captain had rejected at his wife's request a plan to campaign by airplane (he had earlier made tentative plans to campaign by motorcycle). A more basic error was Hobson's last minute effort to assure drinkers of home brew that he did not anticipate any interference with the production of that popular beverage as long as it was not to be sold. Hobson critics took this retreat from his previous fanatical opposition to alcohol as a confession of defeat.[29]

Not all of the frenzy was on one side. Forney Johnston and Phil Painter, editor of Hobson's throw-out paper, *The Advance*, exchanged blows, and Painter was left nursing a black eye and a bruised wrist. W. H. Parker, a political hanger-on subsidized by a close friend of Underwood's, attended Hobson's speaking appointments, heckling him with questions about his absence from Congress. Parker went to Washington in February, 1914, armed with a petition to the sergeant at arms of the House demanding that Hobson's pay be cut off because of his absences. Underwood denied responsibility for Parker while Hobson, still in Alabama, demanded that Underwood prepare a resolution to stop the pay of all congressmen who were out campaigning or put a stop to Parker's actions. The denouement came when Parker was arrested for stealing watches.[30]

At the end of the campaign Underwood returned to Birmingham, as he said, to vote rather than to campaign. A large crowd awaited the returning hero at Jefferson Theater. Congressman J. Thomas Heflin, a raconteur without equal, entertained the crowd with stories but was interrupted by cries of "Oscar" when the crowd recognized Underwood. Nevertheless, Heflin continued to

29. Birmingham *News*, February 26, April 2, 3, 1914; unidentified clipping, April 2, 1914, in Hobson Papers; Grizelda Hobson to her mother, November 1, 1913, in Hobson Papers. O. W. Underwood, Jr., laughingly recalled serving Hobson an alcoholic drink and receiving a temperance speech in return. Interview with O. W. Underwood, Jr., November 24, 1951.

30. Grizelda Hobson to her mother, *ca.* January, 1914, in Hobson Papers; Birmingham *News*, February 4, 13, 1914.

talk for an hour, defending Underwood as a friend of the farmer and explaining why Birmingham lost the Federal Reserve Bank to Atlanta. Heflin left the audience in a festive mood, but as Oscar began to speak, the famous smile disappeared, he lost his composure, and with a quavering arm motioned to the crowd to be quiet. The now solemn group listened as Underwood spoke emotionally of his completion of twenty years of service in the House. He explained that President Wilson had accepted his explanation of why he could not lead the fight for the Panama tolls. Then he addressed Hobson as "one of those men of kid gloves who do not stay on the battlefield but who prefer to follow Indian tactics and lay in ambush, who do not know what it is to fight for a party cause, because their time is entirely taken up in fighting for personal ambition and to create discord." Following a night at the home of his son John Lewis, he cast his ballot. He jestingly denied that he had voted in the senatorial race. The count was slow, and it was noon of the seventh before Hobson conceded Underwood's election and wired his congratulations accompanied by a blast at the whiskey interests.[31]

Underwood ran a surprisingly strong race. Of 144,208 votes cast, he received 89,470, 62 percent of the total. Hobson carried only six counties, five of which were in his own congressional district. In Hobson's home county, Hale, he edged out Underwood by a very slight majority. The supposed Hobson strength in the prohibitionist eastern part of the state proved fictitious, and Underwood ran strong in every section. He carried the more populous counties, Jefferson, Montgomery, and Mobile, by majorities exceeding two to one. The Underwood-Hobson campaign was an expensive contest, but both candidates rendered unrealistic expense statements. Underwood reported expenses of $12,920.01, but he failed to divulge money that he had spent to reimburse local managers. In some cases the campaign was financed locally and no accounting was made. Hobson reported expenses of $16,785.32, but the Anti-Saloon League had spent a great deal on its own to support Hobson.[32]

31. Birmingham *News*, April 5, 6, 7, 1914.
32. Thomas M. Owen (comp.), *Alabama Official and Statistical Register, 1915* (Mont-

Hundreds of friends sent their congratulations to Underwood. Woodrow Wilson telegraphed: "My sincere and hearty congratulations. Now for a triumphant completion of the session's programme." Among the congratulatory messages were greetings from Vice-President Thomas R. Marshall, Speaker Champ Clark, Congressman Nicholas Longworth, and Governor Earl Brewer of Mississippi. One letter, signed "T. F. R." (Thomas Fortune Ryan), said: "I was disgusted because I could do nothing but keep still; I feel now that our day is coming." The press applauded Underwood's victory. The Philadelphia *Press* noted that his leadership was "always suave and generally sane," and the New York *Evening Post* was reassured that the direct primary had not resulted in the election of a demagogue. The Springfield, Massachusetts, *Union* thought Underwood to be far above the "hot-headed radical Hobson." The Birmingham *News* predicted that Underwood "will be a worthy successor to those grand old Romans," Senators John Tyler Morgan and Edmund Pettus.[33]

Underwood had won election to the Senate partially by denying that prohibition was a valid issue. Indeed, it might be said that he won despite his opposition to it. The popularity of prohibition is indicated by the results of another primary on the same ballot. Frank S. White, a prominent prohibitionist, defeated two other candidates, one of them the vice-chairman of Underwood's campaign committee, for the unexpired portion of Johnston's term, ending March, 1915 (in contrast to the regular term for which Underwood was a candidate), by taking 60 percent of the vote. Underwood's victory was also a triumph for the private development of Muscle Shoals, although this had not been an important campaign issue. J. W. Worthington of the Sheffield Company furnished the money for Underwood's campaign in the Eighth District. The campaign was hardly over before Worthington was sending Underwood material to be used in presenting to Congress the power company's case for private development of Muscle Shoals.[34]

Hobson's campaign was notably weak in organization, probably

---

gomery: Department of Archives and History, 1916), 406–407, 450; Forney Johnston to Underwood, April 26, October 21, 1914, in Underwood Papers, Alabama Archives.

33. Underwood Scrapbook, II, *passim*, in Underwood Papers, Alabama Archives.

because of the lack of support among professional politicians. Unlike Underwood, who had not had effective political opposition since the election of 1898, Hobson had experienced three bitter congressional elections in the Sixth District. In addition Hobson inherited the enmity of some of Senator Johnston's friends by announcing for the Senate while Johnston still lived. Hobson fanned this fire of resentment by his accusations against the professional politicians and in particular by his attacks against the state administration.

The Underwood campaigners bear a rather serious ethical burden in their fight against Hobson. The campaign between two national figures had begun as a gentlemanly dispute but descended to the gutter. There were misrepresentations on both sides, but Underwood and Johnston were largely responsible for the low level campaigning. The hiring of a heckler to disrupt Hobson's meetings, the emphasis upon racism, and the accusations that he was mentally unbalanced were perhaps the worst abuses of political ethics.

In one sense Underwood had won a pyrrhic victory over Hobson. The Alabama congressional leader had surrendered his position as House leader for a freshman berth in the Senate. Several years afterward, when he had achieved leadership of the Senate minority, he found himself hamstrung by archaic Senate rules. The prohibition movement was gaining tempo, and by 1916 the "drys" had captured control of the Alabama Democratic party machinery. In 1920, when Underwood might otherwise have bid for the Democratic presidential nomination, he was opposed for his Senate seat by the manager of the Hobson campaign, L. Breckinridge Musgrove, who gave him the hardest political fight of his life.

34. Owen, *Alabama Official and Statistical Register, 1915*, p. 409; Greensboro (Ala.) *Watchman*, April 9, 1914; C. W. Ashcraft to Underwood, April 9, 1914, and J. W. Worthington to Underwood, December 1, 1914, both in Underwood Papers, Alabama Archives.

CHAPTER X

The Politics
of War

Underwood completed his House career on March 3, 1915, by which time most of Wilson's New Freedom had become law. Looking back, he declared that except for the president, the House majority leader has the hardest job in the country.[1] Although he anticipated that the Senate would be a respite from the unbearable burdens of House leadership, by 1917, still a freshman senator, he found himself in a position of leadership.

The Wilson administration had turned its attention to the threat of war with Mexico and the outbreak of the European war, but Underwood continued to devote most of his energy to the domestic sphere. Returning to Alabama in March, 1915, he talked, as he had in his campaign for the Senate, of the railroad problem, which was to be uppermost in his mind until the passage of the Transportation Act of 1920. Before the Sphinx Club in Montgomery on March 9, he declared that the nation had reached the point "where sound progressivism must recognize that the proper regulation of business requires that it must sometimes be helped and not always hindered." He told the Alabama Bankers' Association that the railroads were operating at a reduced capacity with run-down equipment and desperately needed legislative help. Railroads were suffering, he said, from constant governmental interference which made railroad securities difficult to sell. He suggested the creation of a special railroad study commission similar to the National

1. New York *Evening Post*, March 10, 1915.

Monetary Commission from whose work the Federal Reserve System was developed. Such a nonpartisan commission, he said, should investigate and report after the presidential election. The commission could only conclude in favor of a general freight rate increase, he implied, noting that a slight increase would be unimportant to shippers if it would assure good transportation. At Russellville, Alabama, on July 23 he emphasized this theme, saying that "the biggest question before this nation today is the proper regulation of transportation." Then he added, rather startlingly for an advocate of states' rights, that this regulation should be exclusively federal.[2]

Alabama audiences must have been puzzled that their junior Senator considered railroads the nation's number one problem when military preparedness was the talk of the land. Secretary of State Bryan resigned in June, following the *Lusitania* crisis—differing with the administration's tough stance toward Germany. While vacationing at Linville, North Carolina, in early September, Underwood reiterated his dislike for Bryan but denounced heavy military expenditures. He noted that the nation was already spending one thousand dollars per capita for defense (the correct figure was one hundred dollars per capita), that no country could successfully invade the United States, and if further defense were needed he suggested building a large submarine fleet—perhaps as many as three hundred ships. The cost of submarines, Underwood explained, would be small compared with that of the million-man army many were advocating and which he estimated would cost one billion dollars a year. He did not explain why he had opposed the building of submarines a few months earlier, but presumably the sinking of the *Lusitania* had changed his mind. Underwood returned to Birmingham in mid-September ten pounds lighter, invigorated by golfing at Tate Springs, Tennessee, and by climbing Grandfather Mountain. Exultant that there were "runaway prices" and that the recession of 1914 was definitely at an end, he concluded that "democracy has brought a thrust to business," foresaw

2. Montgomery *Advertiser*, March 10, 1915; Birmingham *News*, May 12, July 23, 1915.

"flush times," and predicted that it would tax the resources of the United States to supply Europe's needs.[3]

On December 6, 1915, Underwood was escorted by Alabama's senior senator, John H. Bankhead, Sr., to the vice-president's desk in the Senate and was sworn in. Seated next to the back row in the extreme right-hand corner of the chamber as viewed from Vice-President Marshall's desk, he sat near Bankhead, his long-time friend.

On December 7 Underwood marched into the House chamber to listen to the president's speech before a joint session of Congress. As he reentered the scene of his former triumphs, his former colleagues yelled "Hurrah for Oscar Underwood," and the galleries joined in vigorous applause as Underwood repeatedly smiled and bowed in appreciation of the demonstration.[4] Underwood probably looked upon his former colleagues with envy and perhaps regretted that he had left the body. Already he had expressed unhappiness at the ineffectiveness of the Senate rules in cutting off debate.

Since Underwood had distinguished himself as the chairman of the Ways and Means Committee in the House of Representatives, most observers expected him to serve on the Senate Finance Committee. Indeed, the Democratic majority offered to expand the Finance Committee to make a place for him, but Underwood, surprisingly, declined the proffered assignment. He told about an impecunious cobbler who inherited a fortune, gave up his cobbler's bench for riotous living, and upon exhausting the money returned to the cobbler's bench. When the cobbler was informed of a second legacy, he said: "You mean I've got to go through all that again?" Underwood accepted appointment to the Appropriations Committee, a significant assignment equal to the Finance Committee post

3. Chattanooga *Times*, September 2, 1915; Birmingham *News*, September 14, 1915; Birmingham *Age-Herald*, September 29, 1915. The memorandum of Oscar W. Underwood, Jr., in which he presents his father as an early advocate of preparedness who suggested support for Secretary of the Army Lindley M. Garrison's proposed million-man army to President Wilson as early as late 1914, when Oscar, Jr., returned from France, is unconvincing. "Memorandum Dictated by Oscar W. Underwood, Jr., in Connection with 'The Gold Barrage,'" *Collier's Weekly*, LXXXVI (November 15, 1930), 26, in Letterbox M, Oscar W. Underwood Papers, Alabama Department of Archives and History, Montgomery.

4. Birmingham *News*, December 6, 7, 1915.

he had rejected. He also was given a newly created place on the Interstate Commerce Committee, providing him an opportunity to deal with the railroad problem. And like other Democratic senators, he was given a minor committee chairmanship, that of the Cuban Affairs Committee.[5]

Underwood's Appropriations Committee assignment placed the freshman senator at the side of Democratic majority leader, Thomas S. Martin. Martin, an aging and unambitious leader in ill health, soon formed a five-man subcommittee, headed by Underwood, to steer the unwieldy committee. Underwood's initial task as Democratic aide to Martin was management of the administration's bill to extend the war revenue tax that he had sponsored as a member of the House. He did so by engaging Senator Boies Penrose of Pennsylvania in debate on the merits of protectionism, since the Republicans had charged that the Underwood-Simmons Tariff caused the revenue drop that made the new measure necessary. Egged on by Democratic colleagues, Underwood attacked Republican tariff policy and defended "Democratic prosperity" forcefully. Penrose admitted that protectionism had not helped the iron and steel industry and that the panic of 1914 was not a Democratic responsibility but had been caused by the outbreak of the war. John Sharp Williams gleefully violated Senate rules with handclaps as Democratic senators surrounded Underwood to congratulate him. It was never doubted that the Senate would vote to extend the tax; the vote was 45 to 29.[6]

On other domestic issues Underwood followed a highly independent course. He complained of dilatory tactics that delayed the passage of the rural credits bill, a Democratic measure that had been promised the farmers to compensate for legislation passed to benefit urban areas. He supported the passage of the Bankhead-Shackleford good roads bill, sponsored in the Senate by his Alabama colleague, saying that poor states simply could not build adequate roads with their own resources. On the other hand, he

5. *Ibid.*, December 10, 13, 1915; Champ Clark, *My Quarter Century of American Politics* (2 vols.; New York: Harper and Brothers, 1920), I, 372.

6. New York *Times*, December 18, 1915, p. 3.

opposed confirmation of President Wilson's nomination of George Rublee to the Federal Trade Commission (FTC) and spoke out against secret Senate sessions on confirmations, saying that it was impossible to keep such deliberations secret. Rublee, a Republican friend of Louis Brandeis and an author of the Federal Trade Commission Act, was blocked for the FTC appointment by minority leader Joseph H. Gallinger on the basis of "senatorial courtesy."[7] The president kept Rublee in office through an interim appointment, but he was never confirmed by the Senate.

Immediately after entering the Senate, Underwood opposed an administration bill to expand the Interstate Commerce Commission (ICC) from seven to nine members. President Wilson was displeased and asked Underwood to reconsider, whereupon Underwood denied that he had any objection to increasing the size of the ICC, but feared that the ICC measure would be converted into an omnibus railroad regulation measure without a full investigation of the rail problem as anticipated by the Newlands resolution he supported. The president assured Underwood that he had already asserted his influence to secure passage of the Newlands resolution. The Newlands bill, however, failed to receive House approval, though the administration's ICC bill, which had previously passed the House, received the Senate's blessing soon after the president prompted Underwood.[8]

The four railroad brotherhoods threatened a strike in the early fall of 1916 in the wake of heavy defense orders and anticipating the presidential election in the fall. They demanded an eight-hour day and time and a half for overtime. Francis G. Newlands and Underwood prepared a railway labor bill to meet the emergency, including Section 6, written by Underwood, authorizing the ICC to set wages and hours of railroads. President Wilson sent to the House a bill introduced by Congressman William C. Adamson of

7. Birmingham *News*, March 16, 1916; New York *Times*, April 30, 1916, Sec. 3, p. 2; Birmingham *Age-Herald*, May 27, 1916.
8. Oscar W. Underwood to Woodrow Wilson, May 9, 1916, Wilson to Underwood, May 11, 1916, both in Box 16, Underwood to Wilson, May 24, 1916, in Box 366, all in Woodrow Wilson Papers, Library of Congress.

Georgia, limiting hours on the railroads to an eight-hour maximum in line with the brotherhoods' demands but excluding the ICC labor provisions of Underwood's Section 6. The House quickly passed the Adamson bill, and the Senate faced a choice between the Adamson bill and that of Newlands. The Adamson bill reached the floor first, and Underwood attempted to attach the Newlands bill's labor provisions, arguing that the Adamson bill had no method for permanently solving wage conflicts. Underwood asserted that the nation was being "held up" by the railroad brotherhoods, and he would resist if it were possible to do so without the nation suffering a strike. He defended the president for taking action to stop the strike and for asking authority to use the army to run the railroads if necessary. Opponents of the Underwood amendment replied that it was a repressive proposal for compulsory arbitration, and Senator Furnifold M. Simmons of North Carolina argued that it might well precipitate an extended strike. Underwood's amendment failed by a vote of 14 to 57 and was thus decisively stricken from what became the Adamson Act.[9]

The war that absorbed the senator was not that in Europe but the defense of the Texas border against the depredations of Pancho Villa. Oscar, Jr., who had returned to the United States from France in 1914, was among those called into the National Guard. In the midst of his preparations to leave a lucrative Birmingham law practice to go to the "front" as a private in Battery 6 of the Alabama National Guard, the senator's older half-brother, Will, died suddenly while inspecting his coal mines in Kentucky.[10] The call-up was delayed, and when Oscar, Jr., began active service it was as captain of Troop A of Birmingham's First Cavalry Regiment which, after brief service at Ft. Sheridan near Montgomery, was transferred to Ft. Sam Houston, Texas. Underwood agreed with Wilson's Mexican policy, saying that the president was "absolutely right" in sending troops to capture Villa. In a statement issued on

9. Francis G. Newlands, *The Public Papers of Francis G. Newlands*, ed. Arthur B. Darling (2 vols.; Boston: Houghton Mifflin, 1932), I, 1, II, 359, 363; *Congressional Record*, 64th Cong., 1st Sess., 13557–13649.

10. Underwood to Nita Patterson, July 18, 1916, in Oscar W. Underwood Papers, University of Virginia Library.

the way back from Atlantic City where he had been recovering from a bronchial infection, Underwood said:

> Villa must be suppressed, and I do not think that the Carranza government would make any objections to the United States going into Mexico. On the other hand, I think Mexico will be glad to have the help of the United States. I do not think that permanent intervention will result from sending troops over the border.
>
> If Villa has much of a start and has managed to reach the mountain passes, it will be a hard job to get him. I know this, for I have been through that country.
>
> If permanent intervention must come, I think it would take twelve years to pacify Mexico, and the task would cost hundreds of millions of dollars. Congress is back of the president in sending troops into Mexico, and Congress will, no doubt stand back of him in case of intervention. The Carranza government has shown that it could not cope with the situation. In fact the *de facto* government has shown itself very weak; not only by the results of yesterday, but in many other ways.[11]

Underwood stoutly resisted the heavy expenditures required in the preparedness movement. In early February, 1916, Marian E. Martin, Underwood's trusted secretary, stated that although typewritten, dictated letters to the senator stressed preparedness, those written in ink or pencil, sometimes scrawled on wrapping paper, were opposed. In March he assured a Baptist minister in New Decatur, Alabama, that he was opposed to Americans sailing on belligerent vessels and had so informed the president. In July, 1916, he favored an unsuccessful effort to reduce the administration's naval bill below four dreadnaughts and four battle cruisers. In a speech on the war appropriations bill, he burst out that the nation had gone "war mad" and that he had gone as far as he would go. He unsuccessfully supported an amendment that would have prevented the enlistment of men under twenty-one years of age, maintaining that numbers of Alabama parents complained that their minor sons had enlisted without parental consent.[12]

---

11. New York *Times*, March 11, 1916, p. 3.
12. Birmingham *News*, February 9, March 3, 1916; *Congressional Record*, 64th Cong., 1st Sess., 11372, 11619–20; New York *Times*, July 27, 1916, p. 4.

The Mexican border operation together with mounting preparedness costs created a treasury crisis in that revenues were falling short of expenditures by several hundred million dollars a year. In congressional circles it was thought that some one hundred million to two hundred million dollars in additional revenue must be raised to offset the government's great expenditures. The Democratic caucus met in mid-August, 1916, to consider plans for raising the additional revenue. Underwood and other southern senators favored a bond issue of something more than one hundred million dollars, which they claimed could be issued without congressional approval. Senator Simmons, chairman of the Finance Committee, presented an omnibus war revenue bill to raise over two hundred million dollars in new revenue by increasing the income tax, placing a tax on raw materials used in munitions, and levying an inheritance tax. Substantial raises in the tariff on dye to prevent German "dumping" after the war were also provided, and a tariff commission was attached at the insistence of President Wilson. The Finance Committee's plan was adopted by the caucus despite strong objections from southern congressmen to the munitions tax, which would include cotton.

Underwood was dismayed at the action of the caucus. He felt that the war revenue bill as approved contained features contrary to Democratic doctrine and objectionable to the South because southerners had not stuck together and because so many senators "sneeze when the president takes snuff." He rather petulantly determined, without any hope of success, to attack the dye tariff, the tariff commission, the cotton tax, and the level of income tax exemption.[13]

Under severe criticism from party leaders for having participated in the Democratic caucus yet not abiding by its rule, Underwood presented a series of amendments to the war revenue bill. He proposed that the income tax exemption be lowered $1,000 from the bill's $3,000 for married men and $2,000 for unmarried persons, maintaining that persons at those income levels were not poor. The amendment lost, 31 to 19. The boost in the tariff on

13. New York *Times*, August 19, 1916, p. 3; Birmingham *Age-Herald*, August 17, 1916.

dyestuffs Underwood described as "a stench in the nostrils of the Democratic party," bringing an angry retort from Senator William J. Stone of Missouri that he was engaging in "heroics." Despite Underwood's opposition, the dye item was adopted by a vote of 43 to 7, the minority being composed entirely of Democrats. He made no overt fight on the tariff commission. Embarrassed by the spectacle of their best known tariff expert attacking the war revenue bill, the Democrats made concessions. The Senate Finance Committee halved the cotton tax and then dropped it completely, although an indirect cotton tax appeared in the final bill in a tax on profits from munitions manufacture. The final bill, known as the War Revenue Act of 1916, provided that the dye tariff would be reduced over a period of five years.[14]

Despite his differences with the administration, Underwood campaigned for Wilson and the Democratic ticket in early October. His midwestern itinerary included Cleveland, Ft. Wayne, Indianapolis, Evansville, and Hannibal, Missouri. At Cleveland, Underwood struck the Democratic keynote of "peace and prosperity." Replying to Republican criticism that American honor had not been defended on the high seas, he boasted of Wilson's diplomatic achievement in the *Sussex* pledge that Germany would not sink unarmed merchant vessels without making provision for the safety of the passengers:

> There never has been in the history of the American republic a greater achievement in diplomacy than that accomplished by Woodrow Wilson when he maintained American honor, protected American property in settling the controversy . . . without the cost of a single dollar or the loss of an American life.
>
> I thank God that we have in the White House a Woodrow Wilson

14. *Congressional Record*, 64th Cong., 1st Sess., 13266–67, 13273, 13768; Birmingham *Age-Herald*, August 27, 1916; New York *Times*, September 5, 1916, p. 16; Arthur S. Link, *Wilson: Confusions and Crises, 1915–1916* (Princeton, N.J.: Princeton University Press, 1964), 345, Vol. IV of Arthur S. Link, *Wilson* (6 vols. projected; Princeton, N.J.: Princeton University Press, 1947–). Although Underwood had advocated an inheritance tax, his wife was the heir to one third of her ailing father's estate of over $6 million. He died in 1917, and the inheritance taxes under the Revenue Act of 1916 were almost 10 percent of the estate's value. Charles F. Spear, "The New Taxes," *Review of Reviews*, LIV (1916), 395–98; "Report on the Estate of J. H. Woodward," December 15, 1917, in Underwood Papers, Alabama Archives.

that will not send your boy and my boy to slaughter—unless he is sure
he is right, and then he will say "Go ahead."[15]

The senator's audience must have gagged at the candor of the qualification of the peace statement.

Underwood discussed the Mexican situation in his Ft. Wayne,
Indiana, speech. He maintained that Mexico was small and weak,
yet the administration had not dealt differently with it than it had
with Germany or Russia. "We want to see Mexico right herself and
reestablish organized government. We do not want to fight her,"
he said, declaring that the Republicans might well get the United
States into a war. The Republican nominee, Charles Evans
Hughes, was a good man, Underwood admitted, but was controlled by "the same old machine."

Underwood defended the Democratic economic record, maintaining that the Underwood-Simmons Tariff Act and the new Federal Reserve System were important causes of prosperity which he
maintained was not a war prosperity. He also defended the Adamson Act, denying that it was the surrender of the principle of arbitration since the railroad men would not arbitrate and there was no
principle to surrender. He found the campaigning tiresome although he wrote his wife that his cough was gone. He expressed
the vain hope that he had completed his last campaign out of Alabama. Upon his return to Alabama, he insisted that the tide had
turned strongly in Wilson's favor. "This is not hot air but the situation as I see it," he declared.[16]

Underwood committed himself to preparedness reluctantly and
cautiously in 1917. Following the sinking of the British liner *California* and the detention of Ambassador James W. Gerard, President Wilson broke diplomatic relations with Germany on February
3. Senator Stone sponsored a resolution to endorse the president's
action. Underwood stated that he had not allowed himself to become "a partisan of either of the contending forces" and com-

15. Cleveland *Plain Dealer*, October 6, 1916.
16. Fort Wayne (Ind.) *Gazette*, October 13, 1916; Underwood to Bertha Underwood,
October 13, 1916, in Underwood Papers, Alabama Archives; Birmingham *News*, October
25, 1916.

THE POLITICS OF WAR

plained that although he would vote for the resolution, he thought it ill timed since the president had not requested such an endorsement. Even the sensational Zimmerman note, whereby Germany proposed, in the event of American entry into the war, that Mexico and Japan become allies of Germany and that property ceded by Mexico at the end of the Mexican War be returned, did not alarm him. Commenting on it on March 1, Underwood stated that the note's significance had been overplayed in the press and that the German foreign office's attempt to prepare its ambassador to Mexico for a break in United States relations with Germany was not surprising or alarming. He felt that Germany's note to the United States announcing the resumption of unrestricted submarine warfare was far more significant.[17]

This latter aggression led Underwood to withdraw his opposition to Wilson's maritime policy. In March, 1917, he signed a cloture petition to bring Wilson's bill for the arming of merchant ships to a vote. By late March, Underwood recognized that the United States was virtually at war with Germany. He asserted upon arriving in Birmingham that though President Wilson had been "patient and tactful" and had used "keen discretion" in foreign relations, Germany had committed the overt act that would involve the United States in war. The war would be, for the United States, a naval war, he said, but if it lasted two years, it would be necessary for the United States to raise an army of a million men. "War is inevitable," he told the Birmingham Rotarians.[18]

A month later, in Montgomery prior to the wedding of Oscar, Jr., to Ellen Pratt of Prattville, Underwood stressed that conscripting an army of "a million or two million" would make it unnecessary to "send a single soldier to France." Although Speaker of the House Clark and majority leader Claude Kitchin opposed conscription, he thought they would "come around." Conscription, like war, was repugnant and unpleasant, he said, but the all-volunteer system had failed.[19]

17. *Congressional Record*, 64th Cong., 2nd Sess., 2736, 4603–4604.
18. Birmingham *Age-Herald*, March 4, 5, 1917; Birmingham *News*, March 20, 29, 1917.
19. Montgomery *Advertiser*, April 18, 1917.

Wilson's reelection was accompanied by a fiscal crisis created by the escalating costs of preparedness. The War Revenue Act of 1916 did not solve the treasury's revenue crisis, and the second session of the Sixty-fourth Congress set to work in February, 1917, to raise several hundred million dollars in additional revenue. The Senate Democratic caucus substantially accepted a bill that came over from the House. The president's authority to issue bonds was increased from somewhat over two hundred million dollars to over three hundred million. The inheritance tax was increased by 50 percent, and, most important of all, an excess profits tax required large corporations to surrender in taxes profits in excess of 8 percent of their capitalization. An oleomargarine tax of ten cents a pound on colored and a quarter of a cent a pound on uncolored was proposed. Underwood attacked the oleomargarine tax, using the argument that it would contribute to the high cost of living by discouraging the use of the butter substitute. He eventually lost his battle to reduce the tax to a uniform two cents a pound on all margarine. Having approved the House's bill with minor changes, the caucus seemed anxious to avoid amendments to the war revenue bill. Undaunted, Underwood took his oleomargarine amendment to the Senate floor. His position was consistent with his advocacy of the abolition of the tax early in his career. He urged the adoption of his amendment as a method of holding down the price of butter, preventing the fraudulent sale of margarine as butter, and as a revenue producing measure. He concluded angrily, and somewhat illogically, that the railroads were being used to carry munitions when "the people are crying for bread"—and presumably for oleomargarine. The oleo amendment had no chance of passage, and it was defeated by a vote of 59 to 21, with twenty-two Democrats, including six southerners, voting against the proposal. "I think everything has gone to pot," Underwood told a reporter.[20] His ill-tempered fight was hardly worthwhile in view of southerners' lack of interest in the issue.

The War Revenue Act of 1917 was hardly on the books in March

20. New York *Times*, February 12, 1917, p. 14, March 1, 1917, pp. 1, 3; *Congressional Record*, 64th Cong., 2nd Sess., 3750–62, 4475; Birmingham *News*, February 28, 1917.

before United States entrance into the war made it obsolete, and discussions began in the new Sixty-fifth Congress to increase the rates of the revenue measure and perfect its terms. In May, Underwood acknowledged the necessity of abandoning the Democratic "tariff for revenue only" doctrine, saying that he was not opposed to the waiving for war purposes of duties in the Underwood-Simmons Tariff. He complained, however, that amendments being considered by the House would increase tariff rates by 10 percent across the board and that such adjustments were products of "recklessness and hasty efforts."[21] The boost in tariff rates was later dropped from the bill.

Underwood attacked the Finance Committee's proposal for revamping the war revenue excess profits tax. The Finance Committee proposed to use a prewar period as a base to determine the level above which the 8 percent excess profits tax would apply. Senator Bankhead proposed an amendment whereby 8 percent profit on capitalization would be exempted and above that level a graduated tax would apply—just as the Finance Committee had provided in earlier forms of the bill. Underwood supported Bankhead's amendment, arguing that the Finance Committee's recommended provision would require a "Philadelphia lawyer" to unravel and would favor large corporations. He did not mention the more obvious fact that undercapitalized southern corporations would escape more readily under the Bankhead amendment, which lost by a lopsided 67 to 9.[22]

Although Underwood sniped at, but did not actually oppose administration revenue legislation, he vigorously supported legislation to counter the mounting submarine campaign that threatened the capacity of the United States to supply its allies after American entrance into the war. In the spring of 1917, supporting a Senate joint resolution to regularize United States seizure of enemy ships, he said that he would go further than the proposed resolution and deny German owners access to the court of claims for compensa-

21. Birmingham Age-Herald, May 13, 1917.
22. Birmingham News, August 23, 1917; Congressional Record, 65th Cong., 1st Sess., 6440, 6623.

tion. This resolution was abandoned, but similar legislation, passed in May, authorized the seizures, which had already occurred.[23]

Relatively few enemy ships, either war or merchant vessels, were seized under Congress' resolution, but the extensive British shipbuilding program in American shipyards offered a substantial source of American merchant ships. Working closely with General George W. Goethals, general manager of the Emergency Fleet Corporation, Underwood engrafted merchant marine legislation onto the huge, urgent army navy deficiency appropriation bill of 1917. The mammoth $3,281,000,000 bill, the largest appropriation bill passed by Congress to that time, contained a $750 million item for the expansion of the merchant marine. The president was authorized to comandeer all American shipyards and vessels under construction within those yards. Underwood piloted the bill through and defended one of Senator Thomas Martin's pet projects, the purchase of the Jamestown Exposition site for a naval training station at what House conferees considered an exorbitant $1,400,000 (the site figure was compromised at $1,200,000). Admitting that the appropriation bill was highly irregular in that it contained new legislation and that most of its appropriations were regular appropriations rather than "deficiencies," he clinched his argument for the bill by saying that he had it on the highest authority that if an American army landed in France, all that the French and English could do was to furnish a port—the United States would have to provide supplies to its own troops. The bill passed by a *viva voce* vote.[24]

Underwood was less sympathetic with the administration's program for wartime control of the railroads than he had been with its merchant ship program. The president seized operational control of the railroads in December, 1917, but legislative action was needed to regularize the action and to allow the government to contract for the railroads' services. The administration bill allowed railroads a profit limited to 8 percent, computed upon a three year base period. Although the bill was assured of passage and Under-

23. *Congressional Record*, 65th Cong., 1st Sess., 1572–73.
24. *Ibid.*, 2512–16, 3429; New York *Times*, May 19, 1917, p. 16.

wood favored it, he stridently cautioned the Senate against the allocation of too much power to the president. There was a danger, he said, of allowing America to become an autocracy while sending soldiers to France to make the world safe for democracy. He thought the railroad bill was unnecessary, "crudely drawn," and that its profit limiting features might well violate the Constitution. The ICC, not the president, should have the authority to regulate the railroads in wartime. He was well aware, however, that there was no prospect of substantially altering the bill.[25]

Even American entrance into the war and Underwood's increasing anti-German animus did not completely overcome his objections to the espionage bill of 1917, although he eventually voted for the measure. In the Senate debate on May 11 he defended the self-restraint of the press in reporting military affairs, asserting that if there were danger of invasion he would be more willing to tolerate restrictions, but the censorship part of the bill might gag valuable criticism of government negligence. "I say that a law to suppress the press and free speech in this time is unnecessary," he said, adding that little other than ship sailings need be kept a military secret, and in any case, the espionage bill would not protect military secrets on the field of battle. In July, 1918, Underwood took a more restricted view of wartime civil liberties and sponsored a resolution to give the president standby control over the telephone, telegraph, radio, and cable services. He defended this measure despite senatorial and press uneasiness that it would result in censorship. Brushing aside arguments that adequate hearings had not been held, he said that only emergency powers, not necessary at the moment, were authorized and that "the president wants it."[26]

Underwood initially indicated that he would oppose the Lever food control bill since it would vest comprehensive regulatory powers in an administrator of an additional government agency. He unsuccessfully opposed the Cummins amendment authorizing the president to forbid the use of grain for the manufacture of liquor or

25. *Congressional Record*, 65th Cong., 2nd Sess., 2370–76, 2435–37.
26. *Ibid.*, 1st Sess., 2114–18, 2nd Sess., 8969–70.

beer. He supported a Senate amendment to compensate owners for liquor impounded in warehouses, saying that it would otherwise mean confiscation, which was unconstitutional. The final version of the Lever Act made no specific provision to compensate for seized stocks of liquor, but Underwood joined most of his colleagues in voting for the comprehensive food bill. Several months later Underwood complained that the Lever Act had been passed "under whip and spur" without adequate time to deliberate. Nevertheless, he supported the request of Food Administrator Herbert Hoover for an appropriation of $1,200,000 for his agency, even though much of the appropriation was for propaganda. Underwood noted that he had not talked with Hoover, whom he hardly knew, but that he recognized the necessity for propaganda in his work.[27]

In March, 1918, Underwood expressed reservations about the administration's War Finance Corporation bill. The measure, a forerunner of the Reconstruction Finance Corporation, provided for government lending to corporations engaged in war production. The bill was largely unopposed except for some details, such as a requirement that securities issues of private corporations be licensed by the War Finance Corporation. The Senate struck the compulsory feature of the licensing program to ease passage of the bill. In approving of the Senate's action, Underwood expressed dismay that "it is necessary to carry this government so far afield." He added, however, that he did not believe in fighting a war "halfway" and that almost a year after American entry, "we haven't got the men on the firing line in France or the ships that we ought to have."[28]

Underwood's frustration with the Senate's slow action led him, in the summer of 1918, to sponsor a cloture measure to limit Senate debate. Having noted how much less efficiently the Senate operated than did the House, he proposed an effective cloture rule for the duration of the war. After cloture, debate would be limited

27. Birmingham *News*, May 22, July 8, 1917; *Congressional Record*, 65th Cong., 1st Sess., 2266, 4760, 2nd Sess., 3380–84.
28. *Congressional Record*, 65th Cong., 2nd Sess., 3101–3102.

to an hour (later amended to an hour and a half) and discussion of amendments to twenty minutes. Limitation of debate would allow more time for committee consideration, "where the real molding of legislation is accomplished," he said. Admitting that the cloture proposal lacked presidential endorsement, he reported that the president had stated that if he were a member of the Senate he might well favor it. Critics of the measure noted that Underwood had sympathized with Senator John Tyler Morgan's filibuster against the force bill in the 1890s and that even in presenting the cloture proposal he was quite verbose. Republican Senator Albert Fall attached an amendment exempting all legislation considered in caucus. The Underwood rule itself was then defeated 41 to 34. Defeat was variously attributed to President Wilson, opponents of national prohibition, and opponents of possible treaties to conclude the war.[29] Underwood retained his desire for cloture legislation but deferred further action until late in his Senate career.

The financial demands of the war again escalated after the first year of American participation, and Underwood was unenthusiastic about proposals to finance the war through further war taxes. Whereas McAdoo was suggesting that the nation shoulder 50 percent of the cost of the war through taxation, Underwood thought that perhaps 40 percent was a proper figure. He said that taxes on luxuries were already so high that it was necessary to broaden the tax base to include necessities. During the debate on the measure itself, Underwood urged economy, noting that although ordinary expenses of government had been frugally provided for, war appropriations had been "made blindly." He urged that the Senate adopt a budget system whereby one committee would be responsible for all appropriations measures.[30] Congress and President Wilson failed to agree on the terms of a budget system, and such a system was not adopted until the Harding administration.

Wartime purchases of cotton by England and France caused a dramatic rise in price, and by September, 1918, cotton was selling

29. *Ibid.*, 7704, 7707–22; Birmingham *News*, June 13, 14, 1918.
30. New York *Times*, June 2, 1918, Sec. 7, p. 8, November 16, 1918, p. 5.

at 38 cents a pound—at least a beginning to the southern cotton farmers' dream of "dollar cotton." Government officials, especially those in Bernard Baruch's War Industries Board, thought cotton prices were exorbitant and should be frozen as the price of wheat had been. Selma cotton brokers wired Underwood urging that the "law of supply and demand" be allowed to operate; but if the price of cotton were fixed, it should at least be pegged at a high level. Underwood agreed. The president then told southern congress-men that he had determined not to fix the price of cotton through legislation but to use the government's buying power and its power to allocate cotton to keep prices below a figure that he did not divulge. The price of cotton temporarily dipped because of news stories based on reports of various southern congressmen, includ-ing Underwood, that the government was preparing to institute controls; the prices soon recovered, however.[31] Campaign charges in 1920 that Underwood had caused a dip in the cotton market appear exaggerated.

Despite his lack of military experience and knowledge, Under-wood could not resist commenting on military affairs. Late in No-vember, 1917, visiting in Montgomery for the wedding of his nephew, he stated that the war would be settled on the western front—that the military reverses in Italy and Russia were unim-portant. He thought that the Italian situation was improved but that the Russian situation could get no worse. The senator pre-dicted victory when the British, assisted by the French and the Americans, finished driving a huge wedge into the German lines, which would compel the German evacuation of Belgium and thus signal the end of the war.[32]

By the fall of 1917 Underwood was enthusiastic about prospects for bringing the war to an early end. On October 7 he reviewed the Rainbow Division, of which his son was a member, at Camp Mills, Long Island, prior to its departure for France. He said: "When our troops get over there next spring and hit the blow, it is

31. Montgomery *Advertiser*, September 21, 22, 1918; Selma (Ala). *Times*, September 20, 1918.

32. Montgomery *Advertiser*, November 27, 1917.

going to be all over and settled. The United States is engaged in preparations for two years of war, but I do not believe that the Germans will last that long." In late October, Senator and Mrs. Underwood went to New York in the hope of seeing Oscar, Jr., before he departed for France. They were unable to stay until his troop transport left Hoboken but felt reassured that since he was to travel on the same cruiser as Major General William A. Mann, they would know immediately if anything happened to the ship. Underwood and Bertha drove South by automobile, having a "very delightful trip down the Shenandoah Valley." At Johnson City, Tennessee, however, the battery of their electric car failed, and rather than wait two days for recharging they continued to Birmingham by train.[33]

The war touched the senator personally in July, 1918, when Oscar, Jr., who was a member of the staff of General Charles T. Menoher, commander of the Forty-second (Rainbow) Division, was injured in an engagement on the Oureq River in the Aisne-Marne offense of the Second Battle of the Marne. A shrapnel splinter went through the fleshy part of Oscar, Jr.'s, leg just above the knee, not a very serious wound, but he was returned to New York, promoted to major, and then assigned as acting intelligence officer of the Ninth Division at Camp Sheridan, near Montgomery, although the division itself was in training at Camp Logan, Houston, Texas.[34]

Underwood's closest friend within the executive branch of government during the war was A. Mitchell Palmer, an Underwood aide prior to March, 1915, when both men left the House of Representatives. Palmer was appointed alien property custodian by President Wilson in 1917. Over ten years Underwood's junior, Palmer was a great admirer of his former congressional colleague. Both men lived on G Street in Washington and often rode to work together. As alien property custodian, Palmer had an abundance of jobs for lawyers. One such job, that of general counsel, went to a Birmingham attorney and friend of Underwood, Lee C. Bradley.

33. New York *Times*, October 8, 1917, p. 4; Underwood to Patterson, October 27, 1917, in Underwood Papers, University of Virginia.
34. Birmingham *News*, September 11, October 18, 1918.

Another, that of Alabama counsel for the custodian, went to E. D. Smith, an Underwood ally and Democratic national committeeman from Alabama.

The Trading with the Enemy Act of 1917 gave the president very limited power over enemy properties. Congress restrained itself from authorizing the sale of German properties in the vain hope that Germany would reciprocate by holding United States property in Germany in trust under provisions of a 1799 treaty with Prussia. Meanwhile, Palmer crusaded for the "Americanization" of German industrial holdings, maintaining that Germany was attempting world control through those holdings. At Palmer's request, Underwood vigorously supported riders to the urgent deficiency appropriations bills of March and October, 1918, to amend the Trading with the Enemy Act to give the president extensive new powers over alien property. Prior to the passage of the largely unopposed March amendment, the custodian had almost no authority to sell German property except to avoid waste. In supporting the provision to authorize such sales Underwood said: "I'd rather fire one shot at the Junker clique in Berlin than a round of ammunition on the front that our American soldiers have taken over. Let us down this kaiser-governed Junker regime in Berlin and we'll deliver a staggering blow to Prussianism."[35] Before passage, a provision requiring sale at auction, opposed by Underwood, was added.

In October he proposed a rider to another urgent deficiency appropriations bill to allow the president to sell rather than lease alien patents—the lucrative German chemical patents being the largest stake. President Wilson objected to the Underwood amendment, saying that it placed too much authority in one man, that leasing would provide American familiarity with the German processes that would make purchase unnecessary, and finally that

35. Interview with O. W. Underwood, Jr., June 15, 1951; Stanley Coben, *A. Mitchell Palmer: Politician* (New York: Columbia University Press, 1963), 132, 134–35; A. Mitchell Palmer, "Crushing the German Advance in American Industry," *Scribner's*, LXVI (July, 1919), 17–24; New York *Times*, March 12, 1918, p. 1.

sales would give a larger return to German investors. Underwood defended the patent amendment, saying that it had been prepared by Lee C. Bradley, general counsel for the alien property custodian, and that it had the support of Palmer, Secretary of the Navy Josephus Daniels, and all of the conferees on the urgent deficiency appropriations bill. Underwood professed to think that the president in fact favored the amendment, which he said had now "passed beyond my control." The amendment, Underwood noted, lodged power in the president, and so long as the president did not transfer that power to anyone else no harm was done. The president appeared to have been reassured, but evidently Palmer, Underwood, and Congress had outmaneuvered him. Scandals were indeed to result from the alien property custodian's generous sales of German patents.[36]

Palmer was elevated to attorney general on March 5, 1919. About a month later, he visited Birmingham and paid tribute to its number one citizen. Speaking before World War I veterans, he said: "It may be true that we were unprepared in a military way, but I believe that divine providence gave this nation leaders like your own Oscar Underwood, the safest, wisest and most effective leader the House of Representatives ever had in the history of the nation, and that great man in the White House."[37]

On June 2, 1919, Palmer's Washington home, on the same street as that of the Underwoods, was attacked by an anarchist who blew himself up in an attempt to assassinate the attorney general. Underwood wrote his wife who was vacationing in Asheville, North Carolina:

> I went up to the Palmers house to see if I could be of any service. The windows and doors in the front of the house were all blown to smithereens and most of the houses in the block were injured in the same way, but fortunately the Palmers were sleeping in the rear of the house

36. Woodrow Wilson to Underwood, October 29, 1918, Underwood to Wilson, October 31, 1918, Wilson to Underwood, November 2, 1918, all in Letterbox M, in Underwood Papers, Alabama Archives; Coben, *A. Mitchell Palmer*, 148.
37. Birmingham *Age-Herald*, May 1, 1919.

and were uninjured. Assistant Secretary of the Navy Franklin D. Roosevelt lives across the street. He and his wife had been out to dinner and returning home in their car were within a block of the house when the explosion went off. If they had started just a few minutes sooner there would have been no one left to tell the tale.

Mrs. Underwood must have been astonished and concerned to read further: "Mrs. Palmer did not want to leave Mitchell, so I asked them to come down to our house and stay until they could get things straightened out, which they did and the servants are making them very comfortable. You must not be uneasy. These occurrences do not repeat themselves and at present we are carefully guarded by plainclothesmen." Several weeks later Underwood wrote that the Palmers had left but that "I still see a sleuth standing around on the pavement. I don't need him and don't think I am of sufficient importance for anyone to make a rough house with me."[38]

The bombing and the Palmers' stay tied Underwood and Palmer closer together. While the Palmers were in the Underwood household, Oscar, Jr., who had been mustered out of the service and was looking for employment, was also present, being temporarily employed in checking land titles for the government in the Muscle Shoals area. Palmer first offered him a job in Ranger, Texas, and when the senator objected, Palmer recommended Oscar, Jr., to J. Henry Covington, a former Maryland representative and recently resigned chief justice of the District of Columbia, who was then forming a new law firm. Judge Covington had been Palmer's employee as attorney for the alien property custodian in the state of Maryland. This suggestion resulted in young Underwood's being taken into the Covington law firm on a basis that Oscar, Sr.,

38. Underwood to Bertha Underwood, June 4, 23, 1919, in Underwood Papers, Alabama Archives. Following the assassination of President McKinley by an anarchist, Underwood opposed making anarchism a federal crime. *Congressional Record*, 57th Cong., 1st Sess., 6467. However, in February, 1919, in a debate with Senator Robert M. LaFollette over high living costs, he touched off an angry reply from LaFollette when he said that there was no anarchist sentiment in the United States "no matter what the Wisconsin senator may dream." Birmingham *Age-Herald*, February 21, 1919.

thought "will fix him for life." The senator felt obligated to Palmer, and this was evidently an important factor in his subsequent support of Palmer for the Democratic nomination in 1920.[39]

Underwood applauded peace overtures made by the president during the early part of 1918. Wilson addressed a joint session of Congress on January 8 and stated the war aims of the United States. The president's "frank" and "impressive" statement, Underwood said, "indicates that an opportunity exists in Europe and here for the discussion of peace." In February Wilson again addressed Congress, following peace overtures made by Count Czernin, the Austro-Hungarian minister for foreign affairs. Underwood praised the president's peaceful tone: "It is as if the president had spoken to the world, to Count Czernin, and to the anti-militaristic parties inside the Teutonic alliance rather than delivered an answer to [German Chancellor] Count Hertling."[40]

Germany reeled under Allied blows in October and the president talked of peace with justice. Underwood approved of Wilson's policy and, with the collapse of Bulgaria in late September, said that the president's idealistic view would "bring about peace on our terms and quickly." A few days later Prince Max, the new imperial chancellor of the German government, requested peace on the basis of the Fourteen Points. The president cannily replied that Allied soil must first be evacuated and concluded with the question: "For whom do you speak?" Underwood extravagantly praised the Wilson note as "the smartest utterance a president has ever made," but he insisted that Marshal Ferdinand Foch rather than Allied diplomacy was winning the war. He optimistically predicted that if winter did not interfere there would be peace by Christmas. In late October he described Germany as "fatally stricken" and searching for "a soft spot on which to fall." Following the Armistice, Underwood applauded the announcement that President Wilson would go to Paris, since he would "cause a more hasty consumma-

39. Interview with O. W. Underwood, Jr., November 21, 1951; Underwood to Daniel Pratt, June 1, 1920, in Underwood Papers, Alabama Archives.
40. New York *Times*, January 9, 1918, p. 2, February 12, 1918, p. 1.

tion of peace" and receive the "most enthusiastic reception ever given any citizen of the world."[41]

While the nation awaited the return of President Wilson and the completed treaty, Underwood's constituents eagerly pressed him to approve the Treaty of Versailles with the League of Nations. But unlike the many Democratic senators who endorsed the League of Nations without seeing the final draft, Underwood deferred. At French Lick, Indiana, recovering from an attack of flu, he asserted that speed was essential in completing the peace settlement. The necessity for ratification was so compelling that he felt the league should be withdrawn if the treaty were otherwise to be delayed. Furthermore he stated that he could not commit himself to the league until he could see "what is in the paper."[42]

Underwood's equivocation on the league brought a chorus of criticism in Democratic circles, and upon his return to Birmingham he viewed it more favorably in a speech to the Civitan Club. Predicting that "all of my side" would vote to sustain the president but that the Republicans would oppose him, Underwood indicated that he liked earlier Wilson proposals for a League of Nations that would guarantee disarmament and freedom of the seas better than later drafts. He blamed Britain and France for the scrapping of disarmament features, but said that the war potential of Germany was nonetheless destroyed for a generation and perhaps for a century. In the postwar world, he expected Britain, France, and the United States to be the keepers of the peace. Underwood equated war potential with industrial potential, and industrial potential, he declared, was dependent upon steel making capacity. In addition to Germany, he excluded as powers Russia because of lack of development, Italy because of lack of resources, and Japan unless it could gain access to Chinese resources. "When we organize the League of Nations," he stated, "we can keep the peace of the world

41. Birmingham *News*, October 3, 13, 23, 1918; Birmingham *Age-Herald*, November 20, 1918.
42. Birmingham *News*, March 17, 1919. Underwood had dinner in French Lick with Democratic political leaders such as Charles Murphy of Tammany Hall and created momentary speculation about his running for the presidency in 1920.

through this generation and perhaps for a century." Immediate ratification of the peace treaty would aid the restoration of American business and the return of American troops. Pent-up demand for cotton by the central powers, he said, might require four and a half million bales in the next year and thereby drive the price of cotton up by six or seven cents a pound. He looked forward to peacetime business with Germany, since "Germany has paid the price and you can't crush her people." Although agreeing with a constituent who wrote that the kaiser should not be tried, Underwood answered that it was unwise for him to involve himself in the area of presidential responsibility.[43]

Underwood privately expressed reservations about the League of Nations. He had found, he wrote a close friend, that no one who had given it close study was entirely satisfied, but the prevailing sentiment was that the treaty should be ratified, and if it became burdensome, it should be renounced under the two years notice clause. Despite these private reservations, he wrote the chairman of the League to Enforce Peace in early July that he would "unhesitatingly vote for its ratification." He explained that this had been his intention all along but that he preferred to wait until the president had finished his work before giving his endorsement.[44]

Underwood had assumed most of the duties of minority leader as early as July, 1919, during the illness of Thomas S. Martin, who died on November 12, 1919. After Martin's death the duties were shared by Underwood and Gilbert Hitchcock of Nebraska. Hitchcock was in charge of the Democratic effort to ratify the Treaty of Versailles, whereas Underwood managed the minority's domestic legislation. Underwood addressed the Senate advocating ratification without reservations on July 15. He feelingly stated the need and the "universal sentiment" for a "final court of judgment." Declaring that he had been reluctant to give up the idea of noninvolvement in foreign affairs, he said that "time and space have been

43. Birmingham *Age-Herald*, March 22, 1919; Underwood to J. de B. Hooper, August 26, 1919, in Underwood Papers, Alabama Archives.

44. Underwood to E. D. Kenna, June 23, 1919, in Underwood Papers, Alabama Archives; Tuscaloosa *News*, July 10, 1919.

eliminated," the "era of territorial expansion" had passed, and the era of "social development" had arrived. He found no one disputing the need for a body for international arbitration, although some felt that the league would not be strong enough for the task. Since most wars were caused by territorial aggression, he felt that Article X was the treaty's greatest principle. Underwood concluded that he would vote against all amendments and for immediate ratification. His speech was well received in Alabama, and he assured league advocates that there would be enough votes to ratify the treaty.[45]

By early fall Underwood's optimism for ratification had begun to flag, and he wrote a friend that it "may be defeated or so amended that it may amount to defeat." He added that if it were so amended that it must be sent back to Europe, he was uncertain of the result. Underwood was to reverse his strategy later. In early October, though deploring the serious illness of the president, he wrote that the majority of the Senate favored reservations, but inability to agree on specific reservations enabled the forty antireservationists to dominate the situation. A few days later, following the defeat of Senator Henry C. Lodge's amendment demanding that Japan surrender to China its economic privileges on Shantung, Underwood stated that the opposition was shattered and that he would not be surprised to see the treaty ratified without reservations.[46]

Underwood and Lodge engaged on November 6 in a tedious two-hour debate over the parliamentary status of the treaty. The Senate could not vote on Lodge's reservations without first voting on the treaty itself, Underwood argued. Lodge challenged Underwood to ask for unanimous consent for a vote on the treaty without reservations. Underwood agreed, but Senator Hitchcock quickly objected. Underwood called at the White House and enlisted the support of presidential secretary Joseph P. Tumulty in opposing Hitchcock's strategy of delay. Tumulty approved and transmitted to

45. *Congressional Record*, 66th Cong., 1st Sess., 2600–2602; Underwood to John T. Ellison, July 21, 1919, in Underwood Papers, Alabama Archives.

46. Underwood to E. D. Smith, September 20, Ocober 4, 1919, in Underwood Papers, Alabama Archives; Birmingham *News*, October 20, 1919.

the president Underwood's insistence that Hitchcock demand a vote on unconditional ratification. "This will put the president in a position to dictate the terms of settlement between the different forces in the Senate," Underwood said. Soon afterward Underwood moved in the Democratic caucus that the Democrats vote against the treaty with the Lodge reservations, and his motion was adopted. Tumulty's biographer, John Blum, concludes that Underwood's "unrealistic strategy of deadlock" was calculated to win the president's favor in Underwood's struggle with Hitchcock for the minority leadership.[47]

The Senate cast three votes on the treaty on November 19. Two motions to ratify with the Lodge reservations attached were defeated by votes of 55 to 39 and 51 to 41. Underwood made the third motion, that for unconditional ratification, which failed by a vote of 53 to 38. Underwood sensed the hopelessness of securing ratification or of getting the president to accept a compromise. The day following the treaty's defeat, he found Secretary of State Robert Lansing receptive to his suggestion that the United States withdraw from Europe its troops which had anything to do with the Supreme War Council, leaving only those operating under the terms of the Armistice. The president agreed that this was sound advice and ordered its implementation.[48] Encouraged by the president's response, Underwood, after conferring with Tumulty, left a letter for the president offering a route around the treaty impasse:

> [Any compromise] should be proposed from the other side, and when proposed it can be weighed and considered on its merits. . . . If this government is not willing to accept the league of nations for itself, it should not destroy it for the balance of the world. . . . As a last resort, we would consent to a resolution that ratified the treaty of peace in its integrity for the balance of the world, and by a reservation eliminating Article I, the league of nations, from binding effect on us and our

47. New York *Times*, November 7, 1919, p. 3; Joseph P. Tumulty to Woodrow Wilson, November 17, 1919, quoting Underwood, in John Blum, *Joe Tumulty and the Wilson Era* (Boston: Houghton Mifflin, 1951), 226; Blum, *Joe Tumulty*, 225–28.

48. New York *Times*, November 20, 1919, p. 2; Robert Lansing to Woodrow Wilson, November 20, 1919, in Keith L. Nelson, *Victors Divided* (Berkeley: University of California Press, 1975), 132.

Government alone; and then propose to go to the country on the issue as to whether or not the people of the United States would ask the permission of the other nations that we might hereafter become a member of the league in its full integrity.[49]

Underwood's proposal that the league be separated from the Treaty of Versailles was, of course, unacceptable to President Wilson. The president asked to see the letter from his sick bed, but he did not reply, and the letter effectively ended communication between Underwood and Wilson. The president issued a statement the following day that he would not take part in the Underwood-Hitchcock contest for minority leader. It would thus not appear that Underwood was pandering to the president's desires, or he would not have advocated compromise. More plausibly, Underwood changed his earlier, intransigent position following the rather conclusive votes of November 19. Senator Lodge said later that the vote on Underwood's motion of November 19 demonstrated conclusively that the treaty never would have been accepted by the Senate. Underwood agreed.[50]

Underwood's politics in World War I had been politics as usual rather than "politics is adjourned." He was extremely successful in getting wartime favors from the Wilson administration. To a constituent who wrote that Underwood had not gotten enough for Alabama, the senator wrote:

Birmingham received large numbers of war contracts during the war and the only thing that I know of that Birmingham wanted and did not get was a military camp. Birmingham failed to offer the government a satisfactory plot of land, [and] the War Department did not want a camp near a large city. I aided [Representative Stanley H. Dent, Jr.] in reference to [securing] Camp Sheridan [for Montgomery] and [Rep-

49. Underwood to Woodrow Wilson, November 21, 1919, in Series II, Box 164, Wilson Papers.

50. Tumulty to Mrs. Woodrow Wilson, November 21, 1919, in Series II, Box 164, Wilson Papers; H. Cecil Kilpatrick to author, February 11, 1953, in possession of Evans C. Johnson, DeLand, Fla.; New York *Times*, November 23, 1919, p. 2; Henry C. Lodge, *The Senate and the League of Nations* (New York: Scribner, 1925), 192; Underwood to Frederick Lewis Allen, January 12, 1920, in Frederick Lewis Allen Papers, University of Virginia Library.

resentative Fred L.] Blackmon in securing appropriations for Camp
[McClellan] at Anniston. I was very active in aiding the development
of the ship [building] plant at Mobile.

As far as Muscle Shoals is concerned, I was the original proponent
in the Congress of the suggestion that the power at Muscle Shoals
should be harnessed to make nitrogen in order that the farmers might
have cheap fertilizer.[51]

Underwood's position as a war leader was ambiguous. While he
was House leader, and during the time that he was dependent on
the support of the Wilson administration for help in his Senate
campaign, he was especially amenable to the White House. When
he was elevated to the Senate and became a lieutenant of Democratic floor leader Martin, he followed a more independent course.
An advocate of laissez-faire, who found war repugnant partially because it disrupted the nation's economic life, he was slow to favor
preparedness measures. Underwood was, however, swept along
into a prowar position by the German submarine campaign, and
he developed a strong hatred for the Germans.

Underwood retained his presidential ambitions, and the Wilson
peace program presented him with a difficult dilemma. Although
his constituents generally favored the League of Nations, he could
not possibly hope, as a southern conservative, to be the legatee of
Wilson's political strength. He attempted to foster compromise on
the league, evidently in a genuine desire to see the treaty ratified,
but since Wilson's adamant position made compromise impossible,
he merely created distrust of himself within the Wilson circle. He
was never able to remove the suspicions of the Wilsonians that he
was unfavorable to the League of Nations.

Underwood's basic conservatism, his strict constructionism, and
his belief in strict governmental economy served as a base for his
criticism of some of the Wilsonian war legislation. Even though
these were wartimes, he despaired at the lack of concern with
economy in defense appropriations. He feared the loss of civil lib-

51. Underwood to James M. Parker, March 27, 1920, in Underwood Papers, Alabama
Archives.

erties, the erosion of congressional power, and the growth of presidential domination. These views were reflected in his criticism of large army and navy appropriations (prior to American entry), the Espionage Act, the Railroad Control Act, and the Lever Act. Even so, like most Americans, Underwood could not bring himself, after the entrance of the United States into the war, to directly oppose most war legislation. Indeed, he sponsored many Wilson war measures, including the neutrality legislation, the huge urgent deficiency appropriation bill of 1917, the Emergency Fleet Act, and an act for control of telephone and telegraph communications. As the war wore on, he was increasingly affected by war fever, increasingly anti-German, and there was little consistent pattern between the repressive measures that he had opposed prior to American entry and those that he supported during the war.

In later years Underwood repeatedly asserted his amazement at the lack of preparedness for war of the United States Army and Navy. He did not seem to recognize that some of this lack was caused by a dearth of appropriations by Congress—appropriations that he had fought against. Toward the end of his life he recalled meeting with five other members of the Appropriations Committee in a little room in the Capitol where they fought the war behind the scenes. The group, he said, knew little about war, but the army and navy seemed to have done little planning either. He said:

> I sometimes think . . . that one smart enemy spy at our keyhole would have been a good thing. It would have justified the enemy in ending the war sooner, to hear of the billions in credit we had to spend. Yet there was another side to it. We were all guessing. But so were the Army and Navy heads who came to us with their plans. None of us knew much about the war. One day an officer came in and asked a million dollars for the Army secret service. It took considerable time to convince [Senator John F.] Shafroth of the necessity for spies. Eventually Shafroth voted with us to give the colonel his million.[52]

Wartimes are confusing times, and they were especially confusing for a man of peace and an advocate of laissez-faire like Underwood.

52. William G. Shepard, "The Gold Barrage," *Collier's Weekly*, LXXXVI (November 15, 1930), 26.

CHAPTER XI

The Musgrove
Campaign

Presidential ambition was never far from Underwood's mind after
he reached national prominence in 1911. He felt that he had come
close to victory in the quest for the Democratic nomination in
1912, and that defeat only whetted his desire to pursue the glitter-
ing crown again. Even the popularity of President Wilson was not
too great to prevent speculation that Underwood would seek the
Democratic nomination in 1916. A dinner given for Underwood in
1916 by Thomas Fortune Ryan, that indefatigable financier of
Democratic campaigns, included in the guest list some of the
wealthiest corporate heads in the United States as well as Democratic regulars from Tammany ranks and set political tongues wag-
ging about Underwood's possible presidential candidacy. However,
Underwood's presidential talk in 1916 was stillborn. The Birmingham News, almost an Underwood organ, commented editorially
that Underwood discouraged talk of his opposing President Wilson
and that there was "no warmer admirer" of the president than Underwood.[1] The fact, however, that Underwood retained his presidential ambitions was seen in January, 1917, when he participated
in the observance of "Cardinal's Day" at St. Patrick's Cathedral in
New York. At a luncheon following a high mass, Underwood, together with a number of public officials, paid homage to James
Cardinal Gibbons of Baltimore. Underwood's participation in the
event accorded with his earlier policy of seeking presidential sup-

1. New York World, February 18, 1916; Birmingham News, February 10, 1916.

port in the Roman Catholic community—especially among Irish and Italian voters. No Alabama politician without national ambitions would have knelt publicly near the red carpeted throne of a Catholic cardinal; the event fueled doubts in Alabama about Underwood's devotion to Protestantism that were to remain for the remainder of his career.[2]

Practical considerations kept Underwood from seeking the Democratic nomination in 1920. Faced with a senatorial reelection contest, he could hardly have waged an effective fight for the nomination. Alabama law would have required him to resign from the Senate, and he also considered the political climate unfavorable to Democratic victory. Strange new doctrines, women's suffrage and prohibition, were strong in the Democratic party, and Underwood did not relish these changes.

Underwood's national prominence set the scene for his campaign for reelection in Alabama. With his presidential ambitions in check, he was forced to launch his 1920 senatorial campaign in a highly unfavorable Alabama political climate. Underwood's victory in the 1914 senatorial primary over Congressman Richmond Pearson Hobson inevitably left deep political scars. Hobson and his campaign manager, Lycurgus Breckinridge Musgrove, had questioned Underwood's devotion to Wilsonian progressivism and had identified him with the "interests," with antiprohibition, and with opposition to women's suffrage. He now faced Musgrove in a contest in which the lines were sharply drawn between Underwood's staid conservatism and Musgrove's muddled progressivism.

The prohibition movement flourished in Alabama under the aegis of the Anti-Saloon League. Abetted by the Protestant churches, prohibition appeared to be the wave of the future in Alabama politics. In March, 1916, Underwood had favored the election of Edward D. Smith of Birmingham as Democratic national committeeman over Borden Burr, also of Birmingham, charging that the prohibitionists were attempting to capture the Democratic party by electing Burr. Smith won. Underwood had incurred further

2. New York *Times*, January 15, 1917, p. 8.

prohibitionist enmity when he tried to attach a referendum provision to a 1916 prohibition bill for the District of Columbia. On July 7, 1917, Underwood unsuccessfully sponsored an amendment to the food control bill that would have required the federal government to pay for liquor held in government warehouses for the duration of the war. He voted against the Volstead Act on its initial passage, and when President Wilson vetoed the measure, he opposed passage over the president's veto.[3]

The prohibition question dominated the elections for the legislature as well as those for statewide office in 1918. Underwood returned to Alabama in August to join the antiprohibitionists in opposing ratification of the Eighteenth Amendment. National prohibition, he told north Alabamians, would "centralize the government" and would restrict state influence to only "two per cent" in regulatory legislation. He concluded extravagantly: "If you are in favor of adoption, you should stop fighting the Kaiser, because, he, like the prohibitionists, believes he is ruling by the will of God." Indeed, the prohibitionists were quite self-righteous. Popular Lieutenant Governor Thomas E. Kilby, the author of Alabama's 1915 "bone dry" law, in campaigning for governor called the Eighteenth Amendment, officially submitted in December, 1917, "the greatest Christmas gift since the birth of the Babe of Bethlehem."[4] Kilby swept to victory, and the prohibitionists gained complete control of the legislature. Underwood was shaken by the "dry" victory and wrote gloomily to an old friend:

I came back [to Washington] feeling first rate excepting a bad throat—worn out from campaigning. . . . Part of the result was due to a lack of real organization [among the antiprohibitionists], but it was largely due to the sentiment in favor of prohibition. Of course what I think is disastrous in the situation is the strong tendency which is being developed in the South toward centralizing the Government and the throwing aside of old and fundamental principles. I made an earnest fight in

3. Birmingham *News*, March 21, 1916; *Congressional Record*, 64th Cong., 2nd Sess., 471; Birmingham *News*, July 8, 1917; *Congressional Record*, 66th Cong., 1st Sess., 7621.
4. Birmingham *News*, August 4, 1918; Albert B. Moore, *History of Alabama* (University, Ala.: University Supply Store, 1934), 764.

278 OSCAR W. UNDERWOOD

favor of local self-government, spoke all over the State for nearly three weeks, had large crowds and enthusiastic audiences, but nevertheless we did not succeed.[5]

Underwood conceded that the prohibitionists had better candidates since "it was hard to get the best men to run on our side and in many cases we did not have any candidates at all." Nevertheless, he felt that in a direct vote of the people on prohibition "we would have won."[6] He urged that prohibition now be forgotten as an issue and placed in limbo with "the Civil War and the annexation of Texas."[7]

Underwood was no less opposed to national women's suffrage than to prohibition. He had a Victorian attitude toward women, even opposing their admission to his alma mater, the University of Virginia. When pressed by the suffragists during the Hobson campaign of 1914, however, he had agreed that he would have no objection to women's suffrage if granted by the state legislature. In late June, 1918, he blocked a vote on the women's suffrage resolution despite overwhelming sentiment in the Senate for the measure. Senator Ollie James, ill in a Baltimore hospital, had authorized Underwood to act for him, and Underwood demanded that the suffragists produce two votes to counter the pair he held for James, since a constitutional amendment requires a two-thirds vote in Congress. Suffragists later accused Underwood of bad faith in having presented a pair secured from James for another purpose, but unless Underwood completely misrepresented James's telegram, which he said James had confirmed only an hour before, this appears unlikely.[8]

In 1919 Underwood emphasized that except for the Fifteenth

5. Oscar W. Underwood to Edward D. Kenna, August 20, 1918, in Oscar W. Underwood Papers, Alabama Department of Archives and History, Montgomery.

6. Underwood to Henry St. George Tucker, August 21, 1918, in Henry St. George Tucker Papers, University of North Carolina, Chapel Hill.

7. Underwood to Val Taylor, July 16, 1919, in Underwood Papers, Alabama Archives.

8. Underwood to Eppa Hunton, Jr., December 2, 1913, in Eppa Hunton, Jr. Papers, University of Virginia Library; Pattie Ruffner Jacobs to Underwood, January 20, 1915, in Underwood Papers, Alabama Archives; New York *Times*, June 28, 1918, p. 6; Maud Younger, quoted in Inez Haynes Irwin, *The Story of Alice Paul and the National Women's Party* (Fairfax, Va.: Delinger's Publishers, 1977), 357.

Amendment suffrage was a state question and that although he was not opposed to women voting, such a change should come through a state statute rather than ratification of the Nineteenth Amendment. Federal action, he said, would violate the Jeffersonian principles he had learned under Professor John B. Minor at the University of Virginia. In late May, 1919, Underwood made a last ditch, unsuccessful effort to avoid presentation of women's suffrage to the states by insisting that the measure go to the Women's Suffrage Committee before being placed on the calendar. Committee action delayed the measure only slightly, and the resolution passed on June 4, 1919. The senator wrote his wife that the suffrage defeat was "much to my regret, but everything has its compensations, and thank God that horde of women have left the Capitol."[9] To a constituent he commented:

> I deeply regret that many of our people at home do not realize that the very basis of our civilization in the South is the control of the suffrage by the people of our state, and not by the National Congress. I also realize that a great many of those who favor the Anthony Amendment think that it is only one step, and not a dangerous step, but I do not view it in that way. They overlook entirely the fact that the border states, such as Missouri, Kentucky, and Maryland, have unlimited manhood suffrage, and with unrestricted female suffrage, the vote of the Negro in those states will almost assuredly make them permanently Republican. With these states in the Republican column there is not much hope of the Democratic party electing its candidates for president in our lifetime. This may be a political argument, but when we consider the fact that it is the Democratic party that sustains our civilization, the question of its undoing goes far beyond the mere question of party advantage.[10]

This breathtaking, racist argument left wholly out of account the probability that white women voters, a far larger group than Negro

9. Birmingham *Age-Herald*, April 27, 1919; New York *Times*, May 24, 1919, p. 3; Underwood to Bertha Underwood, June 6, 1919, in Oscar W. Underwood Papers, University of Virginia Library.

10. Underwood to Floyd S. Kincey, June 21, 1919, in Underwood Papers, Alabama Archives.

women voters, would tend to divide in much the same way as did white men.

Meanwhile, Underwood covertly opposed ratification of the women's suffrage amendment by the Alabama legislature. The Alabama senate rejected the amendment, and the Alabama house of representatives failed to act. Underwood expressed the hope that if national ratification were not completed by 1920, those opposed to it would be elected to the Alabama legislature and would reject the amendment through action of both houses.[11] However, the amendment was on its way to national approval.

The defeat of women's suffrage in the Alabama legislature was of limited significance in Underwood's immediate political future, but adverse reaction to his antiprohibition stance showed that he could anticipate difficulty in his campaign for reelection to the Senate in 1920. The Dothan *Daily Eagle* commented that Underwood had been misled by two large "wet" daily newspapers, the Birmingham *News* and the Montgomery *Advertiser*, into thinking that the Eighteenth Amendment would be defeated and that he could come to Alabama and take credit for its defeat. The anti-Underwood vote was at least 40 percent, the *Eagle* claimed, urging that Probate Judge William W. Brandon of Tuscaloosa, runner-up in the governor's race, oppose Underwood for the senatorial nomination.[12]

Judge Brandon did not run, but by the spring of 1919 the prohibitionists were planning to run L. Breckinridge Musgrove of Jasper. Underwood declared that he was "not apprehensive" about Musgrove's candidacy and felt that the "drys" would produce other names before fielding a candidate. Hearing that Musgrove was almost certainly a candidate, he wrote his wife: "I hope this will happen because it will keep everyone else out, and if I can't successfully win over Musgrove, I am sure I could not win over some other candidate."[13]

11. Underwood to Charles McDowell, Jr., September 11, 1919, in Underwood Papers, Alabama Archives.

12. Dothan (Ala.) *Daily Eagle*, quoted in Birmingham *News*, August 22, 1918.

13. Underwood to Bertha Underwood, May 25, 1919, in Underwood Papers, University of Virginia.

"Breck" Musgrove, a sixty-year-old Walker County banker, farmer, mine operator, and publisher of the Jasper *Mountain Eagle*, had achieved statewide attention when he managed Hobson's campaign against Underwood for the 1914 Democratic nomination for the United States Senate. A convivial bachelor and raconteur noted for his lavish 'possum dinners, Musgrove had served as national chairman of the Anti-Saloon League and had attended the Versailles Conference with a group of Methodist clergy in the interest of temperance. Musgrove's grandfather was the founder of Jasper. His father, a major in Nathan B. Forrest's Confederate cavalry, was wounded at the Battle of Murfreesboro and died from his wounds soon after the war. "Breck" Musgrove, hailed as a self-made man who had been gainfully employed since the age of nine, served as a member of the State Board of Education, as a trustee of the University of Alabama, and as chairman of the Walker County Board of Education.[14]

Musgrove formally entered the race in June, 1919. The "paramount issue," he said, was still prohibition. He called attention to the importance of prohibition in conserving food and his opposition to "special favors for the brewers," a reference to Underwood's efforts to exempt beer from the wartime Lever Food Act. He advocated a "more generous policy with the soldiers and sailors," apparently referring to veterans' benefits as most of the troops were on their way home. He warned against a union of church and state, an effort to capitalize on Underwood's identification with Catholic voters in Birmingham and Mobile. The Jasper industrialist favored federal aid to education and vocational training and suggested a grant-in-aid program similar to the Federal Highways Act, although he admitted that he did not know just how such a program would work. He favored women's suffrage, having earlier endeared himself to suffragettes by lending them an automobile and furnishing them with "other incidentals." He favored the right of labor to organize and act collectively and approved of farm extension work.

14. Thomas M. Owen, *History of Alabama and Dictionary of Alabama Biography* (4 vols.; Chicago: S. J. Clarke Publishing Company, 1921), I, 1264–65.

Musgrove effectively removed the Treaty of Versailles from the campaign by urging immediate ratification and by stating that the alternative was an expensive and dangerous arms race.[15]

Meanwhile, a second prohibitionist, Judge Samuel D. Weakley, an associate justice of the Alabama Supreme Court, announced that he would run against Underwood and Musgrove. The senator wrote his wife: "In the last analysis I have ceased to worry about the matter. There are too many things in life worth while to worry about whether I remain in the Senate or not. When I go home next fall if things are propitious, I will announce and if not I won't. In the meantime I shall enjoy life and thank God I have the finest girl in the world for a wife and two of the best boys in the world for sons." Underwood really preferred that both Musgrove and Weakley remain in the contest, but for a time he thought this unlikely.[16] He feared that Governor O'Neal, a "wet," would also enter the race but wrote that although O'Neal "would probably draw more support from my friends than Weakley or Musgrove. . . . I am inclined to think that the more candidates . . . the better . . . as I think that I have a certain following in Alabama that is not likely to be seriously disturbed by the candidacy of anyone else." Although Underwood expected a strenuous campaign, he did not think it could be "any more fierce" than the Hobson contest. He was also undisturbed by rumors that both Musgrove and Weakley would withdraw in favor of another prohibitionist, Colonel Bibb Graves, a popular World War I officer. Other rumors suggested that John W. Altman, a labor union leader, or Congressman J. Thomas Heflin, a notorious demagogue but Underwood's friend, would enter the contest. Heflin, though eager to run, was loath to risk his congressional seat.[17]

No one else entered the race, but Judge Weakley remained in

15. Birmingham *News*, June 2, 1919; Leander Poole to Underwood, September 29, 1919, in Underwood Papers, Alabama Archives; Birmingham *Age-Herald*, June 2, 1919.

16. Underwood to Bertha Underwood, May 25, 1919, in Underwood Papers, University of Virginia.

17. Underwood to William H. Thomas, May 31, 1919, Underwood to Clayton L. Tullis, June 3, 1919, Underwood to John W. Overton, October 4, 1919, Underwood to R. A. Statham, December 16, 1919, Underwood to Charles Sumner, September 22, 1919, all in Underwood Papers, Alabama Archives.

the campaign to the dismay of many prohibitionists who saw him as a far weaker candidate than Musgrove. The Alabama Anti-Saloon League urged that one of the two "dry" candidates retire from the race, but the message was clearly intended for Weakley. Weakley, a Presbyterian, was fifty-nine years old, a year older than Underwood and a year younger than Musgrove. His campaign was quiet and dignified except when he attacked Musgrove, pointing out that Musgrove was not a family man and did not belong to a church.[18]

The fact that Musgrove and Weakley, both prohibitionists, remained in the race was not altogether to Underwood's benefit. The peculiar Alabama primary system allowed the casting of both first and second choice votes. The leading candidate had to receive a majority of first choice votes to achieve victory; otherwise, the second choice votes must be added to the first choice votes in order to determine the victor. With two dedicated prohibitionists as opponents, Underwood could expect few second choice votes, and if he did not win with first choice ballots, he could expect defeat.

Underwood intended to announce his candidacy for reelection in the fall of 1919, but he delayed for several reasons. The minority leader, Senator Thomas S. Martin, whom Underwood had aided in passing World War I measures, died in November, 1919, at the beginning of the fight for ratification of the Treaty of Versailles. Underwood stayed in Washington to aid Senator Gilbert M. Hitchcock of Nebraska in the unsuccessful attempt to push ratification of the treaty through the Senate. Underwood was also interested in the framing of the Cummins bill to regulate railroads and railway labor. Above all, Underwood's Jefferson County campaign manager and closest political advisor, Forney Johnston, preferred a "short and snappy" campaign.[19]

Underwood focused organizational efforts for the Democratic senatorial nomination on Jefferson County, where the heavy Birmingham labor vote was expected to give him difficulty. The state-

18. Birmingham *Age-Herald*, March 4, 1920; Montgomery *Journal*, April 14, 1920.
19. Underwood to James B. Ellis, January 26, 1920, in Underwood Papers, Alabama Archives.

wide campaign manager was Lloyd M. Hooper of Selma, aided by Richard M. Hobbie of Montgomery, the campaign treasurer. Underwood insisted that he intended to stay clearly within the ten thousand dollar limit set by the Alabama Corrupt Practices Act— evidently an attempt to avoid the criticism of extravagance that had marked his 1914 senatorial campaign.[20]

While Underwood's campaign was in the planning stage, Senator John H. Bankhead, Sr., died suddenly at his post in Washington in early March, 1920. Bankhead was nationally known as an advocate of improved transportation, having served as a member of the Inland Waterways Commission in the Roosevelt administration and as a sponsor of the Bankhead-Shackleford Highway Act of the Wilson administration. Underwood accompanied the remains of his colleague and close friend to Alabama. He eulogized Bankhead, saying that the monument to the coauthor of the grant-in-aid highway act should be the completion of the inland waterways system and the building of a system of roads reaching into "every hamlet and neighborhood in Alabama." Noting that Alabama had recently voted a bond issue for highways, Underwood noted the importance to the state of his membership on the Senate Appropriations Committee to supplement the funds that Alabama had determined to spend on highway construction.[21]

Musgrove launched his campaign in Birmingham in late March, 1920, with the claim that he was a "plain farmer and a business man." In an address peppered with mild profanity he said that "there has been started in Alabama a union between the farmers, union labor, and the prohibition forces," a combination he aimed to forge into victory against the "fossiliferous old asses of reaction."[22] Musgrove stated that he preferred to wear the label of the unions, farmers, and the Christian people rather than that of the "stock gamblers," the salaried officials, and the brewers. His father had lost a leg fighting for the South, he asserted, whereas Underwood's family "had deserted the Southland." He vowed that he

20. Underwood to Herbert E. Smith, March 12, 1920, in Underwood Papers, Alabama Archives; Birmingham *Age-Herald*, January 4, 1920.
21. Birmingham *News*, March 7, 1920.

would never be found "truckling to any sinister foreign element." As the campaign developed, the Musgrove forces accused Underwood of advocating special favors for German-American brewing interests and for the Sinn Fein, that "crimson-handed bunch," as Musgrove called them.[23] Certainly, Underwood favored the exemption of beer from the prohibition laws. But though he sympathized with the Irish independence movement, he refused to favor Irish-tainted reservations to the Treaty of Versailles, and he failed to vote when the Senate passed a resolution of sympathy with Irish independence in June, 1919.[24]

Musgrove was angered at his treatment by the press. Especially annoying was the Birmingham *News*, whose Washington columnist, Hugh Roberts, devoted most of his columns to praise of Underwood. The Anniston *Star* paraphrased the Koran: "Great is Oscar, and the *News* is his prophet." Musgrove's claim that the entire "Bolshevik press" of the state, controlled by the "capitalists," was against him hardly inspired confidence in his judgment. Much of his campaign was directed toward the farmers of Alabama. His campaign manager was Circuit Judge Henry B. Foster of Tuscaloosa, but the chairman of his campaign committee was James A. Wade, former state commissioner of agriculture. Underwood was falsely accused both of having opposed the creation of Federal Farm Loan Banks and with having caused a slide in the cotton market during World War I by announcing that he favored a price freeze on cotton. The Musgrove forces charged that Underwood failed to exert adequate pressure to halt rising prices and noted that he had favored repeal of the excess profits tax. Underwood's

22. Jasper (Ala.) *Mountain Eagle*, March 31, 1920. The Underwood Committee distributed Musgrove's basic speech with annotations. Replying to the charge that Underwood was one of "the fossiliferous old asses of reaction," the committee said that to compare Musgrove with the least of these was like comparing a "singed cat with a Royal Bengal tiger." Birmingham *Age-Herald*, April 18, 1920.

23. Birmingham *Age-Herald*, March 26, 1920; Montgomery *Journal*, May 6, 1920; "The Voters' Guide," in Musgrove Family Folder, L. Breckinridge Musgrove Papers, Alabama Department of Archives and History, Montgomery; Jasper (Ala.) *Mountain Eagle*, April 28, 1920.

24. Underwood to Bertha Underwood, June 18, 1919, in Underwood Papers, University of Virginia; Underwood to Joseph H. Lyons, March 16, 1920, in Underwood Papers, Alabama Archives.

unsuccessful bill to lower the tax on oleomargarine and thus bring down the price of butter was ridiculed, and he was nicknamed "Oleo Oscar."[25]

But the central issue was prohibition. Brooks Lawrence, superintendent of the Alabama Anti-Saloon League, campaigned throughout the state, calling Underwood "the leader of the liquor interest in the United States Senate." William Jennings Bryan urged Alabamians to vote first for Musgrove and second for Weakley, describing Underwood as a man "of great personal charm" but one who had made more trouble for prohibition than any other Democrat. Underwood's reelection, Bryan stated, would foreshadow the raising of a large fund by the breweries to carry the Democratic convention for the "wets." The Anniston *Star* objected that though Underwood had campaigned against Hobson in 1914 on the slogan that a public servant should stay on the job, he had neglected his duties while the Germans were hammering at Paris to campaign against prohibition in Alabama. He was tagged as an ingrate for campaigning in 1918 against prohibition in Etowah County, the home county of Thomas E. Kilby, an Underwood supporter and a staunch prohibitionist then engaged in a campaign for governor and for the Eighteenth Amendment.[26]

The rumor that Underwood was covertly a Roman Catholic had plagued him since he had given a toast to James Cardinal Gibbons at a dinner in 1917; the Musgrove press resurrected it, labeling Underwood "[Pope] Leo Oscar." Musgrove charged that there was a Roman Catholic conspiracy against him headed by Cardinal Gibbons, and he darkly identified Underwood with the Sinn Fein and demanded that their leader, Eamon de Valera, be "exported" from the United States. A scurrilous handbill charged that Underwood "has stooped to kiss the ring of the Pope," though there is no evidence that Underwood ever met the Pope. Presumably the charge relates to the high mass of 1917 at which Underwood may have

25. Anniston (Ala.) *Star*, quoted in Jasper (Ala.) *Mountain Eagle*, February 25, 1920; Montgomery *Journal*, May 1, 1920; Jasper (Ala.) *Mountain Eagle*, May 5, 1920.
26. Birmingham *Age-Herald*, March 4, May 8, 9, 1920; Anniston (Ala.) *Star*, quoted in Jasper (Ala.) *Mountain Eagle*, February 25, 1920.

kissed the ring of James Cardinal Gibbons. The handbill tied Thomas Fortune Ryan, Tammany Hall, and the Roman Catholics to Underwood and accused him of having employed Catholics in confidential positions. It concluded: "NO FRIEND OF THE POPE SHALL GO TO WASHINGTON."[27]

Underwood's managers viciously attacked Musgrove in an advertisement accusing the Farmers' Union and several labor unions of "blacklisting" candidates in unsegregated meetings. Musgrove's attorneys secured an injunction blocking publication of the advertisement, but, having made their point, they allowed publication. The Underwood committee published pathetic stories of mortgage foreclosures by the Jasper Bank and Trust Company under the name of its president, L. B. Musgrove. One such case resulted in a judgment against Musgrove in favor of a Protestant minister's daughter, and in another a Confederate soldier was allegedly defrauded. Musgrove called these charges "lies" and showed that Underwood's supporters had their facts confused.[28]

Although both Musgrove and Weakley had begun their campaigns in the summer of 1919, Underwood stayed in Washington except for his attendance at Senator Bankhead's funeral. His campaign was in abeyance until his return to Alabama in early April, 1920. He declined Musgrove's challenge to debate, replying that his time was so limited he must make his own schedule. He stated that although he had voted against the Eighteenth Amendment as a violation of states' rights, he had, as House leader, given the green light for the passage of the Webb-Kenyon Act prohibiting shipment of liquor into "dry" states. He pointed out that he had convinced President Wilson that Muscle Shoals was the proper place for a war nitrate plant, and he predicted that he would soon become Senate minority leader.

Underwood attempted to divert attention from the prohibition

27. Jasper (Ala.) *Mountain Eagle*, May 5, April 28, 1920; handbill in May, 1920 File, Underwood Papers, Alabama Archives.

28. Montgomery *Journal*, May 3, 1920; "Little Journeys into the Record of L. B. Musgrove No. 1," advertisement in Musgrove Family Folder, Musgrove Papers, Alabama Archives; Montgomery *Journal*, April 28, 1920.

issue by focusing attention on labor unrest. He had been deeply affected by the bombing of Attorney General A. Mitchell Palmer's house in June, 1919. As a representative of the Birmingham district in the House of Representatives, Underwood had had an almost perfect prolabor record. His elevation to the Senate, however, meant that he had an agrarian constituency, and he was now able to vote the antiunion views that were more natural to him. At Gadsden, where the labor vote was heavy, Underwood forthrightly boasted that he was responsible for the no-strike provision of the Cummins bill for the regulation of railroads and railway labor. He claimed, however, that as House leader he had guided the bill for the creation of a Department of Labor to passage and had boosted William B. Wilson, a miner, to prominence as chairman of the Committee on Labor. Wilson subsequently became the first secretary of labor. He also pointed out that he had favored the passage of the Adamson Act of 1916 which was popular with labor.[29]

Underwood seemed genuinely disturbed by signs of anarchy which he identified with the labor movement. In Mobile he said:

> Europe is afire. The sparks are falling here. I mean an effort is being made to kindle a fire of revolution in our country. Our government is in danger. . . . And there are men here who would tear down the fundamental principles of government, the principles which our forefathers established when they came from across the water, drove back the savages and with ax in hand hewed their way through trackless forests and established this government. . . . These I. W. W. strikes are being fostered for the purpose of tearing down the government, not for the ostensible purposes which are held out to the public.[30]

Underwood continued by saying that he had been blacklisted by labor, although he had helped pass a law to outlaw the blacklist when used against labor. He declared that Samuel Gompers was working against him because of personal interest rather than in labor's interest.

Underwood denied charges that he had been insulting to labor

29. Birmingham *Age-Herald*, April 4, 6, 8, 1920.
30. *Ibid.*, April 16, 1920.

delegations that had called on him for help during Birmingham mining strikes in World War I. One charge grew out of the Metal Trades Union's attempt to secure an eight-hour day in 1918. Underwood stated that he had expressed himself "vigorously" in opposing any attempt to cut down hours of production as long as the war continued, arguing that labor should be willing to "make the same sacrifice" being made by soldiers in France. He had not said he would have ore miners who attempted to strike in World War I shot as traitors, but had contended only that the dispute should be submitted to arbitration. Labor unions were unconvinced by his explanations, and a meeting of representatives of the Farmers' Union, the railroad brotherhoods, and the Alabama State Federation of Labor endorsed Musgrove and denounced Underwood as a reactionary.[31]

Toward the end of the campaign, Underwood defended himself against rumors that he was a Roman Catholic, that he was financed by the liquor interests, and that he had speculated in stocks and in commodities futures. He said that he had belonged to the Episcopal church for twenty-five years (actually he had belonged for over thirty years) and that he had been active in the Masons, Knights Templars, and the Shriners (organizations to which Roman Catholics do not ordinarily belong). He noted, however, that the Constitution guarantees religious freedom and that he did not "make war on any church." He said that he had indeed once speculated in a mining stock some fifteen years earlier but except for that investment which had netted him a profit of six hundred to seven hundred dollars, he had only invested in "home companies," and in those his investments were small. He denied that he had ever speculated in or received any funds from the liquor interests.[32]

Underwood hardly mentioned the Underwood-Simmons Tariff Act during the campaign, and most of his remarks were defensive in tone. He won the Democratic nomination for the Senate by a vote of 66,871 first choice votes to 56,563 first choice votes for

31. *Ibid.*, April 2, 1920; Jasper (Ala.) *Mountain Eagle*, March 17, 1920.
32. Birmingham *Age-Herald*, April 6, 8, 1920.

Musgrove and 8,640 first choice votes for Weakley. The addition of
second choice votes would have narrowed Underwood's lead to
69,130 for Underwood, 61,360 for Musgrove, and 25,898 for Weakley. Underwood led in first choice votes in forty-three of the sixty-
seven Alabama counties. In Underwood's home county of Jefferson, Musgrove led him by 101 votes and defeated him by
a majority of over two to one in Musgrove's home, Walker County.[33]

Underwood declared himself satisfied with the results, but his
disappointment was apparent. He rationalized that the farmers had
not gone to the polls, and he wrote his former colleague, Congressman Andrew J. Peters of Massachusetts, that it had been a hard
fight, with organized labor, the Anti-Saloon League, William Jennings Bryan, Tom Watson, and Samuel Gompers opposing him. He
wrote a supporter, however, that he did not think Bryan's opposition had much effect, and interestingly enough, there is no evidence that Watson, the aging agrarian rebel, played an active role
in the campaign against Underwood. Underwood wrote his friend,
New York financier Thomas Fortune Ryan, that he was "proud to
say that I have not yielded to class demands." He wrote a constituent, with evident reference to the prohibition movement, that
there were "a great many good people in Alabama who would
rather win with one idea—their own hobby, if you please, and let
the balance of the government go to smash." His "great difficulty,"
as he saw it, was that he had insisted that his campaign committee
stay within the ten thousand dollar campaign limit set by Alabama
law. The last week of the campaign, Underwood said, his committee was out of money, whereas the Musgrove forces were still
spending.[34]

Musgrove, who had maintained that his desire was not so much
to serve in the Senate as to defeat Underwood, accepted the defeat
with apparent good grace saying: "The long and conspicuous career

33. Montgomery *Advertiser*, May 15, 1920.
34. Birmingham *Age-Herald*, May 14, 1920; Underwood to Andrew J. Peters, May 19,
1920, Underwood to H. J. Rowe, May 19, 1920, Underwood to Thomas F. Ryan, May
14, 1920, Underwood to James B. Ellis, May 17, 1920, Underwood to Zach L. Nabors, May
28, 1920, all in Underwood Papers, Alabama Archives.

of Mr. Underwood and the fine service rendered the prohibition cause by Weakley . . . made it well nigh onto a superhuman task for me to win."[35] Unfortunately, Musgrove diminished the lustre of the near win against Underwood by becoming a perpetual office-seeker. In 1924 he ran for the Democratic presidential nomination in an attempt to prevent Underwood from getting Alabama support in his race for the nomination. And in 1926 he attempted to succeed Underwood in the sweepstakes race that followed the senator's retirement, but he made a poor showing. In 1931 the old warrior died at seventy-two, two years after Underwood's death. His fortune was gone, and he was remembered largely for his strong race against Underwood in 1920.[36]

The lavish spending of the Musgrove forces brought demands for an investigation of campaign expenditures. Underwood estimated that Musgrove's campaign cost $250,000—far in excess of the $10,000 legal limit. Musgrove reported expenditures within the legal limit but admitted that he had no way of knowing what his friends had spent in his behalf. Underwood prudently urged that any investigation be made by Alabama courts and that federal action be discouraged. He noted that if the Republicans were victorious, they might well pass another "force bill." The danger, he said, of Republicans forcing Negro participation in white primaries would be accentuated by woman's suffrage—an argument he frequently made but never logically explained.[37] Talk of investigating Musgrove's expenditures soon abated, perhaps because Underwood's campaign must also have exceeded the legal limit.

The Republican party ran Probate Judge Lewis H. Reynolds of Chilton County against Underwood in the November, 1920, election, but Underwood took little notice of his opponent. Reynolds complained that Underwood seemed to have "full control" of the state's newspapers. In September Underwood made a few speeches in Alabama for the Democratic ticket, but by October he was on tour in New England speaking for the Cox-Roosevelt ticket. He

35. Birmingham *Age-Herald*, May 16, 1920.
36. Montgomery *Advertiser*, July 5, 1931.
37. Birmingham *Age-Herald*, September 30, August 1, 1920.

returned to Birmingham in time to vote on November 2, 1920. Underwood received 155,664 votes, Reynolds 71,337, and Andrew M. Forsman, the Socialist candidate, 1984. There were a surprising number of Republican votes, with nine of the sixty-seven counties showing a Republican majority.[38]

Underwood had begun to assume a Cassandra-like view of American politics. He wrote a close friend, relative to the Democratic presidential nomination of 1920, "there is no telling what is going to be the outcome along any line, and I suppose it will be some years before the nation settles down to an even keel." To another political friend he confided that it was a bad year for the Democrats and that if he were nominated and defeated, the South might suffer a setback. To all who inquired, he urged the nomination of his close friend, the vigorously antilabor A. Mitchell Palmer, as Democratic standard-bearer in 1920.[39]

His narrow victory in the Democratic senatorial primary of 1920 showed the ebbing of Underwood's political strength in Alabama. Samuel Gompers prophetically said that six more years was all that would be seen of Underwood in politics.[40] His near defeat resulted from built-up resentment over his positions on several issues. Prohibitionists, strong in rural areas, and labor and women voters, strong in urban areas, coalesced around Musgrove. Underwood attempted, as in his 1914 race, to capitalize on anti-Negro feeling, while his otherwise progressive opponents used anti-Catholic and nativist prejudice against him. The folksy Musgrove, a man of limited ability, education, and vision, had almost defeated a titan of the Senate.

Underwood had always found campaigning distasteful, and the Musgrove campaign was no exception. He preferred to stay in Washington, depend on his national stature, and rely upon his Bir-

38. Birmingham *News*, September 29, 1920; Marie Bankhead Owen (comp.), *Alabama Official and Statistical Register 1923* (Montgomery: Alabama Department of Archives and History, 1923), 348.
39. Underwood to Edward W. Barrett, May 24, 1920, Underwood to Judge James J. Mayfield, May 22, 1920, Underwood to Joseph C. Taylor, May 24, 1920, all in Underwood Papers, Alabama Archives.
40. New York *World*, June 2, 1920.

mingham friends to handle earthy local politics. He seems to have been shocked by the extravagant use of money against Hobson in the campaign of 1914, and Musgrove clearly outspent him in the 1920 campaign. There was less personal vilification against Musgrove than there had been against Hobson, but nevertheless, neither candidate distinguished himself by high ethical standards in the campaign.

CHAPTER XII

Leader of
the Minority

The end of World War I found Underwood dispirited despite talk
that he would become the Senate Democratic minority leader. The
inability of Congress to officially end the war discouraged him, and
he hoped that President Wilson would make proposals for compromise. The chaotic Mexican situation in which President Carranza
was snarling in anger at the United States and Villa was still at large
was, he said, "distressing," and only patience had kept the United
States army from invading—patience that he thought might be
ending. A hundred thousand men "could cross the border and in
four months' time clean things up and with three or four years of
police duty there we might be able to leave the country," he said.
At home he was alarmed about the demands that labor was making—especially railroad labor—and he denounced the closed
shop. He deplored the coal strike, which he said had been ordered
by a few powerful men.[1]

Underwood complained privately at his lack of contact with
President Wilson: "People at the Capitol during this administration
have been far removed from the knowledge of the inner plans of
the White House and now that the president is sick we have no
knowledge whatever of what is going on." Nevertheless, the president's written message to Congress, which made no offer of compromise on the treaty and urged Congress to democratize industry,
cut taxes, and curb the Reds, received his approval as being up to

1. Birmingham *Age-Herald*, November 30, 1919.

"the president's fine standard." In the Senate, Underwood scolded the Republican majority for failing to pass significant legislation in the first session. By his account the Republicans had passed no important legislation except for the supply bills. War taxes had not been reduced, and the majority had dawdled over the Treaty of Versailles without completing ratification.[2]

Both Senators Hitchcock and Underwood sought the minority leader post, and while the leadership lay in the balance, Underwood introduced a resolution calling for the creation of a bipartisan conciliation commission of ten senators to achieve treaty ratification through compromise. He deferred action on his resolution after Senator Lodge told him of informal negotiations through Henry White, who had recently completed his duties as a delegate to the Versailles Conference, that might lead to settlement of the differences over the treaty. President Wilson, however, took a hard line against compromise in a major policy statement at the Jackson Day dinner in New Orleans, and Underwood and Hitchcock vied with one another in complimenting the president. The Democrats, Underwood said, would accept only interpretative resolutions and otherwise the issue must go to the people so that another Congress could determine the treaty's fate. Wilson's statement had scotched the idea that compromise was an immediate possibility, and though there was continued speculation that Underwood might join Lodge in seeking a compromise, he did not press his conciliation commission resolution. Nevertheless, he wrote privately that "we should make a compromise."[3]

Underwood and Hitchcock sought the position of minority leader in an evenly matched contest during these same early weeks of the session. Hitchcock appealed in vain to Wilson for aid, but the president refused to intercede. Following the break between Colonel Edward M. House and Wilson, Underwood denied ru-

2. Oscar W. Underwood to G. W. Pratt, December 2, 1919, in Oscar W. Underwood Papers, Alabama Department of Archives and History, Montgomery; New York *Times*, December 3, 1919, p. 2; *Congressional Record*, 66th Cong., 2nd Sess., 399.

3. New York *Times*, January 8, 1920, p. 3, January 10, 1920, p. 2; Underwood to Frederick Lewis Allen, January 12, 1920, in Frederick Lewis Allen Papers, University of Virginia Library.

mors that House was supporting him for minority leader and would favor him for president in 1920. It was unlikely that he had House's support, he noted, since the senators from House's home state of Texas were for Hitchcock. Such rumors, if not dispelled, could well have cost him the leadership fight. Underwood told friends that the only objections to him were sectional—opposition from northern and western Democrats. He assured Hitchcock's sympathizers that the Nebraska senator would, if Underwood became minority leader, continue to lead the ratification fight with his full support. The initial vote for minority leader in the caucus of January 14 was a 19 to 19 tie. Not until April, late in the second session, did Underwood achieve election through the votes of Carter Glass of Virginia, a new senator, and Senator Hoke Smith of Georgia, who had previously abstained. Senator Hitchcock withdrew, and Underwood was unanimously elected. He received covert help from his New York financier friend, Thomas Fortune Ryan, later writing Ryan that without his help he could not have succeeded. The press generally approved Underwood's election. The New York *Evening Post* commented that he would "reach the scene free of the animosities that gathered about the treaty debate" and that he was "possessed of an unusual quality of leadership."[4] Not since the days of Henry Clay had a former party leader of the House of Representatives led his party in the Senate.

Underwood's elevation to minority leader revived talk that he would seek a compromise with Senator Lodge on the treaty. Underwood wrote a New York businessman, however, that although he was still willing to accept a compromise, he hoped the Senate and the president could agree on ratification with the league attached. "It is nothing but a political move for us to agree to terms that would be rejected by the president," he pointed out.[5] Indeed,

4. New York *Times*, November 23, 1919, p. 2; Birmingham *News*, January 1, 1920; Underwood to Frank N. Julian, December 8, 1919, in Underwood Papers, Alabama Archives; Birmingham *News*, January 15, April 27, 1920; Underwood to Thomas Fortune Ryan, April 27, 1920, in Underwood Papers, Alabama Archives; New York *Evening Post*, April 24, 1920.

5. Underwood to Oscar S. Straus, April 30, 1920, in Underwood Papers, Alabama Archives.

little more was to be heard of the treaty until the campaign of 1920.

The measure that most interested Underwood in the second session of the Sixty-sixth Congress was the Cummins bill, designed to return the railroads to private ownership. Underwood worked closely with railroad lobbyists, especially his close Birmingham political friend, Forney Johnston. Johnston was general counsel of the National Association of Owners of Railroad Securities, a highly lucrative position secured for him by Underwood. Speaking before the Birmingham Chamber of Commerce, Underwood asserted that the Cummins bill marked a new era in the history of railroads. He spoke approvingly of the financial provisions which would provide a modest 5½ percent return to bondholders. Railroad earnings would be limited to 6 percent, with most of the excess going into a loan fund to aid weaker railroads. He brazenly accepted responsibility for the "no strike" provision of the Cummins bill. The provision, similar to one Underwood had vainly tried to add to the Adamson Act, gave the ICC the power to regulate wages and working conditions and therefore outlawed strikes. Underwood maintained that the "no strike" provision would protect labor by preventing general rail strikes. He admitted candidly that he had discussed the provision with Samuel Gompers and leaders of the four railway brotherhoods who opposed it. He said that Gompers, in testimony before the Interstate Commerce Committee, was unable to offer an alternative remedy for general rail strikes. Arbitration through a government court was preferable, Underwood said, to settlement "on the battlefield of a great strike." He concluded defiantly that, though he favored "social justice" for labor, when labor lifted its "mailed fist" against the public: "I will say 'Here you must stop.'" This blunt antistrike speech earned him a first place (in a six-way tie) on labor's congressional blacklist and considerable applause in conservative Alabama circles where the speech was a major ploy in his campaign for reelection. The Cummins bill was amended in the Senate so that the antistrike provision Underwood claimed to have fathered was dropped.[6]

6. Birmingham *News*, January 3, 1920; *Congressional Record*, 66th Cong., 2nd Sess., 1318–19; Birmingham *Age-Herald*, February 22, 1920.

The Jones merchant marine bill, an administration measure supported by Underwood, directed the shipping board to sell government-owned vessels on easy terms, with guarantees against operating losses, and authorized the federally owned Merchant Fleet
Corporation to open new shipping lines and operate surplus vessels. He justified such generosity as necessary to deal with foreign
competition.[7] The bill became law, although it proved far less effective in selling government vessels than had been hoped.

Almost as close to Underwood's heart as the railroad and merchant marine bills was the Canadian wood pulp resolution, which
he sponsored. The yawning maw of the United States paper industry was so great that Canada, experiencing a shortage of newsprint,
had embargoed shipment of newsprint to the United States. Newspaper publishers, thoroughly alarmed, applauded Underwood's introduction of a resolution to create an amply financed commission
to confer with the Dominion of Canada or the provinces in an effort
to revoke the embargo. Critics suggested that it would be better
for the Department of State to seek a remedy. Underwood maintained that although he was an advocate of Canadian reciprocity,
strong, direct, perhaps retaliatory, action was necessary to prevent
serious injury to newspaper publishers. Diplomatic negotiations
through Great Britain was too circuitous a route, he said.[8] The
popular measure easily passed both houses, but it was vetoed by
the president.

Another administration measure strongly favored by Underwood
was the water power bill to create a federal power commission.
Similar measures had been in Congress for ten years and had been
stymied by the inability of conservationists and power interests to
agree. The result was a hiatus in the development of power sites
on navigable streams falling under federal control. The 1920 water
power bill, strongly favored by the power industry, proposed a
board composed of the secretaries of war, interior, and agriculture.
The commission would have been authorized to issue fifty-year li-

7. *Congressional Record*, 66th Cong., 2nd Sess., 6867–68.
8. *Ibid.*, 3436–38, 3560–64; New York *Times*, April 27, 1920, p. 8.

censes for water power development. The bill passed the Senate early in the session although it was stalled in the House, and the president signed it into law late in the session. The new Federal Waterpower Commission proved ineffective in regulating the power industry.[9]

On the foreign scene the Democrats were embarrassed by the prickly Armenian problem. The American people had shown great sympathy toward the Armenians in their suffering and drive for independence from the Turks. In mid-May the Senate responded to the national aspirations of Armenians by congratulating them on their independence and requesting that the president send a warship and marines to protect communication between Armenia's two major port cities—Batun on the Mediterranean and Baku on the Black Sea. Underwood demurred that the Senate was meddling in the president's area of responsibility, but then withdrew his objections, noting that the Senate was only making a "request." The Foreign Relations Committee recommended that the Senate "respectfully decline" the president's request for authorization to accept a mandate of Armenia. Underwood urged delay, as the acceptance of Armenia as a mandate under the League of Nations was, he said, premature since the United States had not joined the league. Democratic delaying tactics were unsuccessful, and when forced to vote on immediate acceptance of the mandate only twelve lonely Democrats favored it—Underwood not among them. The final vote against accepting the mandate was 52 to 23.[10]

Underwood made his first speech as minority leader in opposition to the Knox peace resolution which proposed to end the war by a congressional resolution. He attacked the Republicans for failing to terminate the war by repeal of war legislation and by ratification of the Treaty of Versailles, suggesting that the Republicans could have separated the league covenant from the treaty and brought about lasting peace. He insisted that the question of res-

9. New York *Times*, June 27, 1920, Sec. 7, p. 2.
10. *Congressional Record*, 66th Cong., 2nd Sess., 6978–79, 8067; New York *Times*, June 2, 1920, p. 1.

ervations was unimportant, and he objected to the Knox resolution as a "separate peace." Senator Warren G. Harding replied that the resolution was a means of repudiating one man rule and reestablishing the "coordinate power" of Congress, especially the Senate, in making treaties. The resolution was adopted by a vote of 43 to 38. The Treaty of Versailles was still in limbo.[11]

Underwood completed the session, which ended in June, 1920, in some frustration. He bragged to his wife, who was at Tate Springs, Tennessee, supervising work on the Underwood cabin, that the Senate had passed all of the important legislation and had adjourned on schedule. "My team played good ball," he said, but he added bitterly that the president had vetoed his Canadian wood pulp resolution and was pocket vetoing the water power bill. On the latter he was mistaken; after a delay the president did sign it. Underwood's legislative record as minority leader in the second session of the Sixty-sixth Congress was not quite as good as he indicated. The important bills he backed that became law included the Merchant Marine Act of 1920, the Edge Act for agricultural financing, the Transportation Act of 1920, and the Water Power Act. The Knox peace resolution was passed, but the House's refusal to repass over the president's veto terminated efforts to end the war before the end of Wilson's term. The Armenian mandate, favored by Wilson, failed. The president, in his assessment of Congress' work, complained of the failure to deal with the rising cost of living and the revision of the tax laws.[12]

Despite these frustrations Underwood was enjoying life at 2000 G Street. On the hot nights he slept on the back porch, with "Otto," his trusty German shepherd, guarding him from the backyard. Mrs. Underwood had left her driver in Washington, and it was pleasant, he said, to have "a real chofer [sic] at my beck and call." The day after Congress went home, Underwood went for a relaxing walk in Potomac Park with Otto. He had lunch with his son, Oscar, Jr., his daughter-in-law, Ellen, and a friend of theirs.

11. *Congressional Record*, 66th Cong., 2nd Sess., 7095–98, 7102.

12. Underwood to Bertha Underwood, June 7, 1920, in Oscar W. Underwood Papers, University of Virginia Library; New York *Times*, June 6, 1920, p. 1.

They went to ride on "an unexplored road," and then had dinner together. Oscar, Jr., reported that he had won "a big law case."[13]

While the leadership fight was going on, many of Underwood's friends, especially southerners, had urged him to seek the Democratic presidential nomination in 1920. Early in the year he authorized the use of his name in the Georgia presidential preference primary, but Senator Hoke Smith, whose vote was vital in the leadership contest, objected that the Underwood candidacy would damage the Senate race Smith was conducting together with a "favorite son" candidacy in the presidential preference primary. Underwood deferred to Smith, stating that he was "not really a candidate" and withdrew his name. Faced with his own campaign for reelection to the Senate, Underwood declined to seek the nomination. He said that his chances as a southerner and a "wet" would be slight in 1920. "The Indians have captured our wigwam," and they "desire to administer special nostrums in the name of the Democratic party, forgetting the fundamental principles that have kept our party alive." He reasoned that the "liberal element" in the North was opposed to southern candidates, identifying them with prohibition, and northern prohibitionists naturally favored a proponent of the Eighteenth Amendment. A Republican victory was likely, he said, and though personal defeat would not disturb him, he thought it would be unfortunate for the first southern nominee "since the War Between the States" to be defeated.[14]

Underwood commented to friends on the possible Democratic candidates, each of whom he knew personally. He did not consider Wilson to be a possible candidate, but in the event that someone considered him so, he noted that the president was "much sicker than the country realizes." Herbert Hoover, although "an excellent executive," lacked knowledge of the "working machinery of the national government," and by announcing himself a Republican had removed himself from Democratic consideration. McAdoo had

13. Underwood to Bertha Underwood, June 2, 7, 1920, in Underwood Papers, University of Virginia.
14. Underwood to Clark Howell, February 11, 1920, Underwood to James L. Clayton, undated, in Letterbox N, Underwood to Lee C. Bradley, May 24, 1920, all in Underwood Papers, Alabama Archives.

been an "excellent" secretary of the treasury but had been unsuccessful as railroad administrator and organizer of the Bureau of War Risk Insurance. McAdoo had a strong following among organized labor but would be opposed by labor's opponents. He thought that McAdoo would receive a good vote but that the convention would not nominate him. He referred to James M. Cox, with whom he had served in the House, as "a man of ability and a strong Democrat" who had made "a most excellent Governor of Ohio and showed marked executive ability." He reserved his greatest praise, however, for A. Mitchell Palmer, his friend of many years standing. He described Palmer as "a man of strong personal convictions, high principles and excellent executive ability," who had made an outstanding attorney general and had saved the nation from a disastrous coal strike in the fall of 1919.[15]

The Alabama delegation to the San Francisco convention lacked the services of the state's most famous Democrat. Underwood did not seek election as a convention delegate, and he turned down an invitation to accompany the delegation. He went instead to Atlantic City and later to Tate Springs, Tennessee, for a vacation with his wife. He urged the Alabama delegation to favor a "simple, old-fashioned Democratic" platform without "every fad and fancy that the imagination of man can think of." He favored the endorsement of the Treaty of Versailles but thought that nothing should be said to embarrass those Democrats who, unlike himself, had favored reservations. The Eighteenth Amendment, which he had vigorously opposed, should be "recognized" and its "honest and earnest enforcement" called for, but "not too much should be said about it." The Alabama delegation was dominated by prohibitionists, and here was little reluctance to accept Underwood's decision not to seek the nomination. Nevertheless, Theodore Roosevelt, Jr., smarting over the nomination of Harding who had called former president Roosevelt a "traitor" to his party, lectured the Alabama delegation on the importance of offering Underwood as a candidate

15. Underwood to James A. Mitchell, May 19, 1920, Underwood to Joseph C. Taylor, May 24, 1920, both in Underwood Papers, Alabama Archives.

who could get the votes of the Progressives.[16] On the floor of the convention, however, only a single vote was cast for Underwood. The presidential nomination went to James M. Cox, the former governor of Ohio, and second place on the ticket went to Franklin D. Roosevelt, the former assistant secretary of the navy.

Underwood readily accepted the Cox and Roosevelt ticket as "probably the strongest the party could have named." He restated his favorable views of Cox, calling him "a great Democrat, a progressive statesman, an ideal man to lead the party to victory next November." Arriving in Birmingham from his Tate Springs cabin, Underwood spoke reflectively about his friendship with Cox, which dated back almost to the beginning of Underwood's House career when Cox was secretary to a wealthy tobacco merchant and congressman. Underwood recalled that Cox was "always an active supporter of all party measures and a man of high character and ideals." Unable to contain a dig at Palmer's opponents, who had accused the former attorney general of being repressive, Underwood noted that Cox was an advocate of "law and order" and that he had taken "an energetic stand" during rioting at Cleveland when he restored order with the aid of the national guard.[17]

Underwood, pleased by the nomination of his friend and former senatorial "pair," Warren G. Harding, by the Republicans, sent his congratulations to the Republican nominee. Harding acknowledged Underwood's sentiments as those "that may be becomingly wafted over the party wall" and further stated: "You have always been more than courteous in your treatment of me and I have involuntarily sought to [re]pay in the sincerity of a very high regard. I do not expect you to wish me political success, but I am very happy that if I succeed . . . you will be quite as welcome a visitor at the executive mansion as though your party were the victor. No matter what administration comes into responsibility next March it needs your assistance and advice at every stage."[18]

16. Underwood to W. T. Sanders, June 6, 1920, in Letterbox N, Underwood Papers, Alabama Archives; Birmingham *Age-Herald*, July 3, 1920.

17. Birmingham *News*, July 7, 8, 1920.

18. Warren G. Harding to Underwood, June 26, 1920, in Underwood Papers, Alabama Archives.

Regardless of his friendship with Harding, Underwood campaigned vigorously for the Cox-Roosevelt ticket, and Mrs. Underwood contributed five hundred dollars to the Cox campaign. In a
swing through the East, Underwood defended the Democratic
record on the tariff, the Federal Reserve Act, the building of a
merchant marine, and the return of prosperity. He declared that
although Harding publicly "straddled" the league question, he was
actually opposed to the League of Nations. Underwood emphasized the league as "the real issue" and said that the Treaty of Versailles must be ratified for "the honor of the American people" and
to redeem their obligation to the troops who made victory possible.
With exaggerated campaign rhetoric, he asserted that those who
were for "the advancement of Christian civilization, the rights of
all peoples, and the establishment of justice instead of force," must
vote for Cox. Underwood seemed sincerely convinced that the
league might avert future wars. He told the Birmingham City
Club, "We can't force a millenium, but we can try," adding that
"the old method" of preventing war "has never succeeded, and I
believe this method will, in the main succeed." Supporters of the
league, he cautioned, would not abandon it for a newly constructed
organization such as the League to Enforce Peace. He noted that
although Harding did not favor the League to Enforce Peace, Taft,
Lodge, and former president Theodore Roosevelt did, and the proposed constitution of the new league provided collective action
against aggressors that was "more drastic" than Article X of the
League of Nations.[19]

Although Underwood emphasized "the holy crusade," as he once
termed the fight for the league, he also vigorously attacked the
Republicans on domestic issues. Defending the Democrats from
charges of unpreparedness and inefficiency, he stated that until the
Cleveland administration nothing had been done to build a merchant fleet. He ascribed three panics to the Republican banking
system under the National Bank Act of 1861 and lauded the Federal Reserve Act as a major Democratic achievement. He referred

19. Baltimore *Sun*, October 2, 1920; Waterbury (Conn.) *American*, October 12, 1920; Stamford (Conn.) *Times*, October 13, 1920; Birmingham *Age-Herald*, October 15, 26, 1920.

to the high Republican tariffs and attacked the Republicans for their unwillingness to repeal wartime taxes as recommended by President Wilson. The Wilson administration, he said, had brought prosperity, alleviated unemployment, and made "the bird that used to come to your back door" as extinct as a variety of pigeons he had known in his boyhood in Minnesota. In Louisville he said: "I have known where Warren G. Harding stood since the beginning. He is not for reservations as Republican propagandists would have you believe; he's for rejection. He has told you that he is against the League for Peace. He stands with Senators Borah, Brandegee and Johnson, the bitter enders."[20]

Underwood was reelected to the Senate, having only nominal opposition in the general election, and Harding defeated Cox overwhelmingly. The Republicans regained control of both houses of Congress. Underwood later analyzed the election and said that though the league had been important in the campaign, it was not the "one great issue" that decided the contest. Rather, he said, "reaction from war" was the "controlling element." He quickly adapted to the Republican victory and, asked to anticipate the Republican program, predicted a special session "for reconstruction." Questioned about the Federal Reserve System, he stated that the Republicans might make an effort to set up a "great central bank," but he doubted that the Federal Reserve System would be abandoned.[21]

Underwood viewed the forthcoming period of Republican control gloomily. "The Republicans are paddling the canoes and the Democrats are only passengers," he said. In the lame-duck session the appropriations would be fixed wherever the Republicans wanted them, and President Wilson would see the futility of sending the Treaty of Versailles back to the Senate since it would be pigeonholed by the Foreign Relations Committee. Even if the Democrats could muster a two-thirds vote for the treaty, he said, William E. Borah and Hiram Johnson, with help from a half dozen

20. Birmingham *Age-Herald*, October 26, 1920; Waterbury (Conn.) *American*, October 12, 1920; Louisville *Courier-Journal*, October 24, 1920.
21. New York *Times*, May 28, 1921, p. 2; Birmingham *News*, November 11, 1920.

other senators, could filibuster the measure. He did not expect the Republicans to confirm any of Wilson's appointments except for those of a few postmasters and minor officers in the army. It would be a "quiet session," the lull before the storm. After the inauguration the Republicans would make wholesale personnel changes by allowing all Democratic appointments to expire. He predicted, however, that the Republicans would split on the league, the tariff, and the spoils of office.

Congress assembled on December 6 and heard the written message of the ailing President Wilson. The president did not mention the Treaty of Versailles but asked approval of a loan to Armenia, independence for the Philippines, and a budget system without the objectionable features of the one he had vetoed. Underwood approved of the message, noting that although Versailles was not mentioned, there was no mistaking the president's views. He endorsed the president's recommendations of a budget system and of early independence for the Philippines but expressed reservations about the Armenian loan "until I have studied the question more."[22]

Underwood spoke in Birmingham a month before the December 6 opening of Congress on demands for farm relief. He expressed approval of the Edge Foreign Banking Act, which chartered banking corporations under the Federal Reserve System for long-range credits and the stimulation of foreign trade—a measure generally considered a boon to cotton farmers. This measure was the kind of relief to which he felt farmers were entitled, but he lectured his constituents that farmers were expecting too much of government. Recalling the passage of Wilsonian legislation to regulate cotton warehouses and exchanges, Underwood noted that farmers were still dissatisfied. The American Cotton Association was demanding relief from declining prices. He said that although "sectionalism is past," farmers could not expect the "buying constituency," which forms the majority of Congress, to vote for measures for the benefit of cotton farmers. Farmers were, he said, seeking a political solu-

22. Birmingham *News*, November 28, December 2, 7, 1920.

tion to an economic problem—a problem that might be remedied by marketing farm products throughout the year. He added that as long as the southern farmer saw his salvation in political action, he would stay in the "slough of despondency."[23]

Despite his reservations about federal aid to farmers, Underwood submitted to the demands of his agricultural constituency and favored in 1920 the reorganization and expansion of the War Finance Corporation with the new task of extending loans to farm financing agencies. President Wilson vetoed the measure as violating the spirit of laissez-faire, but Underwood joined with other farm state representatives and overrode the president's veto of the expanded War Finance Corporation, a forerunner of the Federal Intermediate Credit Act and the Reconstruction Finance Corporation.[24]

Impatient to seize the reins of victory, the Republicans presented the Fordney emergency tariff bill to boost the tariff on twenty agricultural products. The bill came to the Senate after passage in the House but had no chance of avoiding a presidential veto. It was designed to curry favor with farmers by advertising Republican intentions to increase the tariff on sugar, meat, and wool. Acknowledging that the rates of the tariff which bore his name did not meet postwar conditions, Underwood insisted that many rates had become protective and should be reduced to a revenue level. The Republicans, he noted, wanted to claim that the Fordney bill had been filibustered to death. Although Underwood assured the Republicans that there would be no "organized" filibuster, in fact a filibuster was underway. Underwood challenged the Republicans to attempt cloture and thereby prove that they would be successful in overriding the president's veto. But Republican cloture efforts failed, and in the general debate Underwood, scorning the bill's ostensible purpose of aiding the farmer, attacked the bill as an effort to aid manufacturers, especially the trusts. He said that if it passed, the Sherman Act might as well be repealed.

23. *Ibid.*, November 11, 1920.
24. *Congressional Record*, 66th Cong., 3rd Sess., 877.

Focusing his attack on the increased duty on sugar, he said, "If we trace the snake to its hole, we find it putting the increased price of sugar into the pockets of the great sugar manufacturers of America." The cotton farmer, who was offered no protection by the legislation, was, he said, as much in need of help as the sheep farmer, yet the sheep farmer was favored with a raise in the tariff although the rate was already prohibitive. The United States, he prophetically cautioned, was now a creditor nation, and passage of the bill would virtually embargo goods from abroad and "force repudiation" of European debts to the United States. Under Republican questioning Underwood revealed that he had not been consulted on the tariff by the White House; Wilson responded by requesting that he give his views of the Fordney bill before the writing of the veto message. Underwood told the president that "no more vicious bill has ever been proposed." The bill, he asserted, was bad from either the Democratic or the Republican viewpoint, it would "not be beneficial to the real producers of farm products," and it would "greatly increase the cost of many of the necessities of life" without increasing government revenues.[25] Wilson's veto reflected Underwood's suggestions. There was no possibility that the veto could be overridden, but time was fast running out for the Democrats.

The last, sad days of the Wilson administration presented special difficulties for Underwood as minority leader. The Republicans blocked the approval of ten thousand Wilson appointments made in the congressional interim. Underwood had had no opportunity to discuss the appointments with the president, but he felt sure that Wilson would sign a bill to extend his own appointments. Senator Lodge, the majority leader, refused to consent to confirmation of the appointments, but after Underwood noted that without legislative action 5,534 army interim appointees would revert to civilian status, Lodge agreed to the passage of a bill limited to army appointees.[26]

As the session ended, tempers were badly frayed. The naval ap-

25. *Ibid.*, 2058, 2312, 2316, 4040; Underwood to Woodrow Wilson, February 7, 1921, in Box 174, Woodrow Wilson Papers, Library of Congress.
26. Washington (D.C.) *Herald*, January 19, 1921.

propriation bill, favored by Underwood, was blocked by isolation-
ist Senator Borah. Senator Miles Poindexter of Washington, who
was managing the bill for the Republicans, blamed Underwood for
the lack of action on appropriations bills in general. He noted that
the sundry appropriations bill had failed to pass because Underwood had attached a ten million dollar appropriation for continued
work on the nitrate plant at Muscle Shoals—a provision the House
refused to allow. Underwood replied tartly that Poindexter had become a "common scold" and was unable to manage his bill, adding
that he would not block the sundry appropriations bill in order to
get the Muscle Shoals item. The sundry appropriations bill passed
without the Muscle Shoals attachment later the same day, but the
navy bill died, creating the virtual necessity of a special session and
the deferring of an ambitious naval program. On the morning of
inauguration day, Underwood accompanied Senator Lodge to the
White House and asked the president if he had any communications to the Congress. President Wilson said that he had none.[27]

Underwood watched the inauguration of Warren G. Harding
from his office in the Senate Office Building with his friend Thomas
Fortune Ryan, his son, Oscar, Jr., and others. He watched the
broken Woodrow Wilson, with whom he had never been close,
walk hesitantly to the platform where Harding was sworn into office. Evidently, Underwood anticipated a political reward because
of his close relationship to Harding. The Birmingham News noted
that Underwood had resigned from the Appropriations Committee
in order to spend more time on the floor and mused that he would
retain his position on the Interstate Commerce Committee unless
he was called to be secretary of state for Harding. The ploy seems
to have reached Harding's attention since he wrote the Birmingham News a few days later that he appreciated Underwood's protection of his "pair" for him through his extended absences from
the Senate.[28] There is no evidence, however, that Underwood was
seriously considered for a cabinet post.

27. New York Times, March 4, 1921, p. 1; Congressional Record, 66th Cong., 3rd Sess.,
4532.
28. Interview with O. W. Underwood, Jr., November 24, 1951; Birmingham News, December 8, 14, 1920.

At the beginning of the Harding administration, Underwood was completely in control of his Democractic minority in the Senate. He was unanimously elected leader of the minority, and Senator William Harris of Georgia described him as the "main hope of the party." On a visit to Harding, Underwood requested that Congress not be called into session until April and that a recess be allowed in the summer. The president was amenable, the special session was scheduled for April 11, and Congress was to be recessed from August 24 to September 21 about as Underwood had recommended.[29]

During the brief delay in the calling of the special congressional session, Underwood visited Bermuda and was received royally by Bermudian authorities appreciative of the tariff advantages of the Underwood-Simmons Tariff Act. Returning to Washington, Underwood urged the repeal of war taxes in order to clarify revenue needs prior to tariff revision. He called for support of Republican Senator Albert B. Cummins' resolution for an investigation of the railroad problem. He denounced Republican talk of a separate peace with Germany, saying that any treaty should be made in collaboration with American allies in the war. In April, Underwood was called to Birmingham to be at the bedside of his ailing mother, and he left his minority leader chores in the hands of Senator Pat Harrison, who was to complete making minority committee assignments, and Senator Gilbert Hitchcock, who was to represent Underwood on the floor. After a brief stay in Birmingham, Underwood returned to Washington to find that the Republicans had reduced Democratic influence on the major committees by increasing their own membership from nine to ten and holding the Democratic positions to six. Senator Frank B. Brandegee explained for the Republicans that Underwood was not consulted because he was away and that Senator Hitchcock had been informed of the change. Brandegee argued that the added Republican positions reflected accurately the Republican majority of twenty-two.[30]

29. Birmingham *Age-Herald*, March 5, 6, 1921; Birmingham *News*, March 7, 1921.
30. Birmingham *Age-Herald*, April 7, 8, 1921; *Congressional Record*, 67th Cong., 1st Sess., 322–24.

Actually, the Democrats had received almost precisely the proper allocation of seats.

The Republicans resurrected the Knox peace resolution with full expectation of success, despite Underwood's vigorous opposition. The president could end the war by signing the Treaty of Versailles, which was "still on his desk," or he could negotiate a treaty with the German government, Underwood said. But one could "declare peace only once," and there was no indication that the German government would accept the terms in the peace resolution. The United States, he claimed, would abandon its rights and those of its allies in the resolution. However, the impending passage of the Knox peace resolution led Underwood to recognize that the League of Nations and the Treaty of Versailles would never be approved in the United States, and he called the defeat "one of the great mistakes of American history."

He supported an administration proposal to hold the navy at the level of 120,000 men as compared with 100,000 favored by a bipartisan minority, stating that the country had attempted to disarm before World War I, but "a war nation struck at our throat," and the United States had been unprepared. Party lines were eliminated as the majority voted to retain the 120,000 man navy. Underwood argued against unilateral disarmament, but he supported Senator Thomas J. Walsh's unsuccessful amendment to the naval appropriation bill to require that President Harding appoint an American representative to the Disarmament Commission of the League of Nations. He said that for half a century prior to the Spanish-American War the United States had practiced disarmament theory, but other nations continued to build up armaments so that the United States was a second-rate power not feared by anyone. If, he said, Borah's and Harding's disarmament theories were to be tested, it should be done in an international conference.[31]

Although Underwood attacked the Republicans for extravagance, he sponsored a bill to liberalize the conditions under which World War I claims could be brought by civilians before the United

States Compensation Commission. Underwood's bill, evidently presented at the request of the commission, would have extended the time for filing a claim from six months after the incident to one year after the passage of the bill. He accused the Republicans of parsimony toward civilian claimants and asserted that Republican Senator Reed Smoot had deliberately misrepresented the Underwood bill as greatly broadening the scope of cases considered by the commission. Smoot, who said that the bill might create "a lot of swivel chair heroes," withdrew his objections after the bill was refined so that only civilians serving on foreign soil were covered. The Senate passed the measure without a record vote, but it died in a House committee.[32]

In the summer of 1921 President Harding wrote Underwood expressing his disappointment that the senator was unable to make a voyage in the *Mayflower* to Portsmouth as a member of the Pilgrim Tercentenary Committee to which both men had been appointed. The president also asked Underwood to see him about a matter of "mutual concern." Underwood received the president's letter at his summer retreat near Tate Springs, Tennessee, and learned that the matter of "mutual concern" was his selection as a delegate to the Washington Conference on Limitation of Armament. Secretary of State Charles Evans Hughes had suggested Underwood's appointment, and it was widely applauded. Former president Taft wrote privately that the presence of Underwood, together with that of Senator Henry Cabot Lodge, meant that the conclusions of the conference would have the "strongest possible support in the Senate." The Memphis *Press* called it "not only an honor to the distinguished Democrat and statesman, but to the Republican party." The Boston *Herald* said approvingly, "a natural choice," and the Pittsburgh *Press* thought Underwood "an ideal representative." The New York *Times* noted sagely and pontifically that the selection would "lessen suspicious partisanship" and that it was also an "irenic and useful piece of political technics." From England the Manchester *Guardian* echoed that Underwood was "undoubtedly

32. *Congressional Record*, 67th Cong., 1st Sess., 2008–11.

the wise choice." But the Louisville *Courier-Journal* vigorously dissented and testily called the appointments of Lodge and Underwood "an insult to the Senate," demanding that they resign from one post or the other.[33]

In accepting the appointment, Underwood said that "party politics" should cease at the "three mile limit" and anticipated that the conference would relieve "this and future generations" of armament burdens. He also stated that the four delegates—Hughes, Lodge, Elihu Root, and himself—could stand together as a unit. He wrote a political advisor who objected to his accepting the appointment that the idealism of the conference was that of the Sermon on the Mount and that although the conference could not satisfy the idealists, "we will go far enough to lift the military burdens from the backs of the great nations of the earth."[34]

At least two leading Democrats, William Gibbs McAdoo and Senator Carter Glass, were acidulously critical of Underwood's acceptance of membership on the United States delegation. McAdoo said that Underwood's acceptance would "compromise the independent position of the minority if its leader is . . . committed in advance to the position the delegation may take"; Glass charged that "Underwood had practically been captured by the Harding administration" and noted that at the recent meeting of Democrats in St. Louis, Underwood was frightfully denounced and some demanded his resignation as minority leader. In fact, Underwood had already offered to resign, but he had done so in a letter to Senator Pat Harrison, a member of the Democratic steering committee and a devoted friend, who strongly favored Underwood's remaining as leader. Following Glass's prodding, Underwood called a conference of Senate Democrats to consider Democratic policy toward the Treaty of Berlin, an administration treaty with Germany

33. Warren G. Harding to Underwood, July 25, 1921, in Letterbox M, Underwood Papers, Alabama Archives; Philip C. Jessup, *Elihu Root* (2 vols.; New York: Dodd Mead, 1938), II, 447; see clippings in Underwood Scrapbook, J, 40, 41, 44, Underwood Papers, Alabama Archives; New York *Times*, September 12, 1921, p. 12. The American delegates were later given the rank of ambassadors plenipotentiary.

34. New York *Times*, September 13, 1921, p. 19; Underwood to J. J. Willett, September 26, 1921, in J. J. Willett Papers, Samford University, Birmingham.

whereby the United States would accept the Treaty of Versailles exclusive of the League of Nations and the boundary settlement. Despite the opposition of Glass and some other Democrats to the Republican proposal, the Democrats were too divided to take a party position.[35] Underwood voted for the treaty as did most other Democrats.

Prior to the assembling of the Washington Conference, Harding acceded to a request from Underwood that he visit Birmingham and speak at the laying of the cornerstone of the Masonic Temple. Both Underwood and Harding were Masons. In introducing the president to a luncheon group at the Tutwiler Hotel, Underwood said: "Although the president and your senator differ on fundamental principles of political policies, there was no one more pleased than I when the Republican party nominated Warren G. Harding for the presidency." Referring to his forthcoming duties at the Washington Conference, Underwood said: "The president and I are not playing party politics. We are out of the three-mile limit, and are fighting the battles of American democracy." In reply, President Harding declared that Underwood would someday be president and explained that he had appointed Underwood a delegate to the Washington Conference because of "a personal regard" and "a high estimate of his statesmanship and his lofty devotion to country."[36]

When the president completed his scheduled day in Birmingham, he asked Senator Underwood to take him to meet his mother, the ninety-one-year-old Frederica Virginia Underwood. The president, Mrs. Harding, and Senator Underwood called unannounced on the little old lady. She elfishly described the visit: "I was *equal* to the occasion. I did not stop to change my dress but walked right in to receive him *as Oscar['s] friend*." Mrs. Harding presented the aged Mrs. Underwood with flowers that had been given her, and after the presidential couple had left, the senator's mother re-

35. William Gibbs McAdoo to Carter Glass, September 23, 1921, Glass to Bernard Baruch, November 15, 1921, both in Carter Glass Papers, University of Virginia Library; Birmingham *Age-Herald*, September 18, 1921.

36. Birmingham *News*, October 26, 1921.

ported that the president and his wife were "very pleasant, social people."[37] Mrs. Underwood, then in the last few weeks of her life and somewhat senile, died in early December, 1921, of a heart attack following an attack of bronchitis at the home of her son, Fred, in Birmingham. Underwood was called to Birmingham from the conference when his mother was stricken, but receiving word that she was dead, went instead to Louisville where the graveside service was held at Cave Hill Cemetery. Bertha did not go as she had a severe cold, and the senator thought it unwise. He reported that a large number of friends and all of Mrs. Underwood's sons and grandsons were present for the services on the lovely December day. He seemed reconciled to the death of his mother, reflecting that she had lived a "great life, so quiet and so full of accomplishment." She had talked so often about going to "my heavenly home," and he thought "she looked very sweet and like herself."[38]

As the Washington Conference convened in November, 1921, it presented an interesting opportunity for Senator Underwood's socially minded and spirited wife. The most elaborate entertainment given by the Underwoods was a dinner for the British delegate and first lord of the admiralty, Baron Lee of Fareham and Lady Lee. The dinner, prepared by a French caterer, featured ham baked by the Underwood cook and bootleg champagne. Bertha pronounced the party, attended by the other delegates, a "great success," despite Lord Lee's absence with tonsillitis. She apologized for her "creaky" French and had compliments for almost everyone in the busy social season, but her strongest praise was reserved for the British. She concluded inevitably: "After all [it is] the same blood which tells."[39]

Senator Underwood chose Tracy Lay, a foreign service officer and son of an Alabama friend and official of the Alabama Power

37. Frederica Virginia Underwood to Sidney S. Underwood, November 22, 1921, in Underwood Papers, University of Virginia.

38. Birmingham *Age-Herald*, December 6, 1921; Bertha Underwood to Mrs. A. H. Woodward, December 11, 1921 (misdated November 11), in Joseph H. Woodward Papers, in possession of Mrs. Joseph H. Woodward II, Birmingham.

39. Bertha Underwood to Mrs. A. H. Woodward, November 30, 1921, in Woodward Papers.

Company, as an aide at the conference. To secure Lay's services Underwood went first to Hughes, and, being turned down on the advice of Wilbur J. Carr, director of the Foreign Service, he secured the help of Senator Lodge who urged that the Foreign Service release Lay. Carr reluctantly agreed.

Secretary of State Hughes viewed Underwood, traditionally a "small navy" man, and Senator Lodge, a "big navy" advocate, as having an intimate knowledge of the mind of the Senate and thus as the men who could give the greatest possible assurance of the Senate's approval of the treaties. Prior to the conference Hughes posed two questions to Underwood and Lodge. First, would Congress provide the money for the exceedingly large navy then under construction. Second, would Congress agree to the large expenditure of money for the creation of a large naval base in the Philippines (and a smaller base in Guam) to rival the fortifications the British were then building in Singapore—or should the United States submit to Japanese insistence upon the maintenance of the status quo in the Pacific. Underwood and Lodge agreed that Congress was in no mood to spend the money required to complete the large navy then under construction or to compete with the British by building a massive Philippine naval base. Hughes was thus provided with the domestic political basis upon which he formulated the Five Power Treaty.[40]

Just after the conference convened, Underwood enthusiastically endorsed Secretary Hughes's proposal for naval disarmament and expressed optimism that an agreement could be quickly concluded. He maintained that the various segments of American society approved of the disarmament proposals, and he denied that the steel industry would be adversely affected by naval disarmament, since steel for battleships was only a small part of the industry's production. Commenting on other phases of the conference, Underwood said that the United States would not take the lead in Far Eastern problems—that questions affecting the Orient were

40. Wilbur J. Carr to Tracy Lay, October 19, 1921, in Underwood Papers, Alabama Archives; David J. Danelski and Joseph S. Tulchin (eds.), *The Autobiographical Notes of Charles Evans Hughes* (Cambridge, Mass.: Harvard University Press, 1973), 240–47.

more in the province of Japan, China, and Great Britain. He supported Elihu Root's submarine resolution, later embodied in a treaty that was never ratified, that bound submarines by the rules of international law governing surface ships in their operations against merchant vessels. [41]

Called away from the conference by his mother's illness, Underwood was not present during the crucial period in which the Four Power Treaty was drafted. Prior to leaving he sided with President Harding when the president dismayed Secretary Hughes by saying that the treaty's defense limitations would not apply to the main islands of Japan. The agreement worked out by the delegates with the president as he left the golf course indeed limited the treaty's sphere to only the outlying Japanese islands.

Underwood served as chairman of the Chinese tariff subcommittee of the conference's Committee on Pacific and Far Eastern Questions. The Chinese delegates were naturally eager that the international agreement governing China's tariff be abolished and that their nation have complete tariff autonomy. The subcommittee declined to agree, and the Chinese delegates, seeing no alternative, acquiesced. Underwood presented the Chinese tariff as a temporary measure necessitated by China's political weakness. The treaty, he said, would aid the Chinese government by raising Chinese tariff rates to an effective 5 percent, and provision was made for the revision of the tariff by a special conference. The committee also recommended that China reduce the size of its army to economize and bring its forces into accord with the spirit of the conference. The Chinese delegate, Dr. Sao-ke Alfred Sze, responded by expressing the thanks of the Chinese people for Underwood's "sympathetic appreciation of their aspiration toward tariff autonomy." [42]

Underwood said relatively little in the discussions that led to the

41. Birmingham *Age-Herald*, November 15, 1921; New York *Times*, December 30, 1921, p. 2.
42. Thomas H. Buckley, *The United States and the Washington Conference, 1921–1922* (Knoxville: University of Tennessee Press, 1970), 139; New York *Times*, January 6, 1922, p. 4, February 5, 1922, p. 18.

Five Power Treaty limiting naval armaments. He favored a committee report recommending that aircraft limitation not be included in the conference's proposals, noting that although he would be happy to see any instrument of war eliminated, aircraft were useful for land armament as well as naval and therefore did not fall within the aegis of the conference. In a similar spirit, he opposed United States admirals who wanted assurances that the United States could convert two unfinished battle cruisers into aircraft carriers. The conference reached conclusions in accord with Underwood's views on these naval aircraft matters, and upon completion of the treaty he stated that he was in "hearty accord" with what had been done.[43]

Senator Thomas J. Walsh precipitated premature discussion of the Washington treaties in January, 1922, by introducing a resolution calling upon President Harding to report to the Senate what steps had been taken to persuade Japan to return the Shantung Peninsula seized from China during World War I. Underwood replied that the Harding administration, like the Wilson administration, maintained that Shantung belonged to China. However, he noted that the conference could not deal with the Shantung problem as seven of the powers at the conference were signatories of the Treaty of Versailles which left Shantung in Japanese hands. He urged that the Senate do nothing to disturb the negotiations by the major powers for the return of Shantung. Senator Lodge seconded Underwood's views, and Walsh's resolution never reached a vote.[44]

Senator Carter Glass, who had objected to Underwood's acceptance of a place on the delegation, threatened to call a conference of Democrats to oppose the treaties. Such a move might have led to an attempt to overthrow Underwood as Senate minority leader. However, former president Wilson's tacit support of the treaties mitigated the attack. Lingering Democratic hopes that Underwood would give only perfunctory help in ratifying the treaties were dis-

---

43. *Conference on the Limitation of Armament* (Washington, D.C.: Government Printing Office, 1922), 793–94; Buckley, *The United States and the Washington Conference*, 120.
44. New York *Times*, January 21, 1922, p. 1.

pelled when he announced enthusiastic support for the entire treaty program. Signing the report of the American delegation and urging ratification without reservations, he said that he would not call a conference of Democrats to explain the treaties as the delegates' report was complete in itself. Clearly, he did not care to meet with the fractious Democrats.

Just prior to the ratification contest, Underwood was stricken with acute bronchitis with indications that pneumonia was developing. President Harding made solicitous inquiries at Underwood's home, but the Alabama senator recovered quickly, and the Senate debate began on schedule with Senator Lodge joining Underwood in leading the proponents of the treaties. Ranged against the ratificationists were most of the Democrats, including Senators Hitchcock, Joseph T. Robinson, and Glass, and Republican Senator Borah. Opponents charged that the Four Power Treaty resulted from an Anglo-Japanese plot to escape the responsibilities of their alliance. Senator Hitchcock offered a resolution asking the president to furnish all drafts of the treaty to the Senate, but Underwood insisted, with Lodge's agreement, that there was only one draft and that the discussions had centered on the effort to get Britain and Japan to cancel their alliance. The suggestion that a treaty be canceled to which the United States was not a signatory was not a matter that could be openly discussed, Underwood said, somewhat inconsistently. Nevertheless, the Senate almost unanimously asked the president for data on the conference. A few days later, on March 9, Senator Robinson drew from Underwood the surprising admission that he did not know who wrote the Four Power Treaty as he had been away from the conference for the funeral of his mother while the treaty was being negotiated.[45]

On March 11, ringed by the treaty's angry opponents, largely from his own party, Underwood defended the treaty in the Senate for three hours. Treaty opponents—Democrats led by Robinson and Republicans by Borah—frequently interrupted the Demo-

45. Birmingham *News*, February 9, 11, 1922; *Congressional Record*, 67th Cong., 2nd Sess., 2637–38, 3607–3608.

cratic leader in an exciting debate that left queues waiting for space
in the galleries. Underwood yielded to each senator who sought to
question him and replied calmly, even to the furiously gesticulating
Robinson. Replying to Robinson's earlier question about the authorship of the treaty, Underwood read a letter from Secretary of
State Hughes acknowledging that he had drafted the treaty and
that in Underwood's absence it had been reviewed by Elihu Root
and Senator Lodge. Underwood argued that the treaty accomplished much of what United States membership in the League of
Nations would have done. It was not an alliance, but even if it were
there was no military obligation, he said. The treaty only applied
to the Pacific, and there was no reason why nonsignatory nations—
notably Russia—should be included in Pacific conferences. Under
questioning, Underwood maintained that though Russia had a
large army it was "not much more than a mob" and that since Russia had no navy, it would have to "swim" to Sakhalin Island in order
to get involved in the Pacific. Germany, he said, was "down and
out for at least fifty years." Arrangements had been made with Hol-
land to extend the treaty to the Dutch East Indies. Referring to
the signatories' promise not to increase fortifications in the Pacific,
he stated that the Philippines and other islands west of Hawaii
were indefensible and "could not be helped in case of war with a
first class power." China, he noted, would be protected by the Nine
Power Treaty. The Lansing-Ishii Agreement, recognizing the special interests of Japan in China, was canceled by the proposed treaties which, he predicted, would presage Japanese withdrawal from
China. The alternative to the treaty, Underwood suggested, might
be an attack on the United States by "two nations"—presumably
Russia and Japan.

Treaty opponents were unimpressed by Underwood's marathon
performance. Senator Glass said they had been subjected to a
"continuous catechism" whereby Underwood, in arguing that the
treaty had no military commitment, made it "meaningless, and if
so, they should not bother to vote." Senator James Reed said that
Underwood had "worked himself into a religious zeal and fervor

seldom manifested outside an old-fashioned camp meeting."[46]

On the eve of the ratification battle Underwood was uneasy about the outcome. He wrote Judge Robert W. Winston of North Carolina that "there is [sic] only barely sufficient votes to ratify . . . and every recruit . . . is of great value now." Unexpected support came from Underwood's longtime foe William Jennings Bryan, who favored the treaty but suggested that a portion of it be changed to the wording of the Bryan arbitration treaties in order to preserve United States independence of action. Underwood graciously acknowledged the superiority of the Bryan clauses but noted the impracticability of such a change. He told the Nebraskan that he regarded the Four Power Treaty as a multilateral extension of the Bryan arbitration treaties.[47]

Senator Robinson's forces failed on March 9 to amend the treaty to stipulate that all powers interested in any controversy would be invited to a conference called to settle it. The vote of 50 to 27 against the effort to amend proved prophetic. On March 22 Underwood conferred with Harding at the president's request and assured him that ratification would be accomplished with a margin of at least three. He stated, however, that the Brandegee amendment declaring that the treaty was not an alliance would be attached. The Senate ratified the Four Power Treaty on March 24 with the Brandegee reservation. The vote was 67 to 27, with twelve Democrats favoring the treaty and twenty-three opposing it.[48]

While the Four Power Treaty discussions were going on, the Senate, under the guidance of Underwood, approved the treaty between the United States and Japan whereby Japan yielded the

46. Birmingham *News*, March 11, 1922; *Congressional Record*, 67th Cong., 2nd Sess., 3711–12, 3716–22. President Harding, informed while vacationing in Florida that Underwood had revealed Hughes's authorship of the treaty said: "That's fine. I'm glad he did it." Birmingham *Age-Herald*, March 13, 1922.

47. Underwood to Robert W. Winston, March 14, 1922, in R. W. Winston Papers, University of North Carolina, Chapel Hill; Underwood to William Jennings Bryan, March 14, 1922, in Bryan Papers, Library of Congress.

48. New York *Times*, March 23, 1922, p. 1, March 25, 1922, p. 1.

right to the establishment of a cable station and radio stations on the tiny Pacific Island of Yap. The Senate quickly approved this treaty by a vote of 67 to 22, with twelve Democrats joining the Republicans to favor ratification.[49]

The Naval Limitations Agreement, or Five Power Treaty, was largely unopposed in the Senate. It was presented by Senator Lodge, and Underwood answered questions regarding it. Opponents complained that the treaty did not cover all naval powers, but Underwood argued that it covered all existing naval powers and that it would be a long time before a naval power not covered by the treaty could be built. As he had done during the crucial days when the treaty was proposed, he emphasized that continuance of the naval program authorized by Congress in 1916 and 1918 would be "very expensive." Few senators were in the chamber and few observers were in the galleries prior to the ratification of the treaty by a vote of 74 to 1.[50]

Debate on the Nine Power Treaty, in which the signatories vowed to respect the territorial integrity of China, came next. Underwood insisted that there was no military obligation in the treaty, but he believed in the effectiveness of its "moral obligation." He described the treaty as "a great onward step" and, with undue optimism, expressed the belief that Japan as well as the other seven signatories of the treaty would respect the rights of China. The Senate ratified the Nine Power Treaty March 31, 1922, by a vote of 66 to 0. In deliberations on the last of the treaties, the Chinese Tariff Treaty, Underwood defended the right of the powers to arrange China's customs, explaining that China had already agreed to this arrangement. The tariff treaty was approved by a vote of 58 to 1.[51]

The ratification of the Washington treaties brought Underwood honor from various sources. Secretary of State Hughes lavishly praised him, saying, "I have never known a finer illustration of

49. *Ibid.*, February 28, 1922, p. 3.
50. *Congressional Record*, 67th Cong., 2nd Sess., 4688–89.
51. New York *Times*, March 31, 1922, p. 1.

non-partisan statesmanship than you have given during this long and difficult period." The New York *Tribune* commented that without Underwood's support the treaty would have failed, and Dr. Sao-Ke Alfred Sze, China's minister to the United States, stated that no native of China could have fought harder or more earnestly for Chinese rights than had Underwood. Underwood's drawing up of the Chinese tariff created interest in China in securing the senator's services as a tariff expert. In August, 1922, the American Chamber of Commerce in Shanghai urged Harding to appoint Underwood to the Chinese Tariff Commission provided for in the Chinese Tariff Treaty. In late October the Chinese government extended an invitation to Underwood to visit China, prepare a tariff, and put it into operation. Although he declined the invitation, Underwood offered aid in securing assistance from tariff experts in the United States. Harvard University recognized Underwood's role in the ratification of the Washington treaties in the June, 1922, commencement by awarding him a doctor of laws degree. The citation proclaimed that he had forgotten partisanship at a time of national crisis.[52]

Underwood's support of the Washington treaties had, however, seriously weakened his position as minority leader. Senator Glass, a fiery redhead who claimed that his vote had made Underwood Democratic leader over Hitchcock, was now snarling in anger. Senator Thaddeus H. Caraway of Arkansas complained that Underwood had conferred with no Democratic senators although he conferred daily with Senator Lodge and occasionally with the president.[53] Although his troubles with his Democratic colleagues were ostensibly over foreign policy, there was also a feeling that Underwood, an outspoken "wet," would be a presidential candidate in 1924. Senator Glass harbored presidential aspirations himself, and he certainly wanted to see a "dry" as the 1924 nominee.

---

52. Charles Evans Hughes to Underwood, April 1, 1922, in Letterbox M, Underwood Papers, Alabama Archives; New York *Tribune*, April 1, 1922; New York *Times*, April 8, 1922, p. 15, August 4, 1922, p. 16; Birmingham *Age-Herald*, October 22, 1922; *Harvard Alumni Bulletin*, XXIV (June 29, 1922), 969.

53. New York *Times*, March 24, 1922, p. 1.

In addition, members of the farm bloc, both Democrats and Republicans, were highly critical of Underwood's lack of enthusiasm for farm relief. Their anger toward him dated from early July, 1921, following a slide in farm prices. The administration had been unhappy with the favorable prospect for passage of several farm relief measures and adamantly opposed the immensely popular veterans bonus bill. Underwood cooperated with Lodge in agreeing to a month's congressional recess. The recess was ostensibly to allow the senators a chance to visit with their constituents, but Underwood stated his agreement with the administration in opposing the bonus bill and denounced the Norris farm relief bill as inadequate.

Norris' bill would have created a one hundred million dollar corporation, authorized to issue a billion dollars in stock, to make loans to farmers. Underwood pointed to the anomaly of attempting to solve the massive farm problem with a one hundred million dollar corporation while paying the soldiers a bonus that would total four billion dollars. Members of the farm bloc were angered by Underwood's support of the Republican-sponsored recess, and Senator Norris moved to block the adjournment. The farm bloc easily won and kept Congress in session for another month by a vote of 27 to 24.[54] It was a shattering loss of face for both majority and minority leaders.

The administration fared no better in keeping the bonus bill off the floor. Underwood, though opposing any bonus plan, argued that the proposal that would pay one dollar for each day of service in the United States and a dollar and a quarter for foreign service made too little distinction between the two. His objections to bringing up the bonus bill were buried in an avalanche vote of 46 to 4, although administration opposition eventually buried the measure for the session. Prior to the recess, the Norris Farm Export Act passed as an amendment to the War Finance Corporation Act. Although Underwood spoke briefly in favor of the measure, he left on vacation for Tate Springs three weeks before it reached

54. *Congressional Record*, 67th Cong., 1st Sess., 3336–38; Winston-Salem (N.C.) *Journal*, September 28, 1923.

a vote at the end of the session, with the excuse that no party matters were scheduled to come up.[55]

In the meantime, the press noted that Underwood had been a frequent visitor to the White House and had been favored with patronage. Frederick I. Thompson, the fiery-tongued publisher of the Mobile *Register* and a vigorous critic of Harding's policies, was appointed to the United States Shipping Board. William H. Barrett of Augusta, Georgia, a kinsman of Birmingham publisher Edward W. Barrett, became judge of the Southern District of Georgia. General John J. Pershing, in reply to an Underwood complaint, assured the Alabama senator that contrary to previous plans Alabama infantrymen would receive their training at Camp McClellan near Anniston, Alabama, rather than at Fort Benning, Georgia. Such favoritism to a Democrat caused grumbling among Harding's Republican friends.[56]

In a like spirit, Underwood supported Harding's appointment of former president William Howard Taft as chief justice of the Supreme Court in June, 1921. Underwood, who had achieved national prominence as an opponent of Taft's tariff policies, admired him greatly and vigorously supported Taft, who was confirmed without difficulty. Underwood also refused to oppose Harding's nomination of Thomas J. Kennemer as United States marshall for the Northern District of Alabama. Kennemer's brother was district attorney in the same district, and there was dissatisfaction in Alabama with the nomination.[57]

Underwood had not gone over completely to the Republican party, however. Among the party matters that vitally interested

55. New York *Times*, July 7, 1921, p. 1; *Congressional Record*, 67th Cong., 1st Sess., 3970; New York *Times*, July 31, 1921, p. 19.
56. Montgomery *Journal*, June 15, 1922; John J. Pershing to Underwood, March 16, 1922, Underwood to Pershing, March 18, 1922, both in John J. Pershing Papers, Library of Congress; O. D. Street to George B. Christian, December 2, 1921, in Box 213, Warren G. Harding Papers, Ohio Historical Society, Columbus.
57. Birmingham *News*, May 16, 1922. According to one report, Underwood dissuaded Harding from appointing Charles Hughes chief justice on the basis that Hughes was needed at the Washington Conference. However, it seems unlikely that Harding would have failed to appoint Hughes because of a relatively temporary duty. Nor is there confirmation of the account in Hughes, Harding, or Taft biographies. *Cushing's Survey*, II (February 7, 1924).

him was the charge that wealthy chain store owner Truman H. Newberry had been elected illegally as a Republican senator from Michigan. Underwood may have been influenced by the fact that Newberry's unsuccessful opponent, Henry Ford, had a pending offer to lease the government plants at Muscle Shoals, a favorite Underwood project. Also, J. Thomas Heflin, who became Alabama's junior senator following the death of Bankhead in 1920, had added Newberry to his roster of enemies—a curious list composed of Negroes, the Federal Reserve Board, and the Roman Catholic Church. Underwood spoke out against Newberry's use of almost two hundred thousand dollars to "buy the seat,"[58] and although Newberry was seated, his reputation was so sullied that he resigned before the end of a year of service in the Senate.

The major issues in the second session of the Sixty-seventh Congress were tariff revision and the soldiers' bonus bill. Senator Reed Smoot was in charge of both measures, although the bonus was not an administration measure. Underwood and the Democrats expected the Republican juggernaut to ram through a tariff measure substantially like the bill vetoed by President Wilson in his last days in the presidency. Underwood objected, however, when Smoot attempted to place the bonus bill ahead of the tariff bill, which would be a time-consuming measure, in the hope of securing quick passage of the controversial bonus measure. He said that though he was willing to go to the "extreme limit" to take care of the disabled veterans, he was opposed to a measure that would attempt "to measure in dollars the services of the man who came back sound and well."[59] The bonus measure was deferred until late in the session.

Underwood demanded that the McCumber tariff bill be thoroughly discussed, arguing that costs of production abroad had risen so that there was less necessity than ever for high tariffs. He insisted that there was no advantage to the farmer in a protective tariff. The Republican proposals removed from the free list fertil-

58. Birmingham *Age-Herald*, January 9, 1922; *Congressional Record*, 67th Cong., 2nd Sess., 1049–50.

59. New York *Times*, February 5, 1922, Sec. 7, p. 1.

izer, binding twine, cotton ties, and bagging used by wheat and cotton farmers. But imports and exports were "Siamese twins," he said, "kill one and you kill the other." The rates of the Senate bill were higher than those of the Payne-Aldrich Tariff Act, and those of the House bill were higher still, he said. The United States economy was plagued by overproduction, which could not be solved by putting a "Chinese wall" around the country but must be solved by finding a market for surplus goods. Denying charges that Democratic delaying tactics amounted to a "filibuster" against the McCumber bill, Underwood pointed out that passage of tariff bills usually took two to three months. The arguments droned on, and Underwood threatened to call for no fewer than eight thousand roll calls that would account for two thousand hours or ten-hour meetings for two hundred days without the Democrats uttering a word in debate. If Underwood and the Democrats were not filibustering, it could at least be described as a legislative slowdown. Underwood objected to increased duties and the removal from the free list of a long series of products, including, as in 1913, those of his own district—especially pig iron and its raw materials. His patience wore thin following an exhibit McCumber made to the Senate of a number of articles on which he said importers were making an exorbitant profit—including a cuckoo clock. The press was critical of McCumber, and Underwood, enjoying the senator's discomfiture, accused him of running a "circus side show." He goaded the Republicans to invoke cloture, knowing that they lacked the votes. McCumber asked for cloture in late July. Underwood noted wryly that the Underwood-Simmons Tariff Act had been passed in seven weeks and that the Senate had already spent ten weeks on the McCumber bill, with only one third of it disposed of. However, the McCumber bill had over two thousand committee amendments as compared to the six hundred on the Underwood bill. McCumber's cloture effort failed by twelve signatures.[60]

Underwood focused his attack on the maximum-minimum pro-

60. *Congressional Record*, 67th Cong., 2nd Sess., 6944, 7038, 7132–33, 7271; Birmingham *Age-Herald*, May 12, July 22, 1922; New York *Times*, June 15, 1922, p. 1.

vision of the McCumber bill authorizing the president to raise or lower the tariff by 50 percent. Vehemently opposing this provision as "a direct retreat" from Congress' responsibility to levy taxes, he expressed doubt that it was constitutional. The provision passed by a vote of 36 to 20, and the McCumber bill passed by a vote of 48 to 25. The final tariff bill returned from conference with a provision that allowed the president to substitute American valuation for foreign valuation. Underwood charged that this conference "joker" would substitute higher rates than either the House or the Senate envisioned. The McCumber tariff bill, now restyled the Fordney-McCumber bill, passed the Senate on September 19 after twenty months of debate—the longest tariff debate in United States history. Underwood gave the final arguments against the bill, reiterating his complaint that the president was being given too much power and insisting that commerce with foreign nations would be brought to a standstill. Nevertheless, the bill passed by a vote of 43 to 28.[61]

While the tariff bill was under consideration, McCumber had presented the soldiers' bonus bill, without any provision for raising the necessary funds. Underwood consistently opposed the measure saying that its cost, alleged by its proponents to be four billion dollars, would amount to about six or seven billion when interest was added. Admitting that the bill would pass by a large majority, Underwood said that the real contest would be to pass the bill over the president's veto. The United States could not have owed, at the outset of World War I, a debt of twenty-five to thirty million dollars and put two million men in France within a little over a year, except for its "virgin credit," which would have been damaged by such an obligation as the bonus debt, argued Underwood. President Harding vetoed the bonus bill, as Underwood had predicted, and the attempt to pass the bill in the Senate over the veto failed by four votes.[62]

Although he had cooperated with President Harding at the

---

61. New York *Times*, August 11, 1922, p. 1, September 17, 1922, p. 20, September 20, 1922, p. 1.

62. *Congressional Record*, 67th Cong., 2nd Sess., 8370, 11742–44.

Washington Conference, Underwood otherwise maintained independence in foreign affairs. When, in September, 1921, France objected to payments to the United States for maintaining troops on the Rhine, Underwood cited the failure of the United States to send a representative to the Reparations Commission as a reason for French noncooperation. When France invaded the Ruhr Valley in January, 1923, after the Reparations Commission declared Germany in default of its obligations, Underwood supported a largely unopposed "sense of the Senate" resolution expressing disapproval of the French action and favoring the withdrawal of some one thousand American troops who remained in the Rhineland. The failure of the United States to ratify the Treaty of Versailles meant that the United States had no right to keep a single soldier in Europe, Underwood said. The only purpose of the troops, he claimed, was to support the decisions of the Reparations Commission on which the United States had declined membership.[63]

Underwood's criticism of the Harding administration's failure to assume its role on the Reparations Commission may have been influenced by suggestions that Underwood be appointed to that commission. On other foreign affairs questions, he generally supported the administration. Thus Underwood and most other Democrats favored the administration's plans for funding the $4,700,000,000 British war debt at 3 to 3½ percent interest; the plan was approved with little opposition. Underwood did not vote on Harding's recommendation that the United States join the Permanent Court of International Justice at the Hague; the measure failed by a lopsided vote.[64]

In the summer of 1922 Underwood embarrassed the State Department with a bill to seize German properties. Underwood had interested himself immediately after World War I in expanding the authority of his friend A. Mitchell Palmer, the alien property custodian, to allow him to sell property seized from the enemy. Underwood's amendment to the Trading with the Enemy Act passed,

---

63. New York *Times*, March 18, 1922, p. 1, January 7, 1923, p. 1.
64. *Congressional Record*, 67th Cong., 4th Sess., 3614, 5272.

to the despair of President Wilson who thought it gave the president too much authority. The failure of the United States to ratify the Treaty of Versailles led to a provision in the Treaty of Berlin that the United States could name a member of the Reparations Commission, which would consider American claims. The Senate, however, refused to authorize the president to name such a commissioner. Underwood sponsored a bill to unilaterally establish an "Enemy Property Claims Commission" with authority to sell all enemy property taken over by the alien property custodian to satisfy American claims. Although maintaining that he had "no bitterness against our late German enemies," he objected to seeing the claims of the heirs of those "murdered in the sinking of the Lusitania" go before a mixed commission. Senator Borah and others objected that it was not right to seize the property of German nationals to pay German government obligations. Underwood bitterly replied that whereas the "old principle of international law" that an invading army should respect the property of the citizens of the country through which it advances was correct in its time, "to-day peoples make war against other peoples." Answering charges that his bill provided for confiscation of private property, Underwood replied that such a danger would be quite a deterrent to the waging of war by monied people. Unless government policies were altered, he said, German dye patents, transatlantic terminal properties at Hoboken, and a wireless station at Sayville, Long Island—some of which had been useful in German spy activities—would be returned to their German owners. He threatened the administration with trouble if it tried to settle the German claims by an executive agreement without submitting it to the Senate for action.[65]

Underwood's attack goaded the State Department into action. Secretary of State Hughes replied that the Underwood resolution dealt with foreign claims as if they were a domestic matter. The Underwood plan, he said, would be embarrassing to President Harding and was "at variance to the principles and practices gen-

65. *Ibid.*, 2nd Sess., 10441–49; New York *Times*, July 25, 1922, p. 19.

erally observed by nations." Hughes also noted that there were not sufficient German assets under control of the alien property custodian to satisfy the American claims. Hughes speedily negotiated the Hughes-Wirth agreement with Germany, providing settlement by a mixed claims commission composed of two Americans and one German representative. Underwood attempted to block the implementation of the agreement and substitute his unilateral commission, arguing that the Hughes-Wirth commission was illegal and would not cover (and indeed it did not) claims against Austria and Hungary. Senator Hitchcock, viewing Senator Lodge's opposition forces, told Underwood that his plan could not be adopted and would only cause delay. Underwood's plan failed by a vote of 39 to 18.[66]

Well before the tariff and bonus bills reached a final vote in the Senate, President Harding recommended congressional action to end the increasingly unpopular rail and coal strikes. The strikes were touched off by efforts of the rail and mine operators to reduce wages to match the price slide of 1922. The coal strike was marked by bloody violence especially at Herrin, Illinois, where strikers murdered twenty-one strikebreakers—an incident named the Herrin massacre. The rail strike also had its share of violence.

Birmingham was only indirectly affected as the area's miners did not strike, and with the rail strike limited to shopmen—the four railroad brotherhoods were not involved—rail transit continued although loadings were restricted. Presidential mediation failed, and on August 18 the president addressed a joint session of Congress, condemning the lawlessness of the strikers and the failure of the state governments to maintain order and promising that "government by law must and will be sustained." He asked that a national coal agency be created to regulate the industry and that the actions of the Railway Labor Board be made binding on the employers as well as employees. The president's address was received with popular favor, and it incited Attorney General Harry M.

66. *Congressional Record*, 67th Cong., 2nd Sess., 13056–57, 13070–71; Birmingham *News*, July 30, 1922.

Daugherty, who opposed labor, to secure an injunction restraining striking shopmen and members of the AFL from interfering with the operation of the railroads. Underwood applauded Daugherty's action although the administration itself, influenced by Secretary of Commerce Herbert Hoover, began to retreat from its antilabor stance.[67]

Underwood criticized the Harding proposals for regulation of the coal industry, since these measures would involve government ownership or regulation of a privately owned industry. He also criticized the administration's Cummins bill that would have granted the ICC the right to seize rail facilities and to grant priorities whereby shipment of coal in interstate commerce would be denied to shippers who failed to accept reasonable prices for their coal. He noted that the proposal had been used on a voluntary basis by Secretary of Commerce Hoover—indeed the bill was Hoover's idea—and it had been ineffective. He urged that a sweeping antistrike provision be incorporated into the bill. The administration lost its enthusiasm for tough new restrictions on the coal and railway industries as both of the strikes ended in the fall of 1922, with victory for the coal miners and defeat for the railway laborers. The Cummins bill, which would have given the Railway Labor Board more authority, died, and in its final form a rather innocuous Coal Distribution and Price Act was passed providing for a fact-finding commission and the fixing of coal prices.[68]

The appointment of W. P. G. Harding, governor of the Federal Reserve Board, expired in 1922, and in August Underwood reluctantly cooperated with Secretary Mellon and others who were eager to see the president reappoint Harding. The Birmingham banker had arrived in the Magic City about the same time as Underwood, and they and their families had become good friends, although Harding had had the misfortune of being president of the Birmingham Chamber of Commerce when the Underwood-Sim-

67. Francis Russell, *The Shadow of Blooming Grove: Warren G. Harding in His Time* (New York: McGraw-Hill, 1968), 546–49; New York *Times*, September 2, 1922, p. 1.

68. New York *Times*, August 29, 1922, p. 2; *Congressional Record*, 67th Cong., 2nd Sess., 12084–90.

mons Tariff was passed and was thus cast in the temporary role of an Underwood critic. At Underwood's request, Wilson had appointed Harding to the Federal Reserve Board in 1914, and in 1916 the genial and able Harding advanced to governor of the board. In 1918 he also became managing director of the War Finance Corporation. Harding, an expert on cotton finance and an able financier, endeared himself to the banking community, but his deflationary policies in the farm price slide of 1922 made him anathema to farm bloc senators. Indeed, Underwood was a critic of his hard-money policies. When Harvard University granted Harding a doctor of laws degree, Senator Heflin of Alabama attacked two of his personal devils, the Federal Reserve System and Wall Street, as responsible for bestowing this honor.

President Harding cannily fended off the pressure to renominate W. P. G. Harding but eventually acceded to Secretary of the Treasury Mellon's importunities for the Birmingham banker, saying that he had "surrendered." The president asked to see Underwood, fearing that farm bloc senators would tie up the Senate in a long confirmation fight. He planned to tie the appointment to that of a farm representative for a second vacancy on the Federal Reserve Board as a sop to the farm bloc. Underwood viewed the prospects for confirmation gloomily, saying that he had to live with Senator Heflin who could prevent confirmation by invoking "senatorial courtesy." Eventually he assured the president that he could secure confirmation, but Congress adjourned without acting. During the interim Senator Charles Curtis of Kansas led a delegation of twelve midwestern senators to the White House to object to Harding's reappointment. It was soon apparent that the reappointment would not go through. [69]

Congress recessed in the fall of 1922 following the passage of the Fordney-McCumber Tariff and the bonus bill, the latter of which

69. Underwood to James E. Caldwell, September 8, 1923, in Letterbox N, Underwood Papers, Alabama Archives; Birmingham *News*, April 7, 1930; New York *Times*, July 12, 1922, p. 17; Charles S. Hamlin Diary, August 8–10, 1922, in Charles S. Hamlin Papers, Library of Congress; New York *Times*, October 17, 1922, p. 8. E. R. Crissinger of Marion, Ohio, a personal friend of the president, was elevated from comptroller of the currency to replace W. P. G. Harding in January, 1923.

the president vetoed. Underwood headed South to join his wife at their cabin at Tate Springs. After a brief return trip to Washington, he joined congressional candidates in the Alabama Democratic campaign—a needless ritual in thoroughly Democratic Alabama. At Aliceville, a hamlet in inland Pickens County, he endorsed an amendment to the Alabama constitution to allow the use of state credit for the building of port facilities at Mobile, using the occasion to recall his role in the canalization of the Warrior River. He reflected on the terrible year 1914 when, at the outset of World War I, Mobile had suffered from the withdrawal of British merchant ships from the American carrying trade. In the absence of a large American merchant marine there had been no way to dispose of cotton, which slid from fourteen to five cents a pound. He noted with pride improvements in the Mobile port in that additional steamship service had been developed and the government had established a coaling and oiling station. Underwood's Alabama campaign was interrupted when he became quite ill with a bronchial ailment that reduced his voice to a whisper. He returned to Birmingham, his speaking engagements were canceled, and his physician insisted that he avoid even ordinary conversation, although the illness was not serious.[70]

Underwood's illness depressed him and led him to reassess his political future. Disgusted with the archaic rules of the Senate and under vigorous attack for his cooperation with Harding's foreign policies, he pondered the desirability of giving up the minority leader's post, which he had not enjoyed. While he was in Birmingham the *Age-Herald* reported that Underwood was being considered for the Supreme Court vacancy created by the resignation of Justice William R. Day. The Birmingham newspapers usually printed what the senator wanted said about him, and the *Age-Herald* story must have reached President Harding. The president wrote Underwood a letter that was tantamount to an offer of appointment to the Supreme Court:

> I am wondering if you would like to be appointed to the Supreme Court. I have such personal affection and such a high regard for your

70. Birmingham *Age-Herald*, October 26, 1922; Birmingham *News*, October 28, 1922.

abilities that if you entertain such an ambition I would like to consider you for nomination. Somehow I have the feeling that service on the Bench would not be in harmony with your preference for a public career. I suspect you of preferring to remain in the big political contest and of nurturing an ambition to be a candidate for president. Of course, I would like to see you the Democratic nominee, though I would not be as favorable to your election as I am to your nomination. I am quite sincere about the matter first referred to in this letter. Please let me have a personal and confidential note as to your feelings.[71]

Underwood replied to the president's letter from Pass Christian, Mississippi, where he was recuperating from the bronchitis attack. His letter declining the offer was a startling and curious statement that he was resigning from the minority leadership on account of his health and for the same reason declined the appointment to the court. Yet he stated that he was available for the Democratic presidential nomination. He said:

> I feel that you honor me greatly, but I cannot consider the question of going on the Bench on account of my health, there is nothing functionally wrong, but the old machine is tired out and my doctor says I must give it a real rest. For this reason I have announced since your letter was written that I would retire from the leadership of my party in the Senate. The man who goes on the Supreme Court must make a contract with himself to work hard, that I cannot do at this time. Don't think for a minute that I would rather run against you than go on the Bench for I would not.
>
> To be nominated by one's party for the greatest office in the world is too great an honor to decline should it come my way. I have recently had a severe attack of bronchitis, the salt sea air here has done me much good and I hope to be able to be back in Washington when Congress meets.[72]

Harding acknowledged Underwood's letter courteously: "I can assure you that I would never wish you to refrain from accepting

---

71. Warren G. Harding to Underwood, November 6, 1922, in Underwood Papers, Alabama Archives.

72. Underwood to Warren G. Harding, November 10, 1922, copy in Underwood Papers, Alabama Archives.

presidential nomination against me, if it should be the wisdom of your party to name you. I should really be glad to see your party exercise such wisdom. I would then feel quite secure about the safety of the country, even though I did not agree with all the policies likely to have your sanction."[73]

Why did President Harding offer to name Underwood to the Supreme Court? Underwood's experience as a lawyer was seriously dated, and he had no judicial experience to qualify him for the post. Harding was an astute political observer, and he could hardly have considered Underwood a dangerous opponent for 1924. Indeed, some of Harding's political advisors were known to prefer Underwood as an opponent who would be seriously handicapped by his identification with "wet" views. More likely, the president felt he had played a part in alienating Underwood from his party, and in Harding's brand of politics such service deserved a reward. There is no indication in Harding's letter that he expected Underwood to accept the nomination. Nor is there any indication that Underwood, who indeed intended another race for the Democratic presidential nomination, seriously considered the Supreme Court offer. Perhaps the president did not really expect that he would accept and merely found it an inexpensive way to fulfill an obligation.

Two weeks prior to the opening of the regular session the president summoned Congress, now a lame-duck body, into special session in order to consider the ship subsidy bill. The president faced a difficult task in securing the bill's passage, since the Republicans had suffered substantial losses in the congressional election, and a Senate filibuster was almost certain in a session that could last only two weeks. While the shipping bill was still in the House, however, a Senate filibuster came first over the administration supported Dyer antilynching bill in which it was proposed to make lynching a federal crime. The measure had passed the House in the previous session, but it had never reached the floor of the Senate. Southern Democrats vociferously objected to the Dyer bill,

73. Warren G. Harding to Underwood, November 13, 1922, in Letterbox M, Underwood Papers, Alabama Archives.

maintaining that it was an election year ploy designed to aid the campaigns of the recently reelected Senators Lodge of Massachusetts and Joseph I. France of Maryland. Underwood denounced the bill as a "force bill," a term usually reserved for laws mandating federal control of elections, and stated that although he disapproved of mob rule, he considered the bill an unconstitutional violation of states' rights. He aided Pat Harrison of Mississippi and other southern Democrats in beginning a filibuster. Until the Dyer bill was withdrawn, Underwood said, he would allow no legislation to be considered, not even the confirmation of Democrat Pierce Butler, a Minnesotan, as a member of the Supreme Court. He wryly calculated that the southerners could stall the ten pending executive appointments for weeks. Meanwhile, he reminisced about his early career in the House, especially about Speaker Reed. After five days Senator Lodge capitulated and promised Underwood that the Dyer bill would not be pushed for the remainder of the session, paving the way for the shipping bill and other legislation. By Underwood's reckoning, it was his first filibuster, and the New York *Times* described it as "practically perfect."[74]

Harding was firmly dedicated to the shipping bill. The inducements offered by the Merchant Marine Act of 1920, sponsored by the Wilson administration and backed by Underwood, had proved ineffective in transferring the merchant marine from governmental to private hands. President Harding asked for a generous subsidy that would enable the government to convert its fleet into a private merchant marine, available for any national emergency, and save substantial sums through the elimination of maintenance costs. But if the president thought Underwood could be depended on to support this cherished bill, he was mistaken. Underwood recalled that he had sponsored the wartime Merchant Marine Act of 1917 and had favored special treatment for the United States merchant marine through discriminating duties, but both the Harding and Wilson administrations had refused to renounce treaty agreements that stood in the way. Although sympathetic with the expansion of

74. *Congressional Record*, 67th Cong., 3rd Sess., 389–92, 450; New York *Times*, November 29, 1922, p. 1.

the merchant marine, he eventually decided he could not vote for
a direct subsidy as provided in the ship subsidy bill.

Despite his opposition to the shipping bill, Underwood declined
to take part in a Democratic filibuster that prevented it from reaching a vote. As a delaying tactic the Democrats cleverly proposed to
substitute a "filled milk bill" to regulate and tax the sale of substitute dairy products. Underwood bitterly criticized his colleagues,
for although he had filibustered against the Dyer antilynching bill
in which the important constitutional principle of states' rights was
involved, there was no great danger in the shipping bill, and it
should be allowed to come to a vote. Senate Democrats, he argued, should meet in caucus rather than in conference (which
lacked the binding nature of caucus commitments) so that they
could have majority rule as the Democrats had when he was in the
House. Lecturing on majority rule, he said that the Senate would
be "discredited by the American people unless it learns how to do
business."[75]

As the Sixty-seventh Congress ended on March 3, 1923, Underwood was discouraged with the Senate. Presidential favor had cost
him Democratic support, and he had resigned in disgust as minority leader. In the House, he had led a majority during the entire
period of his leadership, and the rules were far more effective in
shutting off debate than in the Senate. As aide to Senator Martin,
he played a leadership role, becoming effective minority leader
during Martin's illness in 1919, and was elected leader in 1920.
From 1919 to 1923 his party had been in the minority, and he was
hamstrung by ineffective rules. The last weeks of the Sixty-seventh
Congress were especially exasperating. Underwood's refusal to
lead a filibuster against Harding's shipping bill angered Democrats
yet brought him no favor with Republicans as he did not support
the bill. Among his worst chores at the end of this session was an
attempt to smooth over Senator Heflin's vicious attack on Chief
Justice Taft, Senator James W. Wadsworth, Jr., and newly elected
Senator James Couzens of Michigan, whom Heflin lumped to-

75. *Congressional Record*, 67th Cong., 4th Sess., 3964–67.

gether as representatives of Wall Street. Although Underwood said in sponsoring an agreement for both Couzens and Heflin to withdraw comments made about each other that Couzens would learn that the Senate "is a place, where difficulties among gentlemen can be settled in an amicable way," he must have felt chagrin at the remarks Heflin made toward his friend Taft.[76]

President Harding and Underwood had drifted apart following the ratification of the Washington treaties. They had never been really close personal friends, although both attempted to make it appear that they were. Their friendship had been largely on the floor of the Senate, and such social relations as there were seem to have been through the friendship of the senator and his wife with Evelyn Walsh McLean and her Washington publisher husband, Edward B. "Ned" McLean, whose home, Friendship, was a port of call for both the Underwoods and the Hardings as well as most other Washington greats and near greats. The president had carefully cultivated the senator, having learned well Wilson's mistake in not conciliating Lodge on Versailles. But Underwood could no longer be of service to him, and their differences on domestic issues became more apparent as the election of 1924 approached. President Harding could hardly view with pleasure the idea of further building up a possible competitor for the presidency. Indeed, there is no evidence that Underwood and Harding had any relations after the end of the Sixty-seventh Congress. At the time of Harding's death in August, 1923, Senator and Mrs. Underwood telegraphed very simply "PROFOUND SYMPATHY," to Mrs. Harding. Several months later, however, Underwood paid great tribute to the dead president while he campaigned for the presidency in Akron, Ohio, using Harding's death to buttress a proposal that the president himself had made for a single six-year presidential term, saying: "One of Ohio's great, noblehearted sons has succumbed to the exacting rigors of his office, striving with an exemplary patience and heroic consciousness of duty to crowd into his short four years of office a host of herculean labors. Had he been allotted a larger

76. *Ibid.*, 2865–66, 2874.

space of time, he might have been spared his strength and conserved his powers to their fulfillment." This glowing assessment with which few historians would agree was repeated several months later when the bloom had disappeared from Harding's reputation.[77] There is, however, substantial evidence in the handling of the Alabama senator by President Harding to strengthen the president's reputation as a leader.

Prior to the end of the Sixty-seventh Congress Senator and Mrs. Underwood left on a European tour. The Senate was not to meet again until early December, and Underwood was no longer minority leader. Preoccupied with plans for his presidential campaign, he took little part in the Senate's deliberations. The period of his most effective service to the Senate was at an end.

While Underwood was Senate minority leader, and immediately thereafter, he was concerned with building a platform for his 1924 campaign for the presidency. On the Treaty of Versailles he had obscured his position so thoroughly that he was never able to clarify it. Actually, he had seen that ratification without reservations was impossible, and he was willing to accept such reservations as were necessary to secure ratification—even to separate the treaty from the league if necessary. While Wilson was president, his hard line against reservations made it impossible for Underwood to candidly present his views; he could only hope that the president would modify his resistance to reservations. Underwood's close cooperation with the Harding treaties following the Washington Conference and his acceptance of the Treaty of Berlin alienated many Democratic followers in the Senate and made his position as leader difficult. Although Underwood continued his opposition to the Harding administration's domestic policies—the Fordney-McCumber tariff, the shipping bill, and antilynching legislation—his colleagues nonetheless identified him with Harding's policies.

Underwood's decision to resign as minority leader resulted from dissatisfaction with him among younger members of the Senate—

77. Birmingham *News*, August 3, 1923; New York *Times*, August 4, 1923, p. 8; Address of January 23, 1924, in Letterbox M, Underwood Papers, Alabama Archives; Washington (D.C.), *Star*, May 19, 1924.

especially the southern group who had made him leader. Ostensibly, opposition to Underwood resulted from his cooperation with Harding's foreign policy, but the compelling factors were differences over domestic policy—especially prohibition—and conflict with the incipient presidential candidacy of William Gibbs McAdoo. Despite this criticism, Underwood was remembered in the Senate as a highly effective minority leader. His decision to resign this post was unfortunate in the light of his presidential ambitions.

CHAPTER XIII

Muscle Shoals and the Politics of Power

Underwood's extraordinary interest in the development of Alabama's waterways was, after 1916, focused almost exclusively on Muscle Shoals, which rivaled Niagara Falls in power-producing potential. Differing from those who emphasized the value of the hydroelectric power itself, he envisioned the use of that power for the production of cheap nitrates to fertilize the cotton fields of the South. The outbreak of World War I, Underwood's election to the Senate, rapid advancement in the Senate and assignment to the powerful Appropriations Committee, gave Underwood the opportunity to seek development of Muscle Shoals. As minority leader from 1920 to 1923, he had a strong fulcrum.

At Muscle Shoals, the Tennessee River drops a precipitous 132 feet in the thirty-seven miles east of Florence. This geological marvel was the subject of intermittent engineering surveys dating from the presidency of George Washington. By 1890 lateral canals and locks had been built around the shoals, but the canals were insufficient for navigation. Water transportation at the shoals was nonexistent, and the huge river ran unharnessed into the Ohio. The hardy but poor people of the area were impatient to have the shoals developed.

Underwood had long been associated with J. W. Worthington, a shadowy, backstage electric power lobbyist. Worthington grew up in the Birmingham area and, after graduating in engineering at the University of Alabama in 1882, preceded Underwood to Birmingham. He absorbed the industrial enthusiasm of Henry F. De-

Bardeleben with whom he was in partnership for a time, and by
the 1890s Worthington had shifted his operations to Muscle Shoals,
organized a group of new business enterprises, and lobbied for a
variety of power projects. He unsuccessfully sought, with Underwood's support, franchises for the Birmingham Water Light and
Power Company on the Black Warrior River in 1910 and the Alabama Power Company on the Coosa River in 1912. When Underwood campaigned for the United States Senate in 1914, Worthington quietly and "personally" furnished the money for Underwood's
campaign in the Tri-Cities (Muscle Shoals) area, although it may be
assumed that the funds came from the Alabama Power Company.[1]

Soon after Underwood's victory in his Senate campaign, Worthington, then a vice-president of Alabama Power Company, sent
Underwood by express a number of documents relating to Muscle
Shoals. Worthington argued that Muscle Shoals should be developed with federal subsidies similar to those with which irrigation
of the West had been promoted. He reasoned that navigation costs
should be borne by the government and that the remainder of the
cost should be loaned by the government at a low rate of interest.
Worthington recognized Underwood as the only Alabama politician who had sufficient stature to persuade Congress to develop
Muscle Shoals.[2]

Underwood's support of Worthington's plan was revealed when
he offered in the House a $150,000 amendment to the rivers and
harbors appropriation for a survey at Muscle Shoals preliminary to
the building of a huge dam by a subsidiary of Alabama Power, the
Muscle Shoals Hydro-Electric Company, in partnership with the
government. Opponents of the Muscle Shoals Hydro-Electric
Company's project maintained that Muscle Shoals was primarily a
power project rather than a navigation improvement and that the
proposed amendment amounted to new legislation. Despite strong

1. Adrian G. Daniel, "J. W. Worthington, Promoter of Muscle Shoals Power," *Alabama
Review*, XII (July, 1959), 197–98; C. W. Ashcraft to Oscar W. Underwood, April 9, 1914, in
Oscar W. Underwood Papers, Alabama Department of Archives and History, Montgomery.
2. J. W. Worthington to Underwood, December 1, 1914, in Underwood Papers, Alabama Archives.

opposition from conservationists, Underwood, powerfully aided by Senator John H. Bankhead, successfully fought off efforts to remove the Muscle Shoals survey from the rivers and harbors bill.[3]

Worthington's ambitious plans to develop Muscle Shoals included an immense power-navigation project as well as a nitrate plant. The idea of manufacturing nitrogen from the air through the use of the cyanamid process at a large water power site had been proposed before, but it was given urgency by the outbreak of war. In December, 1914, an engagement between the British and German navies off the southern coasts of Chile and Argentina dramatized the danger that the United States supply of Chilean nitrates might be severed. Nitrates were essential for explosives and large quantities of nitrate of soda were used by southern farmers. The only method well known in the United States for making nitrates was the cyanamid process which required a vast amount of electricity; the more advanced Haber process for producing nitrogen with far less electric power was little known outside of Germany. Muscle Shoals offered an obvious answer to the need.

Some of Underwood's political advisors thought that Worthington's appreciation for Underwood's help was not adequately reflected by support in Alabama politics where prohibitionists had seized control of the legislature. Underwood was distressed over the legislative power of the prohibitionists who, he said, "cause turmoil and endanger good government." The Alabama Power Company, whose political power probably was exaggerated in the minds of Underwood's friends, was charged with aiding prohibitionists who were attempting to pass statewide prohibition without a referendum. Worthington hotly and effectively denied the existence of any coalition between Alabama Power and the prohibitionists.[4] Underwood denied, however, that he had any commitment to the Alabama Power Company: "I am not in any way tied . . . to the Alabama Power Company, but I do believe the development of this power is of great importance to our people. It is not only nec-

3. *Congressional Record*, 63rd Cong., 3rd Sess., 1859–60, 1870–73.
4. Frank P. Glass to Underwood, January 14, 1915, J. W. Worthington to Frank P. Glass, January 16, 1915 (copy), both in Underwood Papers, Alabama Archives.

essary to the development of the Tennessee River, but if the great power that is possible of development at Muscle Shoals is utilized to its fullest extent it means the greatest industrial development in the entire South."[5]

A civic celebration at Muscle Shoals in May, 1915, arranged by Worthington, brought to the site members of the Senate Committee on Commerce and the House Rivers and Harbors Committee. Underwood accompanied the congressmen, who were feted with a barbeque and a steamboat trip through the area. At Sheffield he endorsed the Muscle Shoals project, suggesting that it would cost less than the amount paid by the United States to the Chilean government in severance taxes on nitrates. On the train back to Birmingham, Underwood told reporters that Muscle Shoals "is the greatest waterway proposition in the United States, and I can see no reason why it should not be carried out as the people of the Tennessee Valley desire, if the engineers report it as a feasible proposition, and there appears to be little doubt that such will be their report."[6] In the fall of 1915, "Colonel" Worthington resigned form the vice-presidency and board of directors of the Alabama Power Company to devote all of his energies to the development of Muscle Shoals, evidently objecting to Alabama Power Company's decision to concentrate its efforts on the development of the Coosa River. He retained, however, a directorship in the American Cyanamid Company, which was later shown to have financed the Tennessee River Improvement Association which Worthington headed.[7]

By 1916 the nation was thoroughly committed to preparedness, and Muscle Shoals's date with destiny had arrived. A Muscle Shoals proposal was defeated in the House, but when the army reorganization bill appeared in the Senate, both Underwood and Senator Ellison D. Smith of South Carolina offered amendments for the building of a huge nitrate plant. Both amendments directed

5. Underwood to Forney Johnston, January 16, 1915, in Underwood Papers, Alabama Archives.
6. Birmingham *News*, May 11, 1915.
7. Daniel, "J. W. Worthington," 205.

that the Army Corps of Engineers select a location for a nitrate plant. Underwood's amendment differed from Smith's in that it provided for leasing to a private corporation rather than for government operation of the plant. Underwood's amendment was reported from the Senate Committee on Military Affairs without recommendation on April 7. He estimated that a hydroelectric plant could be built for fourteen million dollars, and a nitrogen plant for thirty-six million dollars. A similar proposal, he said, had been defeated by the DuPont Company, a charge promptly denied by the president of DuPont. On the other hand, Senator Henry Cabot Lodge, the Republican minority leader, feared that the Alabama Power Company, of which he said J. W. Worthington was a director, would be the beneficiary of the amendment under which a plant would be built at Muscle Shoals where the Alabama Power Company had riparian rights.

Underwood replied that it was flattering for Lodge to assume that the plant would go to Muscle Shoals. He pointed out that Worthington was no longer an officer of Alabama Power and that the company, which owned only the "banks" of the river at Muscle Shoals, opposed government development of the shoals. Underwood's proposal for the government to build and then lease a fertilizer plant in peacetime shocked conservatives on both sides of the aisle. Senator Lodge described the proposal as "socialistic," and Senator Thomas W. Hardwick of Georgia, after paying great tribute to Underwood, said that "the Senator from Alabama ought to apologize to Debs and every other Socialist" and that Jefferson would have left the chamber in disgust at the presentation of the Underwood amendment.

Senator Ellison D. Smith's amendment for government operation prevailed over Underwood's proposal to lease by a vote of 43 to 22. The Senate was swayed by suspicions that the leasing plan would have resulted in control of the plant by Worthington and his associates. The House quickly agreed to the Smith amendment in conference, and it became Section 124 of the National Defense Act of 1916, with an initial appropriation of twenty million dollars. To Underwood's dismay, however, Secretary of War Newton D. Baker favored a North Chattanooga site for the dam and the plant. Underwood and Senator Bankhead relentlessly pressured President Wilson to choose Muscle Shoals, charging that the Council of National Defense was dilatory and had abdicated its responsibility to a committee of chemists associated with the fertilizer interests.[8]

Paradoxically, the Corps of Engineers preferred the Warrior River, near Birmingham, as a possible location for the new power and nitrate plants. Underwood opposed this plan, questioning the accuracy of the engineering studies. He maintained that they failed to take account of low water levels for three very dry years and conversely failed to note that during flood seasons the low dams that had been planned could not utilize the heavy water flow. The construction of hydroelectric dams would close the Warrior, Birmingham's only outlet to the sea, to navigation for one to two years, he noted. Indeed, this small river is not comparable to the Tennessee as a source of water power.

Yielding to tremendous pressure from Underwood and Bankhead, President Wilson chose Sheffield, Alabama, as the site of Nitrate Plant No. 1, an experimental Haber process plant. The War Department soon afterward selected Muscle Shoals as the site for Nitrate Plant No. 2, a much larger plant where nitrates would be produced by the cyanamid process. In late February, 1918, Secretary of War Baker announced that Dam No. 2 (later known as Wilson Dam) would be built together with an auxiliary steam plant. A total of some forty-five million dollars was available for the industrial complex. The area boomed, and the influx of workers at Muscle Shoals led immediately to congested conditions and the threat of epidemics. Underwood secured a special appropriation for the Public Health Service to clean up the Muscle Shoals area.[9] The contract for the building of the large Nitrate Plant No. 2 went to the Air Nitrates Corporation, a subsidiary of American Cyanamid Company.

The armistice abruptly terminated most government activities at

8. *Congressional Record*, 64th Cong., 1st Sess., 5145–47, 5646–49, 5970–71, 6125; Birmingham *News*, March 20, May 20, 1917.
9. Birmingham *Age-Herald*, July 22, 1917, February 24, March 14, 1918.

Muscle Shoals. Nitrate Plant No. 2, the cyanamid process plant, performed as expected in a test run in November, 1918, but operation was discontinued at the end of the war. Nitrate Plant No. 1, the experimental Haber process plant, was completely unsuccessful. Wilson Dam, or Dam No. 2, was about 35 percent complete by the end of the war, and work continued on the dam and the hydroelectric plant until April, 1921. On a visit to Muscle Shoals in April, 1919, Underwood assured Tennessee Valley residents that the project would continue. Nevertheless, prospects for immediate action were bleak. The Republican Congress viewed Muscle Shoals as a Democratic project; public enthusiasm was dampened by cost overruns and rumors of vast waste, and Underwood was involved after January, 1920, in a difficult race for reelection that did not end until May of that year. In May, however, he wrote Judge J. J. Mitchell of Florence, "my hands are free to get behind the Muscle Shoals fight."[10]

Meanwhile, the War Department attempted to interest private investors in taking over the huge Nitrate Plant No. 2. Investors were offered the opportunity to convert the plant from the production of ammonium nitrates for explosives to the production of nitrate of soda for fertilizer. These efforts failed, and at the request of Secretary of War Newton D. Baker, Senator James W. Wadsworth, Jr., of New York introduced the Wadsworth-Kahn bill which provided for the creation of a government corporation, similar in some ways to the later TVA, to operate Nitrate Plant No. 2 for the production of fertilizer. Upon completion of Wilson Dam, the surplus power not needed in the production of nitrates would be "sold at the switchboard." The Wadsworth-Kahn bill was favorably reported to the Senate on May 21, 1920, but Congress adjourned a few days later, preventing any action until the next session, which began in December. Ironically, Senator Wadsworth became an advocate of private development after introducing the bill and was its major Senate opponent, whereas its major Senate defenders were Underwood, J. Thomas Heflin, and Ellison D. Smith.

10. *Ibid.*, April 6, 1919; Underwood to J. J. Mitchell, May 13, 1920, in Underwood Papers, Alabama Archives.

The Wadsworth-Kahn bill was just the type of measure that Underwood had consistently opposed as unconstitutional and as a violation of laissez-faire. Yet he argued that Muscle Shoals was an exception to the rule that the government should not interfere in business, since it was clearly authorized under the war powers. He saw it as a solution to the southern farmers' fertilizer problem, even though he admitted that the government's high dam expert and the designer of Wilson Dam, the respected Colonel Hugh L. Cooper, had said that he did not think Muscle Shoals should be used for producing fertilizer. Underwood noted, however, that Cooper had recommended that Muscle Shoals's power potential be developed. He accused the fertilizer companies of opposing the bill because they would receive no royalties from the cyanamid process as they did from the coke-oven by-product business, in which Underwood himself was financially interested. Opponents argued that the bill was a hydroelectric proposal in disguise and that the Alabama Power Company, which had the only lines to take the power from "the switchboard," would be the real beneficiary. The Wadsworth-Kahn bill passed the Senate on January 14, 1921, by a vote of 34 to 29.[11] The House refused to concur, with most Republicans acceding to their leadership and opposing the measure.

The Wadsworth-Kahn bill was unrelated to Underwood's effort in January, 1921, to secure an appropriation for the completion of Wilson Dam. The Senate voted 36 to 27 to appropriate ten million dollars on the sundry civil appropriations bill to complete the dam. Underwood successfully defended the bill against the onslaught of Republican Senators Reed Smoot and Irving Lenroot, and five Republican senators joined the Democrats to pass the appropriation. The Muscle Shoals item in the sundry civil appropriations bill faced a hostile House of Representatives, where the Republican majority was stronger. Underwood wrote his old friend, president-elect Harding, a long (for Underwood) four-page letter detailing the history of the project and asking aid in securing House passage

11. Preston J. Hubbard, *Origins of the TVA* (Nashville: Vanderbilt University Press, 1961), 5–6, 16; *Congressional Record*, 66th Cong., 3rd Sess., 1397–1404, 1196, 1397–1415.

of the appropriation. Underwood estimated that Plant No. 2 had cost seventy-five million dollars. Wilson Dam, to which he did not refer by name, would have cost sixteen million dollars by the time of Harding's inauguration, and its ultimate cost would be fifty million. The House Appropriations Committee was considering, Underwood said, a temporary halt in the construction of the dam or abandoning the project completely. A temporary halt would require an appropriation of four million dollars a year just to keep the dam from "being washed away," he asserted, adding that Wilson Dam was so vital to national defense that its abandonment would be comparable to abandoning the navy. Plant No. 1, a complete failure, was not mentioned in Underwood's letter. Having argued that the completion of the dam was good business and was essential to national defense, he shifted to politics. Abandonment of the plan to produce cheaper and greater quantities of fertilizer would, he said, "produce a very dissatisfied sentiment in the agricultural sections of the country." President-elect Harding denied Underwood's request, saying that "it is not becoming in me to dip into this matter at the present time." Nor did the president agree to Underwood's urging some months later that he include Muscle Shoals on the itinerary of his visit to Birmingham.[12]

The House struck the ten million dollar appropriation for the completion of Wilson Dam by a vote of 193 to 182. Underwood secured reinsertion of the item by a vote of 40 to 31 when the conference report reached the Senate, saying that it would be "an unprecedented thing to deliberately sacrifice the money already spent at Muscle Shoals." The House refused to concede, and in the waning hours of the session Underwood admitted defeat. Forced to withdraw the amendment from conference or bear the responsibility for the defeat of the sundry civil appropriations bill, he withdrew the Muscle Shoals amendment. He did so with a swipe at the "special interests" that he maintained had defeated the bill.

12. Birmingham *Age-Herald*, February 6, 1921; Underwood to Warren G. Harding, December 15, 1920, Harding to Underwood, January 10, September 26, 1921, all in Warren G. Harding Papers, Ohio Historical Society, Columbus.

Underwood characterized the progressives as "dreamers" and charged that Senator Irving Lenroot had "dreamed this dream" that "some power company" in Alabama was going to seize the government's property. He insisted that the dam would pay for itself.[13]

The defeat of the Wadsworth-Kahn bill, together with the defeat of the Wilson Dam item in the sundry civil appropriations bill, ended hope for immediate government completion of Muscle Shoals. The Harding administration could hardly be expected to look favorably on a project that was associated with the Wilson administration, had been widely condemned as a "white elephant," and was regarded by many as a national joke.

Meanwhile, Underwood and other senators from the Southeast urged Secretary of War John W. Weeks to lease the auxiliary steam plant at Muscle Shoals to the Alabama Power Company for a year. The lease was intended to alleviate a power shortage caused by a drought in north Alabama which threatened to close industries in the area. Such a lease, it was maintained, would not affect the disposal of the Muscle Shoals properties. The power was leased to Alabama Power Company and helped prevent a severe power shortage in the Southeast.

The irrepressible J. W. Worthington was still at work, however. At his suggestion, the chief of the Army Corps of Engineers sent Henry Ford an invitation for a bid to operate Muscle Shoals. Ford was interested, and Worthington went to Detroit armed with a letter of introduction from Underwood. Worthington prepared a proposal for Ford to present to Secretary of War Weeks, and he returned from Detroit in triumph with Ford's offer and an appointment as Ford's representative in Washington.[14]

The Ford offer, which was divided into three parts, was vaguely worded and its terms have been subject to great dispute. First, Ford agreed to lease Wilson Dam and Dam No. 3 (later Wheeler

13. *Congressional Record*, 66th Cong., 3rd Sess., 3926, 4432–35; Birmingham *News*, March 4, 1921.

14. Birmingham *Age-Herald*, November 1, 1921; Worthington in Florence (Ala.) *Times*, March 7, 1924.

Dam) for a hundred years if the government would complete construction. Rental payments would be 6 percent annually of the money to complete construction though full payment was not to be made for six years. Ford would pay $46,547 a year into an amortization fund designed to equal the government's earlier investment of $17 million in the power facilities, which was hardly a realistic amount. Ford would pay the government $55,000 annually for maintenance and repair of the dams, power facilities, and navigational structures. Second, Ford offered to purchase outright both nitrate plants including two steam plants—properties that had cost $82 million—for $5 million. Third, Ford agreed to operate Plant No. 2, which many thought to be obsolete, at its capacity for the production of fertilizer and to limit his profits on this venture to 8 percent. Under the proposal, Ford would have acquired properties costing well over $100 million for a relatively small outlay and would have had an enormous amount of surplus power. Several other offers for operation of Muscle Shoals, including one from Alabama Power Company, were largely forgotten in the excitement. The Muscle Shoals area received Ford's offer with jubilation. Land values spurted as speculators claimed that Ford would build a city to rival New York on the banks of the Tennessee. Underwood cautiously said that if Secretary of War Weeks could arrive at an agreement with Ford, he would aid in pushing the necessary legislation through. Thus Underwood appeared in the press as an arbiter of differences between Ford and Weeks. The Ford offer was, at Underwood's request, referred by *viva voce* vote to the Committee on Agriculture and Forestry rather than Military Affairs or Appropriations. Underwood consistently maintained that Muscle Shoals was valuable principally for fertilizer production, but House hearings on the Ford offer produced damaging testimony that the cyanamid process was obsolete. The Haber process was more economical, but Plant No. 2 could not be adapted to that method.[15]

The American Farm Bureau and the Farmers' Union enthusias-

15. Hubbard, *Origins of the TVA*, 28–43; Birmingham *News*, December 17, 1921, January 28, February 7, 1922; Birmingham *Age-Herald*, March 14, 1922.

tically supported Ford's offer, and Underwood was criticized in
Alabama for not pushing it. Actually, he was tied up in the Washington Conference. On April 10, however, he endorsed the Ford
proposal before the Senate Committee on Agriculture and Forestry, saying, "I consider Mr. Ford's offer the best that is before
Congress. Mr. Ford has succeeded in every industrial enterprise
he has undertaken, and I see no reason why he should fail at
Muscle Shoals. He is willing to bet $10,000,000 that he will make
good."[16] Underwood told House leaders that if they would pass a
Ford bill, he could get it through the Senate before the end of the
session, but Senator Norris denounced Ford's offer as an effort to
buy properties which cost $106 million for $5 million.[17]

The Ford offer conflicted with an appropriation of $7,500,000 in
the army appropriation bill for the completion of Wilson Dam. A
House amendment stipulated that the appropriation would be unavailable until October 1, meaning that a summer of good construction weather would be lost. Underwood regarded the House
amendment as "most unfortunate," but he was eager to approve
the army appropriation bill and to move on the Ford offer, fearing
that otherwise the entire Muscle Shoals item might be lost. With
Senator Norris, the chairman of the Committee on Agriculture and
Forestry, objecting vociferously, Underwood acceded to the House
terms that the new appropriation for Muscle Shoals be unavailable
until October 1.[18]

The Senate Committee on Agriculture and Forestry rejected the
Ford bid by a vote of 9 to 7, and several other proposals for the
leasing of Muscle Shoals were unanimously rejected. The majority
report recommended government operation with the original objectives of the National Defense Act of 1916 in mind. The third
session of the Sixty-seventh Congress faded into the fourth without
a vote on the Ford offer. Underwood complained to a Farmers'
Union official that "there has been a great combination for years to

16. Birmingham *News*, December 3, 1921, April 11, 1922; New York *Times*, April 11,
1922, p. 21.
17. Birmingham *Age-Herald*, June 6, 1922; New York *Times*, June 18, 1922, p. 17.
18. *Congressional Record*, 67th Cong., 2nd Sess., 9465–66.

kill the Muscle Shoals proposition." He recalled that he had helped secure passage in the Senate of the Wadsworth-Kahn bill for government operation, but the bill had failed in the House. Underwood mused that Muscle Shoals had been described by its critics as a "junk heap" but when Ford showed interest, "they turn around and say it is too valuable for Ford to keep."[19]

The accession of Calvin Coolidge, following the death of President Harding, appeared to increase the prospects of the Ford offer. Underwood returned to Florence on August 26, 1923, after he had announced his candidacy for the 1924 Democratic presidential nomination. Acclaimed by the largest parade in the history of the Muscle Shoals district, he visited Wilson Dam and spoke at Florence Normal School. Preceded on the platform by Dr. H. J. Willingham, the president of the college, and Congressman Edward B. Almon, Underwood declared that the government would be foolish not to accept Ford's offer. It met all the requirements set down by Secretary of War Weeks, and an adequate supply of nitrates for explosives would thus be assured for one hundred years, asserted Underwood expansively.[20]

The McKenzie bill, embracing the Ford offer, passed the House by a vote of 228 to 142 on March 10, 1924. Two weeks later, after meeting with J. W. Worthington, Underwood predicted that the Ford offer would win in the Committee on Agriculture and Forestry. On May 26 he pleaded with the Senate to bring the McKenzie bill to a vote without amendment, since any alteration would lead to withdrawal of the offer. Underwood recalled that he had cast the deciding vote in committee in passing the first irrigation act and complained that the South had often aided the West, but the West failed to reciprocate.[21]

The Senate Committee on Agriculture and Forestry reported on June 3, but as in the previous session, the majority still opposed the lease. Senator Norris declared that the reduction of the Ford offer to account for the recent sale of the Gorgas steam plant (a

19. *Senate Reports*, 67th Cong., 2nd Sess., No. 831, Pt. 1; Underwood to R. D. Bowen, December 2, 1922, in Box 6, R. D. Bowen Papers, Duke University.
20. Birmingham *Age-Herald*, August 26, 1923.
21. *Ibid*., March 11, 24, May 27, 1924.

plant on the Warrior River—not the one at Wilson Dam) to Alabama Power made the offer even less attractive than before. He
proposed creation of a "Federal Power Corporation" for government production of fertilizer and power. As the session drew to a
close, Underwood reminded Norris that he had promised to dispose of the Ford offer before adjournment. Norris then proposed
to reassemble Congress to dispose of Muscle Shoals legislation
after a recess for the party conventions. Underwood, who hoped to
be his party's nominee, declined, arguing that adjournment was an
"abstract right." Two efforts at securing unanimous consent for consideration of the Ford offer were blocked by western senators who
insisted on immediate consideration of farm price legislation. As
the session ended, Underwood obtained unanimous consent to
present the Muscle Shoals bill at the beginning of the second session in December. He denounced the "filibuster tactics" of "so-
called progressive Republicans" but stated that the Ford offer was
in a "better position" than ever before.[22]

The Ford offer had been popular initially, but Senator Norris'
bill for the creation of a government corporation to develop Muscle
Shoals as the nucleus of a "super power" district incorporating a
series of multipurpose dams gained strength in 1924. Outside of
the Tennessee Valley industries feared the competition to be created by the cheap power at Muscle Shoals and wanted it distributed over a broad area of the Southeast. The Teapot Dome scandal
fueled feelings that Ford's offer was less than a patriotic gesture,
and Underwood's southern following began to fall away.

In October, 1924, Ford withdrew his offer while Underwood was
campaigning in Washington, D.C., for the Davis presidential
ticket. Underwood refused to acknowledge that the offer was withdrawn but said that if it were, he was favorable to a similar offer
from another source. "I believe in utilizing Muscle Shoals to produce nitrate for fertilizer in time of peace and ammunition in time
of war," he said.[23]

Ford's withdrawal reduced the alternatives for operation of

22. *Senate Reports*, 68th Cong., 1st Sess., No. 678; *Congressional Record*, 68th Cong.,
1st Sess., 10278–90, 10474; Birmingham *Age-Herald*, June 18, 1924.
23. Washington (D.C.) *Star*, October 16, 1924.

Muscle Shoals to two power proposals—Norris' government operation plan and the Alabama Power Company's offer to lease and
operate the power facilities. Underwood was still determined that
the lessee be required to produce forty thousand tons of nitrogen
annually at Plant No. 2. He framed a bill similar to the Ford proposal, providing that if no contract were awarded within six months
after the completion of the Wilson Dam, the government itself
would operate the plant. Also, the lease period was reduced from
one hundred years to fifty to counter a major criticism of the Ford
offer. Underwood stated that he would withhold his bill in the hope
of a new bid similar to Ford's.[24]

The Hearst press, which had been critical of the Ford offer, vo-
ciferously attacked the Underwood bill. A reporter from Hearst's
Washington *Herald* interviewed Underwood's brother, Fred V.
Underwood, assistant general manager of Birmingham Electric
Company, who urged private leasing of Muscle Shoals. Since Bir-
mingham Electric Company bought its power from Alabama Power
Company and both companies were allegedly controlled by Gen-
eral Electric through Electric Bond and Share Corporation, the
Herald thought it had confirmed Senator Norris' charges that a
large power trust was attempting to get control of Muscle Shoals.[25]

President Coolidge's message to Congress revived the fertilizer
issue. He called for the use of the Muscle Shoals properties "primarily for the support of agriculture" and suggested his willingness
to lease or sell the property under rigid guarantees of commercial
fertilizer production. The president doubted, however, that immediate large-scale production of fertilizer was practicable. He envisioned sale of the power for general purposes until a lessee of the
fertilizer plant could, in the course of several years, make effective
use of the power. The president's plan did not allow for government operation of the complex.

Underwood played down the differences between the Underwood bill and the president's views. "The president's message," he

24. Birmingham *Age-Herald*, November 22, 1924; Birmingham *News*, November 25,
1924.
25. Washington (D.C.) *Herald*, quoted in Birmingham *Age-Herald*, November 30, 1924.

said, "is well in keeping with the bill that I have introduced."[26]
Meanwhile, he worked with Secretary of War Weeks to reconcile
the two, their differences being not inconsequential. Opposition to
the Underwood bill was far greater than to the Ford proposal, as a
number of southern senators shied away from possible identification with the "power lobby" and began to favor the Norris bill.

The Norris bill was reported to the floor by the Committee on
Agriculture and Forestry, and Underwood offered his bill as a substitute. Recalling the lack of preparation of the United States in
World War I and the shortage of nitrates created by shipping de-
lays, he compared the Muscle Shoals development to a "battleship"
which should be kept in readiness for wartime service. Muscle
Shoals, he said, provided protection against two major forces capable of destroying national life—an invading army and soil deple-
tion. He estimated that by producing fertilizer at the shoals the
price of fertilizer could be dramatically reduced. Replying to extensive public criticism that the millions spent on Muscle Shoals
had been wasted and referring without name to Alabama Power
Company's offer, he said that "a power company" was willing to pay
a rental of 5 percent for the facilities—only half a percentage point
below the figure set by the government as its minimum. He noted
that his bill set a 4 percent figure as a minimum but provided that
a higher figure could be negotiated by the secretary of war. It
would be easy, Underwood said, to lease for a higher figure if fertilizer production were not required, since power production was
more profitable. He defended the lack of a requirement in his bill
for federal regulation of the sale of surplus power under the terms
of the Federal Water Power Act, maintaining that regulation by
the public service commissions of the states involved was preferable.

Norris and his followers—now including a number of southern
senators—vigorously attacked the Underwood bill. Advocates of
government development argued that although the McKenzie bill

26. New York *Times*, December 4, 1924, p. 8; Birmingham *Age-Herald*, December 4,
1924.

embodying the Ford offer had purported to pay 4 percent interest, the actual figure was 2.79 percent. The Alabama Power Company offer, reported by Underwood at 5 percent, was figured at 3 to 3½ percent by other senators. If, Norris said, one dam was so good, why not build a series for full power development as his bill envisioned? Norris argued that production of fertilizer at Plant No. 2 was uneconomic and that the real purpose of the bill was the sale of Muscle Shoals power to Alabama Power which had the only lines to distribute it. He expressed doubt that a satisfactory bid for power and fertilizer production could be found.

Underwood reminded the Senate that there had been a shortage of nitrates in World War I, but there had been no shortage of power. Republican senators were lining up behind the Underwood bill, and four bidders were said to be angling for the project. Coolidge was reportedly opposed to Underwood's plans for financing the operation, but the senator stated that he had drawn his bill in general terms to provide latitude for amendment.[27]

Opponents of the Underwood bill offered a series of amendments—actually amounting to a filibuster. Scholarly Senator William C. Bruce of Virginia wanted civil service rules to apply to the government corporation that might operate the project temporarily. Underwood maintained that the board of five to be appointed by the president to administer the corporation would run the project in a nonpolitical way. He denounced as "ridiculous" Bruce's plan to appoint a board of "school teachers" to determine who was capable of running a great industrial plant. Bruce's amendment was tabled. An amendment proposed by Senator William J. Harris of Georgia, directed at Alabama Power Company, would have prevented subcontracting or any transfer of the lease. The Senate rejected the Harris amendment, together with most of the other obstructive amendments. Underwood defended Alabama Power saying, "I hold no brief for the Alabama Power Company, I have been fighting for Ford's offer against the Alabama Power Co. for

27. *Congressional Record*, 68th Cong., 2nd Sess., 109–27, 527; Birmingham *News*, December 7, 1924; Birmingham *Age-Herald*, December 8, 1924.

four years; but what I want to do is to produce nitrogen and fertilizer under the terms of the bill and sell surplus power to do it profitably."[28] Senator Kenneth McKellar of Tennessee, recently converted to the Norris bill, tried to show that the Underwood bill was in the interest of the Alabama Power Company by printing its offer in parallel columns with the Underwood bill. Underwood denied that he had consulted with Alabama Power Company officials in drawing up his bill and said they did not expect to make a bid. The power companies preferred the more profitable power business to the production of fertilizer, he said. Speaking to McKellar's fear that Alabama Power would control Muscle Shoals, Underwood said that McKellar had "built up a ghost and dreamed a dream."[29] Indeed, McKellar's charges were unfounded. Although Alabama Power Company maintained that its offer to lease Muscle Shoals was still good, the company had no interest in a lease with tight fertilizer guarantees as provided in the Underwood bill.

Underwood told the Senate on December 12 that President Coolidge's message and a "personal conversation" with him indicated that the president would sign his bill. Asked if Coolidge would sign a bill for government operation without leasing features, Underwood said that such was doubtful. A flurry of amendments and substitutes were presented from both sides of the aisle, although none seemed to have administration support.[30]

In the midst of this uproar, the Hearst newspapers charged in an editorial that the Underwood bill was a "steal" and a "greater scandal than Teapot Dome." The editorial, written by E. J. Clapp, continued in a virulent personal attack on Underwood: "He is an able man, capable of high statesmanship but since his entrance into Congress his ability and his statesmanship have often been at the service of the railroads and other great corporations. . . . Now his talents are working for the power trust, General Electric, which owns Electric Bond and Share which owns Alabama Power Company." The editorial asserted that the government had spent $135

28. *Congressional Record*, 68th Cong., 2nd Sess., 271, 299, 303.
29. *Ibid.*, 397.
30. *Ibid.*, 526–27.

million on Muscle Shoals and that it was a crime to "give it away" for a 4 percent rental on the cost of Wilson Dam or about a third of the cost of the entire project.[31]

Underwood irately defended himself on the Senate floor on December 13. Glowering at Senator Norris, he said: "This slimy snake that crawls through an editorial column bearing misrepresentations and slime is too cowardly to attack the president of the United States and seeks by innuendo and charge to attack other people who are only carrying out exactly what the president of the United States recommended." Underwood charged, although he lacked proof, that the editorial was "purchased by interests who are trying to gobble this power." He demanded that the author of the editorial be subpoenaed to appear before the Senate Judiciary Committee.[32] The New York *American*, Hearst's editorial flagship, viewed the ensuing investigation as "a new attack upon freedom of the press." Underwood read on the floor of the Senate a bulletin of the National Fertilizer Association in an effort to prove that the editorial was inspired by the fertilizer trust.[33]

The Senate Judiciary Committee questioned E. J. Clapp, the editor of the Hearst newspapers, on December 19, 1924. Clapp said that he did not question Underwood's motives, but he based his statement that Underwood was a servant of special interests upon his record. He listed numerous measures in which he thought Underwood had served these special interests. The list included the bill for a dam across the Coosa River, vetoed by President Taft, bills for a dam at Muscle Shoals, and the Esch-Cummins Railway Act. Clapp could hardly have expected equitable treatment from Underwood's Senate colleagues, but his listing of the Esch-Cummins Act as a measure passed for the advantage of special interests did not endear him to the Judiciary Committee's chairman, Senator Cummins. The committee concluded that the editorial "was neither fair nor honest" and that Clapp made no

31. Washington (D.C.) *Herald*, quoted in Birmingham *Age-Herald*, December 14, 1924.
32. Birmingham *Age-Herald*, December 14, 1924.
33. New York *American*, December 15, 1924; New York *Times*, December 17, 1924, p. 11.

claim that any evidence existed to reflect on Underwood's integrity. The controversy continued, however, since Hearst reasserted in a personal editorial that Underwood was a servant of the corporations. Hearst said: "My private opinion of Senator Underwood with whom I served four years in Congress is that he is a delightful man personally, but one of the most persistent supporters of the great financial corporations and trusts who ever sat in the Senate."[34] Why had the Hearst press turned against Underwood so strongly? Hearst was Underwood's Democratic colleague in the House from 1903 to 1907, and in 1903 Underwood accompanied Hearst's Committee on Irrigation and Arid Lands to Salt River Valley, Arizona. In 1912 Hearst backed Champ Clark for the Democratic nomination but supported Underwood's Georgia campaign in an effort to block Wilson. In Tennessee an angry dispute erupted between the Clark and Underwood supporters, but relations between Hearst and Underwood remained friendly. In 1913 the Hearst press supported Underwood in two major policy differences with the Wilson administration—Underwood's sponsorship of the clause granting United States merchant ships a 5 percent tariff advantage and his opposition to the repeal of Panama tolls. Hearst and Underwood had no significant relations after 1913. In 1924 Hearst, harboring presidential ambitions of his own, gave a Lucullan dancing party for prominent Democrats at the Democratic convention, but neither Underwood nor Underwood's friend, Governor Alfred E. Smith, was invited. There is, however, no evidence of any direct conflict between Underwood's and Hearst's presidential ambitions. Evidently, Hearst was impelled to attack Underwood because of the publisher's longstanding advocacy of prohibition and of municipal ownership of public utilities; Hearst also may have been angered by Underwood's friendship with Governor Smith, his archenemy, and with Edward B. McLean, his competitor as the publisher of the Washington *Star*.[35]

An amendment to the Underwood bill, offered by Senator Elli-

34. *Senate Reports*, 68th Congress, 2nd Sess., No. 823; Birmingham *Age-Herald*, December 20, 21, 1924.
35. W. A. Swanberg, *Citizen Hearst* (New York: Scribner, 1961), 436–40.

son D. Smith on December 16, required that the government hold the Muscle Shoals property for experimental purposes for an undetermined number of years. The Smith amendment envisioned government operation, and its defeat by a vote of 49 to 32 was a significant victory for Underwood's private operation plan. Underwood said that he was now assured of the bill's passage, but Republican Senator James E. Watson, after a visit to the White House, reflected President Coolidge's doubts about the Underwood bill. Watson said that though he preferred the Underwood bill to the Norris bill, he thought it better to refer the question to a commission for settlement.[36]

Underwood charged on December 17 that Norris was engaged in a filibuster. He ridiculed the Nebraskan as an impractical dreamer who believed, as did the Populists, that "the government had more sense and more capacity to do business than private individuals." Underwood said that Norris' plan to produce a million horsepower on the Tennessee was a "lovely dream" but that Congress would not appropriate the necessary money. In effect, he said, there was only two hundred thousand horsepower available at Muscle Shoals, and half of that would be needed for the production of nitrates.[37]

Senator Norris replied caustically that the Underwood bill was "a concession so great it will make Teapot Dome look like a pinhead." He admitted that since the president was opposed to his bill it had no chance and stigmatized Underwood's bill as an administration measure, despite Coolidge's failure to support Underwood.[38]

Charges in the Hearst newspapers that the Underwood bill served the interest of the power trust drew blood. Senator Smoot, the Republican majority leader, announced after conferring with President Coolidge that the administration favored the setting up of a commission of cabinet members to decide the fate of Muscle Shoals. A few days later the Washington *Star* reported that the

36. New York *Times*, December 17, 1924, p. 11.
37. *Congressional Record*, 68th Cong., 2nd Sess., 712–14.
38. New York *Times*, December 18, 1924, p. 1.

president, influenced principally by Secretary Weeks, had decided that it would be "economically wrong" to allow the lessee to recoup his losses in making fertilizer by selling electricity. Underwood said, however, that he had no information that the president was unfavorable to his bill.[39]

The long, tedious battle over Muscle Shoals was interrupted by the Christmas recess of 1924 during which Underwood was ill with the grippe. Senator Norris, who had been conducting a slowdown that Underwood termed a filibuster, agreed to bring the question to a vote on January 8. Underwood calculated that he had lost two votes during the debate but had also gained two. The Committee of the Whole voted 48 to 37 to replace the Norris bill with the Underwood bill. It was an encouraging majority, but the Underwood bill still faced three major hurdles: the Wadsworth bill, a substitute that did not stipulate the amount of nitrate that must be produced; the Jones bill, which would have referred the Muscle Shoals problem to a commission of cabinet officers; and further dilatory tactics by Norris.[40]

A curious cycle began on January 13 when the Jones bill was substituted for the Underwood bill by a vote of 46 to 33. Later the same day the Norris bill, now "sweetened" to promise the eventual production of forty thousand tons of nitrate annually, was adopted by a vote of 40 to 39. Underwood, however, brought his bill up again. The circle was completed when the Underwood bill replaced the Norris bill 46 to 38, with administration senators swinging behind the Underwood measure again. A second vote on the Underwood bill confirmed its passage by a vote of 50 to 30.[41]

In conference the Senate's Underwood bill normally would have been handled by unfriendly Senate conferees, the three ranking members of the Senate Committee on Agriculture and Forestry, Norris, Charles L. McNary, and Ellison D. Smith. Senator Cummins, the president *pro tem* of the Senate, denied Underwood's

39. Birmingham *News*, December 21, 1924; Washington (D.C.) *Star*, quoted in Birmingham *Age-Herald*, January 5, 1925.
40. Birmingham *Age-Herald*, January 8, 9, 1925.
41. *Congressional Record*, 68th Cong., 2nd Sess., 1736–40, 1795–1808.

request that other conferees be accepted. Underwood was narrowly defeated in an appeal in which he attempted to name his
own slate of conferees, Senators Henry W. Keyes, William B.
McKinley, and Harrison. Norris, McNary, and Smith played the
role of injured martyrs and resigned. They were replaced by Keyes
and McKinley of the Underwood slate and John B. Kendrick of
Wyoming, an opponent of the bill. Underwood declined to serve
on the committee himself but agreed that the new slate was satisfactory.[42]

The conferees attempted to reconcile the Underwood bill with
the House's Ford proposal, basically accepting the Underwood
bill. The lessee's cost was reduced by allocating a third of the cost
of Wilson Dam to navigation. Dam No. 3 was to be built and leased
on terms similar to those for Dam No. 2. The lessee was allowed
ten years (as compared with six in the Senate bill) to reach production of forty thousand tons of fertilizer. The conference bill allowed
a much greater profit for fertilizer production, 8 percent as compared with 1 percent in the Senate bill, but closer scrutiny of profits was provided. A seemingly minor amendment allowed the lessee to use electric production for "other related uses" in addition
to the production of nitrates. Underwood argued that the conference had "perfected the measure" as a fertilizer bill. Norris
charged that the conference bill was new legislation, especially the
provision for the leasing of Dam No. 3. Senator Cummins ruled for
Norris. Underwood's appeal from the ruling lost 45 to 41. The bill
was returned to conference, and there was little hope that it could
be passed before the March 3 adjournment.

Underwood appeared undaunted. Barring a filibuster, he said,
"we will pass the bill before March." A filibuster, he admitted,
would block passage, but, he said, "We will get a bill in another
session, and it will be the fertilizer bill. The president favors a
fertilizer bill and if I know him at all he will stick." But he feared
that they might never get another bill that would provide for the

42. Birmingham *Age-Herald*, January 18, 29, 1925; *Congressional Record*, 68th Cong.,
2nd Sess., 2557.

construction of Dam No. 3 since Secretary Weeks opposed that feature. Underwood sat with the conferees as they recast the conference bill in accordance with Senate rules, a task he described as requiring "scientific operation" and much work. Senator Charles Curtis, the Republican majority leader, aided Underwood in the otherwise hopeless task of securing passage of the modified Underwood bill before the end of the session.[43] The second conference bill was substantially like the first, and Norris again filibustered, aided by Senator McKellar. The Underwood bill died.

Just before adjournment, however, a coalition of those opposed to government operation passed the Madden resolution asking that the president appoint a commission and recommend a course of action on Muscle Shoals. President Coolidge, after conferring with Underwood, announced the appointment of the Muscle Shoals Inquiry Commission. Three members favored private operation: Representative John C. McKenzie of Illinois, chairman and author of the Ford bill; former senator Nathaniel Dial of South Carolina, a University of Virginia classmate of Underwood's; and Russell F. Bower, an official of the Farm Bureau and the National Grange appointed at Underwood's request. The two other members, Harry A. Curtis, a professor of chemical engineering at Yale University, and William McClellan, a former president of the American Institute of Electrical Engineering, eventually favored leasing.

During the Ford fight, Alabama Power Company offered to buy the power produced by Dam No. 2, but neither Congress nor the administration was interested in the proposal. Underwood and the administration were committed to a fertilizer bill, and obviously Norris, with his harsh accusations against the "power trust," could not favor such a lease. Since Congress failed to act, however, the president agreed for Secretary Weeks to ask for short term bids for the power which would soon be generated at Wilson Dam. Underwood attempted unsuccessfully to persuade the president to reverse Weeks's action. But the power was sold, on a short-term ba-

43. Birmingham *Age-Herald*, February 7, 1925; Birmingham *News*, February 15, 1925; New York *Times*, February 20, 1925, p. 5; Birmingham *Age-Herald*, February 24, 25, 1925.

sis, to Alabama Power Company, the only bidder, at two mills a kilowatt hour for an estimated hundred thousand kilowatts a day.

The Muscle Shoals Inquiry Commission reported to the president on November 14, 1925. By a majority of three to two, with the two technicians in the minority, the commission recommended the leasing of Muscle Shoals in a manner similar to that proposed in the Underwood bill. The recommendation that Muscle Shoals be devoted to munitions and fertilizer and that the power and fertilizer facilities be leased together accorded with the Underwood bill. The commission's report, like the Underwood bill, was modeled after the Ford offer.[44]

Underwood and Norris were again locked in combat. Underwood, saying that compromise with Norris was impossible, concluded: "The battle cannot be avoided. The Senate after going to the matter, must vote for private or government operation." Norris reportedly felt the same way.

Underwood and Coolidge conferred immediately preceding the president's annual message to Congress, but the president's message disappointed Underwood. Although Coolidge agreed with the majority report that Muscle Shoals must be dedicated to fertilizer production, he differed in opposing even temporary government operation. Coolidge urged the creation of a small joint congressional committee to make recommendations for sale of the plants to the highest bidder. The House quickly passed the Snell resolution to create a joint congressional committee to seek bids for the leasing of Muscle Shoals—the president's suggestion of an outright sale was rejected.[45]

In the Senate the Snell resolution went to Norris' hostile Committee on Agriculture and Forestry. Underwood opposed sending the bill there, but since Senate majority leader Charles Curtis insisted on the referral, Norris could not be circumvented. Underwood said that he would insist upon a report in a reasonable length of time, and Norris replied reassuringly that he would insist that

44. Hubbard, *Origins of the TVA*, 171–76.
45. Birmingham *Age-Herald*, December 13, 1925; Hubbard, *Origins of the TVA*, 177–79.

some disposition of Muscle Shoals be made before the session's end. Even so, it was February 4, 1926, before Norris' committee reported the Snell resolution favorably by a vote of 11 to 5. Norris had lost control of his committee for the first time.[46]

Underwood was ill and absent from Congress for about a month in late February and early March. In Underwood's absence, Senator Heflin managed the Snell resolution and fought savagely with Senator McKellar, who argued that a large chemical company, presumably American Cyanamid, had conspired with Alabama Power Company to divide profits from the project. Senator Thaddeus H. Caraway of Arkansas succeeded in amending the Snell resolution to require a regional distribution of the power produced at Muscle Shoals. With Underwood off the floor, Heflin stood almost alone among Democrats in fighting to maintain Muscle Shoals for fertilizer production. The resolution cleared the Senate—this time with the Caraway amendment attached. The resolution also permitted separate leases of the power and nitrate facilities. Other amendments to the Snell resolution revealed a growing interest in the power aspect of Muscle Shoals. However, the major pressure on Congress for passage of the Snell resolution was the Farm Bureau, which objected to the Caraway amendment. President Coolidge continued to insist on the production of nitrates, and it was rumored that Ford was again interested.

During the hearings of the joint committee only two bids received serious consideration—those of American Cyanamid and Alabama Power Company. Both companies offered to produce fertilizer at Muscle Shoals, limit profits to 8 percent, and produce whatever the market required. American Cyanamid proposed to produce fertilizer in connection with power and to utilize most of the excess power in the immediate area of the plants. Alabama Power Company, representing a group of southeastern power companies, proposed to create two separate corporations to handle the fertilizer and power aspects. The power companies planned to use the Haber process, thus using considerably less electricity than the

46. Birmingham *Age-Herald*, January 17, February 4, 1925.

cyanamid process and leaving considerably more electricity for distribution over a wider area of the South than was possible under
the American Cyanamid proposal. The power companies offered to
pay some two hundred million dollars during the fifty year lease as
compared to eighty-six million dollars offered by American Cyanamid.

In the hearings on the measures, R. F. Bower of the Farm Bureau and J. W. Worthington appeared as witnesses in behalf of the
American Cyanamid offer. Several government officials testified for
the power company offer and charged that American Cyanamid
planned, once it got the lease, to use the obsolescence of Plant No.
2 as the excuse for abandoning fertilizer production. The joint committee accepted the advice of its advisory board and recommended
acceptance of the Alabama Power Company offer, acknowledging
that the fertilizer guarantee was weak in both proposals.[47]

Underwood endorsed the American Cyanamid Company bid in
late May, 1926. He admitted the superiority of the Alabama Power
Company offer as a power proposition but noted the simplicity
with which the power company with dual corporate organizations
could retire from the fertilizer business and retain its power lease.
On the other hand, he noted that an American Cyanamid subsidiary had built Plant No. 2 and that the company was experienced in
the fertilizer business. Underwood insisted that the guarantees of
fertilizer production by American Cyanamid were better than
those of the power companies.[48]

The split between the administration, which now favored the
power company offer, and Underwood's followers, who favored the
American Cyanamid offer, meant failure for Underwood unless
Coolidge changed his mind. Underwood realized that there was
little hope of the American Cyanamid offer being accepted in the
second or short session of the Sixty-ninth Congress. In February,
1927, Governor Bibb Graves of Alabama asserted rather preposter-
ously that since the beds of rivers belong to the state through

47. Underwood to Braxton B. Comer, March 8, 1926, in Braxton B. Comer Papers,
University of North Carolina, Chapel Hill; Hubbard, *Origins of the TVA*, 181–86.
48. New York *Times*, May 22, 1926, p. 26.

which they run, the federal government was squatting on Alabama's land, and he proposed that the state take over the Muscle Shoals development. This absurd idea was a ploy to force action, and Underwood went with the Alabama congressional delegation and the governor to discuss the claim with the president. On the Senate floor, however, Underwood said that he would have to study Alabama's proposal before committing himself to it. On the more reasonable question of leasing the properties to the power companies or to American Cyanamid Company, Underwood stated that without a "miracle" Muscle Shoals could not be disposed of at that session. Senator Harrison unsuccessfully attempted to reinvigorate the Underwood bill by attaching it to a bill for the building of Boulder Dam.[49] Plagued by illness and ennui and looking forward to retirement, Underwood had lost his zest for the fight.

Underwood was to retire from Congress on March 4, 1927, but the long fight for control of Muscle Shoals was far from over. Norris eventually won the battle. He secured passage of one bill for government operation which was vetoed by Coolidge, another which was vetoed by Hoover, and a third which was signed by Franklin D. Roosevelt, creating the Tennessee Valley Authority. One of the dams in the system is named for Norris, but not surprisingly, none is named for Underwood.

Republican control of Congress, augmented by the accession of Harding in 1921, meant that private leasing was the only way to put Muscle Shoals to work at once. The Ford offer, inspired by Underwood's friend Worthington, seemed to offer great promise to the Alabama part of the Tennessee Valley and to farmers in the state generally. Underwood had been elected to the Senate in 1914 and again in 1920 with powerful majorities in the Tennessee Valley, where his interest in Muscle Shoals was appreciated. To have opposed the Ford offer would have meant risking his strong north Alabama base of support. The declining popularity of private control plans in Congress is shown in Underwood's inability to muster

49. *Ibid.*, February 25, 1927, p. 3; *Congressional Record*, 69th Cong., 2nd Sess., 4535; Birmingham *Age-Herald*, February 26, 1927.

support for the Ford offer from the Democratic senators of the states adjacent to Alabama—Pat Harrison of Mississippi excepted.

Withdrawal of the Ford offer resulted in the Underwood bill, designed in the hope that Ford would renew his interest. Norris viewed Coolidge and Underwood as partners opposed to government operation, but the lack of cooperation between the president and the Alabama senator was seen in Underwood's refusal to endorse the offer of the southeastern power combine favored by Coolidge. Underwood seemed genuinely devoted to the use of Muscle Shoals to produce fertilizer, an obsolete but politically alluring idea. However, Underwood's preference for American Cyanamid's offer, as contrasted with the administration-supported Alabama Power proposal, prevented congressional approval of a lease.

The fight for Muscle Shoals is usually presented as a classic conflict of government versus private control. In the Wilson administration, however, Underwood supported two government operation measures. In the first, Section 124 of the National Defense Act of 1916, though he preferred the inclusion of a leasing feature, he was agreeable to the government operation plan. At the end of the war he favored the Wadsworth-Kahn bill for government operation, preferring government operation to abandonment of the project. After the withdrawal of the Ford offer, Underwood proposed a bill that provided for government operation if leasing plans failed as appeared likely.

A congressional committee in 1930, a year after Underwood's death, investigated the "power trust" and failed to prove the angry charges that Underwood and Norris had hurled at each other. Worthington avoided testifying, taking refuge first in Tate Springs and later, appropriately enough, at the Henry Ford Hospital in Detroit. Nevertheless, ample testimony demonstrated that Worthington's Tennessee River Improvement Association and the American Farm Bureau served as foils for American Cyanamid, a large producer of fertilizer. Underwood's claims that the "fertilizer trust" opposed him were, therefore, ludicrous. On the other hand, Norris' charge that Underwood's plans to produce fertilizer masked a plot to turn the shoals over to Alabama Power, with whom Underwood often had acted in concert until 1916, was erroneous. Alabama Power and American Cyanamid were genuine antagonists for control of the shoals, and Underwood sided with American Cyanamid against the largest corporation in Alabama. Although Worthington's influence on Underwood was strong, the senator was genuinely convinced that the shoals had value principally as a fertilizer producer.[50] And though Norris' plan for the shoals was more practical, imaginative, and comprehensive than Underwood's, without the interest Underwood focused upon Muscle Shoals, the development might well have gone to another area.

50. New York *Times*, February 12, 1930, p. 9, April 2, 1930, p. 5.

CHAPTER XIV

The Democratic Nomination of 1924 and the Fight Against the Klan

Soon after the Democratic victories in the congressional elections of 1922, Underwood had announced that he would resign as minority leader of the Senate Democrats at the end of the Sixty-seventh Congress on March 3, 1923. Despite his health problems, he thought that after a few months rest he could campaign effectively for the Democratic nomination of 1924. Had he been elected, he would have been almost sixty-seven years old at the end of his term.

Although agonizing publicly over the nomination in 1923, Underwood had been planning to make the race for over three years. He wrote a friend who, like himself, had anticipated the defeat of Governor Cox in 1920 that although he was not as "keen about the presidential nomination as I was eight years ago, yet I should be more than glad to have [the nomination] and make the fight win or lose." Bertha, a hero-worshiper almost without peer, urged him to enter the race, although Oscar, Jr., then a Washington attorney, thought the political climate unfavorable with prohibition and Ku Klux Klan sentiment running strong.[1]

The Alabama legislature endorsed his candidacy in January and February, 1923, and by late February the New York *Times* rated him as a "sure candidate." William Gibbs McAdoo was the other major contender, but if Henry Ford entered the race, the Detroit

1. Oscar W. Underwood to J. J. Willett, November 7, 1920, in J. J. Willett Papers, Samford University, Birmingham; interview with O. W. Underwood, Jr., November 11, 1952.

automaker was expected to run strong in the tracks of his Model
T's and gain strength among farmers from his offer to lease Muscle
Shoals. Ford's withdrawal in late 1923 left little doubt in the minds
of most observers that Underwood would overpower the craggy-
faced, Georgia-born McAdoo in much of the South. Governor
Alfred E. Smith of New York, an avowed opponent of prohibition,
was viewed as an effective check to McAdoo's ambitions in the East
and a potential ally of Underwood if Smith himself were eliminated.[2]

Underwood considered his southern background to be his major
asset. He was well and favorably known throughout the South as
an advocate of tariff reduction and the operation of Muscle Shoals
as a source of cheap fertilizer for farmers. Planning his appeal as a
sectional candidate in much the same fashion that he had sought
the Democratic nomination in 1912, Underwood wrote his son: "I
think the South should have a chance to lead the Democratic Party
and if I were the man from the South chosen to lead, I would
appreciate the honor and the opportunity above all things political."[3] Nationally, Underwood was recognized as a hard-working and
astute congressional leader whose name had been before the nation since his election as House majority leader in 1911. A warm,
gregarious person, his career as a parliamentarian gave him an urbanity and suavity that made him an exceedingly attractive personality.

Underwood's political liabilities were less apparent. His opposition to women's suffrage was reflected in a poll of the General Federation of Women's Clubs which gave him seventh place among all
presidential candidates; he trailed President Coolidge 52,274 to
2,366. Fundamentalist southerners disliked his opposition to prohibition and identified him with the Roman Catholic Church. Bob
Jones, the high priest of this group, said that "the whiskey people,
the Roman Catholics and the lawless foreigners" were as much for

    2. New York *Times*, February 26, 1923, p. 2; see, for example, *ibid.*, June 3, 1923, Sec.
8, p. 1.
    3. Underwood to O. W. Underwood, Jr., May 20, 1923, in Oscar W. Underwood Papers,
Alabama Department of Archives and History, Montgomery.

Underwood as they were for Al Smith.[4] Charges that Underwood was pro-Catholic continued despite the fact that he was a member of the Episcopal Church of the Epiphany in Washington. His family were identified with the Church of the Advent in Birmingham, but he seldom attended. In Birmingham the Committee of Allied Labor Organizations denounced his candidacy in August, 1923, saying that his career was "characterized by his lack of sympathy with the great masses of the people and by subserviency to the selfish big business and financial interests."[5] Also, Underwood could expect opposition from the aging but still powerful William Jennings Bryan with whom he had feuded for most of his political career.

Underwood had had strong appeal for Roman Catholic political leaders in his campaign for the presidential nomination in 1912. Yet his capacity to appeal to Irish Catholics was limited in 1924 by his lack of support for Irish independence resolutions passed during the fight over the Treaty of Versailles. Senator Borah had sponsored in June, 1919, a resolution endorsing Irish independence and asking the American delegation to Versailles to hear representatives of the Sinn Fein. Underwood failed to participate in the lopsided 60 to 1 vote approving the Borah resolution, later explaining that he had been "down town at one of the departments" and that he had been paired with Senator Harding. He did not say which way he was paired. Nine months later, in March, 1920, Underwood opposed the Gerry resolution, a reservation to the Treaty of Versailles that advocated independence for Ireland. Widely regarded as the death knell of the treaty, the Gerry resolution was added to Lodge's already lengthy list of reservations by an overwhelming vote. Underwood explained his opposition to this resolution, saying that although he favored Irish independence, he thought that dominion status was as much as Britain would concede and that independence would certainly not be granted at the suggestion of the United States. Neither the Borah nor the Gerry

4. Oxnard (Calif.) *Courier*, January 5, 1924; Bob Jones to Bibb Graves, January 7, 1924, in Campaign File—Alabama, Underwood Papers, Alabama Archives.
5. New York *Times*, August 7, 1923, p. 19.

resolution had any practical effect. The president rejected the advice contained in the Borah resolution, and the Gerry reservation died with the Treaty of Versailles. Nevertheless, Underwood's failure to favor Irish independence legislation was displeasing to Irish-Americans, some of whom had aided his fight for the nomination in 1912.[6]

Highly restrictive immigration legislation was introduced in the spring of 1924, and public sentiment ran strong for shutting off the influx of immigrants—especially from Southern and Eastern Europe. Underwood had long favored restrictive immigration legislation, sponsoring a literacy test bill as early as 1902, voting for the Burnett Act of 1917 which contained a literacy test, and as late as 1921 voting for an unsuccessful amendment to the Johnson Act of 1921 to suspend immigration for two years. Yet the introduction of the Johnson bill of 1924, which proposed to further reduce immigration by cutting the quota from 3 percent to 2 percent, presented a dilemma to Underwood as he busily campaigned for the Democratic presidential nomination. The Johnson bill, which was favored by almost everyone on both sides of the aisle, excluded Japanese immigrants altogether and moved the base for figuring the new reduced quota from 1910 to 1890. The Japanese exclusion feature was hardly an issue after Masanao Hanihara, Japanese minister to the United States, warned of "grave consequences" if that provision became law. The angry senators unanimously voted for Japanese exclusion. Underwood favored the new bill, which would reduce the flow of immigrants by two thirds, and he approved of Japanese exclusion. He objected, however, to moving the date upon which the quota was computed from 1910 to 1890—a feature designed to discriminate against southern and eastern Europeans. Carefully assessing the various nationalities, he objected to the assumption that Prussians were more desirable immigrants than Czechs, Poles, Yugoslavs, and Italians. He was especially solicitous of the Italians, who had fought with his son in battle. Although he

6. *Ibid.*, June 7, 1919, p. 1; Underwood to Joseph H. Lyons, March 16, 1920, in Underwood Papers, Alabama Archives.

did not say so, Birmingham's Italian community had fought for him politically, and his presidential aspirations depended upon Italian support. Despite this frankly racist evaluation, Underwood concluded that the Democratic party had departed from the principles of Jefferson and was submitting to passion and prejudice. His concluding remarks against prejudice were interpreted by the press as a challenge to the Ku Klux Klan. Despite these objections, Underwood failed to vote with the six senators who opposed the new immigration bill with the objectionable 1890 basis intact.[7]

Underwood failed to appreciate the threat of McAdoo's candidacy to his southern base of support. As a son-in-law of Woodrow Wilson, McAdoo was the legatee of much of Wilson's political strength, especially on the League of Nations issue. His fiscal policies as secretary of the treasury when he worked assiduously for agricultural credits had endeared him to farmers, and his labor policies as wartime director general of the railroads pleased the powerful railroad brotherhoods. Veterans were impressed by McAdoo's role in creating the veterans insurance program of World War I and were further ingratiated by his endorsement of a veterans bonus after the war. In 1922 McAdoo moved to California, a more hospitable climate for his prohibition views than was New York. He had strong support in the West and in the South, where he capitalized upon his Georgia birth.[8]

Late in February, 1923, Underwood and his wife left the United States for a tour of Europe and the Middle East with the dual purpose of recovering his health and learning first-hand of the European situation about which he knew so little. Underwood's departing statement that he would give the question of running "very serious consideration" left little doubt that he would announce his candidacy upon his return from Europe. The Washington *Star* cautioned that if Underwood were to become a candidate, it would be

7. *Congressional Record*, 68th Cong., 1st Sess., 6457–60, 6649; New York *Times*, April 12, 1924, p. 1, April 17, 1924, p. 5.
8. Lee N. Allen, "The McAdoo Campaign for the Presidential Nomination in 1924," *Journal of Southern History*, XXIX (May, 1963), 211, 213, 217.

necessary for him to be "clear and unequivocal" in denouncing the Ku Klux Klan.[9]

The Underwoods sailed for Europe on the British ship *Adriatic*, a steerage vessel that had accommodations for 126 cabin passengers for the cold and stormy Atlantic voyage. After stopping at the Madeira Islands, they arrived at Gibraltar. They visited Algeria which Underwood described unimaginatively as "like Florida but drier." Plans for travel in Spain were deferred because of bad travel conditions. They stopped at Nice, drove along the old Roman road to Naples, took the ship again to Athens and left the *Adriatic* again at Haifa, Palestine.

As with so many travelers the Holy Land was the high point of the trip. They went to Acre, then drove to Nazareth by automobile past Jacob's well, where they drank the water. In Nazareth they were shown the room where Joseph's carpenter shop was said to have been. Underwood was moved by the experience, remarking, "I shall not forget Nazareth in Galilee, little and lovely, nestled high in its storied hills." They drove along the Turkish military road from Nazareth to Jerusalem, the route followed by General Edmund H. Allenby who had driven Turkish troops before him. At Herod's Temple, where the Germans had had gun emplacements, they saw "Biblical-looking shepherds with their dogs."

The modern Jewish farms, equipped with tractors, impressed the Alabama senator. In Jerusalem, Underwood was greatly interested in a huge cave known as "Solomon's Stable," allegedly the founding site of the Masonic order. The cave had been rediscovered some fifty years before by an American who had lost his small dog in a crevice leading into the chamber. The evening that Underwood saw the cave, he returned to the Allenby Hotel to awaken Mrs. Underwood and tell her of the huge chamber as large as that of the House of Representatives. Mrs. Underwood's response, the true reaction of a dog fancier, was "Oscar, did they find the dog?"

From Jerusalem the Underwoods traveled by rail to Cairo, ac-

9. Birmingham *News*, February 24, 1923; Washington (D.C.) *Star*, quoted in Birmingham *News*, February 28, 1923.

companied by a Massachusetts couple, Republican Representative Allen T. Treadway and his wife. At the Continental Hotel in Cairo, the Underwoods and the Treadways met Howard Carter, Lord Carnavon's aide in opening King Tut's (Tutankh-Amon's) tomb. Carter gave them passes to the tombs at Thebes, and they traveled up the Nile to Thebes, Karnak, and Aswan Dam. Thinking of his own battles for the utilization of water power at Muscle Shoals, Underwood said: "In that land where the soil is still ploughed with a crooked stick, they are more alive to the value of rivers and water than we are in America."[10] From Cairo they took the *Lotus*, a very good French boat, on a rough crossing of the Mediterranean through the Straits of Messina, viewing the Italian cities along the shore and the Island of Stromboli with its volcano. They landed at Marseilles and registered at the Splendide Hotel, glad to be back "in the Western Europe, so much nearer to home."

Bad weather again forced them to cancel plans to visit Spain, and the Underwoods headed for Switzerland which they found pleasantly clean and prosperous. But after they cabled Oscar, Jr., from Interlaken that they would spend several more days or the rest of April in Switzerland, the weather turned cold, and the Underwoods decided to leave the mountains for Nancy, France. They traveled by rail, stopping in Lucerne, Basel, Strasbourg, and Luneville. In Luneville they rented a car and retraced some of the World War I routes of Oscar, Jr., who had been a captain with the 42nd Division. They drove up the Moselle Valley, followed the German lines to Verdun, thence around the French lines, through the underground passages in Fort Vaux, past the trenches, and back into Verdun for lunch. They returned from Verdun along the Meuse River, observing the German and American trenches. The French monument to American valor at Flirey where the Americans first struck the Germans in the St. Mihiel salient impressed Underwood as "a wonderful piece of art." Soon they came to one of the American cemeteries that "told the price" of American victory.

10. Birmingham *News*, July 8, 9, 1923.

Continuing by way of Toul and Bar-le-Duc up the old Roman road to the Field of Attilla, they went on to the battlefield where the 42nd Division of the United States, aided by the French, halted the last German drive. The senator remarked: "We went for miles when it did not seem to me [that] there was a hundred feet square that was not cut up with trenches or shell holes and the barbed wire was still there. It is a more desolate place than a desert." Noting the poverty, he felt that the French peasants were barely able to eke out a living. Continuing to Paris via the route of the 42nd Division—Rheims, Frimes, Deringes, Fereen-Tardenois, Serges, Chateau Thierry, Belleau Wood, and Meaux—the senator and his wife visited friends in Paris with whom Oscar, Jr., had practiced law after the war. [11]

Arriving in London "fed up with sightseeing" they settled down in a hotel in the center of the city. A few days later they were in Edinburgh. The weather continued cold, and the Underwoods retreated southward to Harrogate in Yorkshire, a spa town and a nice place to rest up before their trip to Liverpool to board the *Adriatic* for the return voyage. Relenting from his decision not to make speeches, Underwood spoke to a civic club at Harrogate, where he described England and the United States as the bulwarks against socialism and communism. [12]

The senator said little about politics while on the trip, although Oscar, Jr., wrote him encouragingly about his presidential prospects and advised him on the proper approach. Writing from Nancy on April 27 Underwood said that the Eighteenth Amendment should be strictly enforced except for the manufacture and sale of sacramental, medicinal, and nonintoxicating beverages. He wrote from Harrogate that he did not feel that the World Court "now meets the real difficulties that confront us in Europe, and its real difficulties will not be changed by our becoming an official member of it." He added, however, that the traditional United

11. Underwood to O. W. Underwood, Jr., April 11, 27, May 12, 1923, all in Underwood Papers, Alabama Archives.
12. *Ibid.*, May 20, 27, 1923; Harrogate (England) *Herald*, June 20, 1923.

States policy of settling international disputes by arbitration was "right and sound."[13]

While in Europe, Underwood seemed fairly popular as a candidate. A *Literary Digest* poll of Democratic officeholders showed him in third place among Democratic candidates with 10.2 percent of the vote, well ahead of Smith who had 6.8 percent, but behind Ford with 11.5 percent, and far behind McAdoo who had 35.3 percent.[14]

By landing at Boston where the boat discharged immigrants rather than at New York where he was expected, Underwood evaded reporters. On the following day, however, he held a press conference, gloomily predicting war in Europe unless there was an end to the "timid" foreign policy of the United States. The failure of the United States to ratify the Treaty of Versailles, join the League of Nations, and play its role in European affairs had led to world disorder, he said. He had been an advocate of the League of Nations but had subsequently differed with President Wilson in advocating compromise on the Treaty of Versailles; he now declared that the league and the World Court were no longer the important issues in American politics. Underwood did not specify the kind of foreign policy that he wanted, and he gave an erroneous illustration of the use of arbitration in citing favorably Cleveland's action in the Venezuelan affair of 1895. He subsequently revealed that he had confused the Venezuelan dispute of 1902 with that of 1895.[15]

Underwood's foreign policy statements were ambiguous and confusing, and editorial writers criticized his failure to offer constructive alternatives to the Harding policies. Some political reporters interpreted his statements as indicating that the United States should guarantee the Franco-German border—a proposal Underwood had favored earlier. Most observers interpreted his

13. Underwood to O. W. Underwood, Jr., April 27, June 17, 1923, both in Underwood Papers, Alabama Archives.
14. *Literary Digest*, LXXVII (June 30, 1923), 6.
15. Birmingham *Age-Herald*, July 3, 6, 1923; Underwood to S. P. Knut, July 7, 1923, in Underwood Papers, Alabama Archives.

position as being anti-League of Nations. Attempting to redefine his position, Underwood advocated United States reliance on traditional diplomatic machinery for arbitration. He thus confirmed doubts of league advocates that he was less than an ardent supporter of the international organization.[16]

Underwood's extreme caution in foreign affairs is seen in the account of William Phillips, undersecretary of state, who dined at the Underwood home at 2000 G Street soon after their return. Phillips later recorded that Underwood, in recalling his trip to Europe, spoke of having walked by the League of Nations without entering (actually it was closed); of being in Lausanne while the treaty with the Turks was being negotiated without consulting with the American representative, Joseph C. Grew; and of declining an invitation of Lord Almerec Hugh Paget, baron of Queensborough, to honor him at dinner. This caution, Underwood explained, insured his freedom to "talk in the future."[17]

Underwood's difficulties in defining his European policy were minor compared to those of reconciling his outspoken antiprohibition position with the vigorous prohibition movement in the southern states where he based his political hopes. Senator Kenneth McKellar of Tennessee stated that if Underwood were associated with the "wets," Tennessee delegates could not favor him, although they admired him.[18]

Despite the strength of prohibition sentiment in Alabama, Underwood was given an emotional reception in Birmingham. Rain drenched the elaborately planned homecoming at East Lake Park, but Underwood was twice reduced to tears by the affectionate tributes of his hometown friends. After a party at the country place of department store entrepreneur, Louis Pizitz, Underwood went to Montgomery where the Alabama legislature listened appreciatively as he told of his willingness to accept the nomination as the candidate of Alabama and the South. He noted that there had been no southern president since James K. Polk, a pronouncement, re-

16. Birmingham *Age-Herald*, July 4, 7, 1923; Chattanooga *News*, July 6, 1923.
17. William Phillips, *Ventures in Diplomacy* (Boston: Beacon Press, 1952), 120.
18. New York *Times*, June 17, 1923, p. 3.

peatedly made, that ignored the presidential terms of Zachary Taylor and Andrew Johnson. The pageantry of Underwood's brilliant reception in Montgomery could not mask the doubts of Alabama prohibitionists, who demanded assurances that Underwood would oppose repeal or abridgment of the Eighteenth Amendment. Declaring that he favored "honest enforcement" of the law and privately assuring prohibition leaders that he would oppose an interpretation of the Eighteenth Amendment that would allow the sale of beer and light wines, Underwood partially succeeded in burying the prohibition question. He was endorsed by the aging Dr. W. B. Crumpton, president of the Alabama Anti-Saloon League, and other state prohibition leaders. [19]

The announcement of Underwood's candidacy received less notice than expected because of the death of President Harding. However, it brought a predictable adverse reaction from Underwood's long-time political foe William Jennings Bryan, then living in Miami, Florida. Bryan charged that Underwood was "wetter" than Governor Alfred E. Smith of New York and was controlled by Wall Street. Underwood replied that he had opposed the Eighteenth Amendment because he thought that temperance could be handled better by the states and that he had no connection with the business interests commonly referred to as "Wall Street." He wrote privately that Bryan's "javelin was long since broken" but that he would not "resist slapping at a mosquito when it comes buzzing about." [20]

Editorial reaction to Underwood's candidacy was generally favorable. The Nashville *Banner* described the candidate as "a big man, a true man, a courageous man." The Cleveland *Plain-Dealer* said apologetically that "it is doubtful whether the North . . . is yet ready to confer the presidency on a man from the South." The Knoxville *Sentinel* regretted that Underwood had brought in the sectional issue. The New York *Journal of Commerce* liked Under-

19. Birmingham *News*, July 29, 1923; Birmingham *Age-Herald*, August 1, 1923; Montgomery *Advertiser*, September 9, 1923.

20. Birmingham *Age-Herald*, August 3, 1923; Underwood to Walter Myers, August 10, 1923, in Letterbox N, Underwood Papers, Alabama Archives.

wood's forthrightness in announcing his candidacy while others were being coy, but doubted that he would make a strong candidate.[21]

Harding's death on August 2, 1923, improved Underwood's chances in the view of some political observers. Although the new president, Calvin Coolidge, was a conservative, if the Republicans gave in to pressure from the LaFollette wing of the party and nominated a moderate progressive for 1924, the conservative ground would be left to the Democrats.[22]

A deep political chasm between the "wets" and the "drys" endangered Underwood's Alabama campaign. Despite the favorable statements of the state's two leading prohibitionists, Dr. Crumpton and Brooks Lawrence, rank-and-file prohibitionists refused to support the state's senior senator. Underwood's supporters were reluctant to pit him against William Gibbs McAdoo, a prohibitionist. The legislature dutifully passed the Verner Act which, assuming that an Alabamian entered the presidential race, restricted the state's presidential primary to Alabama candidates and authorized the primary victor to name the delegation to the convention. Hopes of Underwood supporters that the senator would have a clear field in Alabama were jolted when Lycurgus Breckinridge Musgrove, a prohibition leader and Underwood's foe in the senatorial election of 1920, qualified, presumably in the interest of McAdoo. Characterized by Underwood's followers as "a millionaire with a sore toe," the Jasper coal mine operator could not be laughed off when Bryan joined him in his Alabama campaign. Less disturbing was the candidacy of Marvin A. Dinsmore, an obscure Birmingham attorney who deplored the plight of those who were reduced to living on "sassafras tea, corn bread, and eating swine bosom." Dinsmore was allegedly the candidate of the Ku Klux Klan but was avowedly for McAdoo. Prohibitionist concern that Underwood's candidacy was in the interest of repeal or modification of

21. Nashville *Banner*, Cleveland *Plain-Dealer*, Knoxville *Sentinel*, all quoted in Birmingham *Age-Herald*, August 5, 1923; New York *Journal of Commerce*, quoted in Birmingham *News*, August 5, 1923.

22. Montgomery *Advertiser*, August 10, 1923.

the Eighteenth Amendment led bone dry former governor Braxton
B. Comer to demand that he be allowed to select half of the delegates to the convention—delegates who under the Verner Act
were to be chosen by Underwood if he won the presidential primary. Underwood succumbed to Comer's demands in the interest
of harmony.[23]

Underwood's managers feared that resentment against the Verner Act would lead prohibitionists to embarrass Underwood by
voting against him in the presidential primary. Frank R. Kent, the
Baltimore *Sun* political analyst, quoted an Alabamian who said that
Underwood would be defeated in Alabama for ten reasons. The
first five were the Anti-Saloon League, the WCTU, organized labor, unorganized labor, and the veterans, and the "other five are
the Ku Klux Klan."[24] Gloomy prophecies about Underwood's weakness in Alabama proved largely erroneous. In a light vote, in un-
seasonable, freezing weather, Alabamians gave Underwood 65,798
votes, Musgrove 37,837 and Dinsmore 2,001. Musgrove majorities, notably in heavily unionized Anniston, were overbalanced by
substantial Underwood majorities in the Muscle Shoals area where
Underwood was credited with securing Wilson Dam.[25] Underwood's supporters crowed with delight, but the result could hardly
be described as a major victory in view of the limited choice available.

The national Underwood campaign was organized by Forney M.
Johnston, counsel for the Seaboard Air Line Railway and the National Association of Owners of Railroad Securities which had lobbied through Underwood for the railway bondholders' plan of railroad control. Johnston had secured both of his positions through
Underwood's influence. His selection as campaign manager was
soon recognized as politically damaging, since it would appear that
Underwood's candidacy was in the interest of the railroads. Johnston and Underwood then selected a new manager, Charles C.

23. *Ibid.*, August 30, 1923; Birmingham *Age-Herald*, December 30, 1923; Birmingham
News, March 4, 1924; Birmingham *Age-Herald*, March 10, 1924; Underwood to Braxton B.
Comer, December 10, 1923, in Braxton B. Comer Papers, University of North Carolina,
Chapel Hill.
24. Baltimore *Sun*, February 26, 1924.
25. Montgomery *Advertiser*, March 22, 1924.

Carlin, a former Virginia congressman and manager of A. Mitchell Palmer's campaign for the Democratic nomination in 1920. Carlin, owner of the Alexandria *Gazette* and member of a Washington, D.C., law firm, had strong influence in Virginia and Pennsylvania. The Washington staff had offices adjacent to those of Johnston, and as the campaign quickened an expensive publicity staff was added.[26]

In October, 1923, Underwood left his summer home at Tate Springs to launch his campaign in Texas, where the Ku Klux Klan and prohibition were rampant. At Wichita Falls he addressed a banquet audience and appealed for votes as the South's candidate for president. Condemning a "government of commissions," Underwood criticized Coolidge and the recent Governors' Conference for ineffectiveness in enforcing prohibition. He advocated enforcement by armed federal revenue cutters with the authority to fire on smugglers regardless of national registration. This was only campaign oratory, as there is no convincing evidence that Underwood had softened his opposition to prohibition.[27]

The Ku Klux Klan rather than prohibition itself was the central issue in Texas, and Underwood, normally the soul of caution, had determined to attack the Klan. Although from a city that was perhaps as Klan-infested as any in the United States, Underwood had not spoken out against the Birmingham Klan's depredations in 1921 and 1922. Nonetheless, he had not cultivated the Klan leaders who were attempting political control, and his antiprohibition stand made Klan support unlikely. The Klan covertly opposed him in the Alabama presidential primary. Underwood made his decision to oppose the Klan before opening his Texas campaign, and to a political advisor who wanted to temporize with the Klan, he wrote:

> I have no doubt a great many good people belong to the Ku Klux Klan and many of their principles for which they stand are good. But there are two things that [they represent] that are absolutely un-American. . . . One is to decide political issues and nominate and se-

26. Underwood to L. J. Bugg, November 17, 1923, in Campaign File—Alabama, Underwood Papers, Alabama Archives; Montgomery *Times*, November 19, 1923.
27. Birmingham *Age-Herald*, October 25, 1923.

lect political candidates in secret caucus behind closed doors. . . . The other is without authority of law to set themselves up in place of the government to try and punish men for crime. . . . All men are entitle[d] under the law to a just trial by jury and an appeal to the Supreme Court of the land. Of this they are deprived by a set of men who assume to set themselves up in place of the law.[28]

Underwood's sentiments were doubtless sincere, but the position was also good politics. He noted that it would be "perfect folly" to attempt to win the presidency without meeting the Klan question in the Democratic platform. Otherwise, the Republican party, which was certain to meet the question in its platform, would carry the doubtful states.[29]

Dallas was the most powerful Klan stronghold in Texas, and in that city Underwood held his fire on the Klan issue. At the Dallas fairgrounds where the Klan had held a rally of ten thousand the day before, Underwood drew only one thousand for a discussion of United States foreign policy. Standing at the rostrum where Woodrow Wilson had launched his national campaign in 1912, Underwood based his candidacy on America's duty to assume world responsibility, saying, "America has surrendered leadership in world affairs. We surrendered the leadership in world affairs which our great sacrifice had won for us." Later, addressing a luncheon at the Oriental Hotel, Underwood leaders emphasized that Klan leaders had been invited to the luncheon but none had accepted. Not one member of the city government nor of the Klan was present at either meeting according to Underwood's managers—although one questions if they had such accurate lists of Klan members. While Underwood addressed the luncheon group, Hiram Evans conferred with Klan leaders at a hotel across the street.[30] At San Antonio, Underwood again emphasized foreign affairs as the central issue in the campaign, denying that the Ku Klux Klan issue would be crucial.

28. Underwood to Cecil Beasley, October 18, 1923, in Underwood Papers, Alabama Archives.
29. *Ibid.*
30. New York *Times*, October 26, 1923, p. 19.

Underwood waited until his arrival in Houston, where the Klan had recently suffered a stinging defeat, to launch out against the hooded order. Clearly, the Klan was opposed to him, and he had nothing to lose. Lashing the Klan before Houston civic clubs, he said: "When any group of men unites in a secret order to run the laws and the government, their action strikes at the very heart of government. . . . No class or clan can assume control over a democracy." Fraternal orders and civic clubs were all right, he said, except "for the purpose of governing." He concluded somewhat irrelevantly that the "government governs best which governs least."[31] Underwood's anti-Klan declaration was received with great applause, but the rest of the Texas campaign was an anticlimax. At Beaumont, Underwood spoke only of local issues and assured his followers of his interest in the Sabine River waterway.[32]

Underwood returned to Tennessee on November 2 and was met at the station by Mrs. Underwood. After a fifty-mile drive to Tate Springs over a crooked mountain road, they arrived at their "Log Cabin" for supper and it was, he said, indeed "good to be back." The following day he wrote a Texas supporter who urged that he soft-pedal the Klan issue: "I did not take my position in my Houston speech captiously or without careful deliberation and consideration. You also know me well enough to know that when I have once crossed the bridge where great principles are involved that I do not turn back, even where the opportunity affords itself and of course there is no [such] opportunity left in this instance. . . . The bridge is down and the only thing left for me to do is to fight my way through on the principles I announced at Houston."[33]

The Klan retaliated angrily. *Mayfield's Weekly*, a Klan publication in the Southwest, denounced Underwood as the "Jew, Jug, and Jesuit candidate."[34] The Klan revealed that Underwood was the owner of a one hundred dollar share of stock in the *Fellowship Forum*, their Washington, D. C., news organ. *Our Sunday Visitor*,

31. Birmingham *Age-Herald*, October 27, 28, 1923.
32. Montgomery *Advertiser*, October 30, November 5, 1923.
33. Underwood to Joseph H. Eagle, Jr., November 3, 1923, in Campaign File—Texas, Underwood Papers, Alabama Archives.
34. New York *Times*, November 4, 1923, p. 1.

a Roman Catholic publication, demanded and received Underwood's quite plausible explanation that he had contributed to the *Fellowship Forum* when it was organized under different editorship and when it was devoted to Masonic activities. He regarded the money as a gift and had not known that the paper would become "anti-Catholic, pro-Klan, or a paper designed to promote religious belief of any kind." He turned his stock in, his money was refunded, and the *Fellowship Forum* headlined: UNDERWOOD DESERTS HIS MASONIC FRIENDS." Underwood's friends replied that the Klan attack was designed to keep Underwood from leading the effort to unseat Earle B. Mayfield who had been elected to the Senate from Texas with Klan support in 1923, and whose fight to retain his seat had the support of Alabama's junior senator, J. Thomas Heflin.[35] In fact, Underwood took no part in the attempt to unseat Mayfield, who retained his seat after an extensive investigation in 1924.

As late as February, 1924, Underwood seemed to be attempting to avoid offending Klan supporters. While reiterating his anti-Klan views, he incongruously wrote a constituent that no member of his "campaign committee has in any way denounced the Klan as an organization."[36] Even so, by May, 1924, Underwood was listed as the Klan's number one enemy in their *Who's Who in Congress*. He was accused of "wet and papal influences" as well as opposition to women's suffrage and failure to oppose Senator Borah's Irish independence resolution.[37]

In Kentucky and South Carolina, Underwood shifted his emphasis to economic issues. At Franklin, Kentucky, he reviewed Democratic accomplishments in the Wilson period and called for reduction of the tariff in order to open foreign commodity markets for the farmer. At Bowling Green he condemned the Republican party for its failure to enforce the Eighteenth Amendment. In South

35. *Fellowship Forum*, quoted in Columbus (Ga.) *Enquirer-Sun*, January 21, 1924; Columbus (Ga.) *Enquirer-Sun*, January 21, 1924.
36. Underwood to Horace G. Carlisle, February 28, 1924, in Campaign File—Alabama, Underwood Papers, Alabama Archives.
37. New York *World*, May 7, 1924.

Carolina, Underwood reverted to a sectional appeal. He said at Greenville, South Carolina's textile capital, that the Civil War was as passé as the Wars of the Roses and that the South was entitled to a proper proportion of the membership on regulatory commissions, especially the ICC. He expressed particular interest in ending discriminatory freight rates. At Spartanburg he advocated the leasing of the Muscle Shoals nitrate and power plant to Henry Ford. Before the South Carolina legislature, he denounced the soldiers' bonus as "a mere travesty" and belabored the Republicans for their lack of a foreign policy and for Teapot Dome.[38]

Despite the sectional nature of his campaign and his reference to freight rate discrimination and the nonsouthern composition of the ICC, Underwood avoided making a major issue of economic discrimination against the South. Responding to demands for agricultural relief, he said that though he sympathized with farmers in the severe decline of farm prices, those who were advocating relief through removal of freight rate discrimination were engaging in "vaporing of the mind" and "bunk." In a period of falling prices, he said, the farmers could get no advantage if freight rates were reduced—the advantage would go to the purchaser.[39]

Nor did Underwood mention in his campaign United States Steel's use of "Pittsburgh Plus," a discriminatory pricing policy whereby rolled steel products, made in Birmingham, allegedly were sold at the Pittsburgh price with freight charged from Pittsburgh to the point of delivery. In practice Birmingham steel was sold in Birmingham at the Pittsburgh price plus a fixed differential that was somewhat less than the freight from Pittsburgh to Birmingham. Many southerners felt that "Pittsburgh Plus" was a mark of the South's economic subservience, but United States Steel officials professed that it had been discarded years before. Underwood, who made no claim to understanding the complex pricing system, did not join the clamor against United States Steel. The

38. Montgomery *Advertiser*, November 1, 1923; Birmingham *Age-Herald*, November 3, 9, 1923; Columbia (S.C.) *State*, February 28, 1924.
39. Underwood to W. E. Lea, January 14, 1924, in Campaign File—Texas, Underwood Papers, Alabama Archives.

Federal Trade Commission forbade "Pittsburgh Plus" in August, 1924, but vestiges of the system persisted until the 1940s.[40]

Underwood told reporters in Boston that he had no one great issue with which he hoped to sell his candidacy. "Conditions not men make issues," he said. Declining to comment on his rivals by remarking that running for the presidency was not like running for the justice of the peace in Alabama, Underwood said that he was not opposed to the League of Nations and criticized the Harding administration for failing to do its duty regarding the French occupation of the Ruhr Valley—"the Ruhr War" he called it. Following the French occupation of the Ruhr in January, 1923, Underwood had voted with the overwhelming majority of the Senate in disapproving of the French action, but he now insisted that the United States should have supported France.

Underwood reverted to the Klan theme in his major Boston speech which was favorably received. Indeed, it could not be said that the Klan issue had hurt him in his New England foray. Charles Michaelson of the New York *World* suggested that Underwood could afford to endow a foundation for "goblins, wizards and kleagles in return for services rendered by the Ku Klux."[41]

Democratic party bosses, whose big city constituencies found McAdoo's prohibition ideas and Klan support abhorrent, were disturbed that the Democratic race appeared to be McAdoo against the field. In mid-fall of 1923 several Democratic party bosses assembled at French Lick Springs, Indiana, to develop plans for opposing him. Charles F. Murphy, the "Tiger of Tammany Hall," the most powerful of these leaders, had allegedly favored Underwood's candidacy for the 1912 Democratic nomination, but he now favored Governor Smith. Others present were the new Democratic boss of Chicago, George E. Brennen, Senator Joseph F. Guffey of Pennsylvania, and the host, Thomas Taggert, the Democratic boss of Indiana. Taggert's candidate was Indiana's aging, pro-Klan Sen-

40. *American Economic Review*, XIV (1924), 192–93; *Literary Digest*, LXXXII (August 9, 1924), 12–13.

41. Birmingham *News*, November 13, 1923; New York *World*, quoted in Birmingham *Post*, November 16, 1923.

ator Samuel M. Ralston. Despite the absurdity of an agreement among these disparate elements, subsequent events give credence to reports—evidently from Taggert—that the group would support Underwood for several ballots, hoping to affect a deadlock following which Ralston or another compromise candidate would be chosen.[42]

Underwood dealt with domestic issues with surprising candor in the fall of 1923. Clinging tenaciously to his position on the Klan, he declared his opposition to the soldiers' bonus, for reasons of economy, and favored "immediate consideration" of Andrew W. Mellon's plan to cut income taxes, especially in the higher brackets.[43] To one friend who complained of his frankness on political issues, Underwood said: "I confess that Gum-Shoe politicians who can travel about without making issues often have the best of the political game. But I have never been able to play politics that way, and I think there are some assets as well as liabilities in frank declarations on public issues."[44] Doubtless, Underwood had McAdoo in mind as a "Gum-Shoe" politician who refused to commit himself on the issue of the Klan, who favored both a tax cut and the soldiers' bonus, and whose position on the league was unclear. Underwood did not recognize that his own positions on European foreign policy and on the league were often contradictory.

Underwood invaded the North a second time in January, 1924. At Akron, Ohio, he proposed a single six-year presidential term, reasoning that the president consumed half of his four-year term satisfying party demands. A six-year term without reelection would, he maintained, remove "all temptations to further political ambition." He failed to mention that his somewhat advanced age would almost preclude a second term since he would have been almost seventy-one by its end. Underwood's single-term idea was received with mixed enthusiasm, and his advocacy of this relic of the Confederate Constitution and Populist platforms missed its

42. Springfield (Mass.) *Daily News*, November 26, 1923.
43. Baltimore *Sun*, November 21, 1923.
44. Underwood to Harvey B. Heard, November 17, 1923, in Campaign File—Texas, Underwood Papers, Alabama Archives.

mark. He urged the reduction of bureaucracy through the removal of at least a hundred thousand employees and deplored centralization of government and the loss of states' rights.[45]

Underwood had declared that Mississippi was "his most strategic point" and that its fall to McAdoo would be a "sure omen" for his defeat. Just before his speech to the Mississippi legislature, Underwood received three anonymous notes from Klansmen who demanded that he state his position on the Klan. Underwood denounced the secret organization. Bravely referring to the Klan's efforts to take the law into its own hands, he told Klansmen that if the "laws of your state are being violated, stand up on your hind legs and go to the grand jury."[46]

Underwood had commented on the Harding scandals as early as May, 1922, when, learning of charges that Attorney General Daugherty had cooperated with an attorney to approve parole for a wealthy prison inmate, Underwood urged that it be investigated. In January, 1924, when a Senate resolution was presented condemning the principals in the Teapot Dome affair, Underwood stated that although he was happy to vote for the resolution, it did not go far enough. It was quite clear, he said, that Harry F. Sinclair's and Edward L. Doheny's corporations had received property worth more than one hundred million dollars in excess of what they were to pay for it. He therefore urged that the Senate resolution go further and declare the leases null and void. "This is no time for technicalities," he said, pointing out that it did not take action by the Supreme Court to nullify the leases. About a month and a half later, he wrote a constituent that "we have been surfeited with gossip" and everyone would be glad when one could pick up a newspaper without reading of some new distasteful development in the oil investigation.[47]

45. Address of January 23, 1924, in Letterbox M, Underwood Papers, Alabama Archives; Boston *Daily Herald*, January 24, 1924; St. Louis *Star*, January 24, 1924.
46. Vicksburg (Miss.) *Herald*, January 27, 1924; Jackson (Miss.) *Daily News*, February 22, 1924.
47. Birmingham *News*, May 21, 1922; *Congressional Record*, 68th Cong., 1st Sess., 1688–89; Underwood to Frank B. Shutts, March 8, 1924, in Campaign File—Florida, Underwood Papers, Alabama Archives.

A McAdoo setback suddenly gave Underwood the kind of political break of which politicians dream. Doheny testified in the Teapot Dome hearings that he had paid substantial legal fees to McAdoo in connection with oil leases. Few thought that McAdoo had violated the law in representing Doheny, but the mere association of the two appeared to make the former secretary of the treasury "unavailable" for the nomination.

A few days later Underwood's name appeared briefly in the Teapot Dome investigation. A telegram was introduced before the Senate investigating committee showing that an employee of Edward B. McLean, publisher of the Washington *Post*, had suggested that McLean have his attorney, A. Mitchell Palmer, ask Underwood and others to intervene with the Senate's chief investigator, Senator Thomas J. Walsh, in order to save McLean the embarrassment of testifying. McLean was a friend of Underwood as well as of the embattled secretary of the interior, Albert B. Fall. Senator Walsh assured the Senate that Underwood had never attempted to interfere in any way with his investigation, and Palmer denied having approached Underwood. Underwood admitted having been contacted by Ira E. Bennett, the editor of the Washington *Post*, who requested that he ask Walsh to allow McLean, who claimed to be ill, to give his testimony by deposition. Underwood agreed that he probably would have spoken to Walsh, but before he could act Walsh was authorized to take McLean's testimony at his West Palm Beach home.[48] The revelations of the Teapot Dome investigation were greatly damaging to McAdoo but hardly touched Underwood, whose name quickly disappeared from the investigation.

The campaign in Georgia against McAdoo was both crucial and difficult for the Underwood forces. Clark Howell, editor of the powerful Atlanta *Constitution*, sympathized with Underwood but declined to endorse him because of his own race for Democratic national committeeman, evidently realizing that Underwood faced an uphill fight. Underwood's friend, Senator Walter F. George,

48. Montgomery *Advertiser*, February 29, 1924; Underwood to George M. Bailey, March 4, 1924, in Campaign File—Texas, Underwood Papers, Alabama Archives.

also declined to help, saying that the Georgia situation was "too confusing." Former governor Thomas W. Hardwick, a caustic League of Nations critic, campaigned for Underwood despite Underwood's refusal to assure him of his opposition to the league. Before the Georgia legislature, Underwood denounced Coolidge's lack of a foreign policy, after which pro-Klan Governor Clifford M. Walker refused to pose with Underwood for a picture. At a meeting of Democratic women in Atlanta, Underwood offended his listeners by applauding the Supreme Court's decision declaring the second child labor law unconstitutional. One of Underwood's Georgia campaigners, his Alabama senatorial colleague J. Thomas Heflin, had close ties with the Klan, and at Augusta he violated the canons of the Underwood campaign by praising McAdoo.[49]

In a brief three-day Georgia appearance McAdoo emphasized that he was a native and skillfully evaded the Klan issue. Nathan Bedford Forrest, the grand dragon of the Georgia Ku Klux Klan, gave official Klan backing to McAdoo's cause. McAdoo defeated Underwood resoundingly in the Georgia primary by a vote of 93,000 to 51,000. At Underwood's cue his forces shouted in unison that the Klan had defeated him. Yet this was too simple an explanation for what Underwood privately described as a decisive defeat. Underwood's managers listed a variety of other reasons: Underwood's opposition to women's suffrage and prohibition, McAdoo's Georgia birth, and the support of unpopular former Governor Hardwick.[50]

The Georgia defeat weakened the Underwood campaign, particularly in Florida where the primary battle was going on at the same time. The Underwood committee in Florida avoided an error of the Georgia campaign which had failed to recognize the role of women. Women were featured in Florida campaign publicity, al-

49. Clark Howell to Forney Johnston, October 1, 1923, Walter F. George to William W. Brandon, September 6, 1923, both in Campaign File—Georgia, and Underwood to Thomas W. Hardwick, August 7, 1923, in Letterbox N, all in Underwood Papers, Alabama Archives; Birmingham *Age-Herald*, March 10, 1924; Montgomery *Advertiser*, November 24, 1923; Columbus (Ga.) *Enquirer-Sun*, November 27, 1923; Birmingham *News*, November 24, 1923; Augusta (Ga.) *Chronicle*, March 12, 1924.

50. Birmingham *Age-Herald*, March 19, 1924; Atlanta *Constitution*, April 27, 1924; New York *Times*, March 21, 1924, p. 3; Birmingham *News*, March 20, 1924.

though they took no perceptible role in the leadership of the Underwood campaign. Pleasant A. Holt, Underwood's Florida chairman, said that the McAdoo people were counting on the Klan, organized labor, the Anti-Saloon League, and self-styled Progressives for victory.

Florida voted for McAdoo over Underwood by 11,919 to 8,497. Returns from west Florida, strong Klan country with sentimental ties to Alabama, showed that Underwood broke about fifty-fifty with McAdoo, but in the populous, sophisticated, and non-Confederate Miami area, the vote was two to one for McAdoo. Since Underwood ran better in the Klan-infested area than in the non-Klan area, obviously other factors such as the opposition of organized labor and women voters caused his defeat in Florida.[51]

Underwood campaigns in other southern states were largely unsuccessful. McAdoo won Texas, despite the favorite son campaign of "dry" Governor Pat M. Neff who drew many prohibition votes away from McAdoo. Underwood's Texas manager blamed the Klan for the defeat, and there was some truth in the charge. Underwood expressed disappointment that he had lost Texas but declared confidently that "northern democracy" would adopt an anti-Klan platform. Mississippi was lost partially because of Klan opposition and partially because Senator Pat Harrison, Underwood's erstwhile Senate assistant, faced with his own campaign, declined to help. Underwood's managers made gestures in North Carolina and Kentucky but withdrew and left the field to McAdoo. In Arizona, Underwood picked up a few votes, and in Virginia events later proved that Underwood had second choice support among the delegates pledged to Senator Carter Glass. Glass deprecated Underwood's claims of victory in Iowa, Wisconsin, Missouri, and Arizona, doubting that "he has as many as two of the Southern states."[52]

51. Jacksonville *Florida Times-Union*, April 30, 1924; Pleasant A. Holt to Alfred M. Tunstall, May 2, 1924, in Campaign File—Alabama, Underwood Papers, Alabama Archives; Jacksonville *Florida Times-Union*, June 10, 1924.

52. Wichita Falls (Tex.) *Times*, May 6, 1924; Underwood to Bailey, May 10, 1924, in Campaign File—Texas, and Charles C. Carlin to Tunstall, May 10, 1924, in Campaign File—Alabama, both in Underwood Papers, Alabama Archives; Globe (Ariz.) *Record*, April 2, 1924; Carter Glass to Jouett Shouse, April 7, 1924, in Jouett Shouse Papers, University of Kentucky.

McAdoo's victories throughout the South were disconcerting to Underwood's managers. With the two-thirds rule in effect, a deadlock between McAdoo and Smith was almost a certainty. The Underwood forces expected that Governor Smith, new to national politics, would withdraw soon after the convention opened, and Underwood would become the legatee of Smith's votes. Lacking a substantial block of southern votes, the Underwood forces still hoped that after a McAdoo-Smith deadlock, they would win the nomination through a combination of Smith votes and second choice Underwood support in the South.[53]

The financing of Underwood's campaign is obscure, and unlike his 1912 campaign where expenses were well documented, one is left to speculate on the sources of the funds. The vitriolic Senator Glass charged that Underwood's campaign manager Charles C. Carlin had spent a "large yellow dog fund in Virginia" and was out of jail only because "he has been too clever to be caught as a petty criminal."[54] The Underwood campaigners, however, felt handicapped by a lack of funds, and Underwood wrote a friend that a national campaign was too expensive for him. Expenditures in Florida approximated $6,500, and one may conjecture that the entire campaign cost about $120,000, most of which was spent in the southeastern states. The National Association of Owners of Railroad Securities contributed at least much of Forney Johnston's time and probably much cash. Thomas Fortune Ryan, the New York financier who had contributed handsomely to Underwood's 1912 campaign, also probably contributed heavily. Some money was raised in Birmingham, and Underwood's generous wife was a source of funds.[55]

Underwood stiffened his position on the Klan in the last few

53. New York *Herald Tribune*, May 26, 1924.

54. Carter Glass to Thomas G. McAdoo, April 5, 1924, in Carter Glass Papers, University of Virginia Library.

55. Underwood to Daniel F. Foley, February 28, 1924, Frank M. Merkling to R. B. Evins, April 9, 1924, both in Underwood Papers, Alabama Archives; Carter Glass to Thomas G. McAdoo, May 1, 1924, in Glass Papers. The goal of the Underwood managers for Jefferson County, Alabama (Birmingham), was set at $100,000, but there is no indication that the goal was reached.

months of the campaign. During the Georgia campaign, he denied rumors that he was a Roman Catholic noting that he belonged to the Episcopal church and the Masonic order. He recalled that the Democratic party had gone on record against religious intolerance in the platform of 1856 following the Know-Nothing outbreak. That platform increasingly became a fetish with Underwood, and he proposed that its provisions for religious tolerance be part of the Democratic platform for 1924. In early May, Underwood headquarters announced that Alabama Governor William W. "Plain Bill" Brandon would emphasize the Klan issue in the nominating speech. Former congressman Joseph H. Eagle, a Houston friend, encouraged Underwood to "go resolutely forward on the Ku Klux Klan since it is your only hope and your first duty as well." The Alabama delegation, about a third of whom were prohibitionists named by former governor Comer, refused to support the anti-Klan plank. Underwood magnanimously accepted the entire delegation but noted that they were bound by the unit rule. He wrote Comer that he could not "develop my second choice strength until Mr. McAdoo and Governor Smith have had their tryout." Underwood wrote a supporter that he could not "afford to compromise" on the Klan but that "while I have suffered in the South, my position has won friends in other sections of the country." He stated in an article for the New York *Times* that the Klan was the "chief issue."[56] Suddenly, it was announced that Forney Johnston, not Governor Brandon, would make the nominating speech. This change reflected Underwood's increasing emphasis on the Klan issue, as Brandon's close identification with the Klan would have made his denunciation of it ridiculous. Underwood insisted that members of the Alabama delegation endorse the incorporation of Section 10 of the 1856 platform into the 1924 platform. That platform had specifically denounced "all secret political societies." He

56. Underwood to R. Cuyler Gordon, February 8, 1924, in Letterbox N, Underwood Papers, Alabama Archives; Birmingham *News*, May 12, 1924; Joseph H. Eagle, Jr., to Underwood, May 19, 1924, in Campaign File—Texas, Underwood Papers, Alabama Archives; New York *Times*, June 18, 1924, p. 2; Underwood to Comer, June 19, 1924, in Comer Papers; Underwood to John T. Bashaw, June 7, 1924, in Campaign File—Kentucky, Underwood Papers, Alabama Archives; New York *Times*, June 8, 1924, Sec. 8, p.4.

said: "It may be a new development in modern times that a man's personality is regarded as of more importance than the principles he stands for, but my own viewpoint of party government is that governmental principle comes first and the personality of the candidate is of secondary consideration."[57] Despite Underwood's high-sounding advocacy of Section 10, he failed to note that the same section endorsed free immigration, a principle abhorrent to him.

Except for Alabama, Underwood forces had lost every primary they entered and were very discouraged. Even the senator felt that there was a very small chance for his nomination. If he were to win, he had to have popular strength outside the South where his campaign had been ineffective. A poll in early June, 1924, by the *Farm Journal*, a midwestern publication, placed Underwood in twelfth place with approximately 1.5 percent of the votes cast among candidates of both parties. A deadlock was Underwood's only hope and even that would require the eventual acquisition of Smith's eastern votes and the addition of second choice support in the southern delegations. It was a chimerical hope, and the Smith forces were becoming restive in their second choice commitment to Underwood. Yet Franklin D. Roosevelt, Smith's popular campaign manager, wrote Underwood that it was "anybody's race," and except for his crutches he would enter himself.[58]

The convention was to be held on friendly New York soil—friendly to Underwood and to his potential ally Governor Smith—but it was to be housed in the old Madison Square Garden which was slated for destruction at the end of the convention. Arriving in New York, Underwood delegates knew that their candidate's chances largely depended on the specific denunciation of the Ku Klux Klan in the platform. The Klan plank, originally suggested by Underwood, had become a rallying point for all of the anti-McAdoo forces, including those of Governor Alfred E. Smith. If the convention stigmatized the Klan, it would seriously damage the front-run-

57. Birmingham *News*, June 15, 17, 1924.
58. *Farm Journal*, quoted in Providence (R.I.) *Journal*, June 3, 1924; New York *Herald Tribune*, May 26, 1924; Franklin D. Roosevelt to Underwood, May 23, 1924, in Campaign File—New York, Underwood Papers, Alabama Archives.

ning McAdoo. Upon arriving at his Waldorf-Astoria headquarters, Underwood stated that the Klan was the greatest issue in the campaign: "It is either the Klan or the United States." But the Klan issue was viewed lightly by most delegates, many of whom greeted each other as "Kleagle." Most politicians thought Underwood's anti-Klan position was part of a strategy that assumed southern support and adopted the anti-Klan stance in order to appeal to urban voters in the East. When the Klan fought back, these theorists surmised, Underwood developed a "Klan complex."[59] Indeed Underwood's campaign had been absorbed by this issue, but there is no evidence to indicate that he had the slightest regret for his action.

Underwood's name was placed before the convention by Forney Johnston, a small, unimpressive-looking man who presented his candidate as a genius at the "harmonizing of conflicting economic interests." The convention received the speech quietly, but when the pugnacious Johnston presented the Underwood anti-Klan plank, specifically naming the Klan, the convention broke into pandemonium. There were fist fights in several places in the hall, and Johnston himself fought with an Alabama delegate. Later the strong Underwood plank on the Klan was narrowly defeated and replaced by one that denounced secret societies but did not specifically mention the Klan. Elmer Davis commented that Underwood suffered the misfortune of having the Klan issue eclipse his candidacy. Underwood was discouraged over the defeat of the tough anti-Klan plank, but the near victory showed that McAdoo's nomination was a virtual impossibility.[60]

Johnston's speech emphasized Underwood's opposition to prohibition as well as his insistence that the Democratic party specifically denounce the Klan. Underwood's aging nemesis William Jennings Bryan, a McAdoo delegate from Florida, denounced Underwood for his stance on both these issues. Later, during an interruption in balloting for president, Bryan, in a speech reminis-

59. New York *Times*, June 24, 1924, p. 3; Birmingham *News*, June 24, 1924.
60. Interview with Atticus Mullin, August 15, 1951; Birmingham *Age-Herald*, June 26, 29, 1924; New York *Times*, June 26, 1924, p. 1.

cent of his 1912 convention address, said that no "wet" or "reactionary" candidate could be nominated and that McAdoo, "dry" and "progressive," was strong enough to defeat such a candidate. Underwood assured visitors that he had never expected Bryan's support and that, indeed, he had expected such a thrust against him from Bryan.[61]

Each roll call began with Alabama, and each time Alabama's diminutive but leather-lunged Governor William W. "Plain Bill" Brandon shouted out Alabama's 24 votes for Underwood "like a roll of thunder." Underwood was only one of fifteen candidates, and the total vote for him ranged between 39 ½ and 42 ½ votes in the early balloting. The voting was dominated by McAdoo and Smith, but hardly anyone thought that either of them could muster the 732 votes needed.[62]

Governor Brandon's stentorian shout masked serious dissension in the Alabama delegation. Many were unhappy with the fight against the Klan, and others opposed Underwood's antiprohibition stand. Borden Burr, leader of the Underwood delegates, denied that Alabamians who were talking of switching to McAdoo were members of the delegation. Longtime political opponents of Underwood were there from Alabama, however, and they included L. B. Musgrove, whom Underwood had defeated for the Senate in 1920, and Phil Painter, who had edited Richmond Pearson Hobson's newspaper in the 1914 campaign. Two days before the convention's end eighteen of the forty-eight man Alabama delegation had gone home and twelve more were scheduled to leave that day.[63]

A major disappointment of the Underwood leaders was the failure of the Louisiana delegation, a mixed group of Protestants and Roman Catholics, to support Underwood. Surprisingly, the anti-Klan plank was denounced within the Louisiana delegation as divisive. Louisianians thought they had solved the Klan issue by

61. Birmingham *Age-Herald*, June 27, July 3, 1924.
62. Charles A. Greathouse (ed.), *Official Report [of the Democratic National Convention . . . 1924]* (Indianapolis: Brookwalter-Ball-Greathouse Printing Company, 1924), 339–955.
63. Birmingham *News*, July 4, 8, 1924.

passing an antimasking act and were reluctant to see the issue resurrected. They voted for favorite sons, and, later, for John W. Davis.[64]

On Saturday, July 5, Governor Smith received more than one third of the ballots, thus demonstrating that he could block the nomination of McAdoo. Attention centered upon the six "dark horses"—notably Underwood and John W. Davis. As McAdoo dropped into second place behind Smith on July 7, Underwood noted that the breakup was imminent unless McAdoo was "using strategy." Commenting on the opposition of McAdoo's supporters to the two-thirds rule, Underwood reiterated his support of the rule, saying that although it was not to his advantage, its retention "would keep the South a great power to prevent in the future the nomination of some individual who might be obnoxious to the South."[65]

McAdoo gave in under great pressure and released his delegates on July 9, paving the way for the removal of both himself and Smith as effective candidates. The convention was faced with a choice between Davis, a Wall Street lawyer, and Underwood. On the one hundred first ballot Davis polled 316 and Underwood 229 ½. Underwood's vote included substantial accretions from the "bossed" states—Illinois, Indiana, Pennsylvania, and 86 ½ of New York's 90 votes. The one hundred third ballot saw Taggert, who had split his delegation equally among Underwood, Davis, and Glass, shift most of his delegates into the Davis column on the toss of a coin. New York completed the transition by shifting 60 of its 90 votes to Davis, leaving Underwood with only 44 votes, about the number with which he entered the convention. New York's shift completed Davis' nomination, although the Alabama delegation held fast.[66]

Underwood had developed a deep animus toward McAdoo, but

64. New York *Times*, July 10, 1924, p. 8.
65. Birmingham *Age-Herald*, July 8, 1924.
66. New York *Times*, July 10, 1924, p. 1; Robert K. Murray, *The 103rd Ballot* (New York: Harper & Row, 1976), 204–205. John Quinn, one of Underwood's backers in the 1912 campaign, was dying in New York. The elderly Irish art collector listened, however, to the proceedings on a crystal radio set. Mary A. Conroy to author, June 22, 1958, in possession of Evan C. Johnson, DeLand, Fla.

as he had no substantial chance for the nomination after his losses in the Georgia, Texas, and Florida primaries, he could hardly have been greatly disappointed in the nomination of his congressional colleague, John W. Davis. Before leaving New York he wrote Davis a note that began "Dear John," congratulating him on the "clean and splendid fight" and expressing a wish for a "great victory." Davis made no mention of the Klan in his acceptance statement. Nevertheless, upon returning to Birmingham, Underwood praised Davis' acceptance speech, saying that though he did not name the Ku Klux Klan, "no man can doubt the object [of his comments.]"[67]

Underwood rationalized his defeat as a result of his fight against the Klan. With compromise on the Klan issue, he repeatedly stated, he could have won the nomination. He wrote one disappointed supporter that after the convention refused to adopt an anti-Klan platform "I was not interested in the nomination because I felt that . . . we threw away a large part of our chance for success."[68]

Despite Underwood's privately expressed doubts that Davis and the Democrats could win, he ritualistically stated in public that they would be victorious. Emphasizing the importance of the defection of the newly organized Progressive party and its nomination of Senator Robert M. LaFollette to oppose Coolidge and Davis, Underwood predicted that LaFollette would be a major factor in Coolidge's defeat and in the victory of Davis. Recalling bitterly the failure of the West to cooperate with the South in the fight for private development of Muscle Shoals, Underwood deprecated the view that the West would join the South for a Democratic victory. Rather, he reasoned, LaFollette would draw the labor vote around him more compactly than any other presidential candidate, and, although that would "cut both ways," greater damage would be done to Coolidge than to Davis. Coolidge and LaFollette would

67. Underwood to John W. Davis, quoted in New York *Times*, July 11, 1924, p. 2; New York *Times*, August 13, 1924, p. 2.

68. Underwood to Gertrude, July 19, 1924, in Underwood Papers, Alabama Archives; Underwood to Robert S. Barrett, September 30, 1924, in Robert S. Barrett Papers, University of Virginia Library.

divide the West, and Davis' victory was dependent on a combination of southern and eastern votes, he said. Although Underwood
described this thinking as "simple arithmetic," it was faulty analysis
especially since most of the labor votes were in the East.[69] The
actual result was a landslide for Coolidge who won all electoral
votes except those in the South, which went to Davis, and Wisconsin, which went to LaFollette.

A Washington *Star* reporter, G. Gould Lincoln, noted a few days
after the convention that of the 307 votes received by Underwood
on the one hundred second ballot, only 26 were from the South.
The thirteen southern states, Lincoln said, could, if united, have
given Underwood an additional 269 votes or a total of 576, more
than a majority of the convention. Lincoln did not make clear that
Underwood, like McAdoo, would have then been faced with the
difficult task of securing a two-thirds vote.[70]

Underwood's campaign for the Democratic nomination in 1924
has been badly distorted in the public mind by the media. It was
the first convention to be broadcast, and Brandon's shout was
about all that could be heard on some crystal sets. Will Rogers
seized on the phrase, saying that "Alabama casts twenty-four votes
for Oscar W. Underwood" had become better known than the
Lord's Prayer. Immediately after the convention, Rogers spotted
Governor Brandon in his audience at the Ziegfeld follies and las-
soed him to the stage to give his famous chant. The Brandon cry
was fixed in the public mind as a repeated line in the musical
comedy *Of Thee I Sing*. John F. Kennedy picked up Underwood's
claim and implied in *Profiles in Courage* that Underwood would
have received the nomination except for his refusal to compromise
on the Klan issue.[71] Television writers amplified the same theme in
a program based upon *Profiles in Courage*. Professor Allan Nevins,
a consultant to the program, was a good friend of Oscar W. Underwood, Jr., and may have been influenced by him.

69. Birmingham *Age-Herald*, July 23, 1924.
70. Washington (D.C.) *Star*, July 23, 1924.
71. Birmingham *News*, July 4, 1924; John F. Kennedy, *Profiles in Courage* (New York: Harper & Row, 1956), 226–27.

Underwood had launched his campaign in the same fashion as he had waged the campaign for the Democratic nomination in 1912—that is, as the candidate of the South. But despite his sectional campaign, he failed to develop cogently the issue of economic colonialism—discriminatory freight rates and pricing policies that southern politicians of a later day capitalized on. Favorite son sentiment was enough to win Alabama, a Klan-infested state, for Underwood, but in Georgia, Florida, Mississippi, and Texas, the Klan vote was only one factor to which must be added women, labor, veterans, and prohibitionists as causes for the southern primary defeats. Having been so scarred by a chain of losses, any chance that Underwood might have won the presidency depended on national popularity of the one issue of his campaign that caught fire—the Klan. John W. Davis, the Democratic nominee, said that Underwood's candidacy helped to defeat McAdoo, and "I think his stand against the Ku Klux Klan helped rather than hurt him."[72]

Examination of the Klan's political activities in Texas and Alabama indicates that Underwood's defeat can hardly be attributed to the Klan. The wide publicity given by Underwood's Texas managers to Klan opposition there indicates their hope for political advantage from the issue. In August, 1924, subsequent to the Underwood defeat, Mrs. Miriam A. "Ma" Ferguson and an anti-Klan slate of candidates routed the Klan and destroyed it as a political organization in Texas. Underwood's Texas manager, W. E. Lea, thought that the Underwood campaign was responsible for this, but it seems implausible.

Only in Alabama, the most Klan infested of all states, did Underwood win a primary. McAdoo was inhibited from entering the primary by the Verner Act, and the Klan leaders saw the futility and political danger of trying to block Underwood in his home state. Upon returning to Birmingham, "to let them know how deeply I appreciate the splendid fight," Underwood described Davis as "one of the outstanding figures in the world today," and offered his services to the party in the upcoming campaign. Denying

72. John W. Davis to author, May 16, 1952, in possession of Evans C. Johnson.

rumors that had circulated from the beginning of the convention that he would retire from the Senate if his try for the nomination failed, he asserted: "Those reports are hot air." Nevertheless, Underwood's waning strength in Alabama was seen in editorial criticism by the Birmingham *Age-Herald*. The campaign had been mismanaged, the newspaper stated, in being directed by a railroad attorney and in being directed against McAdoo and the Klan. The *Age-Herald* hinted darkly that Underwood might have trouble being reelected in 1926.[73]

In early September Underwood emerged from a vacation at White Sulphur Springs, West Virginia, and reappeared in Washington. Saying that he had been "lost in the woods," he noted approvingly that Davis and LaFollette had specifically denounced the Ku Klux Klan and that Coolidge had authorized his secretary to make a statement criticizing the Klan.

Underwood then traveled to Maine to repay a political debt to its Democratic gubernatorial nominee, William R. Pattangall, who had supported him in the convention. Pattangall had little chance of election in solidly Republican Maine, but rumors of Klan activity in the state gave Underwood the opportunity to inject the Klan into the campaign. He said: "I come from a state where men and women shudder at night when a knock comes at the door, where men do not dare assert freedom of thought because an invisible hand may fall." The Anniston *Star* commented testily that there was little trouble with the Klan in Anniston and that Underwood was obsessed with the subject.[74]

Pattangall's opponent, Ralph O. Brewster, insisted that the only secret society he had belonged to was a college fraternity and that the Klan was not an issue. Nevertheless, Underwood berated the Klan in four speeches for Pattangall. At Portland, speaking to an enthusiastic crowd of two thousand at the City Hall, he said that the Ku Klux Klan represented a real menace even in Maine. Referring to Stephen A. Douglas as a great man, Underwood cited

73. Birmingham *Age-Herald*, September 4, July 27, August 3, 1924.
74. *Ibid.*, September 4, 5, 1924; Anniston (Ala.) *Star*, quoted in Birmingham *Age-Herald*, September 13, 1924.

Lincoln as being even greater and stated, "You can't be half Democrat and half Klan, and you cannot be half Klan and half Republican and survive as a party." Brewster had help from several Republican senators, and he defeated Pattangall by a majority of 33,000; it was not a bad showing for the Democrats.[75] It is doubtful, however, that Underwood's speeches influenced the result significantly.

Underwood ended his Maine visit in Poland Springs, and while driving back through Portland on his way to Washington, his "machine" struck a small child, Helen Jacobski, who darted against the running board. A cut above the knee was the result—evidently not serious. The senator drove the child and her father home and reported the accident to police headquarters before continuing his trip. Underwood was soon back in Washington, and, as Mrs. Underwood was in Birmingham with her ailing mother, he traded visits with Oscar, Jr., and his wife, who the senator said cooked "grand waffles." He dined one evening at the Ed Campbells and had a visit on another occasion from "my New York friend"—Thomas Fortune Ryan. The weather was bad, and although Underwood was suffering from a cough and a cold, he agreed to campaign for Davis at places nearby. He was assigned to Delaware, New Jersey, Maryland, and Virginia.[76]

Underwood's smashing defeat for the presidential nomination had invigorated the Alabama Klan, and they were infuriated by his Maine speeches. In Birmingham, Circuit Judge William E. Fort charged the October meeting of the Jefferson County grand jury to investigate the statements made "against Jefferson County and Alabama" by Underwood. He said that every flogging case should of course be prosecuted but added injudiciously that Underwood's mind had been "poisoned." If the senator's charges were true, he said, he would resign from the bench.[77]

Judge Fort's politically inspired charge illustrates the strength of the Klan in Birmingham and Jefferson County, which may well

75. New York *Times*, September 9, 1924, p. 1.
76. Birmingham *News*, September 18, 1924; Underwood to Bertha Underwood, September 29, 1924, in Underwood Papers, Alabama Archives.
77. Birmingham *Age-Herald*, October 7, 1924.

have been the greatest Klan stronghold in the nation. In mid-October the Klan staged a giant rally at Rickwood Field, named for Mrs. Underwood's brother, and thousands of Klansmen staged a "funeral" for Underwood before bleachers filled to capacity with twenty-three thousand people. The casket with the effigy of the senator was borne by eighteen pall bearers, representing the members of the grand jury, and the minister was pulled in a cart by two goats for reasons that are less clear.[78]

Arriving in Birmingham as planned on October 20, Underwood said that he had not returned to appear before the grand jury but was prepared to do so. "I told my hearers of some of the crimes which are laid to the Klan in the South. But I did not mention Jefferson County or Alabama," he said, in a canny and strategic retreat from his Rockland, Maine, statement. Asked to comment on the Klan's funeral for him, he quipped, "It must take a good man to get such a public funeral." Judge Fort recommended the cancellation of the investigation, saying that if the alleged attacks had not been made there was nothing to investigate. The charges were dropped by the Jefferson County grand jury in mid-December but not without the judge's parting shot that if Underwood had made such charges, he was "misled."[79]

Underwood's fight against the Klan was an integral part of his strategy in his quest for the presidential nomination in 1924. It was a bid for a national following to match the "favorite son" support he expected from the South. The Klan issue attracted such following as Underwood had outside the South, but his southern base of support collapsed. It is, however, by no means certain that the Klan was responsible for his defeat in the primaries of the South. His unpopular positions on women's suffrage, prohibition, and labor, and his identification with railroad interests also contributed to his defeat. The Klan was indeed a factor, but the Underwood partisans exaggerated its importance and made it a convenient "whipping boy."

78. *Ibid.*, October 16, 1924; *TWK Monthly*, II (November, 1924), 1.
79. Birmingham *Age-Herald*, October 21, 22, December 13, 1924.

Viewed in retrospect, Underwood's campaign had little chance for success. An able parliamentary leader, the aging Underwood no longer had the resilience required of a presidential candidate. His surrender of his position as minority leader of the Senate was a mistake. His effort to capitalize on the Klan issue was the shrewdest move of the campaign, but he failed to counter the consequent loss of southern support with a program attacking a broad range of southern economic grievances. His statements in the field of foreign policy left the public confused as to his attitude toward the League of Nations and security for western Europe. He lacked a sense of humor about himself, and his pomposity led him to a "soft-sell" approach that was inappropriate for a minor candidate. In the end, he had not had as good a chance for the nomination in 1924 as in 1912.

CHAPTER XV

Years of Disillusionment

Underwood's defeat for the Democratic presidential nomination in 1924 ended his quest for the presidency. During most of the years from 1911 until 1924 he had led the Democrats in the House or the Senate. Now he was tired, and the pace of his senatorial activities slackened. He occasionally wore high laced shoes as a mark of his increasing age, and he did not feel well. His chronic respiratory trouble, aggravated by cigarette smoking, persisted, but after several months of daily ultraviolet treatments on his nose, he was pronounced cured—an overly optimistic prognosis. For the first time in many years, however, he had the opportunity to relax. He had always read a good deal on weighty subjects such as economics and taxation, and his reading was expanded to include novels and even a book on the life of Christ. For the first time since childhood he kept a diary. He and Bertha frequently attended plays at Washington's New National Theater, occasionally went to a movie, and also listened to the radio, still a relative novelty. He began a program of exercise, combining automobile trips with walks through Potomac and Rock Creek parks, accompanied by his dogs Otto and Misty. He golfed frequently, and although Bertha occasionally golfed, they did not ordinarily play together. They exchanged visits or luncheon engagements within their Alabama circle of friends or relatives. Occasionally, they attended the Sunday luncheons of Edward B. and Evelyn Walsh McLean at their sumptuous home.

This comfortable existence was not shared by many throughout the country, however. Although the accession of Calvin Coolidge to the presidency in 1923 occurred after the blush of prosperity had begun to return to the nation, farmers—especially Alabama's cotton farmers—were unhappy with low farm prices. The agrarian depression was reflected in price-fixing schemes such as the McNary-Haugen bill. Rural southerners were firmly committed to enforcement of the Eighteenth Amendment, and the Ku Klux Klan thrived through much of the South, surviving as a power in Alabama longer than in any other state. On the foreign scene the Coolidge administration continued the policies of the Harding administration but moved to expand participation in world affairs, especially in disarmament and relations with Latin America.

Underwood was less interested in Democratic party affairs and failed to aid the successful Democratic effort to block President Coolidge's nomination of Charles B. Warren as attorney general. Warren's critics maintained that his close association with the American Sugar Refining Company would inhibit effective action against the sugar trust. He was rejected on two votes, but on the first there was a momentary tie when the Republicans had one Democratic vote, that of Senator Lee S. Overman (he later switched his vote). The tie brought a red-faced Vice-President Dawes running to the Senate chamber only to find that the tie was already broken and confirmation had failed. The Republicans embarrassedly explained that they had expected the vote of Underwood who was "out of town." If Underwood had promised his vote to the Coolidge forces, he had inadvertently dealt a heavy blow to the presidential ambitions of his friend Vice-President Dawes, whose failure to show brought raucous laughter.[1] It is unlikely that Underwood carelessly forgot to attend, as on the second vote, a week later, he was the only Democratic senator unpaired and not voting. Evidently he was committed to the Coolidge administration from which he was anxious for favorable action on his Muscle Shoals bill, but Alabama political pressure—generated in part by Senator Heflin's strong opposition to Warren—made it difficult for him to deliver his vote to the Republicans. So he "went fishing."

1. New York *Times*, March 17, 1925, p. 1.

As an elder statesman of the Democratic party, Underwood maintained a friendship with President Coolidge. Underwood failed to secure Secretary of the Treasury Mellon as a speaker for the Alabama Bankers' Association in 1925, but in the same year the president himself agreed to speak at Birmingham Southern College. In mid-May the Underwoods were weekend guests on the presidential yacht, *Mayflower*. The party of twelve sailed down the Potomac on Saturday afternoon, May 16, anchored off Chesapeake Bay for the night, and steamed slowly into the bay just before breakfast. A navy seaplane brought Sunday newspapers. At 11:00 A.M. the group attended church services on the upper deck, listening to a sermon on "loose talk." Underwood remarked that it must have been directed at the crew and not at the host. On the way back they got a good view of the historic homes along the shores including Mount Vernon and Woodlawn. Underwood had a long talk with Attorney General and Mrs. John M. Sargent in the afternoon, and after dinner there was a travel movie. There is no evidence to confirm Senator Norris' charge that Underwood secured a commitment from his taciturn host for support of his Muscle Shoals bill on this trip; indeed, it is doubtful that he conferred with the president. They returned to Washington Sunday night. On Monday the senator attended a Junior Chamber of Commerce "Alabama Day" banquet in New York, where he was honored as a member of the Alabama Hall of Fame. He was accompanied by a more famous honoree, Lois Wilson, a Birmingham movie actress.[2]

Several months later President Coolidge acquiesced to Underwood's often repeated argument that the South was underrepresented on the Interstate Commerce Commission. In February, 1925, Underwood had joined other southern senators in blocking confirmation of the appointment of Thomas W. Woodlock to the ICC. Woodlock, a New York financial writer identified with the railroads, was opposed by a Gulf states group of senators as well as by Senator Norris. In opposing Woodlock, Underwood said that

2. Birmingham *News*, May 15, 1925. Personal material in this chapter came from an untitled diary, a 3″ x 5″ leather notebook in the last drawer of Oscar W. Underwood Papers, Alabama Department of Archives and History, Montgomery.

four members of the ICC lived on the eight-hundred-mile coast-line from Washington to Maine; not one resided on the three-thou-sand-mile coastline from Washington south to the Mississippi River. Sectional considerations were not so important, he said, in fixing rates as in railroad consolidation. Underwood's comments on the Woodlock appointment were well received in the South but not in the North. The appointment was stymied, however, and President Coolidge resorted to a recess appointment whereby Woodlock served without pay. However, in December, 1925, yielding to pressure, the administration secured passage of a bill to increase ICC membership from eleven to twelve. The president appointed Richard V. Taylor, the mayor-commissioner of Mobile, to the new post. Inevitably, it was charged that Underwood had made a deal with Coolidge to support Woodlock's confirmation in return for the appointment of Taylor to the ICC. Underwood, who indeed now supported Woodlock, said that he and Senator Heflin, who also favored the Taylor appointment, had "no conspiracy" with the president but that "had a conspiracy been necessary, very probably my colleague and I would have conspired." Underwood said that Coolidge had agreed to appoint a southern member if a proper one could be found, and Underwood had suggested Taylor. Two weeks later, Underwood took Taylor to the White House at Coolidge's invitation. The president then asked that Underwood assure him of both Alabama senators' support for Taylor's confir-mation before he would agree to submit the nomination. After con-ferring with Heflin Underwood gave these assurances, and Coolidge sent Taylor's name to the Senate. Underwood announced that he would support Woodlock since his only objection to him was geo-graphic.[3]

Taylor's appointment was not without opposition. Huey P. Long, chairman of the Louisiana Public Service Commission, noted that Taylor, a Mobilian and former general manager of the Mobile and Ohio Railroad, had conferred after his appointment with Forney Johnston who, Long noted, as general counsel for the Seaboard Air

3. Birmingham *Age-Herald*, February 8, October 27, December 22, 1925.

Line Railway had opposed the interests of the port of New Orleans. Defending himself before the Interstate Commerce Committee, Taylor said that he had opposed absorption of the Seaboard by the Southern because the Southern had traditionally favored New Orleans over Mobile. He maintained, however, that he would oppose preference for one port at the expense of another. Long's objections thus appeared actuated by the commercial rivalry between New Orleans and Mobile. The Senate confirmed Taylor and Woodlock, although the latter was confirmed with great difficulty.[4]

The Woodlock appointment was not the only Coolidge appointment on which Underwood balked. In May, 1926, Coolidge reappointed Aubrey Boyles United States attorney for the Southern District of Alabama, based in Mobile. Boyles had been appointed four years earlier and confirmed without opposition. The Judiciary Committee approved the reappointment, there being no apparent senatorial objection. However, twenty members of the Mobile Bar Association, about half the total membership, charged that Boyles over-zealously and illegally enforced the prohibition laws. Boyles had lodged 120 suits based on information furnished by an informer who had collected some twenty thousand dollars from bootleggers who assumed they were buying protection. All but seven of the controversial indictments were dropped. Underwood, supported by Senator Heflin, opposed the nomination as "personally obnoxious" to him. They were supported by the Alabama Bar Association and by the old line Alabama Republican organization headed by national committeeman Oliver D. Street, with whom the Alabama senators often cooperated. Boyles was supported by the Anti-Saloon League. Senate Democrats and a few Republicans supported Underwood and Heflin and refused to confirm Boyles by a vote of 52 to 22. Boyles had claimed to have the support of Attorney General Sargent, but the hasty acceptance of Boyles's resignation together with that of his assistant indicates that the administration was less than ardent in his support.[5]

4. *Ibid.*, January 12, 1926. Taylor was a brother of Hannis Taylor, former United States minister to Spain.
5. Birmingham *News*, May 20, 21, 1926.

In March, 1925, Underwood introduced a cloture rule that he had favored earlier. His comprehensive cloture proposal would have ended debate through the use of the previous question device: a majority of the senators voting could adopt the previous question, and after that an hour would be allowed for each senator to end debate. In a New York *Times* article, Underwood said that rules in the Senate had changed little from 1789 when it had twenty-six men to 1925 when it had ninety-six. Underwood noted that almost every other legislative body, including the House of Representatives, had a cloture rule. There were hundreds of ways a resourceful senator could find to filibuster, he said, inviting his colleagues to "Look at the wrecks strewn along the legislative shores." Vice-President Dawes joined Underwood in Birmingham to support his appeal before the Associated Industries of Alabama for nonpartisan support of effective cloture. Underwood denied that the cloture rule would result in the passage of "force" bills or federal legislation to control elections, declaring that the Alabama Constitution of 1901 gave "absolute assurance of good government"—he meant rule by white men. Underwood gave several illustrations of measures that would have passed the Senate with an effective cloture rule—the ship purchase bill of 1914, the bill to arm merchantmen in 1917, the Treaty of Versailles, and his Muscle Shoals bill. Underwood and Dawes were warmly welcomed, but the audience was uninterested in the cloture proposal. The Birmingham *Age-Herald*, which had become increasingly critical of Underwood, recalled his use of the filibuster to defeat the Dyer antilynching bill of 1922 and printed Underwood's speech alongside remarks made by the late senator John Tyler Morgan in filibustering against "force" bills in the 1890s. There was never a chance that Underwood's cloture proposal would pass. An estimated six senators favored it, together with Vice-President Dawes whom senators resented as a meddlesome newcomer.[6]

Underwood's cloture proposal was not reported by the Rules

6. *Congressional Record*, 69th Cong., Special Sess. of the Senate, 9; New York *Times*, March 15, 1925, Sec. 9, p. 1; Birmingham *Age-Herald*, May 28, 1925.

Committee, and on June 4, 1926, after his retirement had been announced, he introduced a cloture rule that was both narrower and more drastic than his previous proposals. The new proposal applied only to appropriation and revenue bills, and upon majority passage of the previous question called for an immediate vote assuming that a calendar day of debate had passed. Underwood used poker rules as an analogy to show that Senate rules were archaic. He argued that his proposal would avoid the spectacle of Congress failing to pass vital supply bills, insisting that many southern senators, including his grandfather Joseph Rogers Underwood and that noted filibusterer John Tyler Morgan of Alabama had introduced cloture proposals. Underwood said that when he filibustered against the Dyer antilynching bill in 1922, he was merely taking advantage of the existing rules although he did not think the measure would have passed without the filibuster. Underwood concluded sentimentally that the "scars and glory of the Civil War have passed into history" and that force bills were gone.

Underwood's southern colleagues were not so sure that sectionalism was dead, though his poker analogy gave some levity to the otherwise rancorous debate. Senator James Reed said that the Senate had in Underwood "not a deuce but a very fine ace running wild." Senator Joseph T. Robinson of Arkansas shouted that Underwood "discredits and dishonors the brilliant and glorious career which he has enjoyed in the Congress." Neither of Underwood's cloture proposals reached a vote, and four days before his Senate career ended he vainly renewed his pleas for a cloture rule.

Rumors that Underwood would retire developed during the Democratic convention of 1924, and they gained momentum when it was learned that the Underwoods were selling their home at 2000 G Street and moving to Woodlawn, a historic mansion that was part of the Mt. Vernon estate. The Underwoods had lived since 1913 in the comfortable old house, "2000 G," near the White House. The senator had, however, complained on the Senate floor about increasing traffic congestion at his corner lot. The Underwoods felt increasingly affluent after the distribution of income from the Woodward estate began in 1919, two years after Mr.

Woodward's death. After extended bargaining, a price of $115,000 in cash was agreed upon for Woodlawn, which was placed in Bertha's name. President Wilson had made several attempts to buy the house prior to the death of its owner Miss E. M. Sharpe.

Woodlawn was located sixteen miles south of Washington on the Camp Humphreys Road on a tract of 160 acres of an original 2,000 acre tract. George Washington had bequeathed this acreage to his nephew Lawrence Lewis and his wife Eleanor "Nelly" Parke Custis, Martha's granddaughter. The twenty-room Georgian house was planned by Dr. William Thornton, the Capitol architect, and George Washington himself surveyed the property and allegedly reviewed the plans although the building was not begun until 1803. The house, 130 feet wide and 40 feet deep, was surrounded by magnificent trees and fine boxwoods, had frontage on Dogue Run, a creek, and commanded an inspiring view of the Potomac River. After the Civil War Woodlawn had fallen into disrepair, but it had been restored and modernized by Miss Sharpe. Mrs. Underwood took the servants from her Washington house to Woodlawn and added others so that the couple now lived in comparative opulence. The house at 3398 Highland Avenue in Birmingham had long been the residence of the senator's older son, John Lewis, and in 1926 the senator and Oscar, Jr., transferred their interest to John Lewis.[7]

In early June, 1925, former governor Thomas E. Kilby of Anniston, a wealthy industrialist, announced his candidacy for Underwood's seat, noting that he would oppose any change in the cloture rule. Judge J. J. Mayfield announced that he would run if Underwood did not. Former Jefferson County solicitor Hugo L. Black, popular with Protestants and the Ku Klux Klan because of his successful defense of a Methodist minister accused of murdering a

7. *Congressional Record*, 69th Cong., 1st Sess., 10696–703; Washington (D.C.) *Post*, May 16, 1925. The senator sold some Japanese bonds, using the receipts to purchase Woodward Iron Company preferred stock from Mrs. Underwood who thus raised the cash necessary to purchase Woodlawn. The house at 2000 G Street, NW, was sold for $40,000, or $35,000 net to Underwood, to the Washington College of Law. Oscar W. Underwood to O. W. Underwood, Jr., June 21, 1925, in Underwood Papers, Alabama Archives; Deeds Book 1590, p. 27, Jefferson County, Ala.

Catholic priest, added lustre to his political strength through the prosecution of an alleged Mobile "rum runner" and appeared a probable candidate.

With Klan strength at a high tide in Alabama, Underwood faced a difficult race if he chose to run for reelection in 1926. Oscar, Jr., and other members of the senator's family urged him to retire, and he told Mrs. Underwood before leaving for Birmingham in early June, 1925, that he would not run. Yet he harbored hopes that a groundswell of demand would develop for his return to the Senate. Upon arriving in Birmingham, he promised a decision by July 1, saying that he would consult friends before deciding.[8]

Underwood addressed his hometown Rotary Club, which had recently made him an honorary Rotarian, on June 10 at the Tutwiler Hotel. Saying, "that government that governs least governs best," which must rank as his favorite quotation, Underwood denounced the growth of federal bureaucracy, especially that of "independent bureaus." He stated that the ICC was a valuable agency—not one of the useless ones of which he spoke—although he objected to its sectional composition. The Departments of Justice and War he considered necessary, but he singled out the Bureau of Soils of the Department of Agriculture as unnecessary. Noting that he had secured a soil survey for his district twenty-five years ago, Underwood said that since the time of Grover Cleveland a half billion dollars had been wasted on bureaus that were useless or existed only for "convenience." He concluded that "the burden of taxation will hamper business in its development and progress unless it is slowed down."

Indicating that he would run if the people of Alabama so desired, Underwood went by automobile to Montgomery for a major address on taxes to the Alabama Tax Clubs. Telephone lines were installed for transmission of the speech to Atlanta and thence to Pittsburgh for broadcast over radio station KDKA. Underwood boldly advocated the sharp reduction of federal taxes. Denouncing high taxes as socialistic, and as stifling to the American economy,

8. Birmingham *News*, June 7, 10, 1925.

he said, "There is a school of philosophy extant in America that would destroy, if they could the private ownership of all property and mass it in the hands of the state." He equated the destruction of property with the destruction of human life. Noting that the Fifth Amendment prohibited the taking of property without compensation, Underwood said that the taxing power had no limit and thus might be used to destroy private ownership. He argued that high rates had forced capital "into hiding" and that money that would otherwise be invested as risk capital was in bonds, which he considered nonproductive. Underwood's solution was a rollback of tax rates to pre-World War I levels, with a reduction of the maximum income tax from 67 percent to 15 percent and the inheritance tax maximum from 46 percent to 20 percent. He pointed out that as early as 1919 Secretary of the Treasury Carter Glass had stated that the surtax had passed the point of productivity. These lower rates would, he said, give sufficient revenue for the government if the president were given blanket authority to abolish bureaus.[9]

Underwood's drastic proposals were seen by the press in the context of earlier, more moderate proposals for tax reduction advocated by Secretary of the Treasury Mellon and Senator Carter Glass. Mellon had proposed a 25 percent maximum for the income tax and Glass a maximum of 20 percent. Few editors saw any prospect that Underwood could take the Democratic party along with the proposal to "out Mellon Mellon," although there was considerable sympathy with his position. The Birmingham *Age-Herald* noted that Underwood had taken part in the defeat of Mellon's tax reduction plan in the previous Congress.[10]

Underwood's speech inspired Montgomery friends to urge him to run for reelection. Almost all of his political friends assured him that he would win the race, but Underwood recognized that it would be a difficult fight. Victor Hanson, publisher of the Birmingham *News*, told Underwood that he would win, but when Under-

9. *Ibid.*, June 11, 12, 1925; New York *Times*, June 13, 1925, p. 1.
10. Clippings in Underwood Scrapbook, la, 61, 63, 73, Underwood Papers, Alabama Archives.

wood declined to make the race, Hanson agreed that he was wise. Returning to Tate Springs, Underwood issued a handwritten statement that he would not be a candidate for reelection to the Senate and that he was retiring from politics. The New York *Times* remarked editorially on the enemies Underwood had made by his preference for "pondered judgment to the demagoguery of the hour."[11]

Underwood and Bertha relaxed at Tate Springs in August. In an interview relative to the Democratic nomination in 1928, still three years away, Underwood predicted that the religious fanaticism that had been sweeping the country would "no doubt be ended" by 1928, and he saw no reason why a Roman Catholic should not be nominated. He noted Al Smith's powerful eastern support and thought that once Smith was the nominee, the South would rally behind him. By late August the Underwoods were again in Washington, as Woodlawn was not yet refurbished for its new occupants. Underwood predicted that for "about ten days we will find ourselves in a cyclone of kettles and pans."[12]

In October, Underwood addressed the American Bankers Association at Atlantic City. Objecting again to the lack of southern representation on the Interstate Commerce Commission, he urged the appointment of southerners to the commission. He also discussed the problem of railroad consolidation, saying that railroads would ultimately be forced to consolidate simply for economy.[13]

Death was beginning to close in on the senator as family members died. Little Eugenia "Ge Ge" Underwood, John Lewis' daughter and the senator's first grandchild, named for his first wife, died of meningitis following a mastoid operation at the age of seven in 1921. His mother also died in 1921. His half-sister Marinda

11. Birmingham *News*, July 1, 1925; New York *Times*, July 3, 1925, p. 12.
12. Birmingham *Age-Herald*, July 28, 1925; Underwood to R. H. Evins, August 26, 1925, in Retirement File, Underwood Papers, Alabama Archives.
13. Birmingham *News*, October 2, 1925. The New York *Commercial*, October 28, 1925, insisted that the South, counting the District of Columbia, had as many commissioners as the East.

"Rin" died in Birmingham in late November, 1925, followed two days later by his brother Sidney's wife, Clara, who died in Augusta, Georgia.

In early January, 1926, Underwood wrote an article for the New York *Times* commenting on inheritance taxes—especially on a proposal that would levy a federal inheritance tax, 80 percent of which would be remitted to those states with satisfactory inheritance tax laws. Underwood's article was much more extreme than his Montgomery speech on taxation. Declaring that the "surplus wealth that is acquired by man's energies and intellectual service, is recognized by all as an essential to the onward progress of our civilization and to the continuous advancement of man," he stated that rates in excess of 20 percent were confiscatory. He boldly denounced proposals for the federal government to collect inheritance taxes for the states as being for an "ulterior purpose" and "inconsistent with any theory of government except that of the communists." He declared that there was no need to use "the red flag of the anarchists under which to distribute the wealth of the nation."[14]

In mid-January, 1926, Underwood spoke in Congress in favor of seating Senator Gerald P. Nye from North Dakota. Nye, a Republican, had been appointed by the governor of North Dakota despite the lack of a state statute allowing him to do so. Underwood supported Nye's seating on the basis that every state had the absolute right to two senators. Underwood did not explain how his opposition to the seating of Truman H. Newberry in 1919 could be reconciled with such a theory. Most Democrats voted for Nye, and he was seated in a close vote.[15]

Party lines were unimportant in the Coolidge administration's

14. New York *Times*, January 10, 1926, Sec. 8, p. 7. Underwood had personal acquaintance with the inheritance tax since as administrator of the estate of his father-in-law, J. H. Woodward, he had sued the Internal Revenue Service before the court of claims over the inheritance tax owed by the estate. *Congressional Record*, 67th Cong., 1st Sess., 5951, 5953. On one occasion Mrs. Underwood wrote that the government has "rich people by the nose." Bertha Underwood to Mrs. A. H. Woodward, July 31, 1920, in Woodward Papers, in possession of Mrs. Joseph II. Woodward II, Birmingham.

15. *Congressional Record*, 69th Cong., 1st Sess., 1830–32.

advocacy of adherence to the World Court. A resolution of adherence passed the House without difficulty, but in the Senate the "irreconcilable" opponents of the Versailles treaty attached reservations to safeguard United States independence of action in foreign relations. Underwood regarded the Foreign Relations Committee's reservations as unnecessary. He likewise opposed an attempt to add a reservation to the five already attached prohibiting enforcement of the court's decisions by war. Underwood argued that the World Court possessed no power to make war and that had the court been in existence in 1914 the war would have been averted. The amendment was rejected 69 to 22.[16] The resolution of adherence passed, but the reservations to the resolution were not accepted by the other signatories to the court, and the United States did not become a member.

While the World Court battle was going on in January, 1926, Underwood and Bertha had the grippe, but the senator refused to go to bed. Mrs. Underwood recovered, but the senator did not, and by late February he found that he was panting at the least exertion. After thorough examinations, two physicians determined that his heart muscle "was not pulling right" and ordered him to bed. At first he rested at Woodlawn, but in April he went to Atlantic City to complete his recovery.[17]

Returning to the Senate floor in early May, he opposed the arbitration provisions of the railroad disputes bill. The bill provided for arbitration in railroad disputes between railway managers and the railway brotherhoods in order to determine wage rates. Underwood maintained that the railroads no longer resisted railway labor wage raises unless they resulted in rates that were so high as to hamper use of the railroads. The increased wages were paid for by railroad users anyway. Governmental regulation was the only way to protect the public, Underwood insisted and he favored the Curtis amendment, which empowered the Interstate Commerce Commission to set aside wage contracts that placed an "undue bur-

16. *Ibid.*, 2797–98, 2816.
17. Underwood to Sidney Underwood, March 19, April 7, 1926, in Red Folder, Underwood Papers, Alabama Archives.

den" on interstate contracts.[18] The Curtis amendment was rejected
59 to 14, and the arbitration bill became law by a vote of 69 to 13.
In the minority of thirteen opposing the bill, Underwood was one
of only four Democrats. The railway brotherhoods as well as most
railway executives favored the measure.

In the summer of 1926, Underwood joined with twenty-one
Democrats, most of whom were southerners, in aiding the
Coolidge administration to defeat the McNary-Haugen farm bill.
The bill proposed to boost prices of farm staples through a revolving fund for government purchases. Surplus staples would be
dumped on the world market for whatever price they would bring.
Farmers would repay the government's losses for its purchase program through an "equalization fee," which, it was assumed, would
be far less than the farmer gained through the purchase program.
Southern Democrats had been little interested in the bill since it
did not cover the major southern crops, and the measure was first
defeated in the summer of 1924. The 1926 version extended cov-
erage to cotton, tobacco, and rice, reserving half of the fund for
those products. The 1926 bill also provided that the equalization
fee would not be applied for three years. Underwood objected that
the additional price received from farm products would have to be
paid by the "toiling millions" of the country. He could not tax the
bread of iron and steel workers whose products, he said incorrectly, he had placed on the free list in the Underwood-Simmons
Tariff Act. Underwood joined southern Democrats and eastern Republicans to oppose the McNary-Haugen bill, but it passed in February, 1927.[19] Underwood, who was ill, did not vote, and President
Coolidge vetoed the bill.

A speech to college graduates in Dothan in southeast Alabama
revealed Underwood's increasing bitterness and skepticism toward
politics. He advised college graduates to stay out of politics and
said: "You strike out for high accomplishment, but by the time you
get through compromising with the adverse forces in order that

18. *Congressional Record*, 69th Cong., 1st Sess., 8888–89.
19. *Ibid.*, 11870.

you may get your own proposal accepted very often you do not recognize your own child. Compromises in government are more often bad than good—at least they are almost sure to produce undesirable results."[20] It was an ironic note from a master legislative compromiser, who was seemingly unaware that the interests he represented could often be identified by others as "adverse forces."

Senator and Mrs. Underwood embarked on a trip to Europe in early August, 1926, as the Alabama primaries were about to begin. The Klan was heartened by the nomination of Bibb Graves as governor and Hugo Black as senator, both of whom were considered Klan candidates. The Ku Klux Klan held an exultant rally of three thousand in Birmingham's municipal auditorium, and Imperial Wizard Hiram W. Evans attacked Underwood principally for his advocacy of American membership in the World Court.[21]

In England, Underwood told the Harrogate Rotary Club that prohibition was a failure. There was not a town or city the size of Harrogate in the United States, he said, in which one could not get a bottle of liquor: "You may pay a pretty price for it, but you can get it." Even in Washington where unlimited funds for enforcement had been available, it was not effective. No law, he continued, could "rise higher than the jury box," and in those states where prohibition was unwanted it was almost impossible to secure convictions for violations. He continued: "There is no reason for the abatement of your enthusiasm for the high ideals of temperance, but if your enthusiasm for high ideals carries you to the point of demanding Parliamentary enactment, to forcing the way by the strong hand of Government before the peoples are prepared to accept it, you will pay the price that we have paid in America for the experiment."[22]

Upon his return to the United States Underwood expressed concern at the strong underlying anti-United States sentiment in Europe. Europeans thought, he said, that the wealth of the United States had been made out of the war and that America had not

20. Montgomery *Advertiser*, June 3, 1926.
21. Birmingham *News*, September 3, 1926.
22. Yorkshire (Eng.) *Post*, September 15, 1926.

done its part in the fighting. Although cancellation of the war debts would make it appear that the United States was pleading guilty to an indictment, he said, the Fordney-McCumber rates must be reduced or "the American people have no right to expect European nations to pay their war debts." He said that the gold drain from Europe to the United States was caused by restrictive immigration quotas, especially the Italian quota, prohibition, especially relative to shipment of British and French alcoholic beverages, and the expansion of United States shipping. Unless Europe's unfavorable balance of trade were corrected, he said, there would be a day of reckoning when Europe could no longer borrow in the United States.[23] Underwood's analysis accorded with his views favorable to tariff reform, but his denunciation of the low Italian immigration quota, though consistent with his pro-Italian stance, was inconsistent with his earlier fight for immigration restriction.

During January, 1927, Underwood's last days in Congress, illness removed him from the Senate floor. Pleurisy developed into pneumonia, but ignoring his physician's advice he returned to the Senate as soon as he was strong enough to walk. In the last few days of his term the Senate was torn by filibusters, and his final remarks were to encourage the adoption of a cloture rule. There was no opportunity for complimentary speeches when he retired on March 4, but Senator James Watson, a strongly partisan Republican, gave reporters a glowing tribute to Underwood.

Editors generously praised Underwood. The encomiums were mixed with comments that he would probably have been defeated and that his service alongside Heflin, one of the most notorious of demagogues, had been a paradox. The Birmingham *News* editorialized that Alabama had lost its greatest statesman since the 1860s and said, "When the eagle folds his wings from his flight toward the sun, the lesser breeds come forth—the little pee-wee, the ground-skimming chimney sweeps, seeking their small rations of insects—the twittering noisy sparrows."[24] The Birmingham *Post*,

23. St. Louis *Post-Dispatch*, October 24, 1926.
24. Birmingham *News*, March 4, 1927, December 8, 1926.

however, caustically assessed Underwood's career: "His adherents have been those who largely were guided by self-interest and who hitched the tail of their political fortunes to Underwood's kite. There was little personal warmth in those political alliances."[25] The statement that Underwood served his friends was accurate, but no one who knew the senator could accuse him of a lack of warmth.

Underwood felt a sense of relief upon retiring from the Senate. He wrote his brother Sidney in Atlanta: "I am glad to lay aside the burdens of public office for they have been growing heavy for me to carry in the last few years. I have gone through thirty-two years of public service with great opportunities and some achievements without leaving any mark of discredit behind me. That is enough for any man."[26]

Oscar and Bertha spent several weeks in Atlantic City, where he hoped to complete his recovery from the bout with pneumonia. By late May, they were back at Woodlawn, where a Fairfax County justice of the peace issued a warrant for his arrest because Bertha's 1924 Packard had a District of Columbia license plate rather than that of Virginia. The officer was unable to find the senator or his chauffeur, and, apparently because of publicity unfavorable to Virginia, the paper was never served. Underwood purchased the license but wrote a friend and angrily criticized the fee system: "The fact that you and I are annoyed by small officers of the law occasionally because we drive automobiles, I am sure will not hurt us, but there is a real evil in allowing constables and judges to make their living out of fees collected from the public."[27]

Underwood began writing his book, but he was distracted by activities at Woodlawn. There was painting and carpentry to be done as well as the replacement of trees and shrubbery. Then too, Woodlawn was a farm, and Underwood mentioned that they were getting in their spring crops, mainly hay. They planned to spend

25. Birmingham *Post*, March 4, 1927.
26. Underwood to Sidney Underwood, March 4, 1927, in Red Folder, Underwood Papers, Alabama Archives.
27. Underwood to F. M. Carrington, June 11, 1927, in Letterbox N, Underwood Papers, Alabama Archives.

the summer at Woodlawn with perhaps a few days at Tate Springs in the dead of the season. In mid-May they had a two-week visit from Oscar, Jr., his wife, Ellen, and their baby Oscar III, whom the grandfather described as "a fine fellow [who] can say a few words and run about quite well."[28]

In June, 1927, Underwood wrote his friend Edward D. Kenna, a St. Louis railroad executive, analyzing a proposal for the creation of a Democratic advisory group to determine policy long before the convention of 1928. Underwood saw little value in the idea. "In the past we have faced the question of the Democratic party getting together a good many times, especially after the Cleveland-Brian [sic] break in 1896. It can't be done that way. Men's politics are made up of their prejudices and passions rather than their principles, and prejudices and passion is [sic] the last thing they surrender as a rule, except under compulsion."[29]

Underwood planned to write several books, and Tracy Lay, then consul general to Buenos Aires, who had served as Underwood's aide during the Washington Conference, proposed to resign from the Foreign Service to collaborate with him. Underwood at first encouraged Lay but then resisted the suggestion of collaboration, preferring to write on his own and being skeptical of the advisability of Lay's resigning from the Foreign Service. Strangely enough, Underwood looked upon the venture as a lucrative one.[30]

Occasionally, Underwood's bitterness was laid bare. He wrote his brother Sidney that his German shepherd Otto, who was "perfectly kindly with humans, is getting worse than ever with dogs, which is probably an indication of lack of good tast[e] on his part." He added a quotation from Ouida: "The more I know of men, the better I like dogs."[31] The New York *Times*, always favorably dis-

28. Underwood to Sidney Underwood, May 30, 1927, in Underwood Papers, Alabama Archives.
29. Underwood to Edward D. Kenna, June 3, 1927, in Underwood Papers, Alabama Archives.
30. Underwood to Tracy Lay, April 9, June 18, 1927, in Letterbox N, Underwood Papers, Alabama Archives.
31. Underwood to Sidney Underwood, October 11, 1927, in Letterbox N, Underwood Papers, Alabama Archives.

posed toward Underwood, printed an article by him, "The Vanish-
ing Republic of Our Fathers," just before his retirement, which
showed the depth of his disillusionment. He wrote that the end of
the Spanish-American War was the turning point in American history. He regarded the Teller Amendment, which he erroneously
identified as the Platt Amendment, as a grave mistake that led to
the United States denying itself Cuba and adding Puerto Rico and
the Philippines to the national domain. The United States "thus
became a part of the complex politics of the Orient and the legatee
of all the problems that grew out of colonial possessions and the
government of an alien people." He did not explain why Cuba
might not have been as much of a problem as Puerto Rico or the
Philippines.

Underwood contrasted what he called the Mark Hanna "era of
involvement" with Lincoln's "elementary government." He objected to the loss of authority by the Congress to the president,
especially through the creation of "independent agencies," a term
which he seemed to apply to all government agencies. These agencies, he argued, were subservient to the executive and were setting policies over such diverse areas that they could not be fair in
their regulation. He concluded gloomily, "The genius of the Republic of Washington, Lincoln, and Cleveland no longer exists—
the genius of government that sought to interfere with the personal
rights and liberties of the citizen to as small an extent as possible
in order that the government might function."[32]

Underwood continued his interest in foreign affairs after retirement. He privately expressed disappointment in the failure of the
Coolidge administration to "breathe the real spirit of the Washington Conference" relative to China, saying, "We have been too careful about dollars and have not visualized the awakening of a great
people and their movement toward freedom." Evidently, he favored a renunciation of United States extra-territorial rights in
China. He accepted an appointment from President Coolidge as
American member of the Franco-American Commission, estab-

32. New York *Times*, February 27, 1927, Sec. 4, p. 3.

lished under the Bryan Treaty to arbitrate controversies between the two countries. Underwood's appointment may well have resulted from New York *Times* columnist Richard V. Oulahan's suggestion that Underwood be a member of the American delegation to the Geneva Disarmament Conference. Underwood accepted the nonpaying post as "a nice decoration," but it involved no effort since no disputes were presented for adjudication.[33]

Underwood commented on the British-sponsored Geneva Disarmament Conference, called to extend to lesser craft naval limitations established for capital ships at the Washington Conference. He thought that European affairs were disturbed by France's fear that Germany would again attack and England's fear of starvation through submarine warfare. When France declined to attend the conference, he said, Britain proposed a high level of naval strength that the Senate would never have agreed to. Britain had been "honest" in calling the conference, he said, but the British Foreign Office was at times "pig-headed" and "unable to visualize American political conditions at all." When the conference failed, he said that the United States had been made the "goat" in the inability of Britain and France to settle their differences. He commented skeptically on proposals made by French Foreign Minister Aristide Briand that war be "outlawed." Although he found Briand's idea of universal international peace through arbitration and conciliation "a beautiful sentiment," it would not be accepted by the first-class powers. England would never consent, he noted, to submit the problems growing out of her recent acquisition of territory in Africa to international arbitrament. Nevertheless, Underwood endorsed the view expressed by many after Charles Lindbergh's tumultuous reception in Paris that the Coolidge admininistration should explore the Briand proposal.[34]

33. Underwood to Lay, April 9, 1927, Frank B. Kellogg to Underwood, August 3, 1927, both in Letterbox N, Underwood Papers, Alabama Archives; New York *Times*, May 20, 1927, p. 1; Underwood to Kenna, September 19, 1927, in Letterbox N, Underwood Papers, Alabama Archives.

34. Underwood to Kenna, August 6, 1927, Underwood to Marian E. Martin, November 4, 1927, both in Letterbox N, Underwood Papers, Alabama Archives.

Woodlawn was pleasant; the sixteen miles from Washington and several hundred miles from Birmingham insulated Underwood from many of the world's cares. They slept on the back porch in the summer nights and played a little golf in the morning, and he worked on his book, "rather an engaging sport." Underwood maintained contact with Alabama politics through the Birmingham *News*. He felt that his campaign for the presidency had checked Klan outrages in Alabama, though in the summer of 1927 Klan depredations were resumed in Birmingham, and a man who lived across the street from Underwood's former home there formed a Klan "band," which beat an old Negro and forced him to convey his property for a fraction of its value. Underwood endorsed the Birmingham *News*'s editorial war against the Klan and, in a letter to its publisher, Victor Hanson, urged Alabama to adopt an antimasking law. Judge Campbell wrote to Underwood in appreciation of his anti-Klan statements, and Underwood acknowledged the letter sentimentally as coming from one "who started me on the path of [political] life."[35]

A year before the nominating conventions, Underwood analyzed the domestic political situation. He assumed that Coolidge would be the Republican nominee, but when Coolidge said "I do not choose to run," Underwood accepted his statement as sincere. He saw the Democrats in the North as dominated by the foreign-born—liberal in religious viewpoint and antiprohibitionist—and predicted a split with the northern Democrats if the southerners' support of the Klan and the Anti-Saloon League continued. Underwood thought that McAdoo's "sloshing around" indicated that he would again seek the nomination. He noted that McAdoo's followers had wanted to abolish the two-thirds rule at the 1924 convention when their candidate had a majority of the votes and would probably have done so if Underwood had agreed. But the McAdoo people realized that the two-thirds rule might work to their advantage in 1928 in blocking Smith and reversed themselves. Although

35. Underwood to Kenna, July 21, 1927, Underwood to Victor H. Hanson, August 15, 1927, Underwood to Edward K. Campbell, August 30, 1927, all in Letterbox N, Underwood Papers, Alabama Archives.

Underwood saw value for the South in the two-thirds rule, he believed that if the South blocked the majority's presidential choice in 1928, the rule would be abolished in 1932. The McAdoo candidacy failed to materialize.

Underwood consistently supported Al Smith for the nomination. He wrote an admirer of former secretary of war Newton D. Baker that he too admired Baker, who he thought could carry to the presidency "more than the average ability that has hithertofore gone there." But he doubted that Baker could be elected. He saw Al Smith as the only man who could win because "he is the only man that the liberal element of the North visualize as being with them."[36]

In the summer and fall of 1927, Underwood was alone at Woodlawn while his wife was in Tate Springs putting the final touches on the Underwood cabin, a two-bedroom house that must have approached the expense of the Taj Mahal. He wrote some during the day, dictating to his secretary, but much of his time was spent in the management of the old house and its servants. He played golf rather poorly but with interest in imitating the stance of Bobby Jones. Woodlawn proved not so isolated from Washington as he thought. On one occasion he noted that "five thousand cars must have passed this quiet country place yesterday." There were occasional social obligations such as receiving the crown prince of Abyssinia, who urged him to visit his country, and having lunch with Justice and Mrs. Harlan Fiske Stone.[37]

Underwood's repose at Woodlawn was broken by his appointment as a delegate to the Sixth Inter-American Conference. He arrived in Havana four days early for the conference, which began on January 16, 1928, accompanied by Bertha and an aide selected for the occasion, Richard Kenna, son of a railroad executive who was an old friend. Arriving before most of the other delegates, who

36. Underwood to Kenna, August 6, 1927, Underwood to Walter Moore, September 1, 1927, Underwood to James S. Wilson, July 1, 1927, all in Letterbox N, Underwood Papers, Alabama Archives.

37. Underwood to Bertha Underwood, undated [*ca.* June, 1927], September 18, 1927, both in Oscar W. Underwood Papers, University of Virginia Library.

came in a party with President Coolidge, Underwood served on the important Committee on Public International Law and Frontier Police. He was not, however, a member of the crucial subcommittee that dealt with the troublesome movement to repudiate the Roosevelt Corollary to the Monroe Doctrine. The intervention problem was postponed, to the relief of the United States. There is no evidence that Underwood took any significant part in the discussions of the conference, which ended by late February. He remarked, "We have been dined and wined until we appreciate [that] there can be too much of a good thing."[38] He and Mrs. Underwood boarded the *Veendam*, a Holland-America liner, for a Caribbean cruise.

In the Canal Zone, the Underwoods were the guests of Governor and Mrs. M. L. Walker. Interviewed in Balboa, Underwood urged the nomination of Governor Smith and repeal of the Eighteenth Amendment. He expressed assurance that Smith would win the South if Hoover were the nominee although he declined to predict Democratic victory. The remainder of the Underwood itinerary included Jamaica, Panama, South America (presumably Venezuela), the Leeward and Windward islands, Puerto Rico, and Bermuda. Underwood called it "a most interesting and delightful trip," but traveling under the tropical sun was hard on Bertha who became ill on shipboard and returned to Woodlawn the "worse for wear."[39]

On a visit to Birmingham in May, 1928, Underwood predicted Smith's nomination and election although Alabama had just elected a "dry," anti-Smith delegation to the Democratic convention. He also predicted, erroneously, that the Democrats would favor the repeal of the Eighteenth Amendment, declaring that the amendment had not diminished the liquor traffic and that the people "are

38. *Report of the Delegates of the United States of America to the Sixth International Conference of American States* (Washington, D.C.: Government Printing Office, 1928), 8, 88; Underwood to O. W. Underwood, Jr., February 26, 1928, in Underwood Papers, Alabama Archives.

39. New York *Times*, February 28, 1928, p. 3; Underwood to Mrs. William H. Thornton, April 4, 1928, in Underwood Papers, Alabama Archives.

tired of Government intervention in the case of both individuals and business."[40] The following month, he commented on prohibition in writing a friend: "there is no greater danger that can threaten a popular government than for the citizens of a country to treat its laws with contempt. The fault does not lie with the citizen. Often the blame rests with the law-maker. Laws should not be enacted that are not in accord with the true sentiments of the people who live under them, and when a law is enacted that does not meet with popular approval it should be lawfully repealed rather than ignored."[41]

Sporadic efforts were made to draw Underwood back into political life or at least to compliment him with attention. Victor Hanson in 1927 suggested him as a presidential nominee for 1928. In the summer of 1928 there was talk in the Maryland delegation of nominating him for vice-president on the ticket with Smith. Nothing came of either suggestion. Underwood did not attend the Democratic convention at Houston. He thought that Smith had cinched the nomination, and Bertha was not well, having recently suffered the death of her mother. He thought that Smith's nomination would mark a new era in the Democratic party—that it meant a "return to the faith of the fathers, the true principles of government."[42] Another harbinger of good was the birth of his second granddaughter, named Ellen for her mother, on August 14, 1928.

Underwood's book, *Drifting Sands of Party Politics*, appeared in January, 1928. The title indicates the theme, that the United States has slowly drifted from the fundamentals of the Constitution and created a government quite different from that which the framers intended. The 411-page volume is based on wide reading and is laced with quotations from such disparate sources as Montesquieu, Bagehot, Jefferson, James Schouler, Frank W. Taussig, and Claude G. Bowers. Underwood wrote "by way of an apology for the com-

40. New York *Times*, May 10, 1928, p. 2.
41. Underwood to Carlton M. Sherwood, June 9, 1928, in Letterbox N, Underwood Papers, Alabama Archives.
42. Birmingham *News*, February 12, 1927; New York *Times*, June 22, 1928, p. 2; Underwood to Daniel H. Coakley, June 23, 1928, in Letterbox N, Underwood Papers, Alabama Archives.

promises I was at times compelled to accept," but he reveals little of his important role in legislative management. Rather, the book is an arid exposition of his well known states' rights theories.

In it Underwood reassessed legislation passed during his career. He reviewed the free-silver movement of the 1890s as a mistake although he saw virtue in the farmer's demand for more currency. He thought that the issuance of "asset currency," or money backed by bank assets, would have been preferable to free silver. He praised the Federal Reserve Act of 1913, which he credited to Carter Glass, as providing for decentralized regulation of banking, even though it was not in accord with states' rights. Holding fast to his low tariff views he nonetheless criticized vociferously the delegation of congressional power through the flexible tariff provisions of the Fordney-McCumber tariff. He denounced wartime measures passed during World War I, including the draft, the Espionage and Sedition acts, the Committee on War Information, and the Railroad Administration, asserting that the objectives of these measures could have been reached by voluntary action and that they were responsible for the postwar reaction. Child labor, he thought, should have remained under the control of the states. He criticized Congress' delegation of interstate commerce power to the ICC and the Federal Trade Commission rather than setting "fixed and definite" rules for the regulation of commerce.

Above all, Underwood denounced the Eighteenth Amendment as resulting from a movement of people who do not want to be good themselves, but who wish to make others good. Prohibition, he wrote, occurred because Americans have the "softest hearts and the hardest heads." He especially denounced the use of "secret societies" (the Ku Klux Klan) to enforce prohibition.

The book was written with a Jovian detachment and without rancor. Lincoln joined Washington and Jefferson as the nation's great men. Cleveland, whom he opposed in Congress, was honored as were two Cleveland cabinet members—John G. Carlisle, secretary of state, and Richard Olney, secretary of state and attorney general. President Wilson's program was both praised and criticized, but there was no attempt at an overall assessment of Wilson's career.

Even Bryan, Underwood's bitterest enemy, was treated gently. Underwood wrote repeatedly of the capacity of organized minority interests to get their views written into statutes. Such passages could well apply to his own yielding of the public interest to that of railroads and power companies, but he eventually makes clear that he is speaking of groups such as the Anti-Saloon League, the Protestant churches, and the Ku Klux Klan.[43]

Surprisingly, Underwood failed to claim credit for his crucial role in the passage of Wilson's New Freedom and war legislation. His egotism, frequently expressed in other places, was presumably held in check because of his doubts about the wisdom of some of the measures he had supported. Less surprising is his failure to talk of his diplomatic activities of the 1920s—his participation in the Washington Conference and other conferences. He may have recognized that his participation in foreign affairs had been largely ceremonial, or more likely, he intended to talk of these things in another volume.

The reception of Underwood's book was disappointing. The New York *Times* dutifully devoted the front page of its book review section to it, and it was widely reviewed elsewhere. Sales of the book, however, failed to justify the $2,650 advance to the author.[44] Even so, Underwood set promptly to work on a book on Latin America's relations with the United States.

By fall the senator's health was failing, and he apologetically wrote James A. Barnes, biographer of Speaker John G. Carlisle, that he was unable to give his inquiry about Carlisle "the attention it deserves." In early December, Underwood suffered a stroke and canceled a projected world tour. The vision difficulties of which he had earlier complained now became pronounced, and he was placed in the Wilmer Institute of Johns Hopkins for treatment. He was discharged from the hospital in late December, but by early

43. Oscar W. Underwood, *Drifting Sands of Party Politics* (New York: Century Company, 1928), *passim*.

44. *New York Times Book Review*, June 3, 1928, p. 1; Century Company to O. W. Underwood, Jr., May 6, 1929, in Underwood Papers, Alabama Archives. At the time of the senator's death, $1,650.21 of this advance was unearned.

January he was "seriously ill."[45] The senator's older son John Lewis and his wife Mary went to Woodlawn and stayed with the stricken man. Bertha was in a state of nervous collapse.

The senator rallied for a few days. He seemed alert and eager to talk although he was discouraged from doing so. He began eating solid food with a hearty appetite. However, he lapsed into unconsciousness on January 23, and two days later he died at 11:15 A.M. of a stroke. The family had withheld news of his relapse and the death came as a surprise to the public. The Senate and the House adjourned in an unusual tribute to one who was no longer a member of either body. The flags on the Capitol and the Senate office buildings were lowered to half mast. The Alabama congressional delegation went in a body to Woodlawn to offer condolences to the family.[46]

Tributes by the hundreds flowed from the pens of public men of both parties. President Coolidge remarked that "his public service made all the country under obligation to him." Governor Franklin D. Roosevelt of New York described him as a "gentleman of the old school," and former governor Smith recalled him as his "devoted friend." Senator Norris, his longtime antagonist, said "his word was always good." A streetcar conductor in Birmingham recalled that Underwood had ridden his line before the electrification of the Highland Avenue route and remembered the senator's daily comments, his Christmas gifts, the gift of a gold watch, and dinner at Woodlawn.[47]

The body was taken by hearse to the railroad station at Alexandria for transfer to Birmingham. At the station a large crowd awaited the arrival of the Birmingham Special, Congressmen John McDuffie, Henry B. Steagall, Edward Almon, and William B.

45. Underwood to James A. Barnes, November 1, 1928, in Miscellaneous File, Underwood Papers, Alabama Archives; Birmingham *Age-Herald*, January 4, 1929.

46. O.W. Underwood, Jr., to Sidney Underwood, January 10, 1929 (erroneously dated 1928) in Red Folder, Underwood Papers, Alabama Archives; Birmingham *Age-Herald*, January 26, 1929.

47. Calvin Coolidge to Bertha Underwood, January 25, 1929, in Underwood Papers, Alabama Archives; New York *Herald Tribune*, January 26, 1929; Birmingham *News*, January 26, 1929.

Oliver representing the Alabama congressional delegation. The train arrived twenty-five minutes late, and the bronze casket was lifted through the window of the Pullman car "Bordentown." The casket was then enclosed in a gray, steel cabinet in the center of the car, which was between the express car and the first coach of the train.

When the Birmingham Special arrived in Birmingham the following day at 3:40 P.M., an hour and five minutes late, hundreds of the senator's friends had gathered in the drizzling rain. The casket was quickly transferred to a hearse and from there to the Johns Funeral Home. The funeral party went to John Lewis' home on Claremont Avenue (the new name of Highland Avenue). The senator's body was brought from the funeral home to that of his elder son that night.[48]

The senator had not been a conventionally religious man. Oscar, Jr., said that when asked about religion his father talked about nature. Among his last papers was a transcription in the senator's handwriting of a letter of Thomas Jefferson which concluded pragmatically: "I have ever judged the religion of others by their lives."[49]

Plans had been made to have the funeral at John Lewis' home, but public interest in the event led to a change of plans. Charles M. Lewis, a cousin of Underwood's and a lobbyist for distilleries and later the government of China, made the funeral plans. The Independent Presbyterian Church, where Underwood's good friend Henry M. Edmonds was the minister, was selected in preference to St. Mary's Episcopal Church where he had been a member. Underwood had given Edmonds moral support some years before when Edmonds broke with the Presbyterian church in a controversy in which Edmonds favored "modern" theological views.[50]

48. Birmingham *News*, January 27, 1929; Birmingham *Age-Herald*, January 28, 1929.
49. Interview with O. W. Underwood, Jr., November 22, 1953; note in Underwood Scrapbook, I, 150, in Underwood Papers, Alabama Archives.
50. In the fall of 1915 or 1916, Dr. Edmonds was in a restaurant across the room from Senator Underwood. A waiter arrived with a note: "I am with you in this battle for sanity in religion." Henry M. Edmonds to E. C. Johnson, September 5 and October 10, 1951, in possession of Evans C. Johnson, DeLand, Fla.

The casket was moved to the church on Monday morning. When the doors were opened at 9:00 A.M., long lines of people were waiting to file by the open casket. During the brief service, Bertha was seated between Oscar, Jr., and John Lewis, her two stepsons, with A. H. "Rick" Woodward and other relatives in the same row. The second row was reserved for four Negro servants. Pallbearers and other Underwood associates filled the remainder of the reserved section. The service was brief, and there were no eulogies. Dr. Edmonds selected passages from John, Psalms, and Second Timothy: "I am the resurrection and the life"; "as for man his days are as the grass"; and "I fought the good fight."

The pallbearers rose and took their positions in the center aisle of the little church. Among the ten pallbearers and fourteen honorary pallbearers were the friends of Underwood's lifetime. Most were lawyers, a number were fellow Rotarians, and all were political friends from the Birmingham area. Henry R. Howze, Forney Johnston, J. P. Stiles, and Walter Moore were close political associates; M. V. Joseph and Oscar Wells were prominent Birmingham businessmen. At least seven of the twenty-four had received public office through Underwood's influence.

To the slow, majestic chords of Chopin's funeral march, Underwood began the journey to the grave. The procession, led by a police escort, crossed the southside of Birmingham to Elmwood Cemetery. At the cemetery two planes from the 106th Observation Squadron of the Alabama National Guard droned out a farewell. Floral tributes, including wreaths from several foreign embassies, were brought to the cemetery in a moving van and two passenger cars.[51] The graveside service consisted of two brief prayers, the second of which was: "He was the victor. Thanks be unto God who gave him the victory, and gave him to us. To live in hearts we leave behind is not to die."[52]

Oscar, Jr., found in his father's safe deposit box articles associated with his mother Virginia—the first Mrs. Oscar Underwood. Together with trinkets and her wedding ring, there was a poem

51. Birmingham Age-Herald, January 29, 1929; New York World, January 29, 1929.
52. Joseph N. Benners to O. W. Underwood, Jr., January 28, 1929, quoting Dr. Edmonds' prayers, in Underwood Papers, Alabama Archives.

about Genie written by a Confederate veteran who was registered as a student at the University of Virginia but largely confined to his quarters with tuberculosis. The poem was in admiration of the child, later Underwood's bride, who played outside his window on "The Lawn" of the University. Underwood died without a will, an unfortunate situation, especially with two sons and their step-mother as the heirs. There was, however, no indication of any squabbling. Letters of administration were filed at the Jefferson County Court House by Underwood's friend, Probate Judge J. P. Stiles. The size of the estate was estimated at $50,000 and John Lewis Underwood was designated as the executor. He made bond for $100,000. The gross estate, however, amounted to $327,623.83. The senator's conservative nature was reflected in his stock port-folio which consisted mainly of preferred stock in the Woodward companies. He owned two hundred shares of Woodward Iron com-mon worth $12,000 and small amounts of stock in the Birmingham Trust and Savings Company and the Blount County Bank. Bertha generously gave up her interest in the senator's estate to his two sons. A few months later she deeded the Underwood cabin at Tate Springs together with rights to drinking from the famous spring, to the senator's brother, Frederick. The property was returned to her when he died in 1934. A year later, an acre of the property was sold for $2,000. Bertha received in 1941 a payment of $370 from the Tennessee Valley Authority for a part of the Tate Springs prop-erty that was flooded by Cove Creek Dam—an ironic epitaph to her husband's fight for use of Tennessee River power for fertilizer production.[53]

Bertha planned to have an authorized biography of Senator Un-derwood written, and his papers were reorganized. She wanted to hire Allan Nevins, Julian Harris, or Claude G. Bowers for the task. Eventually, she determined to reprint *Drifting Sands of Party Pol-*

53. Interview with O. W. Underwood, Jr., July 7, 1955; Administration Record Book 12, pp. 71–72, Jefferson County Court House, Birmingham; Final Settlement Book 17, pp. 408–10, Jefferson County Court House, Birmingham; Federal Estate Tax Return for Oscar Underwood, Sr., in Underwood Papers, Alabama Archives; Deeds Books 56, p. 587, 61, p. 562, 63, p. 95, 68, p. 442, all in Grainger County Court House, Rutledge, Tenn.

itics and to include a biographical introduction by Bowers. Bowers'
twenty-four page biographical sketch is hardly more than a eulogy.
The volume, reprinted in 1931, was mailed to a long list of friends
and former Underwood constituents. Bertha continued to live at
Woodlawn for several years among the fine antiques that she and
the senator had acquired. A visitor in 1935 was met by Cortez, the
butler who had served in the senator's lifetime. Among the prize
furnishings were a 1665 sideboard, a portrait of Senator Joseph
Rogers Underwood, a life-sized portrait of Senator Oscar Underwood, and a chair owned by Nelly Custis and purchased by the
senator. The senator's office contained framed originals of cartoons
in which he was a principal, notably those of Clifford K. Berryman
of the Washington *Star*.[54]

Something was wrong, however. A newsman recalled that in the
early 1940s Bertha visited Tate Springs, which the senator had
loved so well. Always a devotee of fortune tellers, she lavished
money on a seeress in the hope of contacting "Oscar." In 1944 she
was moved from Woodlawn to an apartment in New York City near
that of Eugenia Woodward, daughter of her brother, A. H. "Rick"
Woodward. The court appointed a guardian *ad litem*, and on February 28, 1945, upon the petition of her brother, she was declared
mentally incompetent. Eugenia was retained at a salary of $350 a
month plus travel expenses to care for her aunt. The court's order
anticipated Bertha's removal to a Philadelphia hospital where she
was placed soon after being declared incompetent. Woodlawn was
sold to the Immaculate Heart of Mary Mission for $165,000 in
1948, but evidently the court did not approve as it was almost immediately resold to the Masonic order.[55]

Bertha Underwood died in the fall of 1948 at the Philadelphia
hospital and was buried in Elmwood Cemetery in Birmingham.
She was survived by her brother Rick and by her stepsons.

54. Birmingham *News*, February 13, 1935.
55. Interview with Hugh Sparrow, June 15, 1960; Chancery Order Book, 1944, No.
5958, Fairfax County, Virginia, 191–93, in Fairfax County Courthouse, Fairfax, Va. The size
of the bond would imply liquid assets of perhaps $200,000. The majority asset being a life
trust, it was not necessary to bond for the corpus of the estate.

Oscar, Jr., who left a Washington law practice in 1940, was a professor of law at the University of Virginia for ten years. When the writer knew him, he and his wife, Ellen, the granddaughter of pioneer Alabama industrialist Daniel Pratt and the daughter of a second industrialist by the same name, lived in an attractive Georgian home in Charlottesville. Mrs. Underwood died in 1960 and Oscar, Jr., in 1962. They were survived by two daughters and a son, Oscar Underwood III. John Lewis Underwood, the senator's older son who died in 1973, was survived by his wife Mary, the daughter of Judge E. K. Campbell, in Birmingham. Retired some years ago from the sand and gravel business, he was the physical incarnation of the senator but was a reticent man who revealed little of his famous father to visitors.

CHAPTER XVI

The Pattern of a Bourbon Elitist

Birmingham was a mining frontier town when Underwood arrived in 1884, and a spirit of camaraderie soon developed among the young men who sought their fortunes in a burgeoning little city. Underwood emerged as a leader of this group who were to be political friends for a lifetime. Victory in the general election of 1894 (later reversed by the House of Representatives) showed the popularity of his quasi-Populist views, as well as astute manipulation of votes by black-belt Democrats. However, he had not permanently rejected the conservative states' rights tutelage of Professor John B. Minor in law classes at the University of Virginia, and as Populism receded he embraced conservative and orthodox Democratic views.

Oratory was not one of Underwood's arts. His early speeches had the florid quality of the Bourbon politician and evoked fears of Negro rule, but his passionless delivery and restrained nature softened the impact of his racism on the northern press. As he matured, he recognized his ineffectiveness at "old school" oratory, and his speeches became surfeited with facts and figures so that many an ardent supporter was "turned off" after the first column of tariff statistics. His serious, stentorian, and verbose delivery, unrelieved by humor or anecdotes, added to the ennui of his listeners. Rarely did he use popular terminology to make a point or excoriate an opponent. Oscar Underwood, Jr., recalled that his father's voice in speeches was not his conversational voice and that it had a "metallic" quality. Underwood explained that he could not be an orator because he was not frightened as orators were when they spoke.[1] If his oratory was mediocre, his written expression was worse. Unlike his prolixity on the floor of Congress, his letters are cryptic and unreflective, marked by poor grammar and confused syntax.

Underwood entered Congress with an anachronistic respect for party platforms, and he took the Democratic tenet "a tariff for revenue only" quite literally. So taken, a tariff pegged at a level to produce sufficient revenue to run the government would furnish incidental protection for the heavy products of Birmingham's mines and furnaces. Even so, his orthodoxy on tariff reform was suspect, and in 1903 when he might otherwise have reclaimed his position on the Ways and Means Committee, he was blocked by the skeptical minority leader, John Sharp Williams. Underwood had presidential ambitions, and even his marriage to the daughter of Birmingham's wealthiest citizen and an independent iron producer did not prevent him from advocating moderate tariff revision. Birmingham was a low-cost producer of iron products, and although Birmingham iron and steel producers opposed a reduction in the tariff on iron products, some recognized that the tariff was irrelevant to the city's inland markets and that cheap access to the sea and an export trade were more important.

Underwood, who had demonstrated organizational ability as Democratic whip between 1900 and 1903, resumed his advancement when he was restored to the Ways and Means Committee by Williams in 1905. Although Underwood participated in the destruction of Speaker Joseph G. Cannon's power in 1910, he secured the adoption of strong House rules when he became majority leader in the special session of 1911, and, more importantly, he reinstituted binding caucus action and disciplined the Democrats. The resulting tariff bills embarrassed the Republicans and prepared the way for Democratic victory in 1912. The combination of Underwood's organizational ability with his membership in the "good old boy" group of southern congressmen made him a na-

1. Interview with O. W. Underwood, Jr., November 24, 1951.

tional leader and catapulted him into the race for the Democratic nomination which he lost to Wilson in 1912.

Except for the tariff and banking, Underwood was little interested in reform, but his pragmatism won out over his states' rights and strict construction views so that he supported most of Wilson's New Freedom. President Wilson cajoled him, rewarded him with patronage, and helped in his successful race for the United States Senate. Not only did Underwood lead the House in passage of the Underwood-Simmons Tariff Act and the Federal Reserve Act with which he was in basic agreement, but he piloted through the House the Clayton Act and other antimonopoly measures about which he was unenthusiastic.

In the Senate, Underwood was more independent of the Wilson administration than he had been in the House, and he viewed much of Wilson's domestic program with a jaundiced eye. During World War I, however, he generally supported Wilson's policies. After the war he advocated ratification of the Treaty of Versailles, although his willingness to accept interpretative reservations or even to drop the League of Nations from the treaty angered Wilson and led to doubts that Underwood genuinely favored ratification.

Campaigning for reelection to the Senate in 1920 against a little-known opponent, L. B. Musgrove, Underwood demonstrated an increasing insularity from and dislike for earthy Alabama political campaigning. Basing his campaign on a reversal of his earlier pro-labor stance, he refused to shoulder the campaign burden, leaving it with Forney Johnston. Underwood attacked Musgrove for liberality on the Negro question, and Musgrove accused Underwood of pro-Catholic sentiments. Underwood was so distraught that he threatened to retire from the race. His narrow victory reflected his lack of contact with Alabamians outside of Birmingham and was a harbinger of his retirement from the Senate in 1927.

Nevertheless, Underwood became Senate minority leader in 1920. Frustrated by the Senate's failure to use binding caucus action and the lack of an effective cloture rule, he found Senate rules a great handicap. Always a vain man, his vanity was played upon by President Harding and Secretary of State Hughes when he was appointed a delegate to the Washington Conference, where his role was largely ceremonial. His support of ratification of the Washington treaties together with his continued opposition to prohibition put him out-of-step with southern Democrats, and in 1923 he resigned as minority leader.

During Underwood's career, the distance between the Capitol and the White House increased. His relations with the chief executive became closer in every presidential administration, reflecting his advancement toward House leadership and reaching a peak in Wilson's first administration. After his transfer to the Senate and American entry into World War I, his relations with Wilson were distant despite the Alabamian's assumption of the duties of Senate majority leader during the war. The complexities of war together with the president's illness after Versailles made communication difficult. President Harding maintained close relations with Underwood while the Washington treaties were pending in the Senate, but with ratification this relationship lapsed. President Coolidge's relationship with Underwood was friendly but not close. The executive had grown to such an extent that the president and an important congressional leader lived in worlds that were essentially far apart.

Underwood's pragmatism and his businessman's viewpoint were seen in his marathon fight for the development of Muscle Shoals. The passage during World War I of legislation for the building of Wilson Dam and two nitrate plants was followed by years of postwar frustration as he fought for completion of Wilson Dam. Underwood favored private development not because of his commitment to laissez-faire but because it was the only hope for immediate development of the shoals in the years of Republican control. Although Presidents Harding and Coolidge favored private control, Underwood was unable to secure their support for his plan of private operation.

Early in 1924 Underwood was considered a formidable contender for the Democratic presidential nomination. His campaign, however, was launched in the unfavorable atmosphere of strong prohibition and Ku Klux Klan sentiment. Well known as an anti-prohibitionist, opposition to the Klan came naturally to him, and, feeling that he must use the Klan issue in order to attract northern voters, he denounced the hooded order. The aging candidate showed courage and candor, but his Klan position was politically popular outside the South. Unable to afford a national campaign, he entered southern primaries, reasoning that he would win southern delegates who would serve as the base upon which eastern support, and to a lesser extent western, would be added in the convention. He had overestimated his strength in the South, and with his loss of the southern primaries that he entered, except that of Alabama where the contest was restricted to state residents, his candidacy had little chance of success. He could only have become a national candidate by reversing his well-known stance against labor and against federal farm price supports. These things he was unwilling to do, and such a reversal would have further eroded his conservative base. There was never a real chance for Underwood's nomination, and even the retirement of Al Smith from the race was not enough to make Underwood a powerful contender.

With the loss of the Democratic nomination in 1924, Underwood began the life of a country gentleman at historic Woodlawn in Accotink, Virginia. He had, as Mark Sullivan had earlier observed, "an excessive urbanity"—at least for an Alabama politician.[2] His respiratory ailments became more acute and were accompanied by heart trouble. He lost interest in the Senate and in his long battle for private development of Muscle Shoals. At the end of his Senate career he joined Vice-President Dawes in unsuccessfully attempting to secure passage of an effective cloture rule. With encouragement he would have sought reelection in 1926, but the increasing power of the Ku Klux Klan and prohibition forces made defeat probable at the hands of Hugo L. Black who had powerful Klan support.

As a member of Congress, Underwood had an advantage over many other members in being identified with a number of states.

2. Birmingham *News*, January 18, 1921.

As particularistic as were members of the House, he could claim common experience with congressmen from Kentucky (the state of his birth), Minnesota (where he lived in his youth), Virginia (where he attended college), Ohio (ancestral home of his first wife), West Virginia (girlhood home of his second wife), Tennessee (where his father lived for a number of years), and Alabama.

From the beginning of his career Underwood carefully cultivated the press. Journalists of the day, often derided as "penny-a-liners," depended so much for bread and butter on their sources that they almost always printed what those sources wanted. He maintained close and friendly relations with members of the press, and even a distinguished reporter like Arthur Krock, bound to Underwood by a common Kentucky background, felt beholden to him for the interviews he received. Occasionally Underwood bought space in special newspaper editions, lent money, or indirectly subsidized reporters or cartoonists—purchasing originals of Berryman cartoons, for example. Friendly reporters were given letters of introduction to William Randolph Hearst or other notable figures. The prohibitionist Montgomery *Journal* was an exception among Alabama newspapers in treating Underwood harshly throughout his political career. [3]

Through the press Underwood constructed an image of himself that was only partially factual. Almost every interview emphasized his geniality, saying "Underwood smiled" or "Underwood laughed." Details of his life were changed in minor ways for his political advantage. For example, after he entered politics the time of the Underwood family's move from Louisville to the North was shifted from late 1864 to late 1865, a less embarrassing time for a son of the South to depart. Having never completed an earned college degree, he was repeatedly said to have graduated from the University of Virginia. In an anachronistic fashion, he emphasized that he

3. Arthur Krock to Oscar W. Underwood, March 4, 1911, in Letterbox M, H. F. Jones to Underwood, June 8, 1911, A. F. Chambers to Underwood, April 30, 1911, in Birmingham File, McLanahan, Burton, and Culbertson to Underwood, October 20, 1914, Aubrey Hardell to Underwood, May 4, 1911, all in Underwood Papers, Alabama Department of Archives and History, Montgomery.

came from a prominent family—as indeed he did. Underwood presented himself as a careful, deliberate, methodical man, who seldom erred and who cleaned his desk every day. Yet the deed to his own home, drawn in his handwriting in 1890, is erroneous in that he failed to complete the description by closing the rectangle on which his home sat. He was accused of having caused financial difficulty for a Kentucky relative by failing to record a mortgage so that years later two mortgages were discovered on the same property. Bills were occasionally left past due, sometimes because of moves between Birmingham and Washington, but often enough to lead one to question if he was as meticulous as he claimed.[4]

Underwood's fierce temper was shown when he challenged a fellow college student to a duel. This temper stayed with him throughout his career although in his later life he learned self-control. In the senatorial campaigns of 1914 and 1920 his opponents attempted, unsuccessfully, to goad him into anger to give lie to the press image of Underwood as "Placid Oscar."

As a politician, Underwood was an "accommodationist," a broker of the interests that surrounded him. He never accepted any form of bribery—if one excludes the financial support given in campaigns by those who sought governmental favors. Underwood's services to Birmingham's industrial interests resulted not from venality, as his enemies argued, or laissez-faire convictions, as his friends claimed. Rather, he favored business interests as a result of the influence of personal friends to whom he owed political debts. An exception to this was in the steel industry where, despite close friendships among the independent producers of Birmingham, he favored tariff reduction. Always favorably disposed toward the railroads, this association deepened in Underwood's eagerness to repay his two most important political friends, railroad attorneys Ed Campbell and Forney Johnston. In public utilities he consistently supported the power projects of J. W. Worthington, a utility lobbyist who combined avarice with a vision for the development of

4. Warner U. Grider to Underwood, June 26, 1909, in Underwood Papers, Alabama Archives; see, for example, University of Virginia to Underwood, May 25, 1910, in Accounts File, Underwood Papers, Alabama Archives.

Alabama—first for Birmingham and later for the Tennessee Valley
area. After World War I, support of Worthington's Muscle Shoals
plans ranged Underwood alternately on the side of Ford and
American Cyanamid and in opposition to Alabama Power, Alabama's largest corporation. Birmingham, unlike its sister city Atlanta, was a "company town" with relatively little indigenous capital. Although Underwood would have preferred native capital to
absentee financing, as a practical matter he decided which interest
to support based on personal considerations. On the national scene
his closest friend in the financial community was Thomas Fortune
Ryan, who had heavy investments in insurance, utilities, and railroads.

Underwood's book, *Drifting Sands of Party Politics*, grapples
morosely with the central problem of democratic government—
protection of individual rights. Repudiating his own role as a compromiser, he advocated a return to simplistic and pristine government. He noted the continuing aggrandizement of political power
by the presidency at the expense of Congress and the loss of individual freedom through attempts of the majority to legislate morality, especially through prohibition legislation. In arguments
similar to those of economists Friedrich Hayek and Milton Fried-
man of a later era, he warned gloomily of the loss of freedom unless
the trend toward statism were reversed. Although these warnings
are trenchant to one writing after the Watergate affair, there is little
in Underwood's career to indicate a concern for minority rights
aside from his opposition to the Klan and to prohibition. Indeed,
there is little indication, either in his career or in his political testament, that he was sensitive to the needs of the blacks who lived
in the most segregated of cities, his hometown. Like John C. Cal-
houn of the previous century, he struggled manfully with the problem of minority rights but found no workable solution. He devoted
little attention to foreign affairs until late in his career, and, though
he was basically a man of peace, his ignorance sometimes led him
to chauvinism. He recognized that war was economically unsound,
and after World War I he shared the desire of most Americans to
avoid a costly arms race and build a world of peace.

Underwood's political idols were Speakers Reed and Cannon, both of whom were autocrats. When Underwood became House majority leader, he shrewdly divested the speakership of its power and thrust the institution into an eclipse from which it did not emerge until Speaker Nicholas Longworth restored much of its power in 1925. As majority leader, Underwood failed to engender the animosity that both Reed and Cannon suffered. His motto, "Always leave 'em happy when you say goodbye," taken from George M. Cohan, was effective.[5]

Knowing the rules of the political game well, Underwood was a "role player" who did not take political animosity off the floor. In only twelve of his thirty-two years of service did the Democrats control both Houses of Congress, and his relations with his Republican opponents were cordial. Republicans played on his vanity at times by praising his leadership, yet it is unlikely that he could have served the minority nearly so well had he not gotten along with the Republicans.

Underwood once said that one of his mottoes was "know thyself," but unfortunately he misunderstood his role as a legislator. His forte was an astute knowledge of parliamentary rules and a nimbleness at accommodating differences among legislators. Although he was not a formulator of broad policy, he was a legislative craftsman of consummate ability. His parliamentary skill was legendary, and both Senator Walter F. George and Speaker Sam Rayburn described Underwood as the greatest party leader they had ever seen.[6]

Underwood was a warm and congenial man. Forney Johnston called him "the most magnanimous man I ever knew," and certainly he was not one to bear a grudge despite the heated politics of the time.[7] Almost every one of his political friends had at one time been an opponent: J. W. Worthington, Senator Joseph F. Johnston, and Senator John H. Bankhead. Even William Jennings Bryan re-

5. Edward G. Lowry, *Washington Close-ups* (Boston: Houghton Mifflin, 1921), 223.

6. Walter F. George to E. C. Johnson, May 23, 1952, in possession of Evans C. Johnson, DeLand, Fla.; interview with Sam Rayburn, June 30, 1951.

7. Interview with Forney Johnston, August 16, 1951.

ceived a courteous letter from Underwood after years of political infighting. Underwood was acutely aware of the necessity for conciliating the opposition.

There is not the slightest bit of evidence, after his unfortunate challenge of a fellow student to a duel, that Underwood's personal life was less than exemplary. His first wife, attractive and easygoing but in bad health, was his true love, and the sons that she bore him were to have Underwood's careful attention—although he had much help in rearing them. His second wife, nine years his junior, worshipped her husband, and their relationship was almost that of father-daughter rather than husband-wife. Bertha, as everyone in the family called her, was an insecure woman who fancied herself an aesthete and, like Eugenia, suffered from ill health. Her bad health, however, appears to have been psychological. She read books on psychology, evidently for introspective reasons, and her insecurity was reflected in profligate spending and in an unquestioning support of her husband in his political career. Evidently it was partly because of her desire that he ran for the Democratic nomination in 1924. Unfortunately, Bertha did not think reflectively about politics, and she was unable to help her husband adapt to the changing postwar world.

Underwood was an eminently rational man, but he seems to have been influenced at least briefly in the 1920s by his wife's interest in the occult. In 1923 he sought a permanent army commission for his brother Sidney, then fifty-nine years old. Sidney, who had been a civil engineer with the Canadian Grand Trunk Railway, had held a temporary commission in army ordnance. He was eager to secure a permanent commission, but turned down as being "too old" by the army, he sought his brother's help. Oscar received the same answer from numerous army officials. One evening, Oscar reported, he sat in his Washington home in front of a wood fire following his defeats in army offices. As he looked into the flames, he saw his mother's face smiling at him. The following day he tried again, secured the support of the surgeon general, and Sidney received the permanent commission.[8] Perhaps more significant than

8. O.W. Underwood, Jr., "Commentary on the Dissertation of Evans Johnson (ms. in possession of Evans C. Johnson, DeLand, Fla.), 11.

Oscar's belief that he had made a foray into the supernatural world was that fact that his mother—not his father—appeared to him. There is little evidence of the influence of his father despite the fact that Underwood was grown before his father died. His mother was the strongest influence in his life although he did not share her religiosity.

Oscar Underwood was a man of moderate ability who through hard work and long service in Congress mastered its rules. With this skill and through personal magnetism he led his party in both houses—the first man since Henry Clay to do so. Underwood was the first Deep South candidate to make an effective race for the Democratic presidential nomination and, because of his subsequent career in the mainstream of national politics, is sometimes cited as a symbol of the decay of sectionalism. This rather romantic picture is inaccurate. Underwood was nationally ambitious, and these ambitions doubtless influenced him toward a more national position than he otherwise would have had. On the other hand, few southern senators were more particularistic and sectionalist in judging nominations or legislation that affected the South. The intriguing parallel between Underwood's quest for the presidency and that of President Jimmy Carter is belied by Carter's lack of congressional experience and his reliance upon Negro support.

Closer parallels than Carter are to be found in other southern statesmen. Senator Richard B. Russell of Georgia, whose career Underwood influenced, was respected as a parliamentarian in the Senate, but Underwood would have disapproved of his use of the filibuster. Russell was the strongest Democratic contender for the presidential nomination from the Deep South between the Civil War and 1976 except for Underwood. Lyndon B. Johnson, although not from the Deep South, parallels Underwood in legislative craftsmanship, and, though Underwood might well have encountered the same problems of unpopularity had he become president, it is difficult to imagine that he would have shucked his regional views as much as did Johnson. Despite apparent similarities with other southern statesmen, Underwood was *sui generis*.

Underwood was stubborn and unresponsive to popular currents. Perhaps the fact that he seldom drove an automobile after he shifted to a gasoline powered engine illustrates his incapacity for change. Although his career has been interpreted by some as that of a national statesman, and indeed there were moments when that appeared to be so, his final tragedy was an incapacity to adapt to the political world of the 1920s. Opposing labor unions, women's suffrage, coeducation, and child labor legislation, Underwood was unattuned to the progressive forces of the age. Yet, one applauds his opposition to prohibition, the Klan, and isolationism.

Underwood had most of the obvious hallmarks of a Bourbon. He identified himself with the Confederate tradition, favored laissez-faire, economy in government, states' rights, and Jeffersonianism. Nevertheless, these shibboleths do not always describe the essence of Bourbons who, after all, were essentially promoters of New South business through generous concessions by government. Although Underwood's advocacy of tariff reform is an exception to his Bourbonism, on economic interests other than the tariff he pandered to business interests and practiced "business interest politics." This was especially reflected in his Senate career in his favoring of the railroads and in his opposition to organized labor. To leave Underwood's political philosophy as that of a southern Bourbon, however, fails to take full account of the fact that despite his advocacy of doctrinaire tenets, he was a pragmatist who made concessions to his fundamental political beliefs in order to reward his friends and maintain himself in power.

In many respects Underwood was the product of elite politics as Gaetano Mosca and Vilfredo Pareto, political theorists of the twentieth century, would have used the term. "Born to the purple" with moderate wealth, he stood apart from the common people, whose judgment he distrusted and whom he was destined to lead in a poverty-stricken South. A man of superior organizational ability and personal attractiveness, he had the family connections necessary for political success. Although his credentials as a "Bourbon" were not flawless—he was too young to have a war record and not all of his family were Confederate sympathizers—he nonetheless arrogated to himself the symbols that made him acceptable to his sectionally oriented electorate, a relatively small percentage of the population. Never in full sympathy with those he learned to refer to in Populist days as "the toiling masses," he ended his career as a Bourbon elitist out of step with his unsophisticated Alabama electorate.

Bibliographical Essay

Most of my research was done in primary sources—manuscripts, newspapers, or government documents. This bibliography is concerned largely with specialized monographs that deal at length with Underwood or with the direct background for his career. A more extensive listing is to be found in the footnotes; no attempt is made to be exhaustive.

ORAL HISTORY: I began this study in 1951 with an appeal through letters to the editors of Alabama newspapers for information about Oscar Underwood. Through these sources and through personal friends, I interviewed Underwood's political associates and a number of men familiar with Alabama politics of the period. The reminiscences were generally of limited value, the interviews having been conducted five to fifty years after the events, with opinions and memories mellowing through the years. Nevertheless, I found this testimony invaluable in setting the stage of Alabama politics and furnishing leads for the location of Underwood manuscripts. The late Oscar W. Underwood, Jr., then a retired professor of law living in Charlottesville, Virginia, furnished a huge mound of Underwoodiana that had not at that time been deposited in libraries. Unfortunately, Professor Underwood's memory of his father was marred by a hero-worshipping filial relationship. An older son, John Lewis Underwood, the physical incarnation of the senator, was uncommunicative. Judge Henry R. Howze of Birmingham was helpful but really had not been a member of the inner circle of

Underwood's advisors. Forney Johnston, whose role in this study is largely confined to Underwood's later career, was too busy with a huge corporate law practice to comply with his offer to help. However, a pamphlet written by Johnston (noted below) is probably the best source for information about Underwood's House career with the exception of the *Congressional Record* and the newspapers. Dalton Swann, a court reporter in Birmingham, furnished candid information based on his observations as a clerk in Underwood's office in 1920. Justice Hugo L. Black received me graciously, but his knowledge of the senator was largely limited to the Ku Klux Klan period about which he was less than candid. Tracy Lay of Orlando, Florida, recalled his service as Underwood's aide at the Washington Conference. Others interviewed were: Senator Lister Hill; Peter Brannon, secretary of Thomas M. Owen in the 1912 campaign; Carroll Kilpatrick, a clerk in Underwood's office; Hugh Sparrow, a Birmingham *News* columnist; Cassius M. Stanley, editor of the Montgomery *Alabama Journal*; Speaker Sam Rayburn; Judge Walter B. Jones; Hugh Morrow, Sr., chairman of the board of directors, Sloss-Sheffield Iron Company; Judge Oakley Melton; and Frederick I. Thompson, editor of the Mobile *Register*.

MANUSCRIPTS: The mother lode for the study of Oscar W. Underwood is the Underwood Papers at the Alabama Department of Archives and History in Montgomery. This collection, thirteen file drawers of correspondence and three file drawers of clippings and scrapbooks, is extremely voluminous but of low quality. Carbons of Underwood correspondence were not regularly saved until 1910. However, the quality of the materials in the basic collection was enriched while this study was in progress by the addition of newly discovered files of letters that had been received in Birmingham (rather than Washington). Also, two letterboxes, "M" and "N," consisting of correspondence with prominent people, especially presidents, were added. Other collections at the Department of Archives and History containing significant Underwood correspondence are those of Joe Wheeler, John H. Bankhead, Sr., and Thomas Goode Jones.

Duke University Library contains a number of collections that have a few Underwood letters. The James Hemphill papers contain numerous references to Underwood's 1912 campaign in the Carolinas. The Neyle Colquitt papers provide a surprising insight into the Georgia and Florida campaigns in 1912. The Richard L. Maury collection has one highly significant letter relating to Underwood, from Maury's son. The Southern Collection of the University of North Carolina at Chapel Hill has several collections of incidental value to the Underwood scholar: Braxton B. Comer, Daniel A. Tompkins, Robert W. Winston. The Library of Congress has energetically collected the papers of twentieth-century United States government officials, and within the period in which Underwood served in Congress, 1895–1927, one can find a few Underwood letters in many of these. Those collections that contain valuable Underwood material are: Richmond Pearson Hobson, Woodrow Wilson, George W. Norris, Charles S. Hamlin, and John Sharp Williams.

The most valuable Underwood papers in private hands are those owned by Mrs. Joseph H. Woodward II of Birmingham. These papers, a microfilm copy of which is retained by the author, contain correspondence from 1904 to the early 1920s between Bertha Underwood and her father, Joseph H. Woodward, who died in 1917, and between Bertha and the senator. They are the most candid Underwood letters seen by the author. Papers of the New York law firm of Davies, Hardy, Schenck & Soons include files of Joseph S. Auerbach, a confidant of Underwood in his 1912 campaign.

The University of Virginia Library contains valuable Underwood material in papers bearing on the history of the university itself. Papers of the Jefferson Society and faculty minutes of the University of Virginia were especially useful. The most valuable collection is a special one of Underwood papers that were withheld by Oscar Underwood, Jr., until his death. These papers (identified as Underwood Papers, University of Virginia in the text) contain letters from Underwood's first wife and correspondence between Underwood and the sister of his first wife, Mrs. Malvern C. "Nita" Patterson, who cared for his two sons during most of their childhood.

Professor Underwood considered the letters to be too personal for viewing by scholars, and although they are invaluable, there are no shocking revelations in them. The collection is much smaller than that in the Alabama Department of Archives and History, but its quality is much higher. Other collections containing some Underwood material include: Carter Glass, Jouett Shouse (copies of originals in the University of Kentucky Library), and E. A. Alderman.

The files of the Ways and Means Committee in the National Archives proved valueless. Only one letter of Underwood's was located among the official papers of Judge Edward K. Campbell, Underwood's closest political associate. A vigorous search for personal papers of Judge Campbell has yielded nothing.

The Historical and Philosophical Society of Ohio at Cincinnati has the Judson Harmon papers, which contain a few Underwood letters in the period 1910–1912. The Ohio Historical Society at Columbus, Ohio, contains a few highly significant letters exchanged between President Harding and Underwood. The New York Public Library contains the papers of John Quinn, an Irish bibliophile and art collector, which are of some value for the 1912 campaign. Other letters of interest are in the Albert Shaw, Robert Underwood Johnson, and R. R. Bowker collections. The University of Alabama Library at Tuscaloosa contains a few Underwood letters in the Henry D. Clayton and J. Thomas Heflin collections. Yale University Library contains a few Underwood letters in the papers of Edward M. House and, more importantly, William C. Beer, a tariff lobbyist. Columbia University has a few Underwood letters in the papers of Nicholas Murray Butler and George W. Perkins. Samford University Library contains the Joseph J. Willett, Sr., papers which are significant for Alabama politics. Correspondence developed by this author in the writing of this study is retained by the author.

Much information may be found about the Underwood family in the property records in Ramsey County, Minnesota (St. Paul) and Jefferson County, Kentucky (Louisville). The Jefferson County Court House in Birmingham contains numerous court records relative to Underwood's law practice in addition to records of his real estate transactions.

ARTICLES: Popular magazines gave considerable attention to Underwood during the period 1910–1912. Among the more useful articles are Burton J. Hendrick's "Oscar W. Underwood, a New Leader from the New South," *McClure's Magazine*, XXXVIII (February, 1912), 404–20, and Alfred Henry Lewis' "Underwood—House Leader," *Cosmopolitan*, LII (December, 1911), 109–14. Paul B. Worthman treats a neglected area of Birmingham history in "Black Workers and Labor Unions in Birmingham, Alabama, 1897–1904," *Labor History*, X (Summer, 1969), 375–407.

Some of the material in this book was previously published in periodicals: "Underwood and Harding: A Bipartisan Friendship," appeared in the *Alabama Historical Quarterly*, XXX (Spring, 1968), 65–78. "The Underwood Forces and the Democratic Nomination of 1912" appeared in *The Historian*, XXXI (February, 1969), 173–93. Four of my Underwood articles appeared in the *Alabama Review*: "Oscar W. Underwood: An Aristocrat from the Bluegrass," X (July, 1957), 184–203; "Oscar W. Underwood: A Fledgling Politician," XIII (April, 1960), 109–26; "Oscar Underwood and the Hobson Campaign," XVI (April, 1963), 125–40; "Oscar W. Underwood and the Senatorial Campaign of 1920," XXI (January, 1968), 3–20. The *Alabama Review* contains numerous articles by other authors that relate to this study. Charles G. Summersell's "The Alabama Governor's Race in 1892," *Alabama Review*, VIII (January, 1955), 5–35, is a valuable treatment of Reuben F. Kolb and Alabama Populism. Martin Torodash gives a general view of Underwood's tariff position in "Underwood and the Tariff," *Alabama Review*, XX (April, 1967), 115–30. Lee N. Allen, "The McAdoo Campaign for the Presidential Nomination in 1924," *Journal of Southern History*, XXIX (May, 1963), 211–28, and by the same author "The 1924 Underwood Campaign in Alabama," *Alabama Review*, IX (July, 1956), 83–99, have been relied upon heavily. Adrian G. Daniel, "J. W. Worthington, Promoter of Muscle Shoals Power," *Alabama Review*, XII (July, 1959), 196–208, throws light on a shadowy power lobbyist who was close to Underwood.

Background for Underwood's House career is found in Arthur S. Link, "The South and the 'New Freedom': An Interpretation," *American Scholar*, XX (Winter, 1950–51), 314–24, and Richard M. Abrams, "Woodrow Wilson and the Southern Congressmen, 1913–1916," *Journal of Southern History*, XXII (November, 1956), 417–37. Underwood's career as House leader is dealt with effectively in James S. Fleming, "Re-establishing Leadership in the House of Representatives: The Case of Oscar W. Underwood," *Mid-America*, LIV (October, 1972), 234–50.

PAMPHLETS AND BOOKS: At the time this study was begun in 1951 very little that had been published among volumes of memoirs and general history gave much help relative to Underwood. An exception was Thomas M. Owen's *History of Alabama and Dictionary of Alabama Biography* (4 vols.; Chicago: S. J. Clarke Publishing Company, 1921), which is indispensible for the study of Alabamians up to 1921. Albert B. Moore's *History of Alabama* (University, Ala.: University Supply Store, 1934) was quite helpful. There is no satisfactory history of Birmingham. John W. Dubose, *History of Jefferson County and Birmingham, Alabama* (Birmingham: Teeple and Smith, 1887) still has value, however, and Ethel Armes, *The Story of Coal and Iron in Alabama* (Birmingham: Chamber of Commerce, 1910) is invaluable. For Underwood's side in the election contest in which he was unseated, see Edward K. Campbell, *Aldrich vs. Underwood, Brief for Contestee* (Birmingham: Leslie Brothers, ca. 1898).

Some of the best material on Underwood appears in intensely partisan campaign pamphlets, copies of which may be found in the Underwood Papers at the Department of Archives and History in Montgomery. The best account of Underwood's House career is in [Forney Johnston], *Democratic Senatorial Campaign: The Issue and the Facts* (Birmingham: Roberts & Sons, ca. 1914); although published anonymously, the pamphlet is the work of Forney Johnston. See also J. H. Patten, *Truth about Underwood, Hobson, Clark, McElderry and Others* (Birmingham: Roberts & Sons, ca.

1914) which defends Underwood from charges made by agrarian radicals; *The Unparalleled Record of Oscar W . Underwood of Alabama on Legislation of Interest to Labor* (Birmingham: Dispatch Printing & Stationary Company, *ca.* 1920); and Forney Johnston, *Democratic White Paper* (Birmingham: Roberts & Sons, 1916). For anti-Underwood views see L. Breckinridge Musgrove, *Facts About the Senatorial Campaign: The Vital Issues* (Birmingham: Musgrove Volunteer Committee, 1913).

Recent years have brought an outpouring of books useful to this study. The history of the South for the period of Underwood's political life is covered generally in C. Vann Woodward's *Origins of the New South* (Baton Rouge: Louisiana State University Press, 1951) and George B. Tindall's *The Emergence of the New South, 1913–1945* (Baton Rouge: Louisiana State University Press, 1967). The Bourbon period of Alabama history is ably treated in Allen J. Going's *Bourbon Democracy in Alabama, 1874–1890* (University: University of Alabama Press, 1951). Alabama politics in the Populist era is brilliantly reassessed in Sheldon Hackney's *Populism and Progressivism in Alabama* (Princeton: Princeton University Press, 1969). Carl V. Harris' *Political Power in Birmingham 1871–1921* (Knoxville: University of Tennessee Press, 1977) is an excellent study of elitist politics in Birmingham. There is no satisfactory history of the United States House of Representatives or the United States Senate, but for the House, Randall B. Ripley, *Party Leaders in the House of Representatives* (Washington, D.C.: Brookings Institution, 1967) and Richard Bolling, *Power in the House: A History of the Leadership of the House of Representatives* (New York: Dutton, 1968) are useful.

Memoirs of prominent figures in the Wilson era generally lack important information about Underwood. Lawrence F. Abbott (ed.), *The Letters of Archie Butt: Personal Aide to President Roosevelt* (2 vols.; Garden City, N.Y.: Doubleday, Page, 1924) is an exception and is valuable for the relations between Underwood and Taft. Champ Clark's *My Quarter Century of American Politics* (2 vols.; New York: Harper and Brothers, 1920) and George F. Sparks (ed.), *A Many Colored Toga: The Diary of Henry Fountain*

Ashurst (Tucson: University of Arizona Press, 1962) are also valuable.

Recent biographers have begun to include Underwood importantly, as earlier biographers did not. Arthur S. Link's *Wilson* (6 vols. projected; Princeton, N.J.: Princeton University Press, 1947–) is seminal to this study as are other works by the same author. Among the biographies of Underwood's colleagues that devote substantial attention to Underwood are: Paolo F. Coletta, *William Jennings Bryan* (3 vols.; Lincoln: University of Nebraska Press, 1969); Paul W. Glad, *The Trumpet Soundeth: William Jennings Bryan and his Democracy, 1896–1912* (Lincoln: University of Nebraska Press, 1960); John Blum, *Joe Tumulty and the Wilson Era* (Boston: Houghton Mifflin, 1955); Stanley Coben, *A. Mitchell Palmer: Politician* (New York: Columbia University Press, 1963); Richard Broesamle, *William Gibbs McAdoo: A Passion for Change* (Port Washington, N.Y.: Kennikat Press, 1973); Virginia Hamilton, *Hugo Black: The Alabama Years* (Baton Rouge: Louisiana State University Press, 1972).

THESES AND DISSERTATIONS: A number of theses and dissertations, most of them in southern universities, have been done on Underwood and related topics. Shelby S. Walker, "Oscar Wilder Underwood: His Political Career" (Senior thesis, Princeton University, 1935) is largely obsolete but has some value. Nancy Ruth Elmore's "The Birmingham Coal Strike of 1908" (M.A. thesis, University of Alabama, 1966) deals with neglected Alabama labor history.

The lack of a good history of Birmingham is partially filled by Martha C. Mitchell, "Birmingham: A Biography of a City of the New South" (Ph.D. dissertation, University of Chicago, 1946). And Martin Torodash, "Woodrow Wilson and the Tariff Question: The Importance of the Underwood Act in His Reform Program" (Ph.D. dissertation, New York University, 1966) is valuable.

DOCUMENTS: The *Congressional Record* is of central importance to this study. Reports of tariff hearings before the Ways and Means

Committee, together with reports on legislation in which Underwood was interested, are to be found in the serial set of government documents. A valuable source of election returns for the Alabama historian is the *Alabama Official and Statistical Register*, published quadrennially by the state of Alabama. The official record of the Washington Conference is given in *Conference on the Limitation of Armament* (Washington, 1922) in both French and English.

NEWSPAPERS: Most of the newspaper research contained herein was done at the Library of Congress and at the Alabama Department of Archives and History in Montgomery. The Underwood Collection in Montgomery contains clippings of many of the articles cited. These clippings are chronologically arranged in scrapbooks except for those for the 1924 campaign which are in folders arranged by states.

Index

Tennessee River Improvement Association, 345, 370

Tennesee Valley Authority, 369

Thach, Robert H., 19n, 49, 68

Thompson, Charles Willis, 138

Thompson, Frederick I, 325

Thornton, Dr. William, 416

Thurman, Allen L., 20

Titanic (Vessel), 193

Tombigbee River, 109

Trading with the Enemy Act of 1917, pp. 264, 329–30

Transportation Act of 1920, pp. 113, 245, 300

Transylvania College, 3

Treadway, Allen T., 378

Trent, William P., 16, 20

Trotter, Eliza McCown. *See* Underwood, Eliza McCown Trotter

Tumulty, Joseph P., 270–71

Turpin, Lewis W., 25–28, 30

Tuskegee Institute, 53

Unanimous Consent Calendar, 142

Uncompahgre Reservation, 54

Underwood, Bertha Woodward: 89–91, 100, 104, 118, 149, 173, 193, 231, 263, 315, 376–80, 406, 409, 415–16, 419, 425, 430–31, 432, 437–39, 450; political interests, 304, 372, 396; health, 421, 435, 439

Underwood, Catherine R. Thompson (Mrs. Eugene, Sr.), 5–6

Underwood, Clara, 420

Underwood, Eliza McCown Trotter (Mrs. Joseph Rogers Underwood), 3

Underwood, Elizabeth Taylor (Mrs. Thomas William, Sr.), 2

Underwood, Ellen Pratt, 255, 300–301, 400, 426

Underwood, Ellen (granddaughter of O. W. Underwood, Sr.), 432

Underwood, Eugene, Sr., 5, 6, 9–11, 23, 106

Underwood, Eugene, Jr., 5

Underwood, Eugenia Massie, 15, 20, 21, 36, 48, 63, 65, 450

Underwood, Eugenia "Ge Ge", 231, 419

Underwood, Frances Rogers (Mrs. John), 2–3

Underwood, Frederica Virginia Wilder (Mrs. Eugene, Sr.), 6, 7, 7n, 9, 10, 12, 65–67, 310, 314–15, 437–38

Underwood, Frederick, 12, 315, 356, 438

Underwood, John, 2–3

Underwood, John C., 96

Underwood, John Lewis, 21, 36, 59, 65–66, 231, 242, 416, 419, 435–38, 440

Underwood, Joseph Rogers, 3–5, 12, 227, 415, 439

Underwood, Marinda Burnett Wilder (Mrs. William T.), 6, 9, 12, 20, 21, 65–66, 419–20

Underwood, Mary (Mrs. John Lewis), 435, 440

Underwood, Oscar W.:

—as campaigner and speaker, 26, 49, 149, 195, 292–93, 337, 441–42

—as leader, 23, 138, 142, 154, 163–65, 167, 168, 199, 201, 202, 210, 223–25, 245, 273, 300, 308, 310, 313, 318–19, 323–24, 334, 335, 338, 340–41, 372, 434, 442, 449

—early political involvement, 23–28

—economic views, 93, 103, 105, 117, 146–47, 417. *See also* monetary policy, tariff, taxation

—elitism, 45–46, 68, 452–53

—finances, personal, 21, 23, 36, 93–94, 193, 253n, 289, 416n, 434n, 438

—health, 174, 199, 210, 231, 246, 251, 254, 268, 277, 319, 334–35, 363, 367, 369, 372, 376, 406, 409, 421, 422, 424–25, 434–35, 445

—law practice, 18–19, 21–22, 23n

—patronage, 80–81, 196–97. *See also* each president

—personal habits and home life, 94, 148–49, 193, 225–26, 300–301, 409, 415–16, 429, 430

—personality and temperament, 15, 17, 203, 373, 446–47, 450, 451–52

—political philosophy, 17, 95, 166, 167–68, 225, 273–74, 292, 422–23, 426–27, 432–34, 448, 452–453

—political supporters, 447–48. *See also* individual elections

—presidential aspirations, 139, 149, 154, 165, 170, 227, 268n, 275–76, 301, 323, 409, 432. *See also* Democratic presidential nomination 1912 and 1924

—press relations, 446. *See also* individual newspapers

—religion, 10–11, 13, 233–34, 276, 286–87, 289, 373–74, 397, 436; belief in occult, 450–51

—travel, 93, 310, 340, 376–80, 381, 423,